Shaping Israelite Identity through Prayers in the Book of Chronicles

Shaping Israelite Identity through Prayers in the Book of Chronicles

The Chronicler's Hope for Liturgical Community

Kiyoung Kim

WIPF & STOCK · Eugene, Oregon

SHAPING ISRAELITE IDENTITY THROUGH PRAYERS IN THE BOOK OF CHRONICLES
The Chronicler's Hope for Liturgical Community

Copyright © 2021 Kiyoung Kim. All rights reserved. Except for brief quotations in critical publications or reviews, no part of this book may be reproduced in any manner without prior written permission from the publisher. Write: Permissions, Wipf and Stock Publishers, 199 W. 8th Ave., Suite 3, Eugene, OR 97401.

Wipf & Stock
An Imprint of Wipf and Stock Publishers
199 W. 8th Ave., Suite 3
Eugene, OR 97401

www.wipfandstock.com

PAPERBACK ISBN: 978-1-6667-0691-8
HARDCOVER ISBN: 978-1-6667-0692-5
EBOOK ISBN: 978-1-6667-0693-2

11/16/21

To Minhee,

my love and friend,

and to

Timothy, Andrew, and Shahron,

my forever reward and delight

Contents

Figure and Table | ix
List of Abbreviations | xi
Preface | xvii

1: Introduction | 1

2: Past Prayer Shapes Contemporary Identity | 13
    Definition and Identification of Prayer | 13
    Shaping Identity through Prayer | 15

3: Recorded Prayers in Chronicles: Literary Rhetorical Analysis | 26
    Introduction | 26
    First Chronicles 4:9–10: Jabez's Prayer | 26
    First Chronicles 16:8–36: Israel's Jubilant Overture | 34
    First Chronicles 17:16–27: David's Prayer | 52
    First Chronicles 29:10–19: David's Final Prayer | 67
    Second Chronicles 6:14–42: Solomon's Prayer | 75
    Second Chronicles 14:10: Asa's Prayer | 88
    Second Chronicles 20:5–13: Jehoshaphat's Prayer | 95
    Second Chronicles 30:18–20: Hezekiah's Prayer | 106

4: Tracing Israelite Identity in Its Sociohistorical Context in the Post-Exilic Biblical Literature | 119
    Introduction | 119
    The Post-Exilic Biblical Literature and Its Testimony | 120

Achaemenid Imperial Influence: Policy and Its Ideology
(539–332 BCE) | 123
Tracing Israelite Identity in Its Sociohistorical Context | 129

5: Conclusion | 168

Bibliography | 177
Subject Index | 197
Ancient Document Index | 215

Figure and Table

Figure: Rhetoric of Prayer in Relation to Identity Formation | 25
Table: Historical-Sequential Projection of Nathan's Oracle | 62–63

List of Abbreviations

AIL	Ancient Israel and Its Literature
AJS	*American Journal of Sociology*
ANEM	Ancient Near East Monographs
AOTC	Abingdon Old Testament Commentaries
AT	*Acta Theologica*
ATLA	American Theological Library Association
AYBC	The Anchor Yale Bible Commentary
BCBC	Believers Church Bible Commentary
BCOT	Baker Commentary of the Old Testament
BDAG	*A Greek-English Lexicon of the New Testament and Other Early Christian Literature*
BI	*Biblical Interpretation*
Bib	*Biblica*
BibSac	*Bibliotheca Sacra*
BIS	Biblical Interpretation Series
BJSUCSD	Biblical and Judaic Studies from the University of California, San Diego
BTB	*Biblical Theology Bulletin*
BWANT	Beiträge zur Wissenschaft vom Alten und Neuen Testament
BZAW	Beihefte zur Zeitschrift für die alttestamentliche Wissenschaft
CBC	Cornerstone Biblical Commentary

CBET	Contributions to Biblical Exegesis and Theology
CBOT	Coniectanea Biblica Old Testament Series
CBQ	*Catholic Biblical Quarterly*
CBQMS	Catholic Biblical Quarterly Monographs Series
ContC	Continental Commentary
CPNIVC	College Press NIV Commentary
CR:BS	*Currents in Research: Biblical Studies*
CTM	*Concordia Theological Monthly*
CTQ	*Concordia Theological Quarterly*
CurTM	*Currents in Theology and Mission*
DCH	*The Dictionary of Classical Hebrew*
DSD	*Dead Sea Discoveries*
EBC	The Expositor's Bible Commentary
EDNT	*Exegetical Dictionary of the New Testament*
EJL	Early Judaism and Its Literature
FAT	Forschungen zum Alten Testament
FOTL	The Forms of the Old Testament Literature
FrThst	Freiburger Theologische Studien
HALOT	*Hebrew and Aramaic Lexicon of the Old Testament*
HAT	Handbuch zum Alten Testament
HBM	Hebrew Bible Monographs
HCOT	Historical Commentary on the Old Testament
Herm	Hermeneia: A Critical and Historical Commentary on the Bible
HJ	*Heythrop Journal*
HSM	Harvard Semitic Monographs
ISBLS	Indiana Studies in Biblical Literature Series
JBL	*Journal of Biblical Literature*
JBQ	*Jewish Biblical Quarterly*

JAOS	*Journal of the American Oriental Society*
JETS	*Journal of the Evangelical Theological Society*
JHS	*The Journal of Hebrew Scriptures*
JSJ	*Journal for the Study of Judaism in the Persian, Hellenistic, and Roman Period*
JSJSup	Journal for the Study of Judaism Supplement Series
JSOT	*Journal for the Study of the Old Testament*
JSOTSup	Journal for the Study of the Old Testament Supplement Series
JSS	*Journal of Semitic Studies*
JTS	*The Journal of Theological Studies*
KEOTS	Korean Evangelical Old Testament Study
KJOTS	Korean Journal of Old Testament Studies
LHBOTS	Library of Hebrew Bible/Old Testament Studies
LXX	The Septuagint
LSTS	Library of Second Temple Studies
MBS	John MacArthur's Bible Studies
MSJ	*The Master's Seminary Journal*
MT	Masoretic Text
NAC	The New American Commentary
NDBT	*New Dictionary of Biblical Theology*
NICOT	The New International Commentary of the Old Testament
NIVAC	The NIV Application Commentary
NSBT	New Studies in Biblical Theology
NTC	A New Translation and Commentary
OBT	Overtures to Biblical Theology
OTE	*Old Testament Essays*
OTL	Old Testament Library
OTS	Old Testament Studies/Oudtestamentische Studiën
PCP	Perspectives in Continental Philosophy

PEQ	*Palestine Exploration Quarterly*	
PFES	Publications of the Finnish Exegetical Society	
PHSC	Perspectives on Hebrew Scriptures and Its Contexts	
PSPR	*Personality and Social Psychology Review*	
RQ	*Restoration Quarterly*	
RTR	*The Reformed Theological Review*	
SBL	Society of Biblical Literature	
SBLDS	Society of Biblical Literature Dissertation Series	
SBLMS	Society of Biblical Literature Monograph Series	
SBLSS	Society of Biblical Literature Symposium Series	
SBLHS	Hervormde Teologiese Studies	
SemeiaSt	Semeia Studies	
SJOT	*Scandinavian Journal of the Old Testament*	
Soc.Res.	Social Research	
SPT	Studies in Philosophical Theology	
SR	*Studies in Religion/Science Religieuses*	
STDJ	Studies on the Texts of the Desert of Judah	
TCLBS	T&T Clark Library of Biblical Studies	
TCSGOT	T&T Clark Study Guides to the Old Testament	
TBN	Themes in Biblical Narrative	
TCBC	The Cambridge Bible Commentaries	
TDOT	*Theological Dictionary of the Old Testament*	
TLJS	The Taubman Lectures in Jewish Studies	
TLOT	*Theological Lexicon of the Old Testament*	
TLZ	*Theologische Literaturzeitung*	
TOTC	Tyndale Old Testament Commentaries	
TR	*Theologische Rundschau*	
TrinJ	*Trinity Journal*	

TSAJ	Texts and Studies in Ancient Judaism
TWOT	*Theological Wordbook of the Old Testament*
TynBul	*Tyndale Bulletin*
UBC	Understanding Bible Commentary
USFISFCJ	University of South Florida International Studies in Formative Christianity and Judaism
VE	*Verbum et Ecclesia*
VT	*Vetus Testamentum*
VTSup	Supplements to Vetus Testamentum Series
WBC	Word Biblical Commentary
WBBC	Wiley Blackwell Bible Commentaries
WLQ	*Wisconsin Lutheran Quarterly*
ZAW	*Zeitschrift für die alttestamentliche Wissenschaft*

Preface

THE FOLLOWING STUDY IS a revision of my doctoral dissertation (PhD in Old Testament at Southwestern Baptist Theological Seminary, 2020), entitled "Shaping Israelite Identity through Prayers in the Book of Chronicles," completed under the supervision of Joshua E. Williams. My scholarly interest initially did not lie in the book of Chronicles but in the Pentateuch. I still remember a conversation with my supervisor regarding a research topic for the dissertation. Since Dr. Williams had been writing a commentary on Chronicles, I asked him whether it would be wise to write about Chronicles. Dr. Williams answered, "That makes sense." A short conversation with him thus began my long journey of delving into the world of Chronicles. Indeed, the decision was the right one, since Dr. Williams's abundant knowledge on Chronicles and the post-exilic period has been a tremendous help in my completing this research. Yet, as I have studied Chronicles more, I have realized that stepping into the scholarly dialogue on Chronicles was, in fact, a timely and meaningful decision. Considering the many divisive issues surrounding us in the present age, the Chronicler's concerns about the post-exilic community are worth heeding. Chronicles portrays a better future for the Yehud community as it suggests core elements of it. The shape of the Chronicler's envisioned future is not a divided community but an integrated one, which shares the community members' solid roles and characteristics. Also, in people's hoping for and bringing about a better future, prayer has taken a critical role in religion, regardless of the times. Thus, the Chronicler's use of prayer in his writing is sufficient to draw our attention. Therefore, I hope this study may assist not only those who want to study the book of Chronicles but also those who desire to bring about a sound community and to study the rhetoric of prayer.

This study discusses the prayers and post-exilic Yehud community's identity formation as depicted in the book of Chronicles. In this study, the book argues that prayers in Chronicles rhetorically function to persuade the post-exilic community to become a liturgical community. This liturgical community is composed of worshiping, praying, monotheistic-believing members who are citizens of the Davidic kingdom. This project will demonstrate that the prayers in Chronicles provide pictures of a desired Israelite community and that such a portrayal, by the Israelites' perception of the roles and characteristics described in Chronicles, is intended to assist the post-exilic community's understanding of their own identity. Therefore, through the prayers, the Chronicler intends to convey model roles and characteristics, thereby further persuading readers to enact such roles and characteristics to become his desired liturgical community.

I thank my wife, Minhee, for her ceaseless prayer and help. She is loving, wise, and kind, and, most of all, she loves the Lord Jesus Christ. I also thank my three children, Timothy, Andrew, and Shahron. They are forever my delight and reward. I appreciate my parents, Jaehun and Jaehee. They have sacrificed many areas of their lives by supporting me spiritually and financially. Without them, it would not have been possible for me to finish this research. I also thank my parents-in-law, who have exhibited what model Christians are. I am grateful to my friend Torey Teer for his editorial assistance on an earlier draft of this manuscript. I appreciate Wipf & Stock for accepting my proposal and publishing my work. It has been a good journey working with many experts during the publication process. Lastly, I praise and thank the Lord Jesus Christ, my Savior and forever King.

— *Chapter One* —

Introduction

BABYLONIAN EXILE SEEMED TO have utterly shattered the identity of the Israelites. The demise of the state, the elimination of the temple, and the deportation of its people led to significant social, political, and religious changes. These changes pressed the post-exilic community to reconstruct its identity.[1] The Israelites wanted to understand who they were, and they had to struggle to retrieve what they had lost under foreign rule.

---

1. Blenkinsopp, "Judeans, Jews, Children of Abraham," in Lipschitz et al., *Judah and Judeans in Achaemenid Period*, 463. Note that under the Persian Empire, there was no kingdom of Israel or Judah. In this book, therefore, the term Yehudite refers to inhabitants of the Jewish community who were located in the Persian province of Yehud. Also, Israel refers to the people of Israel portrayed in Chronicles beyond their political and historical reality during the Persian period.

The book of Ezra exhibits a strong interest in identifying Judah or Israel. E.g., "The people of Judah" (Ezra 4:4, 6, 9:1), "people of Israel" (2:2); "descendant from Israel" (2:59), "all-Israel" (2:70, 8:25, 35, 10:6), "descendant of Israel" (3:1, 6:21, 7:7). In Nehemiah, "people of Israel" (Neh 7:7), "descendant of Israel" (1:6, 2:10, 7:72, 8:14, 17, 9:1, 10:40, 13:2), "all-Israel" (7:72, 12:47), "seed of Israel" (9:2), "descendant of Judah" (11:4, 25, 13:16), "all the house of Judah" (4:10), "all Judah" (13:12), "the inhabitant of Judah" (4:6), and "the nobles of Judah" (6:17, 13:17) (Grabbe, *Yehud*, 170; Becking, *Ezra, Nehemiah, and Construction*, 45; Levine, "Jewish Identities in Antiquity," in Stern, *Jewish Identities in Antiquity*, 12–15). See also some other scholars who have contributed to this subject: Jonker, *Defining All-Israel*, 19; Moffat, *Ezra's Social Drama*; Southwood, "And They Could Not"; Tiemeyer, *Ezra-Nehemiah*; Durant, *Ezra Pound*; Wright, *Rebuilding Identity*; Thiessen, "Function of a Conjunction"; Washington, "Israel's Holy Seed"; Esler, "Ezra-Nehemiah"; Knoppers and Levinson, *Pentateuch as Torah*; Watts, *Persia and Torah*; Kennedy, *Seeking a Homeland Sojourn*; Collins, *Invention of Judaism*; Crouch, *Making of Israel*; Bautch, "Function of Covenant," in Boda and Redditt, *Unity and Disunity*, 8–24.

The difference between the Israelites' current situation in the post-exilic period and the past that they remembered created discontinuity.[2] The textual resources in this particular situation played an important role in overcoming the gap created by such discontinuity. Two important types of textual resources to bridge the gap were historiography and recorded prayers. These resources allowed the post-exilic community to retrieve the past and examine themselves in light of these resources. They even allowed the members of the community to see future possibilities for overcoming the gap between past and present. For instance, the ancient historiographers (e.g., of Kings, Chronciles, Ezra-Nehemiah) did not report the complete demise of Israel's history but the life of the people continuing.[3] The texts provided a blueprint for their lives—in this sense, a forward-looking, promising (or hopeful) presentation. Through the textual sources (e.g., Chronicles, Daniel), the post-exilic community remembered their past in order to understand themselves and hope for a better tomorrow. In a similar manner, the recorded prayers played a part in the post-exilic community's reflections as they attempted to understand their painful experiences, deal with current matters, or bring about their desired future.[4] For instance, prayers such as psalms often recorded Israel's suffering in the past (e.g., Babylonian exile or the destruction of Jerusalem [Pss 74; 79; 137]). Ezra's prayer (Ezra 9:6–15) reflected the community's present ethnic issue regarding intermarriage. The penitential prayer in Nehemiah 9 looked forward to covenant renewal and a better future (vv. 32–38).[5]

Hence, as Israelites lived amidst the post-exilic circumstances, it would have been natural for the readers to perceive their identity from the texts (i.e., historiography and recorded prayer) through the process of searching for who they should be. Consequently, as the post-exilic community perceived the ancient traditions in their own life context, these textual sources provided a chance for them to formulate their identity.[6]

---

2. Mermelstein, *Creation, Covenant*, 1.

3. Knoppers, "Exile, Return, and Diaspora," in Jonker, *Texts, Contexts and Readings*, 38.

4. O'Kennedy, "Prayer in the Post-Exilic," 9.

5. "Nehemiah 9 expresses an eschatological hope, that is, a hope for a future far better than the present conditions, even though there is cause to celebrate even these" (Satterwaite and McConville, *Exploring the Old Testament*, 252).

6. Jonker, *Defining All-Israel*, 201–6; Mtshiselwa, "Remembering and Constructing," 4; Mtshiselwa, "Introduction," in Jonker, *Texts, Contexts and Readings*, 3; Esler,

This book is particularly interested in the book of Chronicles in relation to the post-exilic community's identity reconstruction. This research presupposes that the Chronicler wants to bring about a desired community and that it does not come about *ex nihilo*; instead, it is a prerequisite that the members of the community recognize that there may be better circumstances for them to actualize. Then, they need to possess a shared picture of a hopeful tomorrow and the desire to bring about that future. Authoritative sources could be useful and provide hopeful images for this process. In this regard, the Chronicler's history is a meaningful consideration for the present research undertaking. Since Chronicles records the historical reality of Israel, it includes Israel's failures. However, the perspective through which the Chronicler views Israel's history differs from its *Vorlage* (Samuel–Kings).[7] Israel's history in Chronicles' *Vorlage* serves to present the fatalistic failures of Israel that eventually led the people into exile. However, the Chronicler suggests to his audience hopeful perspectives through the history of Israel (e.g., the author's optimistic perspective even through his description of Judah's demise [2 Chr 36:21–24], the characterization of King Manasseh [2 Chr 33:10–13]).[8]

"Ezra-Nehemiah"; Bosman, "Social Identity in Nahum," 88–89.

For recorded prayers, see Neh 9:4–37 and Ezra 9. Eskenazi, "Nehemiah 9–10," §1.1, 1.7; Newman, *Praying by the Book*, 115; Mtshiselwa, "Remembering and Constructing," 4–5; Moffat, *Ezra's Social Drama*; Tucker, *Constructing and Deconstructing*, 165–85.

Hereafter, this book will use the terms readers and audience interchangeably. Furthermore, unless otherwise noted, these terms will refer to the Chronicler's target audience and readers in the post-exilic period.

7. *Vorlage* refers to prior versions of the text; *Sondergut* refers to material particular to a text and not found in other versions of the text. Concerning Chronicles' *Vorlage* and *Sondergut*, see Willi: "Die vorliegende Arbeit hat sich zum Ziel gesetzt, die Methodik und damit die Form der Chronik in ihrer Wechselbeziehung zu den erhaltenen Vorstufen, den hier als 'Voralge' bezeichneten Büchern (Genesis-) Samuel-Könige, zu erklären; es liegt daher nicht in ihrem Rahmen, die Frage nach möglichen Quellen des chronistischen Sondergutes zu stellen. Wohl aber sollte von den in den letzten Kapiteln gewonnenen Ergebnissen her ein Ausblick auf diese eigenen chronistischen Partien gegeben werden. Jene Ergebnisse erlauben es auch, gewisse Grundsätze zu formulieren, die für die Interpretation dieser Stücke von Bedeutung sein dürften. Wenn der Chronist außerkanonische Quellen benützt hat, so scheint es ihm doch weniger um ihre Vermittlung als vielmehr um ihre Angleichung an die einzig gültigen, weil prophetischen, Quellen gegangen zu sein. Er hat die wohl nur zur Erläuterung des in den Samuel- und Königs-Büchern gebotenen Stoffes in sein Geschichtswerk aufgenonmmen" (Willi, *Chronik als Auslegung*, 188).

8. The audience of Chronicles are the groups for whom the Chronicler desires to form a particular identity. Although there is no concrete answer concerning who the

Thus, the Chronicler's history presents his vision of a desired community, a vision which he hoped the post-exilic community would actualize.[9] In addition, this book believes that simply knowing and sharing what a desired community should be does not change the status quo of the community; instead, the members of the community need to internalize who they should be and what they should do in order to actualize such a community. In this sense, the Chronicler's hope for a better future for the community is intrinsically linked to the identity of Israel. Therefore, the present investigation on post-exilic Israelite identity will be one way of providing the vector for how the Israelites were eventually supposed to actualize the desired better community.

This book recognizes several problems from scholarly researches on the subjects of identity formation and prayers in biblical books. With the emergence of sociological methodologies,[10] scholars have contributed to

---

Chronicler's audience was, the textual evidence (i.e., 1 Chr 1–9) suggests that it was those who had returned from Babylon and remained in the promised land during the exile period (Ahn, *Persuasive Portrayal*, 53–55).

9. Scholars have discussed different hopes presented in Chronicles. Hwang, *Hope for the Restoration*; Hahn, *Kingdom of God*, 44–47; Dempster, "Servant of the Lord," in Hafemann and House, *Central Themes*, 163–64; Kelly, *Retribution and Eschatology*, 13–15; Selman, "Purpose of Chronicles," in *NDBT*, 192–93; Duke, *Persuasive Appeal*, 74; Wilcock, *Message of Chronicles*, 83–86.

For some scholarly discussions regarding a better future or utopia, see Schweitzer, *Reading Utopia in Chronicles*. See also Boer, "Decentered and Utopian Politics," in Boer, *Jameson and Jeroboam*, 198–285; Boer, "Utopian Politics," in Graham and McKenzie, *Chronicler as Author*, 360–94. Boer indicates that utopian theory cares less about the members and their identity in the society: "A Levite utopia may not be all that positive for women, for example, or foreigners, or anyone else who is not part of the in-group" (Boer, "Utopia, Dystopia," 13). See also Ben Zvi, *Utopia and Dystopia*; Blenkinsopp, "Ideology and Utopia," in Ben Zvi and Edelman, *What Was Authoritative*, 89–103; Boda, "Identity and Empire," in Knoppers and Ristau, *Community Identity*, 249–72; Boda, "Encountering an Alternative Reality." Ian Douglas Wilson indicates the possible conflict between the Chronicler's utopia and other Biblical utopias (Wilson, "Chronicles and Utopia," in Edelman et al., *History, Memory, Hebrew Scriptures*, 154, 158–59).

10. Duke, "Recent Research in Chronicles"; Ben Zvi, "In Conversation and Appreciation," 34–35; Wright, "A Commentary on Commentaries," 63–64, 67. See also Willi, "Zwei Jahrzehnte Forschung," 61–104; Jonker, "Reforming History"; Jonker, "Within Hearing Distance?"; Jonker, *Defining All-Israel*, 17; Jonker, "From Paraleipomenon to Early Reader," in C. Maier, *Congress Volume Munich 2013*, 217–54; Dyck, *Theocratic Ideology*, 1; Yamauchi, "Exilic and Postexilic Periods," in Grisanti and Howard, *Giving the Sense*, 202; Berquist, *Judaism in Persia's Shadow*.

Here, the definition of sociology follows Pagán's explanation: "In a narrow sense, the word 'sociology' refers to a branch of the social sciences concerned with the behavior

diverse discussions on the subject of Yehudite identity during the Persian period. Scholars have tried to understand the various social factors (e.g., political, sociohistorical, economic, religious, cultural, psychological) in the life matrix of this community under the influence of the Persian Empire. Specifically, recent studies on identity in Chronicles have expanded with regard to both number and scope as they give more attention to the Chronicler's rhetorical strategies and intentions instead of the book's historical value.[11] However, those studies exhibit weaknesses or limitations. The fundamental issue in employing sociological models is that they often fail to observe biblical writings' unique presentation of the Yehud community's life matrix. The life matrix described in biblical texts could be radically, if not completely, different from its surrounding world.[12] Therefore, identity formation through biblical texts should be dealt with in consideration of the peculiarity of this community as presented in the texts. However, socioscientific models often try to understand identity

produced by human interaction and values. In a more general sense, 'sociology' refers to the study of society as it relates to any of the social sciences (e.g., sociology, economics, or anthropology), or it may describe the analysis of one aspect of social life" (Pagán, "Poor and Poverty," 69–70).

11. Ramírez Kidd, *Alterity and Identity*; Watts, *Persia and Torah*; Knoppers and Levinson, *Pentateuch as Torah*; Ben Zvi and Edelman, *Imagining the Other*; Lipschitz et al., *Judah and Judeans in Achaemenid Period*; Lipschitz et al., *Judah and Judeans in Fourth Century B.C.E.*; Lipschitz and Oeming, *Judah and Judeans in Persian Period*; Grisanti and Blenkinsopp, *Judah and Judeans in Neo-Babylonian Period*; Jonker, *Historiography and Identity*; Jonker, *Defining All-Israel*, 19; Jonker, "Who Constitutes Society?"; Jonker, "Textual Identities," in Knoppers and Ristau, *Community Identity*, 197–217; Jonker, "Rhetoric of Finding." See also Moffat, *Ezra's Social Drama*; Southwood, "And They Could Not"; Becking, *Ezra, Nehemiah, and Construction*; Tiemeyer, *Ezra-Nehemiah*; Durant, *Ezra Pound*; Wright, *Rebuilding Identity*; Thiessen, "Function of a Conjunction"; Washington, "Israel's Holy Seed"; Esler, "Ezra-Nehemiah"; Ben Zvi, "Book of Chronicles"; Boda, "Identity and Empire," in Knoppers and Ristau, *Community Identity*, 249–72; Willi, "Late Persian Judaism" in Eskenazi and Richards, *Second Temple Studies 2*, 146–52; Willi, *Judah–Jehud–Israel*, 119–68; Joo, "Past No Longer Present"; Dyck, "Ideology of Identity," in Brett, *Ethnicity and the Bible*, 89–116; Dyck, *Theocratic Ideology*; Siedlecki, "Foreigners, Warfare and Judahite Identity," in Graham and McKenzie, *Chronicler as Author*, 229–66; Throntveit, *When Kings Speak*; Duke, *Persuasive Appeal*; Schweitzer, *Reading Utopia in Chronicles*; Ristau, "Reading and Rereading Josiah"; Schweitzer and Uhlenbruch, *Worlds That Could Not Be*; Lynch, *Monotheism and Institutions*; Ahn, *Persuasive Portrayal*.

12. For instance, Lynch's book, *Monotheism and Institution*, shows that one needs to be aware of the uniqueness of the Yehud community. He explains that Chronicles embraces both particularism and universalism. In his view, Israel is peculiar in relation to the universe; Israel witnesses God's supremacy (e.g., the temple) even as it does not reject the existence of other gods.

formation through the lens of interpreting the relationship or conflict between an inner and an outer group (i.e., how other groups see Jews and vice versa). In other words, rather than focusing on internal factors, sociological studies often are concerned with external factors (e.g., foreign hegemony surrounding the post-exilic community).[13] Therefore, scholars have suggested different methodological presuppositions concerning identity and have noticed diverse social factors at play during the Persian period. Unfortunately, such suggestions have created difficulties in grasping a concrete or unified understanding of the concept of identity.[14]

In relation to this present scholarly trend, it is questionable whether the exclusive use of socioscientific models on the texts is appropriate. First, it could be anachronistic to apply those models to ancient historiography. Various contemporary socioscientific models may not apply to the ancient Persian period. Second, it could be difficult and unverifiable to determine the best socioscientific method for interpreting the texts.

Even though scholars had earlier recognized the importance of the prayers in Chronicles,[15] few had devoted much research to the subject of prayer in both the Old Testament and Chronicles until the 1980s.[16] At that time, scholarly attention on prayer shifted from the form critical analysis of the prayers (i.e., Psalms) to rhetorical, literary, and ideological concerns related to the biblical narrative and prose prayer.[17] Recent

---

13. Levine suggests the following internal factors: group self-definition, geography, leadership, institution, worship, holidays, and sacred literature (Levine, "Jewish Identities in Antiquity," in Stern, *Jewish Identities in Antiquity*, 12–13).

Jonker, acknowledging the existence of diverse factors, chooses four different methodologies that he considers to be the best for his research in order to understand the different dynamics that may play a role in Chronicles: postcolonial, utopian, social memory, and social psychology studies (Jonker, *Defining All-Israel*, 18–24, 64–65).

14. Mulholland, "Sociological Criticism," in Black and Dockery, *Interpreting the New Testament*, 176–77; Berquist, "Constructions of Identity," in Lipschitz and Manfred, *Judah and Judeans in Persian Period*, 54, 63.

15. Driver, "Speeches in Chronicles" (*Expositor I* and *II*); von Rad, *Problem of the Hexateuch* (see the chapter "Levitical Sermon in Books of Chronicles"), and Plöger, "Speech and Prayer," in Knoppers and McConville, *Reconsidering Israel and Judah*, 31–46.

16. Balentine, *Prayer in Hebrew Bible*, 226–30; Widmer, *Moses, God, and Dynamics*, 5.

17. Matlock, "Traditions of Prose Prayer," 11–13; Wendel, *Freies Laiengebet*; Krinetzki, *Israels Gebet*.

Balentine, "Prayers for Justice," 601. See some other contributions, see Balentine, *Prayer in Hebrew Bible*; Greenberg, *Biblical Prose Prayer*; Miller, *They Cried to the Lord*; Newman, *Praying by the Book*; Schuller, "Penitential Prayer in Second Temple

notable research by Throntveit, Pratt, Rigsby, Duke, Mason, and most recently Ahn explores the Chronicler's prayers and speech.[18] Although these studies have contributed to the field of Chronicles studies, they exhibit several weaknesses or limitations. First, all the studies fail to distinguish between speeches and prayers and do not recognize prayer's unique rhetorical features.[19] Second, even though the studies often acknowledge the issue of identity in Chronicles, most of them do not exhibit extensive concern for it. There is no presentation of a particular methodology for determining identity within the text of Chronicles.[20] Third, the studies rarely cover all of the prayers presented in Chronicles; instead, they often deal only with the royal (David-Solomon) prayers.[21] Fourth, some studies contain methodological fallacies or a different research scope.[22]

Therefore, while this study recognizes the significance of the sociohistorical contexts during the Persian period, it does not attempt to demonstrate every aspect of identity in post-exilic Israel. Such a project is basically sociological and is secondarily concerned with Chronicles as evidence within a sociological model. Instead, this book is interested only in the pictures of a desired Israel that emerge from all the prayers recorded in Chronicles by recognizing their unique rhetorical features. This book focuses on interpreting the texts as literary theological or literary ideological documents in order to describe more clearly how the Chronicler envisions a desired Israel.

In addition, it is necessary to inform several backdrops or key concepts for the current study. First, although this book's primary purpose is not to discuss the historical value of Chronicles, this research affirms that the Chronicler's purpose was to write a historiography in alignment with

---

Judaism," in Boda et al., *Development of Penitential Prayer*, 1. For a more recently published work, see Millar, *Calling on the Name*.

18. Throntveit, *When Kings Speak*; Rigsby, "Historiography of Speeches"; Pratt, "Royal Prayer"; Duke, *Persuasive Appeal*; Mason, *Preaching the Tradition*; Ahn, *Persuasive Portrayal*.

19. Boda insists that differentiating between speech and prayer is unnecessary. Boda, "Prayer as Rhetoric," in Kalimi, *New Perspectives*, 272.

20. Ahn, *Persuasive Portrayal*, 41–62.

21. Pratt, Throntveit, and Ahn.

22. Duke anachronistically employs Aristotle's rhetoric in order to understand the Chronicler's perspective. Mason researches the addresses in Chronicles and examines them together with Ezra-Nehemiah, Haggai, Zechariah, and Malachi to show the Chronicler's special concern for worship and the temple.

his theological and ideological intentions—so, a theological history.[23] In addition, the fact that Chronicles contains the form of narrative does not mean that it is a work of fiction; instead, the Chronicler's concerns in writing could be both information concerning past events and the literary/rhetorical style of his account.[24]

Second, even though the Chronicler adopts prayers from other textual sources (e.g., Solomon's prayer in 2 Chr 6 from 1 Kgs 8), they serve as the Chronicler's strategic literary artifacts. Considering that Chronicles, as a whole, is the Chronicler's ideological and theological presentation, prayers contribute as a part to the whole within the literary context. Therefore, others' prayers (i.e., prayers through the mouths of the characters in Chronicles) become a part of the Chronicler's message, so that prayers can contribute to the presentation of his ideology and theology.

Third, the texts of Chronicles serve as a medium for identity formation. First, the texts serve the significant function of remembering past history.[25] The remembering of past history is significant because it

---

23. This book opposes a view particularly represented by William Johnston, who denies the Chronicler's historiographical aims and distinguishes history from theology. Johnstone, therefore, refers to Chronicles as a theological essay. Johnstone, *First and Second Chronicles*, 1:22; Johnstone, *Chronicles and Exodus*, 166. Also, this book disagrees with Ackroyd's ideas that the Chronicler dehistoricizes history, and thus, only parts of texts are real (Ackroyd, *Chronicler in His Age*, 66–67, 264).

As Provan writes, "Nor can it be justified on the grounds that the biblical testimony is ideologically loaded—that is, that it carries a particular perspective on Israel's past and has an intention to persuade others of the truth of that perspective. No account of the past anywhere is free of ideology, and thus principle is to be trusted more than other accounts; nor should one presume that an ideological account cannot also be historically accurate" (V. Long et al., *Biblical History of Israel*, 62, 68, 96).

In regard to the Chronicler as historian, see Kalimi: "The author deals with the past; he collects material from the earlier books and perhaps additional sources; he selects from the sources, evaluates, and interprets them; he makes connections between the sources; and above all, his work as a whole is imprinted with a unique 'philosophy' of history.... Chr also articulated his views in the guise of speeches and prayers by the heroes in his narrative ... he did not sit and 'dream' about the past but studied it in order to learn about the present and perhaps about the future as well" (Kalimi, "Was the Chronicler a Historian?," in Graham et al., *Chronicler as Historian*, 83–85).

24. V. Long et al., *Biblical History of Israel*, 86. See also Marc Zvi Brettler: "It is likely that authors who feel that their stories are important will have the good sense to offer them in a pleasing form, so that they will be listened to, remembered and transmitted further" (Brettler, *Creation of History*, 139). See also Sternberg, *Poetics of Biblical Narrative*.

25. Ben Zvi, "Book of Chronicles," 271; Ben Zvi, "Reading Chronicles," in Evans and Williams, *Chronicling the Chronicler*, 122; Ben Zvi, "Toward a Sense of Balance,"

provides an opportunity for readers to sense who they were and what they lost. It also suggests a desired blueprint for which the community could hope. Second, the Chronicler recalls history via authoritative texts (*Vorlage*) so that his readers will accept Chronicles as a veracious account of history to share with other members in the community.[26] Therefore, as readers engage in the same memory (i.e., Israel's past), the text allows community members to share essential ground on which they can answer questions about their existence and identity.[27]

Fourth, this book will investigate the Chronicler's depiction of the roles or characteristics of the Israelites in order to seek their identity as portrayed in Chronicles.[28] The fundamental question for this book is

---

in Evans and Williams, *Chronicling the Chronicler*, 52, 55, 57; Ben Zvi, "One Size Does Not Fit All," in Ben Zvi and Edelman, *What Was Authoritative*, 13–36. See others who discuss social/collective memory: Eskenazi, "Imagining the Other," in Ben Zvi and Edelman, *Imagining the Other*, 230–56; Ben Zvi and Edelman, *Memory and the City*; Ben Zvi and Edelman, *Remembering Biblical Figures*; Ben Zvi and Edelman, *Leadership, Social Memory*; Merrill, "Remembering," 28.

26. Ben Zvi, "Introduction," in Ben Zvi and Edelman, *What Was Authoritative*, 4. Although Newman's main focus is Neh 9:5–37, he discusses the scripturalization of prayer (Newman, *Praying by the Book*, 55–116). Mtshieslwa, then, argues based on Newman that retelling past history can confer an authoritative status to the text (Mtshiselwa, "Remembering and Constructing," 2).

27. Ben Zvi, "Introduction and Invitation" in Ben Zvi and Edelman, *Memory and the City*, 3; Ben Zvi, "On Social Memory and Identity Formation," in Jonker, *Texts, Contexts and Readings*, 98–99; Ben Zvi, "Reading Chronicles," in Evans and Williams, *Chronicling the Chronicler*, 129; Ben Zvi, *History, Literature and Theology*, 79; Ben Zvi, "Book of Chronicles," 264, 267. See also others: Hendel, "Exodus in Biblical Memory," 621; Tavani et al., "Tell Me What You Remember," 92–93, 104; Hirst and Echterhoff, "Creating Shared Memories," 188.

See also Jonker: "This notion [textual identities] emphasizes the close interrelationship between the social environment within which a group exists, the textual resources that are available in the given culture, and the role that renewed textual construction plays in the process of identity formation" (Jonker, "Textual Identities," in Knoppers and Ristau, *Community Identity*, 205). See also Jonker, *Defining All-Israel*, 17–24; Dyck, "Ideology of Identity," in Brett, *Ethnicity and the Bible*, 89–116.

28. Scholars have pointed out this aspect by the use of various terms, such as behavior, role, characteristics, norm, attitudes, beliefs, and values. Ben Zvi, "Book of Chronicles," 267; Boda, "Identity and Empire," in Knoppers and Ristau, *Community Identity*, 255, 270–71; Willi, "Late Persian Judaism," in Eskenazi and Richards, *Second Temple Studies 2* 146, 161; Lau, *Identity and Ethics*, 159. Although these terms have slightly different senses, they share the core idea that the members of the community are required to do certain actions/behaviors or exhibit certain characteristics (Stets and Burke, "A Sociological Approach," in Leary and Tangney, *Handbook of Self and Identity*, 136–37).

this: what roles or characteristics does the Chronicler expect from his desired Israel? In order to answer this question, one needs to understand two concepts concerning identity: community identity and identity that exhibits multiple roles and characteristics.

In terms of the former, this book does not pursue the identity of a particular individual or a group within Israel. Although the Chronicler occasionally describes the roles of certain groups (e.g., 1 Chr 23–27), the present research undertaking is interested, instead, in the Chronicler's picture of all-Israel (כָּל־יִשְׂרָאֵל). For instance, the conventional understanding of the image of America could be described as pioneerism, freedom, patriotism, etc. These spirits/characteristics are acquired when members of the country actively render particular roles as they pursue those values. In the same manner, the members of the Yehud community can function in designated roles or exhibit particular characteristics as they pursue the actualization of a better future. Even if the Chronicler demonstrates different group roles, those roles eventually contribute to an indication of the overarching identity of the community.[29] For instance, even though 1 Chronicles 23–27 lists various roles,[30] the lists as a whole point out that Israel should be a liturgical community.

In terms of the latter, this research understands that a desired Israelite community could have multiple roles and characteristics. Identity cannot be defined as one fixed role or characteristic, but it could be constructed by the sum of roles or characteristics; thus, this book observes that Israel may have more than one role or characteristic portrayed in Chronicles. One community is hardly defined in a singular way in relation to the internal dynamics of, and external factors surrounding, the community.[31]

---

29. Ohad David and Daniel Bar-Tal employ the phrase *collective identity* instead of community identity. However, their understanding of the concept of identity in a collective manner is similar to this book, since they observe that an individual member of the community can share an identity with other members of the community. These scholars provide the following general features of communal identity: (1) "a sense of a common fate"; (2) "the perception of the uniqueness of the collective and its distinction from other collectives"; (3) "coordinated activity of the collective's members"; (4) "commonality of belief, attitudes, norms, and values"; (5) "concern for the welfare of the collective and mobilization and sacrifice for its sake"; and (6) "continuity and consecutiveness in the dimension of time" (David and Bar-Tal, "Sociopsychological Conception" 359–65).

30. For instance, priests, Levites, singers, gatekeepers, treasurers, and other officials, etc.

31. Jonker, *Defining All-Israel*, 13, 64–66. Stets and Burke, "A Sociological

The primary argument of this book is as follows: through the recorded prayers, the Chronicler intends to define Israel as a liturgical community that is composed of worshiping, praying, monotheistic believing members who are citizens of the Davidic kingdom. This project will demonstrate that the prayers in Chronicles provide pictures of a desired Israelite community and that such a portrayal, by the Israelites' perceiving of the roles and characteristics described in Chronicles, is intended to assist the post-exilic community's understanding of their own identity. Therefore, through the recorded prayers, the Chronicler intends to convey model roles and characteristics and further persuade readers to enact such roles and characteristics in order to become his desired liturgical community.

The Chronicler's specific presentation of roles and characteristics and their aspects will be discussed throughout chapter 3. Yet, it is helpful to provide the following overview in the understanding of those roles and characteristics. First, concerning the characteristic of monotheistic believer, this book finds Lynch's definition of monotheism particularly helpful. Lynch defines monotheism as "*the assertion of Yhwh's categorical supremacy (or supreme uniqueness)*."[32] Yhwh does not simply take a higher position over other gods; instead, he is perceived as categorically different. In other words, other divine beings are not able to share in God's sole supremacy, since Yhwh is categorically supreme.[33] Second, worshiping community is the term characterizing the members of the community who actively worship their God Yhwh. This statement does not mean that each member of the community shares particular roles as worshipers. The Chronicler holds the Levites and the priest to a unique position in the worshiping community as they render their technical roles (e.g., playing music; 1 Chr 16:4–6; chs. 23–27). Thus, the notion concerning the community's role as worshipers (or the worshiping community) refers to the collective nature of the community's role as a liturgical community. In addition, the ideal form of Israel's worship is sacrificial ritual accompanied by musical performance, which occurs as all-Israel gathers in Jerusalem.

Approach," in Leary and Tangney, *Handbook of Self and Identity*, 136–37. Sociologists especially uses the term *the role identity* instead of role.

32. Lynch, *Monotheism and Institutions*, 27 (italics in original). He continues to explain that the biblical writers, including the Chronicler, admit the existence of other divine beings (e.g., אֱלֹהִים, אֱלוֹהַּ, or אֵל), yet they insist on Yhwh's sole divinity. He warns readers not to understand the existence of Yhwh and other divine beings according to a spatial concept (Lynch, *Monotheism and Institutions*, 27–31).

33. Chapter 3 will address ways in which the Chronicler understands Yhwh's position in the universe and his relationship to other gods in a specific way.

Third, regarding a praying community, the term refers to the community members who are characterized by their acts of prayer, which includes both individual and communal prayers. The praying community could praise Yhwh, ask for God's deliverance in their distressing situation, or repent of their sins in hope of the revival of the community. Fourth, Davidic citizenship (or citizens) refers to the membership or inhabitants of those who dwell in the revived Davidic kingdom.[34]

This book examines Chronicles' use of recorded prayer in shaping the post-exilic identity as follows. Chapter 2 deals with the methodology of this research. It argues for the recorded prayers' unique rhetorical effect in Chronicles by demonstrating how the recorded prayers could serve to shape the identity of readers/participants of the prayers. Chapter 3 undertakes a literary and rhetorical analysis of the recorded prayers in Chronicles to uncover the messages in the literary historical context. Chapter 4 attempts to trace community identity in the sociohistorical context of Yehud. This book examines the implications of the roles and characteristics that are portrayed in the Chronicler's literary historical matrix in light of the reality that members of the Yehud community lived under the Persian Empire's influence and control.

---

34. Since there was no tangible structure of the kingdom in the post-exilic era, scholars have articulated different interpretations on the nature of the Chronicler's hope for restoration.

― *Chapter Two* ―

Past Prayer Shapes Contemporary Identity

Definition and Identification of Prayer

IT IS IMPERATIVE TO define and identify prayers in Chronicles for the present research undertaking. Scholars have defined and identified prayer in different ways.[1] This book understands prayer as communication

---

1. See the following scholarly discussions: "In this study I define prayer as an address to God (or perhaps another being), who is perceived 'as somehow supporting, maintaining, or controlling the order of existence of the one praying, and performed with the purpose of getting result from or in the interaction of communication" (Penner, *Patterns of Daily Prayer*, 1). Heiler calls it "a living communion of the religious man with God" (Heiler, *Prayer*, 358). Eichrodt indicates, "The act of kneeling and raising the hands, followed by the bowing of the face to the ground, correspond to the behavior of the vassal in the presence of his king, and symbolize the submission of the supplicant to a will higher than his own" (Eichrodt, *Theology of the Old Testament*, 2:175). Balentine tries to find particular a Hebrew lexicon such as "to pray" or "to call on the name," or a specific expression that opens the prayer, "X prayed saying" (Balentine, *Prayer in Hebrew Bible*, 30). In another article, Balentine emphasizes the intentionality and purpose of communication (Balentine, "Prayers for Justice," 599–600). Chazon defines prayer "as any form of human communication directed at God" (Chazon, "Prayers from Qumran," 266). Corvin understands "where a text is preserved, if it is addressed to God in the second person, it is prayer" (Corvin, "Stylistic and Functional Study," 23). Greenberg defines it as "non-psalmic speech to God—less often about God—expressing dependence, subjection, or obligation; it includes petition, confession, benediction, and curse (but excludes references to nothing more than oracle-seeking)" (Greenberg, *Biblical Prose Prayer*, 7). Staudt gives good explanations of "explicit communication with God," "communication initiated by an individual or the people as a whole," and "such communication that brings response from God," while "prayer is motivated by a situation which is fraught with confusion, fear, and uncertainty" (Staudt, "Prayer and the People," 58–59, 66). Kaufmann

initiated by a human and offered to God. So, a human has a clear object to whom he prays (i.e., God) and a clear intentionality for what he prays; thus, it is not a monologue or self-confession, but a form of communication.[2] However, prayer does not require that God answers as one would in a conversation. This differentiates prayer from direct speech that takes place in a human-human conversation (i.e., a dialogue). In prayer, a human believes that God listens and hopes for God's answer to the prayer, but there might not be a divine response to the human while the prayer is being offered.

This book will identify prayer in Chronicles according to the following considerations. First, it is initiated by a human with direct first person speech. Second, since prayer has clear intentionality and an object, the texts often signal where or in what manner prayer may take place, such as the acts of kneeling, raising hands to heaven, calling on God's name, praising/blessing the Lord, or an explicit verbal signal of prayer in narration (פלל, תְּפִלָּה) followed by direct speech to God before the congregation. Third, this book differentiates between prayer and prayer scene. A

---

compares and contrast between psalm and prayer: "They both have a characteristic of repetition, though the former is fixed and styled in priestly cultic setting but the latter is independent and spontaneous in public cult" (Kaufmann, *Religion of Israel*, 305–9). Newman writes: "Prayer is address to God that is initiated by humans; it is not conversational in nature; it includes address to God in the second person, although it can include third person description of God" (Newman, *Praying by the Book*, 6–7). Peterson adopts Staudt's definition, saying, "First, while the question of divine response is obviously appropriate for the texts of his study, prayer could be recognized even where no divine response is taken for granted." Yet he excludes Staudt's unstated prayer: "As part of literary texts, however, only the 'stated' prayers are actual passages of prayer whereas 'unstated' prayers in the texts are references to the fact of prayers" (Peterson, "Theology and the Function," 40–41). Werline says, "Penitential prayer is a direct address to God in which an individual, group, or an individual on behalf of a group confesses sins and petitions for forgiveness as an act of repentance" (Werline, "Defining Penitential Prayer," in Boda et al., *Origins of Penitential Prayer*, xv). Thompson says prayer is "uttered by individuals or in the liturgy of the Church" (Thompson, *I Have Heard Your Prayer*, 5). MacArthur writes, "Prayer is generated by the Word of God"; "prayer is grounded in the will of God"; "prayer is characterized by fervency"; "prayer is identified with God's people"; "prayer is strengthened in confession"; "prayer is dependent on God's character"; "Prayer consummates in God's glory" (MacArthur, *Elements of True Prayer*, 44–45). FitzGerald understands, "I argue that prayer is . . . relationships between the human and the divine" (FitzGerald, *Spiritual Modalities*, 4, 39). Talsta writes, "Rather, it is *communication*, based on a long tradition of texts about God, his people and their common history" (Talsta, "Discourse of Praying," in Becking and Peels, *Psalms and Prayers*, 235–36).

2. E.g., Jer 29:13; 33:3.

prayer scene is a recorded indirect speech prayer contained in a narrative. Technically, a prayer is embedded in a story, but a prayer scene is part of a story; a prayer scene does not stop the flow of a story. The narrator (third person) usually conveys this scene briefly,[3] whereas in a prayer, a particular character in the narrative provides a direct first person speech form of prayer. Based on these considerations, this book will discuss the following prayers from the book of Chronicles: 1 Chronicles 4:9–10; 16:8–36; 17:16–27; 29:10–19; 2 Chronicles 6:14–42; 14:10 (Eng. v. 11); 20:5–13; 30:18–20.[4]

Shaping Identity through Prayer

The critical question that this book previously raised is: what roles or characteristics does the Chronicler expect from a desired Israel? Discussion of prayer's unique rhetorical features provides an answer to this question. Three ideas are especially significant. First, Chronicles should provide relevant roles or characteristics (presenting). Second, since the identity is constructed by the sum of roles or characteristics, the audience should perceive what they should be and do (perceiving). Third, the audience needs to internalize the roles and characteristics that they discern (performing). The significance of prayers is apparent since the rhetoric of prayers can accomplish these three tasks. Below, therefore, the following sections will examine how recorded prayers describe the pertinent roles and characteristics and will further discuss in what manner the prayers effectively persuade the members of the community to internalize and enact particular roles or exhibit certain characteristics.

---

3. E.g., 2 Chr 32:24; 33:10–13. See below for further discussion on the rhetoric of prayer.

4. This book does not consider 1 Chr 21:8 and 17 as prayer, since there is no conclusive signal for identifying vv. 8 and 17 as prayer. Both simply begin with וַיֹּאמֶר (to say), and it is doubtful that this word strongly serves as a signal for informing readers of the recorded prayer in the narrative, since there are too many occurrences of this word in Chronicles. The function of a signal is important from the Chronicler's rhetorical purpose in this book. Note that 1 Chr 17 begins a direct speech with וַיֹּאמֶר, but the text particularly writes לְהִתְפַּלֵּל לְפָנֶיךָ (to pray before you [God]) later in v. 25; thus, the text clearly suggests that the words of David are a form of prayer.

The Rhetoric of Prayer

One way to understand the Chronicler's communication with his audience is to investigate the rhetoric of prayer. In this regard, the first basic premise for understanding prayer's rhetoric is that the prayer conveys the Chronicler's ideology. The rhetor, in general, often aims to persuade the audience of his ideology in his writing.[5] Thus, he can use particular literary techniques or tools to convince his audience of his views.[6] In the same manner, if the Chronicler uses prayers to accentuate his messages, especially with his careful modification, then it is a reasonable presupposition that the Chronicler conveys his theology and ideology through the prayers.[7] Thus, when considering the fact that the Chronicler's history presents a hopeful agenda of Israel's future, the prayers' rhetorical features can highlight his vision of a desired community.

The second premise is that the prayer can invite the audience to pray, and the audience can respond to the invitation. Then, they are no longer observers, readers, or hearers of the story but serious prayer participants.[8] Since the prayer is communication between God and a supplicant, when the audience participates in the prayer, they could

---

5. Gring, "Rhetoric and Ideology," 192.

6. Edelman writes, "'Rhetoric' in particular is used in the sense of strategies or techniques used to persuade an audience to adopt a particular view or position. There can be a large amount of overlap with ideology, since the latter represents a particular view or position being asserted over against a competing one, which will be developed using rhetorical strategies designed to be as persuasive as possible" (Edelman, "Introduction," in Ben Zvi, Edelman, and Polak, *Palimpsest*, 1–2). See also Burke, *Rhetoric of Religion*, v. Matlock says, "The study of ideology involves a discussion of the context in which the prayer appears, its apparent function, and a brief description of beliefs as relevant to the prayer.... A prayer text tells those listening to the prayer a great deal about an author and his ideas either in regard to the story and how this author sees the character or regarding his theology and his image of God" (Matlock, *Discovering the Traditions*, 8). See also Werline: "A person within a culture knows how and when to draw on any particular pattern of speaking, with its own unique vocabulary, according to what the situation demands.... Thus, the way of speaking is in constant flux, depending on the author/speaker's personality, worldview, social location, and even personal whim, and the author/speaker's perceived understanding of the audience or other participants in the cultural acts" (Werline, "Reflections on Penitential Prayers," in Boda et al., *Development of Penitential Prayer*, 211).

7. Plöger, "Speech and Prayer," 42. Theology and ideology, in other words, refers to how the Chronicler understands God and his people and the world surrounding him (Japhet, *Ideology of the Book*, 5, 8).

8. FitzGerald, *Spiritual Modalities*, 7, 12–13, 15, 18–19, 35, 40, and 133. See also Giffone, "Timeless, Unifying Rhetoric," 551; Staudt, "Prayer and the People," 43–44.

recognize the divine-human analogy that the prayer presents to readers, such as father-son, king-servant, redeemer/savior/deliverer-receiver of divine performance, and God-worshiper.[9] In other words, the participating process includes their now recognizing the object to whom they pray (i.e., God) and their evaluating situations in both Chronicles and their own life setting. Since the recorded prayer reflects the supplicant's view toward God and his situation in the narrative, each prayer reveals something of the divine-human relationship. Hence, when participants pray, they not only recognize the object of their prayer but also understand the divine-human relationship implied by a recorded prayer and thus assimilate their life setting to the prayer's situation by evaluating their own current situation in light of the prayer. Therefore, this process confers rhetorical force to prayer participants, because the recorded prayers are now no longer stories; instead, as participants engage prayers, they transform stories (i.e., prayers) into their own truth claims about their life setting.[10]

One should notice, however, that those truth claims may not include the idea that participants perceive a prayer and its surrounding situation as identical to their contemporary circumstances. Obviously, there is no single situation that can perfectly mirror another. Thus, the divine response to prayer in the story, on a superficial level, may not be entirely appropriate for the supplicant's contemporary situation. For instance, the situations of Asa and Jehoshaphat may not be suitable for the post-exilic situation. The post-exilic community was not engaged in fierce, nationwide battle. And so, God-granted victory against one's enemy—in response to prayer—may not be directly relevant to the post-exilic community. Such an expectation would indicate that participants remain at the superficial level of the prayer. They need, instead, to understand the deeper level of the Chronicler's message. In other words, the participants must engage in the hermeneutical task of transforming the embedded message of the stories into a message relevant to their life setting. This means that the divine-human analogy in Chronicles has a significant function. As the participants are invited to the prayers and

---

9. David P. Wright refers to this as anthropo-metaphorical context. He says, "For example, the description of God as redeemer, savior, father and king all stem from human institutions—the economy, the military, the family, and the monarchy" (Wright, "Study of Ritual," in Greenspahn, *Hebrew Bible*, 129).

10. Psalm 145:18: "Yhwh is near to all who call on him, to all who call on him in truth" (קָר֣וֹב יְ֭הוָה לְכָל־קֹרְאָ֑יו לְכֹ֤ל אֲשֶׁ֖ר יִקְרָאֻ֣הוּ בֶאֱמֶֽת).

engage their context in Chronicles, they discern this analogy that the Chronicler designed. Also, they could apply the theological principles or messages contained in the texts to their present life setting. For instance, in Jehoshaphat's prayer and story, readers could learn that God is described as the God of justice. The post-exilic community could then hope that that particular attribute of God (i.e., justice) would work in their own circumstances. Consequently, the historical prayer could be suitably assimilated into the readers' present life situation.[11]

One should also notice that this participating process does not take place automatically or every time an audience reads or hears prayers, because it requires the readers' particular attention to the prayers. The readers' special attention is critical, since it transforms readers into supplicants. Participating in prayer includes the acts of humbling one's heart and listening, agreeing, partaking with prayer's pleas, lamenting, questioning, praising, or hoping.[12] Therefore, the texts provide a chance for readers to be attentive to prayers by providing signals that summon readers to the prayers, thus allowing the invitation to occur. Also, the Chronicler deliberately chooses to let his readers listen to the prayer's own verbal formulation.[13] The recorded prayer is the Chronicler's literary artifact, in which he presents prayer's unique communicative nature between the divine and a human and reflects the prayer's particular purpose and form.[14]

Prayer as Memory and Hope

Prayer enables the readers to mediate between the past and their present circumstances. The prayers in Chronicles contain memories (i.e., ancient history) like other aspects of narrative. Praying through these memories is effective because God is responsible for them (as the Sustainer), and the prayer participant is an inheritor of them.[15] The people in the past prayed

---

11. Wirzba, "Attention and Responsibility," in Benson and Wirzba, *Phenomenology of Prayer*, 89.

12. Wirzba, "Attention and Responsibility," 89.

13. I.e., direct speech, particular grammatical, literary structure, tone, unique word choices, etc. These could separate prayers, make them distinct from the flow of narratives, and extend a fresh invitation to readers.

14. Greenberg, *Biblical Prose Prayer*, 8.

15. Jeremiah 31:33 implies a connection between memory and devotion (FitzGerald, *Spiritual Modalities*, 102, 113). Although Daffern focuses on the psalm, her idea

to God, and so the present audience (i.e., the post-exilic community) prays to the same God as they apply the prayer to their own unique situation.

Prayer hopes for God's aid, protection, intervention, forgiveness, etc. The supplicants expect God to respond to their prayer and change their current situation.[16] The supplicants are not satisfied with maintaining their status quo but try to actualize a better situation.[17] In the case of the post-exilic community, then, the people could have hope and express that hope to God. Postulating that the post-exilic community was familiar with passages from the book of Jeremiah,[18] the people believed that they would be able to change their situation because God promised them that when they pray (קְרָא), he would provide them with transformative ability (וְאַגִּידָה לְךָ גְּדֹלוֹת וּבְצֻרוֹת לֹא יְדַעְתָּם [I will tell you great and hidden things you do not know (Jer 33:3)]).[19] The people knew that God is the source of hope (תִּקְוָה) and that he could bring about a better future if they prayed to him (Jer 29:10–13).

The Chronicler's Intention: Past Prayer as a Model

The Chronicler intends to provide model prayers for the post-exilic readers. As is stated before, the Chronicler's intention does not mean that the readers always mimic those prayers in an exact manner; rather, they

---

is linked to Chronicles. She points out that certain psalms (e.g., Ps 132) encourage people to remember David and his covenantal relationship with God. This actually happens in the book of Chronicles (1 Chr 16:4, 12, 15). She writes further, "Humans as the readers or performers of the text are the agents of remembering, while God is the fundamentally most desirable agent of remembering. Prayer, then, involves both God and humans both as effective agents of remembering, and also as the object of memory" (Daffern, "Semantic Field," 79, 85, 95).

16. Heschel, *Prophets*, 442; FitzGerald, *Spiritual Modalities*, 69. See Ps 5:4 (Eng. v. 3), "O Yhwh, in the morning, you shall hear my voice; In the morning, I will order my prayer to you and eagerly watch" (יְהוָה בֹּקֶר תִּשְׁמַע קוֹלִי בֹּקֶר אֶעֱרָךְ־לְךָ וַאֲצַפֶּה). See also v. 3 (Eng. v. 2) where is written אֶתְפַּלָּל (to pray).

17. Even if supplicants are in a desperate situation and are not able to seek hope, the prayer itself still has the power to transform their hearts and allow them to hope for a better world. For example, David's prayer in Ps 77 shows how David's inner mind is changed as he prays to God.

18. See Jer 29:1; 43; 44; 51:59–62. It seems that the Chronicler knew Jeremiah's oracle. See also Warhurst, "Chronicler's Use of Prophets," in Ben Zvi and Edelman, *What Was Authoritative*, 179–80.

19. The context of Jer 33:3 communicates that God brings about the needed changes (see 33:2, 6–11).

perceive, interpret, and apply relevant principles to their current circumstances. His intention is revealed through a few instances in the book. First, in Jehoshaphat's prayer, the king keeps in view how his ancestors prayed and what God had done for them (2 Chr 20:7–12). As Jehoshaphat asks for God's intervention in Israel's difficult situation, he brings up God's promise to Abraham in 2 Chronicles 20:7. This reminds readers of the prayer in 1 Chronicles 16, which also mentions the Abrahamic covenant (vv. 16–18).[20] It is further noticeable that the literary context of this forefather's prayer (1 Chr 16:16–23) strongly encourages people to remember and praise God for his protection of Israel. In Jehoshaphat's perspective, then, God, the Savior (יְשׁוּעָתוֹ [his salvation (1 Chr 16:23)]) in Israel's past, could still work for him now. Second, Jehoshaphat's words of prayer in 2 Chronicles 20:8–9 appropriate what Solomon prays to God in 2 Chronicles 6:28, and God answers him in 7:13–16. Jehoshaphat's word choices (e.g., דֶּבֶר and רָעָב) and the way he appeals to God show that the king is not mimicking an ancestor's prayer, but that he perceives, interprets, and applies it as a model prayer to his particular situation. In sum, although these three prayers (1 Chr 16:8–36; 2 Chr 6:12–38; 20:5–12) occur in different literary historical situations, Jehoshaphat is able to adopt his ancestor's prayers and appropriate them into his own situation as he is eager to overcome his imminent difficulties. Third, the prayer of 1 Chronicles 16 can be another example which is composed of Psalms 96, 105 and 106. This prayer also shows that different prayers can be combined, interpreted in a new way (e.g., descendants of Abraham [Ps 105:6]; descendants of Israel [1 Chr 16:13]), and applied to a particular situation (i.e., transferring the Ark to Jerusalem). Therefore, both prayers (1 Chr 16 and 2 Chr 20) show that the Chronicler intends for the prayers to serve as models for the post-exilic readers.

The notion that prayers serve the readers as models indicates then that readers receive prayers more than merely as isolated historical narratives. In other words, prayers become a part of their life. If ancient supplicants adopted other prayers for dealing with their contemporary concerns, then a door opens for the readers of Chronicles to be able to do the same, adopting and utilizing prayers from Chronicles. In the process of identity reconstruction, model prayers provide a chance for supplicants to identify elements or principles which they can possibly apply

20. The name of Abraham appears eight times in Chronicles, and only these two instances in prayers clearly connote God's promise to Abraham (1 Chr 1:27, 28, 32, 34; 16:16; 29:18; 2 Chr 20:7; 30:6).

to their life settings, such as model prayers' description of the vertical relationship between a human and God, or particular roles and characteristics of characters in a story.[21] Jehoshaphat's prayer again provides an example relevant to this matter. Jehoshaphat identifies Israel as God's people (2 Chr 20:7) as he recalls Abraham in 1 Chronicles 16. Concerning roles or characteristics, Jehoshaphat brings up the act of prayer (2 Chr 20:9) from Solomon's prayer (2 Chr 6) and adopts the role of a supplicant in order to defeat his adversaries (2 Chr 20:12–13).[22]

Transformation of Attitude through Prayer

When supplicants desire to change their situation for the better, prayer can function to motivate and transform those individuals.[23] The process

---

21. Although this book does not wholly adopt Kugel's view, Kugel provides a similar view on this book's observation regarding past prayer as a model. His argument assumes a situation that a supplicant cites the Scriptures which were given in the days prior to a current supplicant. Kugel argues that citing the past Scriptures in a prayer functions to "(1) evoke biblical instances of divine intervention so as to suggest a parallel with one's present situation and hence to spur a new divine intervention now; (2) mention illustrious biblical ancestors in the hope of having some of their luster reflect on oneself; (3) use today the same biblical words that had 'worked' in the past in the hope of obtaining the same result; (4) praise God with the same words that He had apparently ordered His angels to use in praising Him; (5) speak to God in the elegant idiom of His own choice biblical servants" (Kugel, "Scripturalization of Prayer," in Kugel, *Prayers That Cite Scripture*, 3).

Now, the citing of past Scripture is not technically different from a situation that this book assumes (i.e., a supplicant adopting or citing a past prayer and transforming it into his own prayer). This book argues concerning the recorded prayers in an authoritative writing, Chronicles. In other words, when the audience of the post-exilic community received the past prayers in Chronicles, they essentially received the authoritative Scriptures.

22. Not only does the scene of prayer itself in 2 Chr 20:5–13 show that Jehoshaphat and his people pray to God, but also the Chronicler specifically indicates through the contents of the king's prayer that the king and people take up the role of supplicant (what Solomon prays: יִתְפַּלֵּל עַבְדְּךָ אֶל־הַמָּקוֹם הַזֶּה, "your servant prays toward this place" [2 Chr 6:20]; Jehoshaphat's prayer according to his model prayer: נַעַמְדָה לִפְנֵי הַבַּיִת הַזֶּה וּלְפָנֶיךָ, "we will stand before this house and before you" [2 Chr 20:9]; עָלֶיךָ עֵינֵינוּ, "our eyes are on you" [2 Chr 20:12]; וְכָל־יְהוּדָה עֹמְדִים לִפְנֵי יְהוָה, "all Judah were standing before Yhwh" [2 Chr 20:13]).

23. Job 22:27–28 implies that the supplicant may want to behave as one who prays to God: "You will pray to Him, and He will hear you; and you will pay your vows. You will decide on a matter, and it will be established for you, and light will shine on your ways," תַּעְתִּיר אֵלָיו וְיִשְׁמָעֶךָּ וּנְדָרֶיךָ תְשַׁלֵּם וְתִגְזַר־אֹמֶר וְיָקָם לָךְ וְעַל־דְּרָכֶיךָ נָגַהּ אוֹר.

of participation in prayer includes the refinement of the individual's passions as he or she follows up the recorded prayer's model language or behavior with his or her own truth claims.[24] Specifically, when the readers of Chronicles witness that a supplicant receives God's positive answer in the story (i.e., effectiveness of prose prayer), then the prayer effectively motivates and transforms the audience's attitude to fulfill a perceived role or characteristic.

Identity and Effectiveness of Prayer

Identity in the prayers in Chronicles is not always revealed explicitly. The Chronicler's primary purpose is not in formulating a particular identity; instead, he records the history of Israel, not according to a thematic (systematic) method but according to the historical timeline, with the addition of his own modifications (strategic). Thus, understanding prayer's effectiveness in its literary and ideological (theological) contexts assists in determining the described roles or characteristics of the audience.

Hence, this book does not insist that prayers are the only vehicle to convey the Chronicler's message; instead, they are embedded in different genres consistent with the rest of Chronicles, and they imprint the Chronicler's messages within them.[25] This indicates that a particular prayer's message should be confirmed throughout Chronicles. Also, the near context of a given prayer enhances the effectiveness of that prayer. Although God's instant response is not guaranteed during the prayer, the near context often offers responses to that particular prayer. For instance, the prayer in 1 Chronicles 16:8–36 praises God and encourages the people

---

24. Mooney, "Becoming What We Pray," in Benson and Wirzba, *Phenomenology of Prayer*, 51.

25. Peterson writes, "And it is inherent in the very nature of prayer that its function reaches beyond its role in the structure and the plot, its thematic relationship to the narrative context, and its depiction of the characters" (Peterson, "Theology and the Function," 43–44). Gilmour argues that writers of historiography use various literary devices to emphasize their particular view, for instance, the repetition of key ideas, the careful choice of words, and the imposition of structure. This implies that the Chronicler could use prayers in order to accentuate his message (Gilmour, *Representing the Past*, 16). Balentine says, "I suggest that prose prayer and the narrative context which embrace them provide an important opportunity to view the literary and theological function of prayer, an opportunity not generally afforded in the poetic traditions where the relation of the text to context is so often inherently ambiguous" (Balentine, "Prayers for Justice," 601).

to be worshipers of him. Verses 37–43 go on to describe the scene of worship, which could be an example to the Chronicler's audience of what they should do and how they should do it, as they pray. Solomon's prayer in 2 Chronicles 6 is another example. The king's prayer is not answered during his speech (vv. 14–42); but, when he finishes his prayer, fire comes down from heaven (2 Chr 7:1), implicitly indicating that his prayer is answered. Later in chapter 7, God answers Solomon's prayer explicitly (vv. 11–16). Further, other royal prayers (e.g., 2 Chr 14:11; 20:5–12), which follow Solomon's supplication, are answered by God (2 Chr 14:12–15; 20:22–30). Therefore, these confirmations give hope to the audience that the prayer they offer in the present would be answered in the future; thus, the prayer could provide more persuasive power.

Identity Identification in Prayer

The discussion on prayer's rhetoric suggests two basic considerations regarding what this book should seek to determine concerning identity in Chronicles: how the prayer understands God and oneself (vertical) and how it understands the situation/world (horizontal). First, since the prayer is communication between a human and the divine, the way the Chronicler projects the supplicant's perspective toward God and oneself is critical. This vertical relationship between two parties defines the supplicant's identity (i.e., characteristic). In other words, the Chronicler's characterization of a supplicant and God is one way to determine an identity. Furthermore, since the prayer is embedded in the narratives, the way the prayer's context describes the characters also can be meaningful. A character's particular attitude or perspective toward God and oneself is shaped throughout the narratives and is highlighted through the prayer's unique features. Thus, a character in a prayer should be evaluated in line with the related narratives.[26] Overall, this book will investigate the Chronicler's depiction of characters in both prayers and narratives.

Second, identity can be determined through analysis of the situations of prayer (horizontal), because people perceive their identity as they relate to two situations: the situation in Chronicles (literary historical) and their own contemporary situation (sociohistorical). The primary task for this book is to analyze the literary historical situation, since the prayer participants are invited to participate in and interpret the prayers

---

26. Watts, *Psalm and Story*, 17.

in Chronicles and then apply them to their life setting (heuristic task). In a given literary historical situation, the Chronicler's particular message or theological principle which is embedded in prayer enables the prayer participants to discern the model language or ideal behavior that a supplicant should manifest. The Chronicler's intended message or principle often stretches across the prayer's near contexts and even repeats in the metanarratives, further assisting the prayer participants to perceive their identity. Therefore, investigating the literary historical situations will be a critical task for this book.

In summary, the criteria for identification of identity (roles or characteristics) are as follows: (1) how the Chronicler reveals God and supplicant (characterization); (2) what the given situation is which surrounds the prayer and its contexts, what the explicit or implicit message is or what the theological principles are in the context, and how the prayers and contexts communicate with each other (literary historical context); (3) what the exegetical/literary indicators are (e.g., word, phrase, grammatical/syntactical relations, literary structures) which specifically enable readers to perceive identity (roles or characteristics) from prayer and its context; (4) how the metanarrative confirms a theme/message of prayer (thematic unity); and (5) how effective prayer is as it relates to its contexts. This research recognizes that, first, these considerations could serve each other in the process of identifying identity, and, second, that one should not presume that each prayer would equally reflect each of the five considerations listed above.

Tracing Israel Identity in Sociohistorical Context

Chapter 4 will trace the roles and characteristics portrayed in chapter 3 within the post-exilic sociohistorical situation under Persian governance. The post-exilic community needed to properly interpret the message of the Chronicler, since the book records Israel's pre-exilic history; thus, it is essentially anachronistic for the community's particular situation. In this regard, this book will examine the roles and characteristics—revealed in the literary historical context in chapter 3—within the sociohistorical situation of the community, in order to reveal the Chronicler's intended messages and hope toward the post-exilic community. This task will eventually reveal possible implications of these roles and characteristics in the community's particular situation.

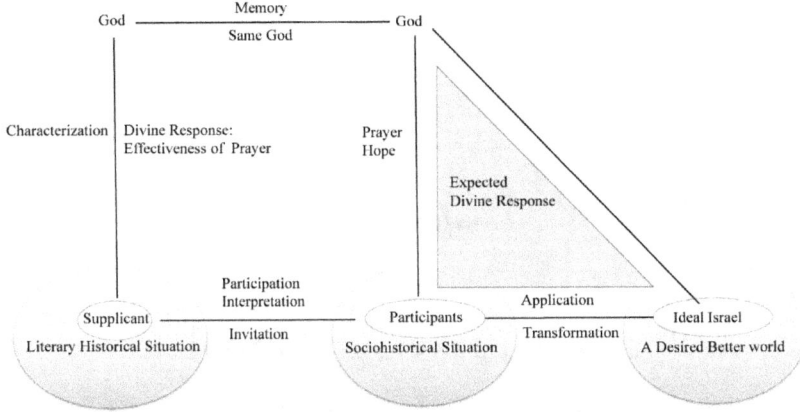

Figure. Rhetoric of Prayer in Relation to Identity Formation

— *Chapter Three* —

Recorded Prayers in Chronicles
Literary Rhetorical Analysis

Introduction

THIS CHAPTER PROVIDES THE exegetical, literary, and rhetorical analysis of eight prayers in Chronicles (1 Chr 4:9–10; 16:8–36; 17:16–27; 29:10–19; 2 Chr 6:12–38; 14:10 [Eng. v. 11]; 20:5–12; 30:18–20) according to the methodological considerations introduced in the previous chapter. These prayers portray the Chronicler's vision for the Yehud community's identity through descriptions of particular roles or characteristics. Since each prayer can exhibit different aspects of each role or characteristic, a careful examination of each prayer will reveal the multifaceted nature of the roles and characteristics that are portrayed throughout Chronicles. This chapter will reveal the roles or characteristics of the community in the Chronicler's portrayal as follows: the praying, worshiping, and monotheistic believing community that is composed of the citizens of the Davidic kingdom.

First Chronicles 4:9–10: Jabez's Prayer

Introduction

The recorded prayer of Jabez in 1 Chronicles 4:9–10 is embedded in the genealogy section (chs. 1–9) in Chronicles. This prayer has become world renowned through Bruce Wilkinson's book *The Prayer of Jabez: Breaking Through to the Blessed Life*, yet the prayer has still been peripheral in the scope of scholarly research.¹ Despite the paucity of studies, several scholars have contributed to deciphering some enigmas of the text, such as the nature of Jabez's pain, the meaning of his request to God, the identity of the supplicant, and the literary function of the text of the prayer in relation to the genre of genealogy.² Yet most commentators agree that the

---

1. Bruce Wilkinson's publication became a worldwide bestselling book exceeding 20 million books sold and receiving the Christian Retailing's Best Award (2001), the ECPA Book Sales Achievement Award (2001), and the Christian Book Award (2001).

The database of the ATLA showed for 1954 only one result of a sermon reprinted concerning the prayer of Jabez, yet even in 2018, it still results in only eleven indexed publications that are specifically devoted to the prayer of Jabez (Heard, "Echoes of Genesis," §1.2).

2. For instance, Heard's main points are basically two: (1) understanding בְּעֹצֶב (1 Chr 4:9) not as pain but as pastureland, and (2) the reason that Jabez receives honor is due to his non-violent way of acquiring the land, as opposed to the Simeonites, Reubenites, and Manasites (Heard, "Echoes of Genesis," §2.7, 2.10, 2.1.2, 3.1.3). See Pechawer, who also insists that Jabez's request is pastureland (Pechawer, *Lost Prayer of Jabez*). Iain Provan's question lies in the nature of Jabez's problem. Provan believes that Jabez's problem was not simply his given name as an omen (future threat or destiny) but that the supplicant actually experiences pain in his life (Provan, "Pain in Childbirth?," in Boda and Provan, *Let Us Go Up*, 285–96). French's contribution is to provide the history of scholarship on this particular text from the early rabbis, medieval times, post-Reformation ages, and to the modern period by introducing some of the major figures such as R. Simon b. Pazzi, Rabbi Ishmael, Saadia Gaon, Stephen Langton, Daniel Turner, Charles Spurgeon, and, most recently, Bruce Wilkinson (French, *Chronicles through the Centuries*, 32–37). Sparks explains the prayer in relation to the genre of narratives and genealogy. He observes that there are seven narratives embedded in genealogy that raise particular attentions. He compares and contrasts six narratives to the narrative of Jabez's prayer and concludes that the positive description of the person Jabez emphasizes the efficacy of prayer (Sparks, *Chronicler's Genealogies*, 237–39). Although Japhet is not the only scholar who argues for an etiological characteristic of the text, she espouses it by comparing the pattern of other typical datum in Scripture and of Jabez's prayer, which highlights the theme of prayer (Japhet, *First and Second Chronicles*, 108–11). For futher information, see Bonder, "Reading the Lists," in Evans and Williams, *Chronicling the Chronicler*, 29–41.

Commentators have also argued that genealogy in Chronicles introduces the major themes, including the theme of prayer, in the following narratives (i.e., 1 Chr 10–12, 2 Chr 36) (Heard, "Echoes of Genesis," §3.2.1). Duke writes, "They [chs. 1–9] establish the principal subjects of the narrative, the theological concerns of the narrator, the general time parameters and the laws of reality at work within the story's world-view" (Duke, *Persuasive Appeal*, 55). Duke sees that Chronicles consists of three sections: (1) genealogy (1 Chr 1–9), (2) David and Solomon narratives (1 Chr 10–12, 2 Chr 9), and (3) stories of the kings of Judah (2 Chr 10–36). He argues that these three sections function rhetorically as an introduction, the presentation of argument, and the proof of argumentation. See also Duke, "Rhetorical Approach," in Graham and McKenzie, *Chronicler as Author*, 119. See also other commentators, who insist on the

major theme of the text is the effectiveness and importance of the prayer.³ In light of this thematic concern, this book particularly argues that Jabez is a model figure, whose recorded prayer is intended to encourage the post-exilic audience to be an active praying community, especially during times of tribulation.⁴

Shaping Israelites as Active Supplicants

Several aspects receive attention in the given passage as they contribute to forming the audience into active supplicants: (1) the Chronicler's esteem of Jabez among his brothers (v. 9a-b), (2) the etiological structure concerning Jabez's name and his life report (v. 9b and v. 10b), and (3) the establishing of a contrast between Jabez's life story (4:9–10) and other figures' stories in genealogies (2:3, 7; 2:18–19, 21–23, 24, 34, 35).

First, the Chronicler writes that Jabez was honored by his brothers; the anecdote of Jabez's life reveals that this was due to his prayer to God. The Chronicler does not provide a reason for this respect for Jabez in his initial introduction. Then, the Chronicler provides the negative origin of Jabez's name by recording his mother's first person speech (v. 9).⁵ Thus, as readers receive the negative impression of Jabez's name, they might raise an etymological question regarding his name (i.e., עֹצֶב [pain (v. 9)]): Why

---

introductory function of genealogy in light of the entire book of Chronicles. Knoppers refers to the genealogies as a prologue (Knoppers, *First Chronicles 1–9*, 259–60). See also McKenzie, *First and Second Chronicles*, 60; Hill, *First and Second Chronicles*, 47; Boda, *First-Second Chronicles*, 57; Schweitzer, "Genealogies of 1 Chronicles 1–9," in Evans and Williams, *Chronicling the Chronicler*, 13–16. For an extensive study of the genre of genealogies in the Bible, see R. Wilson, *Genealogy and History*.

Scholars have discussed the formulation of the book from the standpoint of redaction of the book. This book is not interested in sources of the book; instead, it focuses on the final form of the book. For further information concerning the source and composition of the book, see DeVries, *First and Second Chronicles*, 12–13; McKenzie, *First and Second Chronicles*, 27–29; Williamson, "Sources and Redaction."

3. Sparks, *Chronicler's Genealogies*, 239; Provan, "Pain in Childbirth?," in Boda and Provan, *Let Us Go Up*, 285–96; Heard, "Echoes of Genesis," §3.2.1; Japhet, *First and Second Chronicles*, 110–11; Williamson, *First and Second Chronicles*, 59–60; Pratt, *First and Second Chronicles*, 74–75; Hill, *First and Second Chronicles*, 95–96; Knoppers, *First Chronicles 1–9*, 346; R. Klein, *First Chronicles*, 132–33.

4. Hahn similarly observes, "Perhaps we are being invited to see Jabez as an ideal or model citizen of God's kingdom" (Hahn, *Kingdom of God*, 41).

5. It reads, וְאִמּוֹ קָרְאָה שְׁמוֹ יַעְבֵּץ לֵאמֹר כִּי יָלַדְתִּי בְּעֹצֶב ("His mother named him Jabez, saying, 'Because I bore him in pain'").

did the person whose name had been cursed receive such honor?⁶ The tension between the positive historical report (i.e., נִכְבָּד [honored (v. 9)]) and the negative meaning of the name (i.e., pain) create a rhetorical effect for readers, but this tension is quickly resolved as they witness Jabez's act of prayer and God's answer to the prayer with blessing (v. 10b). The positive ending of the story indicates that Jabez received honor because, through the prayer, he had overcome his sinister omen (i.e., the prediction of a troubled life).⁷

Second, an etiological observation regarding Jabez's name and life story also provides a clue to understanding how the prayer of Jabez is able to persuade readers to be a praying community. In the Hebrew Bible, the text often provides stories that explain the origin of the names.⁸ Interestingly, in Jabez's story, Chronicles provides more information about Jabez's life after he received his name. Therefore, three elements should be considered: (1) the story that explains the cause of the appellation (i.e., Jabez's mother's birth pangs), (2) the particular name of the person (i.e., Jabez), and (3) the additional report after the naming (i.e., the subsequent description of Jabez's life story).⁹ The third element is often

---

6. Pratt, *First and Second Chronicles*, 74; R. Klein, *First Chronicles*, 133; Japhet, *First and Second Chronicles*, 109; Mabie, *First, Second Chronicles-Job*, 62.

Note that the Scripture does not directly note that the meaning of the name Jabez is pain, and there is no definite connection between the name and its meaning. The most probable assumption, therefore, would be the text's comment (i.e., the mother's first person speech), which provides the hint for the origin of Jabez's name. Further, a few scholars have provided an observation on Gen 3:16, to which they believe the name Jabez alludes (Japhet, *First and Second Chronicles*, 109; McKenzie, *First and Second Chronicles*, 80; Ruiten, "Eve's Pain in Childbearing?," in Luttikhuizen, *Eve's Children*, 41).

7. The text does not clarify the nature of his trouble. It seems that a majority number of scholars believe it to be Jabez's mother's omen, though Provan insists that Jabez's pain was real and experienced in his life (Provan, "Pain in Childbirth?," in Boda and Provan, *Let Us Go Up*, 285–96). Several scholars who believe it to be omen are as follows: Williamson, *First and Second Chronicles*, 59; Dirksen, *First Chronicles*, 70; Tuell, *First and Second Chronicles*, 28; Boda, *First-Second Chronicles*, 57.

8. Japhet, *First and Second Chronicles*, 109. See also DeVries, who particularly explains about name etiology. He writes, "NAME ETIOLOGY (Namensätiologie). The explanation of a name by association with an event, commonly involving wordplay or punning (alternate name: ETYMOLOGICAL ETIOLOGY). 1 Chr 1:19; 4:9, 14; 7:23; 13:11; 14:11; 22:9; 2 Chr 20:26" (DeVries, *First and Second Chronicles*, 432).

9. It seems that many times in the Hebrew Bible, etiology offers the first and the second elements. For instance, 1 Chr 1:19 writes the cause (כִּי בְיָמָיו נִפְלְגָה הָאָרֶץ, "for in his days the earth was divided") and names only Peleg and Joktan. First Chronicles 4:14 also provides the cause (כִּי חֲרָשִׁים הָיוּ, "for they were craftsmen") and names only Ophrah and Joab. First Chronicles 7:23 also shows the cause (כִּי בְרָעָה הָיְתָה בְּבֵיתוֹ,

supplementary information that further emphasizes the significance of the given name.¹⁰ However, in Jabez's story, this third element does not emphasize the significance of the name but presents something different; so, it betrays readers' anticipation concerning Jabez's destiny.¹¹ In other words, the passage opens up the possibility of Jabez's life being a miserable journey, but Chronicles does not report his life as painful but as prosperous.¹² This twist creates a rhetorical effect and tells readers that the prayer has the power to change the presumed destiny of one's life.¹³

Third, the characterization of Jabez as an exemplary model compared to other figures in the genealogy is able to shape the post-exilic readers into active supplicants. There are seven life stories, including the person of Jabez, in the genealogies, and the story of Jabez marks a unique contrast to the other narratives in the Judahite genealogy.¹⁴ Unlike Jabez's

---

"because misfortune had come upon his house"), naming only Beriah.

10. E.g., Gen 21:32–34; 26:20–22; 27:20–22; 31:50–53; Judg 15:19b; 1 Sam 7:13–14; 2 Sam 5:21; 6:8b (cf. 1 Chr 13:11b); 1 Kgs 9:13b; 1 Chr 22:9b; 2 Chr 20:26b.

11. Japhet's etiological observation is not adequately observant. She writes, "In general, an aetiology offers an explanation for a given datum (commonly, but not always, a name) by recounting the causes from which it arose and demonstrating a positive connection between datum and causes. . . . While this story contains several aetiological elements, its core is contradictory rather than causal: how did it happen that a man by the name of 'Jabez' was, nevertheless, prosperous!" (Japhet, *First and Second Chronicles*, 109). When reflecting on Japhet's own words, "a positive connection between datum and causes," Jabez's story follows the usual pattern. He received his name because of his mother's birth pangs, so it is not unusual but normal. There is no shift in this relationship; the shift occurs only in the additional report of Jabez's life.

12. Japhet, *First and Second Chronicles*, 109.

13. Interestingly, Exod 15:22–25 exhibits high similarity with Jabez's prayer concerning the pattern of etiological presentation and the effectiveness of the prayer. The passage provides the cause of the place's name (כִּי מָרִים הֵם, "they were bitter") and then writes its name (עַל־כֵּן קָרָא־שְׁמָהּ מָרָה, "therefore, its name was called Mara") in v. 23. The following additional note, however, does not emphasize the significance of the name; rather, it reports the event that does not cohere with the meaning of the name (וַיִּמְתְּקוּ הַמָּיִם, "the water became sweet"), and this positive result was made possible through Moses's prayer (וַיִּצְעַק אֶל־יְהוָה, "he cried to the Lord") in v. 25. Therefore, this exodus report is also one good example, showing that just like Jabez's prayer, Moses changed a miserable circumstance into a preferable one through his prayer.

14. See 1 Chr 2:3, 7; 2:18–19, 21–23, 24, 34, 35; 4:9–10. Sparks's observation is particularly helpful for this book (Sparks, *Chronicler's Genealogies*, 236–46). Millar expands the scope of his research to include the prayers in other genealogies of tribes, yet he similarly notices the function of the prayers: "In order to encourage God's people to throw themselves on him, these prayers [i.e., the prayers of Jabez, Reubenites, Gadites, and Manassites] are embedded in the middle of the long section designed to expound

life, the portrayed lives in the other six stories are unfavorable and show somewhat negative aspects of life in the community.[15] Although Jabez's life begins with a negative report on the background of his birth (i.e., his accursed name), the passage ends with the account of God's blessing him without any negative evaluation. This ending demonstrates a clear contrast with the other narratives and conveys the message that there is a unique element in Jabez's life: prayer.

In sum, the rhetorical effect that Jabez's prayer produces is sufficient to persuade the post-exilic readers to pray. The Chronicler's portrayal of Jabez, the etiological structure of the prayer, and the comparison between the life of Jabez and others in the surrounding genealogies show the post-exilic community that prayer has the power to change an individual's life.

Praying like Jabez

If the text tells the community that prayer has the power to change a person's life, then the next step would be to determine the manner of prayer. A closer investigation of the prayer reveals three essential principles of the prayer: (1) the God of Israel as the object of the prayer, (2) the reason that God is the object of the prayer, and (3) the situation for offering the prayer. The structure of the passage depicted below helps to clarify these principal aspects of prayer.[16]

---

the heart of the Israelite problem" (Millar, *Calling on the Name*, 126).

15. For instance, 1 Chr 2:3 writes about Er, who was evil in the eyes of the Lord (רַע בְּעֵינֵי יְהוָה); v. 7 provides a negative description of Achar, who makes trouble on Israel (רַע בְּעֵינֵי יְהוָה); v. 19 reports the death of Caleb's wife, Azubah (וַתָּמָת עֲזוּבָה); in vv. 22–23, Segub and his son Jair lost their town by Geshur and Aram (וַיִּקַּח גְּשׁוּר־וַאֲרָם אֶת־חַוֹּת יָאִיר); v. 24 conveys the death of Hezron (וְאַחַר מוֹת־חֶצְרוֹן); and finally, in v. 34, the Chronicler writes that Sheshan had no sons (וְלֹא־הָיָה לְשֵׁשָׁן בָּנִים).

16. In this book, the rules of diagramming the passage are as follows: (1) when there is more than one verb or any part of speech that acts like a main verb in a sentence or clause, the line is divided into two or more lines (if the verb is implied, then it qualifies as one line); (2) an exception to the previous rule is that the lines are separated if there is any particular parallel that may show the emphasis of the passage; (3) the diagram notes direct speech separately with a marker (e.g., לֵאמֹר); and (4) the relative clause (e.g., אֲשֶׁר) goes with the next line of an independent clause.

וַיְהִי יַעְבֵּץ נִכְבָּד מֵאֶחָיו
וְאִמּוֹ קָרְאָה‎ᵃ שְׁמוֹ יַעְבֵּץ לֵאמֹר
כִּי יָלַדְתִּי בְּעֹצֶב
וַיִּקְרָא‎ᵇ יַעְבֵּץ לֵאלֹהֵי יִשְׂרָאֵל לֵאמֹר
אִם־בָּרֵךְ תְּבָרֲכֵנִי
וְהִרְבִּיתָ אֶת־גְּבוּלִי
וְהָיְתָה יָדְךָ עִמִּי
וְעָשִׂיתָ מֵּרָעָה לְבִלְתִּי עָצְבִּי
וַיָּבֵא‎ᶜ אֱלֹהִים אֵת אֲשֶׁר־שָׁאָל

First, Jabez's prayer elucidates the object of prayer: the God of Israel. The different acts of three characters in the prayer support this notion. The mother calls (קָרְאָה [named (a)]) her son Jabez—the sign that there is the problem. But, the son reacts to his name by calling (וַיִּקְרָא [prayed (b)]) on the God of Israel—the attempt to solve the problem. Then, God answers (וַיָּבֵא [granted (c)]) Jabez's prayer—the resolution of the problem. The above literary analysis of the passage shows that these three acts stand separately from the mother's appellation or the contents of the prayer by the direct speech marker (לֵאמֹר [saying]). Now, the passage shows that both the acts of the mother and Jabez share the same verbal root קרא (to call), but the former act brings about a problem to one's life, and the latter brings about the solution of the problem, which ultimately leads to Jabez receiving God's blessing. In order to maximize this antithesis, the Chronicler locates the subject (וְאִמּוֹ [his mother]) before the main verb (קָרְאָה) in verse 9; hence the text highlights the origin of the problem (i.e., the mother); whereas in verse 10, the Chronicler evidently provides the object of the prayer, לֵאלֹהֵי יִשְׂרָאֵל (the God of Israel). Therefore, the Chronicler conveys that Jabez's response to his trouble (i.e., וְאִמּוֹ קָרְאָה שְׁמוֹ [his mother's calling]) is to lift it up to God (i.e., וַיִּקְרָא יַעְבֵּץ לֵאלֹהֵי יִשְׂרָאֵל [praying to the God of Israel]). The Chronicler tells his readers that praying to the God of Israel is the way to solve the problem.[17] The final report of Jabez's life enhances this message, as it clearly notes that God grants what Jabez asked for (v. 10b).

---

17. The Chronicler emphasizes that the object of prayer is God (of Israel, of fathers, etc.) throughout other narratives and recorded prayers in Chronicles. See 1 Chr 5:20; 2 Chr 6:14–15, 20; 7:14; 14:10 (Eng. v. 11); 20:6; 30:18–19.

Japhet observes this epithet (i.e., the God of Israel) and says, "It testifies to a direct bond between YHWH and His people" (Japhet, *Ideology of the Book*, 16). See also pp. 67–70 of her book for "The Relationship between YHWH and the People of Israel."

Second, the contents of the prayer provide the reason that God should be the object of the prayer. Jabez begins his prayer by saying אִם־ בָּרֵךְ תְּבָרֲכֵנִי (if only you would bless me) in verse 10. The function of the word אִם is somewhat obscure in this phrase. The word is usually employed in a conditional clause (i.e., if), but there is no apodosis in the following clause.[18] The most probable translation would be "oh that you would bless me" or "if only you would bless me" as the expression of Jabez's desire or request.[19] The infinitive absolute form of ברך (to bless) reinforces the message that Jabez strongly desires to receive God's blessing upon his life. Jabez requests that God's hands would be with him (וְהָיְתָה יָדְךָ עִמִּי [v. 10]), and in Chronicles, God's hands represent a source of power, strength, and abundance (1 Chr 29:16; 2 Chr 6:32; 20:6).[20] Jabez's desire is not hopeless since he believes that God's hands (יָדְךָ [your hands]) would work for him. Therefore, Jabez's prayer tells the reason for praying to the God of Israel: he has power and strength to fulfill supplicants' requests (שָׁאַל [v. 10b]).

Third, the content of the prayer specifically speaks about Jabez's miserable circumstances, so this prayer can tell readers to which circumstances this model prayer may apply in their own lives. Scholars have observed that Jabez's requests for the enlargement of territory (וְהִרְבִּיתָ אֶת־גְּבוּלִי) and the protection from evil and pain (וְעָשִׂיתָ מֵּרָעָה לְבִלְתִּי עָצְבִּי) reflect the difficult situations that the post-exilic community might encounter; the prayer is appropriate for the circumstances of the post-exilic community.[21] Thus, Jabez's prayer is able to help the readers in the post-exilic community cope with their own difficult circumstances.

18. Japhet, *First and Second Chronicles*, 110.

19. ESV, NASB, NIV, NKJ, NLT, NRS, etc. In other words, אִם has a desiderative function in this passage (Joüon, *Grammar of Biblical Hebrew*, §163c). See also Pss 81:9; 139:19.

20. God's hands are certainly at work in the Chronicler's history: his hands hold strength and might (2 Chr 29:12). Through God's hands, he fulfills his promise (2 Chr 6:4, 15); establishes and prospers the kingdom (2 Chr 17:5); and gives the commandment (2 Chr 29:25). His hands change one's heart or mind to obey his commandment (2 Chr 30:12).

21. Pratt writes, "Jabez's prayer related directly to the needs of the Chronicler's original readers in at least three ways. First, the Chronicler's readers had experienced much pain during and after the exile. They certainly would have identified with Jabez's desire. Second, Jabez's prayer touched on the issue of expanding the territories of post-exilic Judah . . . . Third, the Chronicler pointed to Jabez as an example of an appropriate way to gain relief from the problems of suffering and territorial expansion" (Pratt, *First and Second Chronicles*, 100). See also Jonker, *First and Second Chronicles*,

Conclusion

The prayer persuades the post-exilic community in order to shape them into actively praying people. The Chronicler characterizes Jabez as an exemplary model who prayed during difficult times; consequently, the prayer could encourage the post-exilic community to follow the same path that Jabez walked. The prayer exhorts supplicants to recognize the object of prayer (i.e., the God of Israel) in their prayers, since God has the power, strength, and abundance to transform a miserable life situation into a blessed one.

First Chronicles 16:8–36: Israel's Jubilant Overture

Introduction

The prayer in 1 Chronicles 16:8–36 jubilates over the installation of the ark in Jerusalem, which portrays the scene of Israel's worship.[22] This particular prayer does not appear in Chronicles' *Vorlage* (i.e., Samuel–Kings) but consists of portions of three different psalms (Pss 96; 105; 106). Therefore, it is not complicated to perceive the Chronicler's

---

51; Frankel, *Land of Canaan*, 8; Kartveit, *Motive und Schichten*; Mabie, *First, Second Chronicles-Job*, 62.

Note that not all scholars translate מרעה (v. 10) as מֵרָעָה (evil); but a few scholars introduce another possibility, reading it as מִרְעֶה (a pastureland).

22. Based on the definition and identification of the prayer, this research sees 1 Chr 16:8–36 as a prayer. The prayer is given in first person speech, initiated by a human (e.g., David, Asaph, Levites) and offered to (praise) God before the congregation. One may argue that prayer does not explicitly reveal the object of the prayer. However, the introduction (v. 7) of this prayer indicates that Yhwh is the object of prayer. Verse 7 says בַּיּוֹם הַהוּא אָז נָתַן דָּוִיד בָּרֹאשׁ לְהֹדוֹת לַיהוָה בְּיַד־אָסָף וְאֶחָיו ("On that day, David first appointed Asaph and his brothers to praise to Yhwh"). The sentence begins with "On that day," a phrase that introduces the events of the day when the prayer is given. Thus, the prayer is not a repetition of vv. 4–5; instead, it opens the following prayer. Now, the preposition לְ attached to יהוה indicates that Yhwh is the one who receives the praise (i.e., prayer). Thus, v. 7 provides the purpose of the prayer, the object of the prayer (to/before Yhwh) and the central figures of the prayer (Asaph and his brothers). Therefore, in terms of the notion/definition concerning "directed to Yhwh," v. 7 confirms that this prayer is given to praise Yhwh. Concerning the placement of v. 7 in relation to vv. 4–6 and 8–36, see Japhet, *First and Second Chronicles*, 315; Williamson, *First and Second Chronicles*, 129.

intention vis-à-vis the prayer in chapter 16 as conveying his particular message toward the post-exilic readers.[23]

This book argues that the prayer's particular intention concerning the identity of the post-exilic community is to encourage members of the community to become worshipers who have a clear monotheistic understanding of Yhwh. The unique value (i.e., aspect) of this prayer lies in motivating the post-exilic community to perceive the appropriate expression and attitude of worshipers and the object of worship.[24] In addition, the prayer is able to persuade the audience to perceive God as their special and unique God.

The literary structure of the prayer outlined below provides an overview of the prayer. The first section deals with the proper manners of worship (vv. 8–11). The second section (vv. 12–33) contains two subsections. It recognizes Israel's special relationship to God (vv. 12–22) and conveys that the worshipers should have a monotheistic perspective in acknowledging God as supreme (vv. 23–33). The final section affirms the messages of the prayer by reemphasizing the theme of worship and monotheistic belief and presenting the application of the prayer to the post-exilic community's circumstances (vv. 34–36).

Section 1: Israel as Worshipers
    Manners of Worship Practice (vv. 8–11)
        Worshiper's outward expression (vv. 8–10a)
        Worshiper's inward attitude (vv. 10b–11)
Section 2: Israel as Monotheistic Believers
    Israel's Relationship with God (vv. 12–22)
        Remember: Israel as God's People (vv. 12–14)
        Remember: God's Covenant (vv. 15–22)
    God's Supremacy over the World (vv. 23–33)
        Yhwh Is the God of Gods (vv. 23–26)
        Yhwh Receives What He Deserves (vv. 27–29)
        The Universe Recognizes God's Sovereignty (vv. 30–33)
Section 3: Revisiting Role and Characteristic of the Community: A Final

---

23. For Chronicles' dependency on Psalms, see Williamson, *Israel in Books of Chronicles*, 47–52; Welten, "Lade-Tempel-Jerusalem," in Gunneweg and Kaiser, *Textgemäss*, 179–83; Riley, *King and Cultus*, 34. See also Butler, "Forgotten Passage."

24. Hooker says, "David not only provides for the work of the Levitical singers but also teaches Israel itself the songs to sing" (Hooker, *First and Second Chronicles*, 72). In a similar manner, the Chronicler adopts psalms in order to teach the post-exilic community how to sing (i.e., pray) in their situation, just like David did in his days.

Affirmation
  Summary and Application of Prayer (vv. 34–36)
  Summary of Principles of Worship and Monotheistic Belief (vv. 34–35)
  Israel's Ultimate Prayer and Final Acclaim (vv. 35–36)

Chronicles' Invitation to Israel to Be Worshipers

The prayer in 1 Chronicles 16 portrays the community's role as worshipers. In the prayer, the Chronicler conveys his desire to actualize the worshiping community through the lips of Levites who lived in the days of David.[25] A series of several imperative verbs (vv. 8–13, 23–24, 27–30, 34–35) and the explanatory recollection of the past history (vv. 12–22) of the prayer create an authoritative and didactic tone, and such a rhetorical impetus enables the post-exilic readers to realize their role as a worshiping community.[26] The post-exilic community witnesses Levites and priests leading the worship (e.g., playing music), the participants responding to the prayer (with the determined speaking of amen [וַיֹּאמְרוּ כָל־הָעָם אָמֵן] (v. 36)]), and the setting up of personnel (esp. musicians [vv. 41–42]) for sacrifice toward God (vv. 37–43).[27] The message of the prayer, together with the preparation of Israel's sacrifice, motivates the members of the community in the same manner—to become active worshipers.

---

25. See "Characterization" for the characterization of the Levites in Watts, *Psalm and Story*, 160–61.

26. E.g., to give thanks (הוֹדוּ [x2]), to call (קִרְאוּ), to make known (הוֹדִיעוּ), to sing (שִׁירוּ [x2]), to sing praise/make music (זַמְּרוּ), to tell/speak/muse (שִׂיחוּ), to glory (הִתְהַלְלוּ), to seek (בַּקְּשׁוּ; דִּרְשׁוּ), to remember (זִכְרוּ [x2]), to tell (בַּשְּׂרוּ), to ascribe (הָבוּ), to give (הָבוּ [x2]), to lift (שְׂאוּ), to bow down (הִשְׁתַּחֲווּ), to tremble (חִילוּ), to say (וְאִמְרוּ).

27. The Chronicler changed the verb tense of Ps 106:48b; so, he creates a new sense in v. 36b. He replaces וְאָמַר כָּל־הָעָם (let all the people say [*weqatal*]) to וַיֹּאמְרוּ כָל־הָעָם (and all the people said [*wayyiqtol*]); thus, the expression no longer has liturgical instruction but becomes a historical record. The readers (i.e., prayer participants) may abide in the prayer as long as they want, but eventually they need to resume the story and follow the Chronicler's guidance. This can be the Chronicler's strategy of motivating the audience of the prayer into following their forefathers in Israel's history (Hooker, *First and Second Chronicles*, 73).

The Manners of Worship Practice

Verses 8–11 reveal worshipers' proper practice of worship.[28] Worship involves the outward expression of worshipers. The verbs הוֹדוּ (to give thanks [v. 8]), קִרְאוּ (to call upon [v. 8]), הוֹדִיעוּ (to make known [v. 8]) שִׁירוּ (to sing [v. 9]), זַמְּרוּ (to sing praise [v. 9]), שִׂיחוּ (to tell [v. 9]), and הִתְהַלְלוּ (to boast/glory [v. 10a]) represent what worshipers should actively do in their worship.[29] Together, these verbs reveal three basic aspects of the outward expression of worshipers: (1) the direction/axis of worship, (2) the instrument of worship, and (3) the content of worship.

First, worship operates in two directions: God and people. The worshipers should focus on God by giving thanks, calling upon his name (v. 8a), and playing music (v. 9a).[30] Then, the worshipers should let others know about God by making his deeds known among people (v. 8b), telling of his wonderfulness (v. 9b), and boasting in God's name (10a).[31] In short, the worshipers have to praise God and make him known through their outward expression of worship; consequently, they show their reverence to God (1 Chr 16:8, 23, 25, 27, 29), and they expect their worship to have an impact on others (1 Chr 16:30–33; 2 Chr 15:8–9, 15; 20:28–29; see 1 Kgs 10:1).

Second, the outward expression of worshipers is closely related to music as the instrument of expression in worship (i.e., musical/choral presentation). In the prayer and its related context, the Chronicler shows

---

28. Although Deems and others do not give in-depth exegetical notes, they view the beginning of the prayer with regard to two aspects. They note this section in light of "practical seeking of the Lord" and "mindful obedience to him" (Deems et al., *First Chronicles*, 247).

29. Boda indicates this as verbal worship (Boda, *First-Second Chronicles*, 147–48).

30. Note that לְ is used as an object marker (*to* God).

31. One may argue that the indirect object (i.e., one who listens) of שִׂיחוּ בְּכָל־נִפְלְאֹתָיו (tell about his wonderfulness) is obscure. However, the object of this phrase is most likely not God but people or nation. The verb שִׂיחַ can be translated in different ways in the MT such as "to tell," "to meditate," or "to complain." The most probable meaning in the verse is "to speak." When the verb takes its object as God or his deed, the subject of the verb often relates to one's wretched situation (Job 7:11, 13; Pss 55:3, 18; 64:2; 77:4, 7 [Eng. v. 6], 13; 102:1; 119:23, 27 [see vv. 25 and 28], 48 [see vv. 42 and 46], 78, 148 [see v. 150]; 143:5). The most comparable text to 1 Chr 16:9 would be Ps 145:5. This psalm records David's praise to God. In the psalm, the verb in v. 5 appears with נִפְלְאוֹתֶיךָ as in 1 Chr 16:9 (בְּכָל־נִפְלְאֹתָיו). The context of Ps 145:5 is to proclaim God's wonderfulness to people (דּוֹר לְדוֹר יַגִּיד, generation to generation [v. 4]; אֲסַפְּרֶנָּה, make known" [v. 6]).

See also Kleinig, *Lord's Song*, 65–66.

his consistent interest in the musical nature of worship,[32] because through playing music, the congregation witnesses God's presence (1 Chr 16:33; 2 Chr 5:12–13).[33] Before the prayer begins, David appoints Levites and priests and explains the purpose of the worship: וּלְהַזְכִּיר וּלְהוֹדוֹת וּלְהַלֵּל לַיהוָה (to commemorate/to bring to remembrance, to give thanks, and to praise the Lord [v. 4]).[34] Then, the following passage describes the king's further commission regarding the specific musical roles of those leaders (vv. 5–6).[35]

In other words, in verse 4, David's elucidation of the purpose of worship reflects the general roles of Levites and priests. Those general roles are basically worshiping God, defined according to the king's particular requirements. Then, verse 5 provides more specific descriptions of how to accomplish the king's requirements by designating the particular tasks of each person (i.e., musical activity).[36] In the text of the prayer, worship leaders (i.e., Levites) not only render their given roles by means of music but also call for Israel to join in the same musical performance by issuing commands or invitations (i.e., הוֹדוּ [give thanks (v. 8)] and שִׁירוּ [sing (v. 9)]).[37] The narrative confirms music as an instrument of wor-

---

32. Kleinig, *Lord's Song*, 13–14.

33. Mayer, "ידה," in *TDOT*, 5:427–43. See also Kleinig: "The significance of choral music was therefore largely implicit, since it was determined by its ritual context and the tradition of worship in Israel. In his narrative, the Chronicler, however, takes up what was theologically implicit and makes it more explicit. He is particularly interested in showing its theological significance as a ritual performance in the LORD's presence at his temple in Jerusalem" (Kleinig, *Lord's Song*, 133). See also Lynch, who says, "In sum, Levitical music offered the Chronicler a means of depicting the arrival of Yhwh's presence in the cult, and of conveying continuity between the Levites' earlier role as ark-bearers and their new roles as musicians" (Lynch, *Monotheism and Institutions*, 173–74).

34. Infinitive construct with לְ indicating purpose or result (Waltke and O'Connor, *Introduction to Biblical Hebrew*, §36.2.3d).

35. E.g., playing harps, lyres, cymbals (נְבָלִים וּבְכִנֹּרוֹת . . . בִּמְצִלְתַּיִם) in v. 5 and trumpets (בַּחֲצֹצְרוֹת) in v. 6. See 2 Chr 7:5–6; 29:25–30; 30:21–22; 31:2. Williamson, *First and Second Chronicles*, 127; Hill, *First and Second Chronicles*, 239; Lynch, *Monotheism and Institutions*, 155; Hill, "Patchwork Poetry or Reasoned Verse?," 99.

36. See also vv. 37 and 42, where instruments are used during the sacrifice. Although v. 5 is not linked to v. 4 sequentially (e.g., no *waw*-consecutive), it is natural to understand that the musical roles in v. 5 are coupled with the duties of Levites and priests in v. 4. Also, the verb ידה can be translated as give praise, praise, give thanks, or lead worship, act as choir. In v. 4, this verb means lead worship, act as choir, or orchestra (Clines, "ידה," in *DCH*, 95–97).

37. Among various imperative verbs, two verbs "to give thanks" and "to sing"

ship in the historical report that follows the prayer (vv. 36–42), wherein the Chronicler writes of the perennial musical duties of the Levites and priests in association with the sacrifices. Therefore, throughout the prayer and its context, the Chronicler shows his consistent interest in music and imprints it on the readers, for them to acknowledge music as an instrument of worship.

Third, the outward expression of worshipers is related to the contents of the prayer: God's name.[38] In verses 8 and 10, the worship leaders command calling upon and glorifying/boasting in his name.[39] This should be done, because God has promised Israel that he would present himself where his name is called (Exod 20:24).[40] Thus, the pronouncement of God's name does not simply convey information concerning God but makes it possible for worshipers to manifest the actual presence of God (2 Chr 7:16; 14:10–11).[41] In sum, the three observations regarding

---

receive attention in the first section of the prayer because of their frequent occurrence in Chronicles. One should carefully examine imperative verbs in this section. Although this book argues that this section presents the attributes of worship by focusing on imperative verbs, this research does not take those axiomatically. In other words, a few verbs can receive much more attention than others. Thus, verbs should be examined in accordance with the Chronicler's interest, reflecting particular verbs appearing throughout the book of Chronicles. Further note that, in the prayer, even these words appear at the seams of the psalms (i.e., 1 Chr 16:23, 34) (Boda, *First-Second Chronicles*, 239).

The verb "to give thanks" appears seventeen times throughout Chronicles, yet its *Vorlage* appears only three times (1 Chr 16:4, 7, 8, 34, 35, 41; 23:30; 25:3; 29:13; 2 Chr 5:13; 6:24, 26; 7:3, 6; 20:21; 30:22; 31:2; vs. 2 Sam 22:50; 1 Kgs 8:33, 35). Also, the verb "to sing" appears thirty-two time in Chronicles, whereas its *Vorlage* appears only six times (1 Chr 6:16, 17, 18 [Eng. vv. 31–33]; 9:33; 13:8; 15:6 [x2], 19, 27 [x2]; 16:9, 23, 42; 25:6, 7; 2 Chr 5:2, 13 [x2]; 7:6; 9:11; 20:21; 23:13 [x2], 18; 29:27, 2 8[x2]; 34:12; 35:15, 25 [x2]; vs. 1 Sam 18:6 [x2]; 2 Sam 19:36 [x2]; 1 Kgs 5:12; 10:12).

The Chronicler introduces a few other scenes which describe the worship of God by all-Israel or even all the land (1 Chr 16:23, 33; 2 Chr 13:8).

38. The prayer gives special attention to God's name. For instance, the tetragrammaton (יהוה ["Yhwh"]) appears fourteen times in the prayer (vv. 8, 10, 11, 14, 23, 25, 28 [x2], 29, 31, 33, 34, and 36 [x2]) (R. Klein, *First Chronicles*, 364).

39. In Chronicles, worshipers relate to God's name by calling upon him (1 Chr 16:8), glorifying him (1 Chr 16:10; 17:24; 29:13), recognizing his holiness (2 Chr 29:16), and experiencing God's presence (1 Chr 16:33; 2 Chr 6:20; 7:16).

40. בְּכָל־הַמָּקוֹם אֲשֶׁר אַזְכִּיר אֶת־שְׁמִי אָבוֹא אֵלֶיךָ וּבֵרַכְתִּיךָ (in every place where I cause My name to be remembered, I will come to you and bless you) (Kleinig, *Lord's Song*, 145–46).

41. Pratt points out that "God's Name was the way of access to divine power." He recounts that this idea appears forty-three times in Chronicles (1 Chr 13:6; 16:2, 8,

the outward expression of worshipers demonstrate that the community should praise God and make him known by calling on his name through the instrumentalists' playing of music, so that they may experience and manifest God's presence.[42]

Worshipers should pursue an appropriate inward attitude of worship in order to experience the presence of God. Verses 10b–11 reveal the core of the inward attitude of worshipers by focusing on the motif of seeking Yhwh (יִשְׂמַח לֵב מְבַקְשֵׁי יְהוָה [let the hearts of those who seek Yhwh (v. 10)]; דִּרְשׁוּ יְהוָה וְעֻזּוֹ בַּקְּשׁוּ פָנָיו [seek Yhwh, his strength, and presence (v. 11)]).[43] The Chronicler reveals that the act of seeking Yhwh relates not only to the manner of outward expression but also to one's inner attitude, indicating that those who seek (מְבַקְשֵׁי יְהוָה) should rejoice (יִשְׂמַח) in verse 10. Chronicles' *Sondergut* also confirms that the act of seeking Yhwh is closely related to devoting one's heart to the Lord (i.e., wholehearted devotion [1 Chr 22:19; 28:9]).[44]

The reason for the specific aim of maintaining one's appropriate heart/attitude for worship is to seek God's presence. In verse 11, the prayer connects the notion of seeking Yhwh with the act of seeking

---

10, 29, 35; 21:19; 22:7–8, 10, 19; 23:13; 28:3; 29:13, 16; 2 Chr 2:1, 4; 6:5–10, 20, 24, 26, 32–38; 7:14, 16, 20; 12:13; 14:11; 18:15; 20:8–9; 33:4, 7, 18; 36:13). Pratt further explains that since God is transcendent and unapproachable (2 Chr 6:18), he makes himself accessible through his name in the temple (6:20) and that God gives attention to the temple by directing his eyes and heart toward it (7:16). This act of God is identical to his name being in the temple. Hence, God's people could perceive God's name as the source of power as they deal with trouble (6:24, 26; 14:11). In addition, God's name is the object of prayer and praise (1 Chr 16:8, 10, 29; 29:13). God's name bestows the authorization of God upon people's speeches or writings (1 Chr 16:2; 21:19; 23:13; 2 Chr 33:18) or upon their oaths (18:15; 36:13) (Pratt, *First and Second Chronicles*, 39).

42. Lynch, *Monotheism and Institutions*, 134.

43. In fact, the Chronicler emphasizes this motif throughout the transfer of the ark narrative (chs. 13–16) alongside the theme of worship. In David's second attempt, David indicates their failure of seeking God in their first attempt because they did not follow the rule (כַּמִּשְׁפָּט [1 Chr 15:13]). Between the two attempts, the Chronicler emphasizes the significance of seeking Yhwh, even in the story of the battles against the Philistines (14:10, 14).

44. עַתָּה תְּנוּ לְבַבְכֶם וְנַפְשְׁכֶם לִדְרוֹשׁ לַיהוָה אֱלֹהֵיכֶם (set your hearts and spirits to seek Yhwh your God [1 Chr 22:19]), כָּל־לְבָבוֹת דּוֹרֵשׁ יְהוָה וְכָל־יֵצֶר מַחֲשָׁבוֹת מֵבִין אִם־תִּדְרְשֶׁנּוּ יִמָּצֵא לָךְ (for the Lord searches all the hearts and understands all the intention behind thoughts if you seek Him, He will be found by you [1 Chr 28:9]). See also Deut 4:29.

For further study of Chronicles' motif of seeking Yhwh, see Kelly, *Retribution and Eschatology*, 52; Begg, "Seeking Yahweh"; Schaefer, "Significance of Seeking God"; Duke, *Persuasive Appeal*, 50–51.

God's presence (פָּנָיו [his face]) and strength (וְעֻזּוֹ). It is not explicitly clear what God's strength indicates, but considering the literary context of the prayer (chs. 13–16), it most likely refers to the ark, which often represents the presence of God (2 Chr 6:41).[45] Therefore, the appropriate inward attitude of worshipers refers to a worshiper's devotional heart to seek God's presence.

To sum up, the discussions concerning the outward expression of worship (i.e., the music [the instrument of expression] and God's name [the content of expression]) and the inward attitude/heart of worshipers (i.e., wholeheartedly seeking Yhwh) corporately point out a major teaching of this section: the worshipers should wholeheartedly commit to seeking God's presence by calling on God's name and letting others know God's wonderful deeds alongside instrumentalists' playing of songs.

Israel as Monotheistic Believers

The prayer contributes to shaping the post-exilic community into monotheistic believers. It is reasonable to expect that in order to become faithful worshipers of any divine being, members of a believing community should establish their relationship with that divine being and understand the nature of the divine being's existence according to their worldview.[46] Verses 12–33 are the main texts in this prayer that espouse the Chronicler's monotheistic perspective concerning Israel's religion. The section has two subsections (vv. 12–22, 23–33). The first subsection (vv. 12–22) consists of two further subsections (vv. 12–14, 15–22) and reminds the readers of their long history of a special relationship with God. The second subsection (vv. 23–33) has three further subsections (vv. 23–26, 27–29, 30–33), and it switches its focus from the people of Israel to God to the universe, characterizing him as Yhwh who is supreme over the world.[47]

---

45. R. Klein, *First Chronicles*, 364; Knoppers, *First Chronicles 10–29*, 646. Japhet also agrees with this opinion. She argues against the way the LXX reads ("be strong") and connects this expression to Ps 78:61, where she believes "his power" (עֻזּוֹ) is parallel to the ark (Japhet, *First and Second Chronicles*, 318).

46. Clayton, who agrees with McKenzie, notes that "the psalm's function in this context, then, is both liturgical and theological" (Clayton, "Symbol, Service, and Song," 290–91); McKenzie, *First and Second Chronicles*, 148.

47. Knoppers, *First Chronicles 10–29*, 647.

Israel's Relationship with God

The first section (vv. 12–22) addresses Israel's special relationship with God. The literary analysis of this passage is as follows:[48]

¹² זִכְרוּ נִפְלְאֹתָיו
אֲשֶׁר עָשָׂה מֹפְתָיו וּמִשְׁפְּטֵי־פִיהוּ
¹³ זֶרַע יִשְׂרָאֵל
עַבְדּוֹ
בְּנֵי יַעֲקֹב
בְּחִירָיו
¹⁴ הוּא יְהוָה אֱלֹהֵינוּ בְּכָל־הָאָרֶץ מִשְׁפָּטָיו
¹⁵ זִכְרוּ לְעוֹלָם בְּרִיתוֹ
ᵃדָּבָר צִוָּה לְאֶלֶף דּוֹר
¹⁶ אֲשֶׁר כָּרַת אֶת־אַבְרָהָם
וּשְׁבוּעָתוֹ לְיִצְחָק
¹⁷ וַיַּעֲמִידֶהָ לְיַעֲקֹב לְחֹק
לְיִשְׂרָאֵל בְּרִית עוֹלָם
¹⁸ לֵאמֹר
לְךָ אֶתֵּן אֶרֶץ־כְּנָעַן חֶבֶל נַחֲלַתְכֶם
¹⁹ בִּהְיוֹתְכֶם מְתֵי מִסְפָּר כִּמְעַט וְגָרִים בָּהּ
²⁰ וַיִּתְהַלְּכוּ מִגּוֹי אֶל־גּוֹי וּמִמַּמְלָכָה אֶל־עַם אַחֵר
²¹ לֹא־הִנִּיחַ לְאִישׁ לְעָשְׁקָם
וַיּוֹכַח עֲלֵיהֶם מְלָכִים
²² אַל־תִּגְּעוּ בִמְשִׁיחָי
וּבִנְבִיאַי אַל־תָּרֵעוּ פ

Remember: Israel as God's People

Each subsection hinges on the repetition of an imperative verb (זִכְרוּ [vv. 12 and 15]), and the rhetorical impetus (*anaphora*) created by these two verbs in the prayer is noticeable from the above literary structure.[49] The

---

48. See superscript *a* in verse 15. Kraus notes, "כרת cannot be made to refer to דבר," and "8b [1 Chr 16:15b] is parenthetical"; thus, v. 15 is not parallel with v. 16 (Kraus, *Psalms 60–150*, 310).

49. The imperatives in this section should receive attention. In Ps 105:8, the verse begins with זָכַר (perfect) but in Chronicles, the Chronicler replaces it with זִכְרוּ (imperative). Now the two repeated commands together create a strong rhetorical force (Ahn, *Persuasive Portrayal*, 117).

first call to remember (vv. 12–14) characterizes Israel as God's people, referring to his wonderful deeds (נִפְלְאֹתָיו), signs (מֹפְתָיו), judgments (וּמִשְׁפְּטֵי), the various appellations of Israel (עַבְדּוֹ בְּנֵי יַעֲקֹב בְּחִירָיו [his servant, sons of Jacob, his chosen ones (v. 13)]), and the people's exclusive recognition of God as their own (הוּא יְהוָה אֱלֹהֵינוּ [he is the Yhwh, our God (v. 14)]).[50] The passage reminds the readers of their special relationship with God (i.e., God's people) through these particular references. For instance, the Chronicler is careful to associate the passage with the post-exilic context by replacing Abraham (Ps 105:6) with Israel (1 Chr 16:13).[51] In addition, the appellation sons of Jacob (בְּנֵי יַעֲקֹב [v. 13]) helps to clarify that the Chronicler is concerned with all twelve tribes of Israel.[52] Moreover, the expression his chosen ones (בְּחִירָיו [v. 13]) is the only explicit note in Chronicles that God has specifically chosen the people of Israel.[53] Therefore, the Chronicler tries to appropriate the texts for his readers' contemporary context in order to teach them that God has still been working for them throughout their days of turmoil and to convey the same message that Yhwh is still their God (הוּא יְהוָה אֱלֹהֵינוּ [he is the Yhwh, our God (v. 14)]).

Dirksen believes that the imperative in v. 15 is the Chronicler's scribal error, since the LXX uses μνημονεύων (participle form); yet he does not provide any further reason of argument (Dirksen, *First Chronicles*, 223).

50. Braun, *First Chronicles*, 192.

51. See Doan and Giles, "Although the Chronicler favors the name 'Israel' over the pseudonym 'Jacob,' the substitution of 'Israel' for 'Abraham,' especially when quoting a psalm most likely familiar to the readers, could only have a surprise effect. The Chronicler's readers are met with the unexpected mention of Israel, which would have drawn attention. The Chronicler's use of 'Israel' drew the audience into the performance of the song as they—those now reading or listening to the Chronicler's work and considering themselves 'Israel'—suddenly found the song to be about them!" (Doan and Giles, "Song of Asaph," 36).

Note that Klein says his wonderfulness and signs primarily indicate David's accomplishment and army; thus, Klein relate these expressions to their literary historical context (R. Klein, *First Chronicles*, 364).

52. Williamson writes, "By this device [Israel] the Chronicler probably wished to stress that the Israel of his day, if it was to be true to its history, could consist only of the full complement of twelve tribes" (Williamson, *First and Second Chronicles*, 44). See also Williamson, *Israel in Books of Chronicles*, 62; and Hezekiah's story, where the Chronicler shows his interest in all-Israel (2 Chr 30:1–12).

53. Knoppers, *First Chronicles 10–29*, 646.

Remember: God's Covenant

The second call to remembrance (vv. 15–22) develops the message of the first call by examining Israel's special relationship with God—that is, Israel is God's elected people who received his covenant.[54] The prayer explicates the Abrahamic covenant and stresses its eternity (בְּרִית עוֹלָם [v. 17]) by introducing the origin and nature of the covenant.[55] It also addresses why the post-exilic community should remember this covenant (זִכְרוּ לְעוֹלָם בְּרִיתוֹ [v. 15]) by reviewing Israel's past history and contextualizing it to the audience.

With regard to the former, the prayer recounts the three patriarchal origins: כָּרַת אֶת־אַבְרָהָם (made with Abraham [v. 16]); וּשְׁבוּעָתוֹ (oath [v. 16] unto Isaac); לְחֹק (a statute [v. 17] to Jacob).[56] God's intention to make a special relationship with his people is revealed by the making of the covenant, along with repeated affirmations to these patriarchs. In addition, the established relationship (i.e., the nature of the covenant) is an everlasting one (בְּרִית עוֹלָם [v. 17]), which its recipients should perpetually remember (זִכְרוּ לְעוֹלָם בְּרִיתוֹ [v. 15]). With regard to the latter intention of the second call to remembrance, the Chronicler reviews the history of Israel (vv. 20–22). The prayer records that God protected his people from surrounding nations in Israel's past. In particular, the Chronicler replaces the word בִּהְיוֹתָם (when they were [Ps 105:12]) in the *Vorlage* with בִּהְיוֹתְכֶם (when you were [1 Chr 16:19]). Hence, the text creates an impression that God's promise is still relevant and effective in the post-exilic period.[57] In sum, Israel is God's special people who made a covenant with God and are thus under his protection.

---

54. Hill, *First and Second Chronicles*, 239; Dempsey, "Psalms and Israel's Three Covenants," in Knoppers and Bautch, *Covenant in Persian Period*, 335–36.

55. Gentry and Wellum observe that "it is interesting to note that the term 'everlasting covenant' occurs sixteen times in the Old Testament: two times of the covenant with Noah (Gen. 9:16; Isa. 24:5), four times of the covenant with Abraham (Gen. 17:7, 19; Ps. 105:10; 1 Chron. 16:17), once of the covenant with David (2 Sam. 23:5; cf. 2 Chron. 13:5), six times of the new covenant (Isa. 55:3; 61:8; Jer. 32:40; 50:5; Ezek. 16:60; 37:26), and three times of covenant signs (Gen. 17:3; Ex. 31:16; Lev. 24:8)" (Gentry and Wellum, *Kingdom through Covenant*, 475).

56. Mention of the covenant with reference to the patriarchs appears only here in Chronicles (Japhet, *Ideology of the Book*, 81).

57. For this purpose, Ps 105 is surely a good source for the Chronicler. The palmist exercises much freedom in his treatment of the Patriarch narrative. Allen notes, "The oath of v 9 (1 Chr 16:16) harks back loosely to Gen 26:3, though it was not sworn to Isaac himself. The promise of v 11 (1 Chr 16:18) is not found in this exact wording: it

God's Supremacy over the World

The second subsection (vv. 23–33) has three further subsections. The first of these (vv. 23–26) assists the readers to perceive God's place within their worldview. The second of these (vv. 27–29) focuses on the praiseworthiness of God, who deserves offerings from all nations (מִשְׁפְּחוֹת עַמִּים [families of the people (v. 28)]). The final subsection (vv. 30–33) deals with the motif of universal recognition of God's sovereignty.

Yhwh Is the God of Gods

The central theme of this first subsection (vv. 23–26) appears in verses 25 and 26, where the Chronicler evidently writes of God's supremacy over other gods. Both verses begin with the conjunction כִּי (because), and the conjunctions indicate the reasons that the cosmos should worship God (שִׁירוּ [sing], בַּשְּׂרוּ [tell about], and סַפְּרוּ [declare]; vv. 23–24).[58] The Chronicler's reasoning for worship is that Yhwh is great (גָּדוֹל יְהוָה), he is creator (וַיהוָה שָׁמַיִם עָשָׂה [the Lord created the heaven]), he is to be feared (וְנוֹרָא) and praised (וּמְהֻלָּל), and he maintains his position above all idols (כָּל־אֱלֹהֵי הָעַמִּים אֱלִילִים; הוּא עַל־כָּל־אֱלֹהִים [he is above all gods; all the gods of people are idols]). Two phrases are especially notable in relation to God's character as the supreme divine being: "above all gods" and "all the gods of people are idols." The former implies God's status over other gods; thus, he deserves great praise (כִּי גָדוֹל יְהוָה וּמְהֻלָּל מְאֹד [for Yhwh is great and greatly be praised]).[59] The latter phrase emphasizes

---

is the psalmist's own free reformulation" (Allen, *Psalms: 101–150*, 54). Klein also notes that Isaac and Jacob did not make a covenant with God, but "strictly speaking, only a covenant with Abraham is recorded in Genesis (17:7, 13, 19; see 15:18). Isaac and Jacob did not make the covenant with Abraham as well. But, in both Psalm 105 and 1 Chronicles 16 Isaac and Jacob receive the attention in parallel with Abraham. This can be much effective to emphasize the Abrahamic covenant" (R. Klein, *First Chronicles*, 365).

58. כִּי (because) is highlighted below,

כִּי גָדוֹל יְהוָה וּמְהֻלָּל מְאֹד
וְנוֹרָא הוּא עַל־כָּל־אֱלֹהִים
כִּי כָּל־אֱלֹהֵי הָעַמִּים אֱלִילִים
וַיהוָה שָׁמַיִם עָשָׂה.

Throntveit observes this as well. See Throntveit, "Psalmic Structure," in Bowen et al., *God So Near*, 170.

59. The expression "above all gods" appears very rarely in the MT (e.g., Pss 95:3; 96:4; 97:9; 1 Chr 16:5, 25). This phrase does not function to define the ruling

that the Lord is the creator. The word idols (אֱלִילִים [v. 16]) is generally understood as a divine icon, yet it also carries the meaning of "vain, hand-made, or worthless ones."[60] Based on these two points, therefore, the prayer conveys that God is the creator who stands above any other divine being, whereas other divine beings are human-made, weak, and vulnerable creatures.[61]

Yhwh Receives What He Deserves

The second subsection (vv. 27–29) describes God as Yhwh, who receives what he deserves. A series of imperative verbs strengthens this motif by depicting a scene of worshipers making offerings to God. The verbs הָבוּ (to give [vv. 28 (x2), 29]) and שְׂאוּ (to carry [v. 29]) serve to admonish worshipers to offer (or to give [הַב]) glory and strength (כָּבוֹד וָעֹז) and to bring (or to carry [נשׂא]) sacrifice (or tribute [מִנְחָה]) with prostration (הִשְׁתַּחֲווּ [bow down (v. 29)]) to God. With respect to the verb הַב, glory (כָּבוֹד) and strength (עֹז) originally belong to God (וְעֻזּוֹ [his strength (v. 11)]; כְּבוֹדוֹ [his glory (v. 24)]; עֹז וְחֶדְוָה בִּמְקֹמוֹ [joy and strength in his place (v. 28)]; וְהַכָּבוֹד מִלְּפָנֶיךָ [glory comes from you (1 Chr 29:12)]); so, the expression of giving glory and strength implies that the worshipers should recognize the source of glory (כָּבוֹד) and strength (עֹז) and then ascribe them to God.[62] The word מִנְחָה could mean either sacrifice or tribute,

---

relationship between God and other gods, since God is not comparable to others; rather, it rhetorically emphasizes God's non-limited supremacy over other divine beings. For further information see Lynch, *Monotheism and Institutions*, 158–59.

60. Lynch, *Monotheism and Institutions*, 159; Tuell, *First and Second Chronicles*, 68. See also Isa 2:8, 20; 31:7; 40:18.

61. The prayer particularly notes that God created the heaven. The Chronicler describes heaven in various ways throughout the book. The heaven is where God exists or is located (1 Chr 21:26; 2 Chr 7:1, 14; 18:18; 30:27). Although he says that "heaven and the heaven of heavens" cannot contain God (2 Chr 2:5 [Eng. v. 6]; 6:18, 21, 23, 25, 27, 30, 33, 35, 39; 7:1), it should be understood as a rhetorical expression that insists upon God's greatness and supremacy. Heaven in Chronicles is also the source of life (2 Chr 6:26, 27; 7:13). In addition, the God of heaven has everything in the heaven and the earth (1 Chr 29:11). He rules over all the gentile nations (הַגּוֹיִם) in the earth (2 Chr 20:6). The God of heaven has the authority to give all the kingdom of the land to the earthly king (i.e., Cyrus [2 Chr 36:23]); thus, the expression "God created heaven" could imply that God rules over and controls the universe.

62. Some English translations, such as the ESV, NAS, NET, NIV, NRS, and TNK translate this verb as ascribe, whereas the NLT translates it as recognize. The NKJ follows a more literal translation, rendering it as give.

and this word and נשׂא (to carry) together convey the image of offering as well. On the one hand, the expression could instruct worshipers to offer sacrifices to God. In this case, the reference to the word sacrifice (מִנְחָה) should not be limited to a specific type of sacrifice only (e.g., grain offering [Lev 2]); instead, it probably relates to sacrifices, including both meat and grain, in the general cultic sense.[63] On the other hand, these words could portray Yhwh as a king, and the people should treat him as such (e.g., 2 Chr 32:23); thus they bring their tribute to Yhwh. Therefore, verses 27–29 communicate that the worshipers should offer sacrifices/tribute and praises (i.e., glory and strength) to God (see 1 Chr 16:39–40; 21:24; 2 Chr 1:6; 7:4–7; 32:23).[64]

The verb הַב occurs thirty times in the MT, and there are ten occurrences which describe the image of worshipers' offerings to God (Deut 32:3; 1 Chr 16:28 [x2], 29; Pss 29:1 [x2], 2; 96:7 [x2], 8). Considering the fact that Ps 96 is the *Vorlage* of 1 Chr 16:23–33 and has a close parallel relationship with Ps 29, this portrayal of worshipers' offerings to God is rare in the MT, occurring only in these related texts (Pss 29, 96, and 1 Chr 16), with one exception in Deut 32:3. Jamieson et al., *Commentary Critical and Explanatory*, 375; DeClaissé-Walford et al., *Book of Psalms*, 721; Tuell, *First and Second Chronicles*, 68; Broyles, *Psalms*, 376. See Clines, "יהב," in *DCH*, 114.

Interestingly, the LXX of 1 Chronicles uses δότε (give, imperative), whereas Ps 96 uses ἐνέγκατε (bring/carry) for the word הַב (give, imperative). Although these two words occur widely in Greek texts and are sometimes used interchangeably, the sense they carry seems slightly different. The former δίδωμι refers to the "*deliberate transfer of something to someone or something*," whereas the latter φέρω means the "*relocation of something or someone*" (Gilchrist, "יָהַב," in *TWOT*, 368; italics added). See also Popkes, "δίδωμι," in *EDNT*, 1:320–22; and Wolter "φέρω," in *EDNT*, 3:418–19.

63. Clines, "מִנְחָה," in *DCH*, 350–53; Lynch, *Monotheism and Institutions*, 250. The expression בְּהַדְרַת־קֹדֶשׁ (in holy apparel) implies that this particular word probably relates to the sacrifice before God.

64. R. Klein, *First Chronicles*, 367. Commentators on Ps 96 give similar observations regarding the picture of offering. Broyles writes, "We must recognize that the courts of the sacred temple were also regarded by the ancients as those of the divine, royal 'palace.' And the offering (Hb. *minḥâ*) was not only a religious sacrifice but also a political tribute to the king (e.g., 72:10; 2 Sam. 8:2, 6; 2 Kgs. 17:3–4). The qualities that the nations are to ascribe to the LORD are simply those that are inherently his, especially glory (Hb. *kābôd*, cf. v. 3; the Hb. word translated 'glory' in v. 6 is *tip'eret*, which is usually rendered 'splendor') and strength (cf. 6). The repetition simply acknowledges what is already an existing state. As is appropriate before royalty, especially divine royalty, the nations are to 'bow down' (NIV worship). Commands for this posture also appear elsewhere in connection with the cherubim-ark (97:2, 7; 99:1, 5; 132:7–8)" (Broyles, *Psalms*, 366–67). Also, "in Psalm 29 it is the 'sons of gods' that are called to 'Ascribe to the LORD, sons of Eliym! Ascribe to the LORD, glory and strength! Ascribe to the LORD the glory of his name! Worship the LORD in holy splendor!' Here [Ps 96] it is the *families of peoples* who are to *bring an offering and come into his courts*. The worship here on earth is the same as the praise given to God in the

The Universe Recognizes God's Sovereignty

The final subsection (vv. 30–33) broadens the scope of prayer from the realm of human beings (מִשְׁפְּחוֹת עַמִּים [all the clans of nations (v. 28)]) to all creation. It summons all the earth (כָּל־הָאָרֶץ [v. 30]) and commands the universal praise of God: יִשְׂמְחוּ הַשָּׁמַיִם וְתָגֵל הָאָרֶץ וְיֹאמְרוּ בַגּוֹיִם יְהוָה מָלָךְ (Let the heaven be glad, and let the earth rejoice, and let them say among the nations, 'Yhwh reigns' [v. 31]).[65] The particular literary device employed in this verse is personification. Hence, it impresses on the audience that even the heaven and the earth praise Yhwh (i.e., יִשְׂמְחוּ [be glad (v. 31)]; וְתָגֵל [rejoice (v. 31)]; יַעֲלֹץ [rejoice (v. 32)]) and recognize him as the ruler over the world.

Verse 33 reaffirms God's sovereignty over the world. The verse begins with the adverb אָז (then/at that time), which stresses the following phrase: יְרַנְּנוּ עֲצֵי הַיָּעַר מִלִּפְנֵי יְהוָה כִּי־בָא לִשְׁפּוֹט אֶת־הָאָרֶץ (the trees of the forest will shout out joy before Yhwh for he is coming to judge the earth).[66] The received focus in verse 33 is essentially identical to the message in verses 31–32. All the created beings (e.g., עֲצֵי הַיָּעַר [trees of the forest (v. 33)]; הַשָּׁמַיִם [heaven (v. 31)]; הָאָרֶץ [earth (v. 31)]; הַיָּם [sea (v. 32)]; and וּמְלֹאוֹ [all that fills it (v. 32)]) should extol Yhwh and recognize his sovereignty (יְהוָה מָלָךְ [Yhwh reigns (v. 32)]; כִּי־בָא לִשְׁפּוֹט אֶת־הָאָרֶץ [for he is come to judge the earth (v. 33)]). In sum, the whole universe should offer joyful worship in recognition of God's sovereignty, and this scene of worship is sufficient to draw the readers' attention and stimulate them to radiate that same joy in their worship with a clear view of God's sovereignty.[67]

---

heavens" (DeClaissé-Walford et al., *Book of Psalms*, 721; italics in original).

65. Even though many English translations translate the verbs in vv. 31–32 as jussives, the MT is not clear whether the tense/mood of the verbs is imperfect or jussive, except וְתָגֵל (jussive) and מָלָךְ (perfect). This book provides their translation with the jussive mood; in fact, understanding those verbs as either imperfect or jussive does not harm this book's arguments. On the one hand, if one takes the verbs as jussive, then the intention could be a strong desire or command/request. On the other hand, if one understands them as imperfect, then the verse conveys a stronger sense of certainty (i.e., "The heavens *will* be glad, the earth *will* rejoice . . . [italics added]). In other words, the personified creatures will have a desire to praise Yhwh (figuratively). See Waltke and O'Connor, *Introduction to Biblical Hebrew*, §31.4g, 34.3d.

66. Köhler et al., "אָז," in *HALOT*, 26.

67. Concerning the theme of joy, the Chronicler has continually noted joy as one of the core elements of worship throughout the prayer. Verse 10 writes that the act of worship involves the worshiper's joyful response (יִשְׂמַח) to God's presence. In a

Overall, verses 12–33 contribute to shaping the readers' monotheistic belief in God by providing the essential elements of a monotheistic perspective. It characterizes the Israelites as God's special and chosen group (vv. 12–14) who made a covenant with him (vv. 15–22) and presents God as the supreme divine being (vv. 23–26) who is praiseworthy and deserves offerings (vv. 27–29). The section even contends that all God's creation should worship him and recognize his sovereignty (vv. 30–33).

Revisiting Roles and Characteristics of the Community: A Final Affirmation

The final section (vv. 34–36) has two main purposes: first, to provide a concise summary of the theological principles of worship and monotheistic belief presented throughout the prayer (vv. 34–35), and second, to provide a model prayer for the post-exilic community with the prayer's final acclaim (v. 35–36).

Summary of Principles of Worship and Monotheistic Belief

Concerning the former, verse 34 reiterates the very beginning of the prayer (הוֹדוּ לַיהוָה [give thanks to the Lord]) in order to reemphasize the prayer's command or invitation that the readers be a community of worshipers. Further, verse 35 instructs the audience that this role should be the community's desire (לְהֹדוֹת [to give thanks (v. 35)]).⁶⁸ Next, verse 34 reaffirms the reasons⁶⁹ that the members of the community should be worshipers by commenting on God's covenant relationship with Israel (חַסְדּוֹ [his *hesed*]).⁷⁰ In addition, verses 35–36 recall Yhwh as a special

---

series of imperative verbs, a jussive verb (יִשְׂמַח [v. 10]) stands alone (*Oratio Variata*) and receives attention. See also v. 27, which observes the existence of joy (חֶדְוָה) in the place of God. The Chronicler replaces תִּפְאֶרֶת (beauty [Ps 96:6]) with חֶדְוָה (joy [1 Chr 16:27]). This substitution shows the coherence of the Chronicler's emphasis on joyful worship. In Chronicles' other reports and the MT, this joyful expression is what worshipers should emit as the result of worship or as they are influenced by worship (1 Chr 29:9, 17, 22; 2 Chr 6:41; 7:10; 30:25; Neh 8:10; 12:43). Thompson correctly observes the importance of joy. See Thompson, *First, Second Chronicles*, 39.

68. Infinitive construct with לְ indicating purpose or result (Waltke and O'Connor, *Introduction to Biblical Hebrew*, §36.2.3d).

69. כִּי (for or because [v. 34 (x2)]).

70. Zobel, "חֶסֶד," in *TDOT*, 5:44–64; Glueck, *Hesed in the Bible*. Psalm 136 is the

God (אֱלֹהֵי יִשְׂרָאֵל [the God of Israel (v. 36)]) and desire God's capability to deliver Isarel from other nations (הוֹשִׁיעֵנוּ [save us]; וְהַצִּילֵנוּ מִן־הַגּוֹיִם [deliver from the nations]), just as he did in Israel's past (אֱלֹהֵי יִשְׁעֵנוּ [God of our salvation (v. 35)]; c.f. בַּשְּׂרוּ מִיּוֹם־אֶל־יוֹם יְשׁוּעָתוֹ [tell his salvation from day to day (v. 23)]).[71]

Israel's Ultimate Prayer and Final Acclaim

The Chronicler's literary strategy in verse 35 also shows the latter purpose of the final section. In this verse, the Chronicler provides a model prayer that the audience could follow (i.e., application of the prayer). First, the Chronicler adds וְאִמְרוּ (say [v. 35]) to the *Vorlage* creating another level of the direct speech discourse. It is a direct speech (v. 35) embedded in a direct speech (vv. 8–36). This literary strategy is compelling, since now a designated speaker of the deeper level of direct speech (v. 35) is the audience of the prayer (vv. 8–36). In other words, the Chronicler provides words for the audience of the prayer, in order to teach them how to pray.[72] The audience, who are joining the prayer of 1 Chronicles 16, encounter and receive an escalated direct invitation from the Chronicler to mimic the embedded prayer (v. 35).

Second, the literary structure of this given prayer also creates sufficient rhetorical force to encourage this mimicry, since the structure emphasizes the contents of this embedded prayer. The literary structure of verse 35 is as follows:

וְאִמְרוּ
הוֹשִׁיעֵנוּ אֱלֹהֵי יִשְׁעֵנוּ
וְקַבְּצֵנוּ
וְהַצִּילֵנוּ מִן־הַגּוֹיִם
לְהֹדוֹת לְשֵׁם קָדְשֶׁךָ
לְהִשְׁתַּבֵּחַ בִּתְהִלָּתֶךָ

The structure shows that three imperatives stand parallel, and the two following infinitive clauses also construct a parallel structure. Hence, it could pinpoint the Chronicler's intended message. The imperatives may

---

one of the biblical writings that attests well to the covenantal aspect of the word חֶסֶד (*ḥesed*).

71. See also 16:21.
72. Miller, *Representation of Speech*, 230.

reflect the Chronicler's desire to see the scattered people gather together and overcome the tumult of their Persian context (i.e., lack of or limited freedom) when considering the post-exilic Yehud community's pregnable status as a trivial community surrounded by great powers.[73] The following two parallel infinitive clauses note the Chronicler's hope for the Yehud community.[74] The Chronicler's desire does not simply reside in the hope of deliverance but in worshiping God through such deliverance. Therefore, through the act of prayer, the members of the community should become worshipers of God among other nations (מִן־הַגּוֹיִם לְהֹדוֹת לְשֵׁם קָדְשֶׁךָ לְהִשְׁתַּבֵּחַ בִּתְהִלָּתֶךָ). The final acclamation (v. 36) certainly reflects this desire toward the community (i.e., that its members would fulfill the role of worshipers): "Blessed be the Lord God of Israel from everlasting to everlasting" (בָּרוּךְ יְהוָה אֱלֹהֵי יִשְׂרָאֵל מִן־הָעוֹלָם וְעַד הָעֹלָם).

Conclusion

The prayer of 1 Chronicles 16:8–36 suggests that the post-exilic community should become worshipers who have a robust monotheistic belief in God. In order to render these roles, in the first section, the prayer characterizes worshipers as those who maintain the appropriate manner of worship. The worshipers should sing music and call on God's name with the commitment of seeking his presence. In the second section, the prayer attempts to get the audience to perceive their identity as monotheistic believers. The prayer conveys the message that Yhwh, as supreme over the universe, is their special God and therefore deserves their offerings. In the final section, the prayer reemphasizes that the audience should become worshipers and monotheistic believers and encourages them to expect God's deliverance during their period of turmoil by providing a model prayer for the audience to follow.

---

73. Street, "Significance of the Ark," 213. See also Klaus Seybold: "Wie aus der Zusammenstellung zu ersehen ist, ist das bedrängende Problem dieser Zeit offenbar das des reinen Überlebens, der Existenz Israels im 'Lande Kanaan' (V. 18), die offenbar bedroht ist von Staaten und Mächten (V. 19ff.), konkret von der Zerstreuung unter verschiedene Völker" (Seybold, *Studien zur Psalmenauslegung*, 107). Williamson notes that this verse is far more appropriate to the Chronicler's own day (Williamson, *First and Second Chronicles*, 131). See also R. Klein, *First Chronicles*, 367; Dirksen, *First Chronicles*, 225.

74. Infinitive construct as purpose (Waltke and O'Connor, *Introduction to Biblical Hebrew*, §36.2.3d).

First Chronicles 17:16–27: David's Prayer

Introduction

First Chronicles 17:16–27 records David's prayer to Yhwh in response to Nathan's prophecy (vv. 1–15). Scholars have focused on these passages with a great interest in God's promise making with David.[75] This book likewise recognizes the significance of the passage's presentation of God's promise to David, especially in relation to the prayer's function to shape the post-exilic community as citizens of the Davidic kingdom. In addition, the manner which David exhibits in his prayer can motivate the members of the community to become active monotheistic believers and supplicants. Since the prayer is offered in response to God's prophecy through Nathan, one needs to investigate both David's prayer and Nathan's prophecy in order to reveal the roles or characteristics portrayed in the passages.

David as a Monotheistic Believer

The prayer of David reflects his solid monotheistic belief toward God; as the post-exilic community observes the king, the prayer can motivate them to become monotheistic believers themselves.[76] First, David's humility before his Lord is a model attitude for the post-exilic community.[77]

---

75. Due to the significance of Davidic covenant in the scholarship, it would be impossible to list all the publications that are dedicated to the subject of Davidic covenant. Some recent research for further study is offered as follows: Hwang, *Hope for the Restoration*; Hwang, "Coexistence of Unconditionality"; Janzen, *Chronicles and Politics*; Steinmann, "What Did David Understand"; Lynch, "Davidic Covenant," in MacDonald, *Covenant and Election*, 169–88; Gentry and Wellum, *Kingdom through Covenant*, 389–431; Grisanti, "Davidic Covenant"; Levenson, "Davidic Covenant"; Dumbrell, *Covenant and Creation*, 197–241; Dumbrell, "Davidic Covenant"; Kruse, "David's Covenant." Herrmann observes and evaluates the state of research concerning the king David. See Herrmann, "King David's State," in Barrick and Spencer, *In the Shelter of Elyon*, 261.

76. See Selman's overview as he focuses on vv. 16–22 in relation to the subject of monotheism (i.e., David's monotheistic perspective toward God). "Three rhetorical questions . . . and a statement of faith, *There is no-one like you, O Lord, and there is no God but you* (v. 20), form the backbone to the first part of this prayer. The prayer is not just a conventional religious response to good news, for God's word has brought about a marked change in David's perspective" (Selman, *First Chronicles*, 190–91).

77. Pratt agrees that David's prayer represents the model attitude for the post-exilic community. He points out that God's rejection of David's appeal to construct the

David recognizes God's benevolence and abases himself before God (1 Chr 17:16b–19). The king's rhetorical questions well attest to this attitude. He says, מִי־אֲנִי יְהוָה אֱלֹהִים וּמִי בֵיתִי (who am I, Yhwh God, and what is my house? [v. 16b]). This type of self-abasing expression similarly appears in the MT (e.g., Exod 3:11; 5:2; 16:7, 8; Num 16:11; Judg 9:28; 1 Sam 17:26; 2 Kgs 8:13), and the answer is implicitly negative (i.e., nothing or nobody).[78] In other words, David's rhetorical question to Yhwh is a humble expression that he and his house have done nothing to deserve receiving God's promise.[79] David's other rhetorical question in verse 18 enhances the text's portrayal of his humility more vividly, as the king replies to his own question (i.e., *hypophora*).[80] He says, מַה־יּוֹסִיף עוֹד דָּוִיד אֵלֶיךָ לְכָבוֹד אֶת־עַבְדֶּךָ וְאַתָּה אֶת־עַבְדְּךָ יָדָעְתָּ (what more can David your servant add to you concerning the honor given to your servant? You know your servant [v. 18]). Like the rhetorical questions in verse 16, the question in verse 18 implies that there is nothing that David can do to increase his honor. Yet this time, the answer immediately follows the question. Thus, it clearly indicates what the notion implies in the question: God knows about his servants, and David does not need to add anything to what God has done (עָשִׂיתָ אֵת כָּל־הַגְּדוּלָּה הַזֹּאת [you have done all this great thing (v. 19)]). These three rhetorical questions (vv. 16 [x2], 18) at the beginning of David's prayer set the tone of the prayer. David's words of appeal to God in the rest of the prayer (vv. 20–27) are grounded in his humble submission to God in recognition of his greatness and plan (וַתְּדַבֵּר עַל־בֵּית־עַבְדְּךָ לְמֵרָחוֹק [You have spoken concerning the house of your servant for the future (v. 17)]; see vv. 10–13).[81]

---

temple can harm his authority, yet the king still submits himself to his God (Pratt, *First and Second Chronicles*, 211).

78. Adina Moshavi defines the rhetorical question as follows: "The rhetorical question is a sentence whose meaning is that of a question, but which is used to indirectly express an assertion." She continues, "Rhetorical questions have one of three types of implications: negative, specific, and extreme scalar implications" (Moshavi, "What Can I Say?," 95–96).

79. R. Klein, *First Chronicles*, 383; Knoppers, *First Chronicles 10–29*, 681.

80. Ahn, *Persuasive Portrayal*, 138; Bullinger, *Figures of Speech*, 980.

81. Regarding God's greatness, see Ahn: "David further confesses God's mighty acts in 1 Chr 17:19, mentioning the phrase, 'for your servant's sake' (בַּעֲבוּר עַבְדְּךָ) and repeating the phrase, 'all this greatness' (כָּל־הַגְּדוּלָּה הַזֹּאת) or 'all the great things' (אֵת כָּל־הַגְּדֻלּוֹת). The latter phrase forms an *epiphora* (conversio) that repeats a word or words at the end of two successive lines. These phrases emphasize that God Himself has done great things for David" (Ahn, *Persuasive Portrayal*, 139). See also Japhet, *First and Second Chronicles*, 336.

In addition, the text shows the king's humble submission to Yhwh as David characterizes himself as a servant. The king utters עַל־בֵּית־עַבְדְּךָ (on the house of your servant [17:17]) and repeatedly confesses אֶת־עַבְדְּךָ (your servant [vv. 18, 19, 23, 24, 25, 26, 27]).[82] The LXX is careful in describing David as God's servant, and an observation concerning the LXX's use of terms helpfully espouses how David defines his relationship to God. The LXX mostly refers to the king as God's παῖς (vv. 17, 19, 23, 24, 25, 27), yet in verses 18 and 26, it refers to David as God's δοῦλος. The former term, παῖς, normally refers to "one who is in the younger ages (e.g., puberty or child) as an immediate offspring of another" or "a person who obeys another with total commitment."[83] When the text shows παῖς in the prayer, it seems that the context relates to future events or blessings that God promises (e.g., וּכְלִבְּךָ עָשִׂיתָ אֵת כָּל־הַגְּדוּלָּה [for the future (v. 17)]; לְמֵרָחוֹק הַזֹּאת [according to your own heart you have done this greatness (v. 19)]; וְעַל־בֵּיתוֹ יֵאָמֵן עַד־עוֹלָם [and regarding his house, be established forever (v. 23)]; עַד־עוֹלָם [for forever (v. 24)]; כִּי אַתָּה אֱלֹהַי גָּלִיתָ אֶת־אֹזֶן עַבְדְּךָ לִבְנוֹת לוֹ בָיִת [for you, my God, you have revealed to the ear of your servant that you *will* build a house for him (v. 25; italics added)]). The latter term, δοῦλος, generally means a servant or slave who submits or is solely committed to someone else's total control.[84] When δοῦλος is used in the prayer, the context concerns establishing the direct master-servant relationship. For instance, in וְאַתָּה אֶת־עַבְדְּךָ יָדָעְתָּ, Chronicles indicates the subject of the

---

Hill provides the literary structure of the prayer as follows: "(1) introduction (1 Chr 17:16a); (2) invocation (vv. 16b–19); (3) declaration (vv. 20–22); (4) petition (vv. 23–24); (5) recognition (vv. 25–27)" (Hill, *First and Second Chronicles*, 244).

82. The expression "your servants" occurs nineteen times in Chronicles (1 Chr 17:17, 18 [x2], 19, 23, 24, 25 [x2], 26, 27; 21:8; 2 Chr 6:15, 16, 17, 19 [x2], 20, 21, 42), and each of them particularly refers to the king David, except 2 Chr 6:19 [x2], 20, 21.

83. Danker, "παῖς," in *BDAG*, 750–51.

84. Danker, "δοῦλος," in *BDAG*, 260. One should not dismiss the importance of the use of the word δοῦλος in Chronicles. The Chronicler consistently uses the word παῖς for עֶבֶד. In Chronicles, עֶבֶד appears sixty-nine times. The LXX writes παῖς fifty-eight times (1 Chr 2:34, 35; 6:34; 16:13; 17:4, 17, 23, 24, 25 [x2], 27; 18:2, 6, 7, 13; 19:2, 3, 4, 19; 20:8; 21:3; 2 Chr 1:3; 2:7 [x2 (Eng. v. 8)], 9 [Eng. v. 10], 14 [Eng. v. 15]; 6:14, 15, 16, 17, 19 [x2], 20, 21, 27, 42; 8:9, 18 [x3]; 9:4, 7, 10 [x2], 21; 10:7; 12:8; 13:6; 24:9, 25; 25:3; 32:9, 16; 33:24; 34:16, 20; 35:23, 24). The LXX rarely shows δοῦλος, only in 1 Chr 17:7, 18, 26; 2 Chr 2:7 (Eng. v. 8); 6:23; 28:10; 36:20. Note that the LXX 1 Chr 17:19 does not translate עֶבֶד. Therefore, the result shows that the Chronicler's use of the word δοῦλος can be meaningful. Although Jong-Hoon Kim's study particularly focuses on 2 Chr, his observation is helpful. See J. Kim, "열왕기와 역대기 평행본문의 칠십인경 본문 형태에 관한 연구 [Observations on the LXX Parallel Text Forms]," 22–25.

phrase (i.e., the second person pronoun אַתָּה); so, the text portrays a much clearer picture of antipode—the one as the master and the other one as the servant (v. 18). Verse 26 further clarifies who is the master in this relationship by stating וְעַתָּה יְהוָה אַתָּה־הוּא הָאֱלֹהִים (now Yhwh, you are God) and immediately providing וַתְּדַבֵּר עַל־עַבְדְּךָ הַטּוֹבָה הַזֹּאת (you have spoken to your servant [δοῦλόν]). The observations on the LXX's use of two terms reveals that David, as a child of God (i.e., παῖς with a familial portrayal), desires to receive God's promise, and, at the same, he is a servant (i.e., δοῦλος), who should obey his master with total commitment.[85]

Second, David recognizes God's unique and incomparable position (1 Chr 17:20). He utters יְהוָה אֵין כָּמוֹךָ וְאֵין אֱלֹהִים זוּלָתֶךָ (O Yhwh, there is none like you, and there is no god besides you). A similar phrase occurs in several places in the MT to further demonstrate this notion of incomparability and uniqueness (Ps 86:8; Isa 45:5; Jer 10:6; 2 Chr 6:14).[86] The text acknowledges God's uniqueness by indicating the word of invocation at the beginning: his name Yhwh (יְהוָה). It further addresses God's incomparable position by pointing out the nonexistence of divine beings comparable to Yhwh.[87]

Third, the text makes clear that Israel is God's special people by portraying David, who recalls God's salvific deeds in Israel's history in the prayer (1 Chr 17:20–22). In verses 21–22, the Chronicler denotes Israel as God's people (וּמִי כְּעַמְּךָ יִשְׂרָאֵל גּוֹי אֶחָד [what one nation is like your

---

85. The familial image is not limited to David. God promises that Solomon will be his son (1 Chr 17:13) and that Israel is also God's people (vv. 21–22), his firstborn (Exod 4:22–23; Hos 11:1–2).

86. Knoppers, *First Chronicles 10–29*, 683. Jonker also sees a strong theme of monotheism in this verse. "Moses had articulated this truth early on (Deut 4:35, 39; 32:39) and prepared for the monotheistic faith by urging worship of Yahweh alone (Exod 23:13; 34:14; Deut 6:4, 14; 7:4; 13:2; 17:3; 28:14; 31:18, 20). The prophets and poets enlarged on this concept by declaring that Yahweh is incomparable (Isa 26:13; Jer 10:6, 7; Hos 13:4; Mic 7:18; Pss 18:22; 35:10; 50:21) and only he is God (e.g., Isa 37:16; 43:11; 44:6; 45:5, 6, 21; Pss 18:6; 38:21; 83:18; 86:10). The Chronicler's declaration, then, is based on a long tradition regarding Yahweh's exclusivity" (Jonker, *First and Second Chronicles*, 226).

87. See Exod 3:13–15, where Moses asks God's name and receives an answer from Yhwh. It reads, וְאָמְרוּ־לִי מַה־שְּׁמוֹ מָה אֹמַר אֲלֵהֶם (and they [the sons of Israel] shall ask me, 'what is his name?' what shall I say? [v. 13]). Then, God replies to Moses by saying אֶהְיֶה אֲשֶׁר אֶהְיֶה (I am who I am [v. 14]). Now, in continuing God's answer to Moses, God himself refers to his name as יְהוָה (Yhwh): כֹּה־תֹאמַר אֶל־בְּנֵי יִשְׂרָאֵל יְהוָה אֱלֹהֵי אֲבֹתֵיכֶם אֱלֹהֵי אַבְרָהָם אֱלֹהֵי יִצְחָק וֵאלֹהֵי יַעֲקֹב שְׁלָחַנִי אֲלֵיכֶם זֶה־שְּׁמִי לְעֹלָם (thus you shall say to sons of Israel, *Yhwh*, God of your fathers, God of Abraham, God of Isaac, and God of Jacob has sent me to you, *this is my name* forever [v. 15; italics added]).

people Israel? (v. 21)]; לִפְדּוֹת לוֹ עָם [to redeem people for himself (v. 21)]; וַתִּתֵּן אֶת־עַמְּךָ לְגָרֵשׁ מִפְּנֵי עַמְּךָ [by driving out before your people (v. 21)]; יִשְׂרָאֵל לְךָ לְעָם עַד־עוֹלָם [you made your people Israel to be your people forever (v. 22)]). The notion of Israel as God's people first appears in verse 21 in David's prayer. Verse 21 begins with a rhetorical question: וּמִי כְּעַמְּךָ יִשְׂרָאֵל גּוֹי אֶחָד (what one nation is like your people Israel?). Similar to the previous rhetorical questions in the prayer (vv. 16–17), this question also implies a negative answer: there is no other nation that can be like Israel. Thus, even from the beginning of David's historical review, the text impresses the message and sets the tone that Israel is God's special people, as it repeats this notion in following phrases. Tuell's observation shows how verse 21 possibly encourages the post-exilic people to become monotheistic believers:

> Alone among all the world's peoples, *Israel is a nation created by God*. God's mighty acts, manifest in victory over Israel's enemies, but particularly in the deliverance from Egypt (17:21//2 Sam. 7:23; note that, while the NRSV does not reflect this, Egypt is mentioned in the MT of 2 Sam. 7:23), show Israel to be a people much loved by God. But Israel's past is also a reminder of Israel's dependence upon God's grace, and so a reminder of the need for faithfulness.[88]

The Chronicler replaces וַתְּכוֹנֵן (you established [2 Sam 7:24]) with וַתִּתֵּן (you made/chose/created [1 Chr 17:22]). When God is the subject of the action of the verb נתן, this verb, together with its object and accompanied by לְ, refers to God's special appointment of someone or a people in the MT (Deut 28:13; Ps 106:46; Isa 42:6; 49:6, 8; Jer 1:18; 15:20; 20:4; 2 Chr 9:8).[89] Knoppers agrees that this text portrays God's particular election of Israel in his observation on אֲשֶׁר הָלַךְ הָאֱלֹהִים לִפְדּוֹת לוֹ עָם (whom God went forth to redeem as a people for himself [v. 21]), arguing that "this language is typical of Deuteronomy" in referring to Israel as God's elected people (Deut 7:8; 9:26; 13:6 [Eng. v. 5]; 15:15; 21:8; 24:18).[90] Thus, as David and the community remember God's deeds in the past, the prayer motivates the community to imprint on their hearts the notion that Yhwh is their special God.

---

88. Tuell, *First and Second Chronicles*, 76 (italics added).
89. Clines, "נָתַן," in *DCH*, 784–813.
90. Knoppers, *First Chronicles 10–29*, 684.

In terms of remembering God's salvific deeds in Israel's past, the Chronicler noticeably does not omit the exodus event from his *Vorlage* (cf. 2 Sam 7:23) in verse 21.[91] Scholars have observed the Chronicler's particular strategy of frequently omitting the exodus event from his historiography.[92] Yet, the Chronicler retains this event and also repeats the word redeem (לִפְדּוֹת ;אֲשֶׁר־פָּדִיתָ [v. 21]), which shows the Chronicler's concern for describing God as Israel's redeemer. In addition, Chronicles writes הָלַךְ הָאֱלֹהִים (God went [singular form (1 Chr 17:21)]) instead of the word הָלְכוּ־אֱלֹהִים (God went [plural form (2 Sam 7:23)] from its *Vorlage*. Although it is possible that the text in Samuel was corrupted, the intention revealed in Chronicles by clarifying the subject of the action with the plural verb is that Israel's special God delivers his people.[93]

The notion of Israel as God's people is further affirmed in verse 24.[94] David says יְהוָה צְבָאוֹת אֱלֹהֵי יִשְׂרָאֵל אֱלֹהִים לְיִשְׂרָאֵל (Yhwh of hosts, God of

---

91. Unlike 1 Chr 17:22, the prayer's near context deletes the word Egypt from its *Vorlage*; see 1 Chr 17:5 and 2 Sam 7:6. For this passage (1 Chr 17:16–27), MT Samuel serves as the *Vorlage*. For a detailed comparison between this particular passage (i.e., MT Chronicles) and MT Samuel and 4QSama, see Lynch, *Monotheism and Institutions*, 222–26; see also Avioz, "Nathan's Prophecy."

92. Japhet writes, "In a general historical system of slavery, exodus, and conquest of the land, the settlement in Israel represents something of an innovation, a surprising change in the people's fortunes, the ultimate expression of the bond between the people of Israel and the God of Israel. Chronicles presents a different view of history: the dimensions of the Babylonian conquest and exile are reduced considerably, the people's settlement in the land is portrayed as an uninterrupted continuum, and, in the say way, the constitutive force of the exodus from Egypt is eliminated" (Japhet, *Ideology of the Book*, 301). For detailed discussion, see Japhet, *Ideology of the Book*, 296–301; Japhet, *From the Rivers of Babylon*, 38–52.

93. The Chronicler's intention is obvious in v. 21: God delivers Israel for himself (לוֹ [himself]; לְךָ שֵׁם [for your name sake]) since Israel is God's possession (עַמְּךָ [your people]).

Japhet writes: "The precise rendering of 'went' is of significance for its interpretation, since a plural (as in MT) would render 'God' as a common noun, referring to the God of Israel.... In Chronicles, with the verb in the singular, whether the change reflects a better original version or the editing of the Chronicler, the matter is clear: the uniqueness of Israel is that their God has redeemed them in order to make them his people" (Japhet, *First and Second Chronicles*, 340).

94. In vv. 21–22, the word עַם (people) stands alone (עָם [v. 21]) or with a preposition (לְעָם [v. 22]). It also appears in a construct form (כְּעַמְּךָ יִשְׂרָאֵל [v. 21]; עַמְּךָ יִשְׂרָאֵל [v.22]) and with the pronominal suffix (i.e., your; vv. 21, 22). In v. 24, however, the relationship between the people/Israel and God is recorded in a more intense sense. It repeats the word יִשְׂרָאֵל (Israel) and the referent to God (יְהוָה ;אֱלֹהִים).

Israel, God to Israel).⁹⁵ The Chronicler adds אֱלֹהֵי יִשְׂרָאֵל to his *Vorlage* (2 Sam 7:26), further affirming that Israel belongs to God.⁹⁶ These repeated epithets enhance the notion of Yhwh as Israel's special God.⁹⁷

In sum, the prayer shows David's recognition of God's character, deeds, and intention to make a special relationship with his people. The prayer speaks to its audience that Yhwh is the unique and incomparable God who made Israel as his people and delivered them from their enemies. The post-exilic community should serve Yhwh with humility by following the servanthood represented by King David.

Davidic Covenant: Hope of Davidic Citizenship

The recorded prayer of David and Nathan's oracle motivates the audience to hope for the revival of the Davidic kingdom.⁹⁸ The core contents

---

95. The syntactical observation does not provide a clear picture, since there is no verb involved in this phrase. It could be a combination of three vocatives (the Lord of the hosts, God of Israel, God to Israel) as the LXX understands it. The LXX writes κύριε κύριε παντοκράτωρ θεὸς Ισραηλ (Lord, Lord of almighty, God of Israel). Many English translations understand that one could supply a linking verb (i.e., is), in order to understand something similar to what follows: "Yhwh [the Lord] of hosts, the God of Israel *is* Israel's God" (ESV, NIV, NKJ, TNK) or "Yhwh [the Lord] of hosts is Israel's God, *even* a God to Israel" (JPS, NAS). Either position is sufficient to emphasize God's direct relationship to his people, Israel. If one interprets these phrases with an implied linking verb, then one is simply able to establish a direct syntactical relationship between "Yhwh of the hosts" and "God of Israel," so that the verse carries a sense that "Yhwh of the hosts is God of Israel, God even to Israel."

See also Klein: "The tautological confession in the present verse [17:24] affirms David's exclusive allegiance to the God who raised him up as king and established Israel as his people" (R. Klein, *First Chronicles*, 384).

96. Construct as possession or belonging (Joüon, *Grammar of Biblical Hebrew*, §92).

97. Ahn, *Persuasive Portrayal*, 142.
The pattern in these three phrases is as follows:

יְהוָה ᵃ צְבָאוֹת ᵇ
אֱלֹהֵי ᵃ¹ יִשְׂרָאֵל ᵇ¹
אֱלֹהִים ᵃ² לְיִשְׂרָאֵל ᵇ²

In these phrases, יְהוָה (a), אֱלֹהֵי (a1), and אֱלֹהִים (a2) stand in parallel, so it is intelligible for the audience that Yhwh (a) of the hosts (b) and Israel (b1) is God (a1, a2) to Israel (b2).

98. Boda, "Gazing through the Cloud of Incense," in Evans and Williams, *Chronicling the Chronicler*, 216; Kelly, *Retribution and Eschatology*, 135–55.

of the Davidic promise are given through Nathan's oracle in 17:10b–14.⁹⁹ The text begins with a solid statement of God, which promises God's willingness to build a house (וּבַיִת יִבְנֶה־לְּךָ יְהוָה [Yhwh will build a house for you (v. 10b)]). The text further articulates that God would establish the kingdom (וַהֲכִינוֹתִי אֶת־מַלְכוּתוֹ [I will establish his kingdom (v. 11)]) and the throne would be forever (וְכֹנַנְתִּי אֶת־כִּסְאוֹ עַד־עוֹלָם [I will establish his throne forever (v. 12)]). The oracle concludes with an asseveration of God's promise with וְכִסְאוֹ יִהְיֶה נָכוֹן עַד־עוֹלָם (and his throne will be established forever [v. 14]).

Now, in David's prayer, the king affirms God's revelation of his dynasty. David hopes for the fulfillment of God's word (וַעֲשֵׂה כַּאֲשֶׁר דִּבַּרְתָּ [do as you have spoken (v. 23)]), and his promise is effective to the king, his house (עַל־עַבְדְּךָ וְעַל־בֵּיתוֹ [to your servant and his house (v. 23)]) and the people of Israel (אֱלֹהֵי יִשְׂרָאֵל אֱלֹהִים לְיִשְׂרָאֵל [God of Israel, God to Israel (v. 24)]).¹⁰⁰

Therefore, Nathan's oracle and David's prayer function as meaningful rhetorical impetus for the post-exilic community.¹⁰¹ God has promised the everlasting nature of the Davidic royal line through his own prophet (i.e., Nathan), and David believes the promise. When the post-exilic community confronts the prophetic messages and joins in the

---

99. Since David's prayer is given in response to Nathan's prophecy, one must understand what God promises through Nathan in order to reveal the nature of God's promise to David. First Chronicles 17:10b–14 says, "I declare to you that Yhwh will build a house for you. When your days are fulfilled to walk with your fathers, I will raise up your descendants after you, who shall be one of your own sons, and I will establish his kingdom. He will build a house for me, and I will establish his throne forever. I will be to him a father, and he shall be to me a son. I will not take my steadfast love from him, as I took it from him who was before you, but I will confirm him in my house and in my kingdom forever, and his throne will be established forever."

100. In the Chronicler's historiography, the text repeatedly affirms God's promise. See 2 Chr 21:7, where the text says, וְלֹא־אָבָה יְהוָה לְהַשְׁחִית אֶת־בֵּית דָּוִיד לְמַעַן הַבְּרִית אֲשֶׁר כָּרַת לְדָוִיד וְכַאֲשֶׁר אָמַר לָתֵת לוֹ נִיר וּלְבָנָיו כָּל־הַיָּמִים (Yet Yhwh was not willing to destroy the house of David because of the covenant that he had made with David, and since he had promised to give a lamp to him and to his sons forever). Regarding the Chronicler's direct comments, note that in the narrative, the narrator's (third person) comment often conveys increased persuasiveness (Longman, *Literary Approaches*, 85–86).

David affirms God's promise again as he prepares for the temple construction, saying to Solomon, וַהֲכִינוֹתִי כִּסֵּא מַלְכוּתוֹ עַל־יִשְׂרָאֵל עַד־עוֹלָם ([I God] will establish his throne of the kingdom over Israel forever [1 Chr 22:10]).

101. One may then ask a question: "How is it possible for Israel to have an exile?" See "Citizens of the Davidic Kingdom" in ch. 4 regarding this question. See also Hwang, *Hope for the Restoration*, 147; Hwang, "Coexistence of Unconditionality," 242.

prayers of David (esp. 1 Chr 17:23–27), who hoped for the fulfillment of God's promise, these stimuli motivate the members of the community to have the same hope of bringing about the Davidic kingdom.

The Davidic Temple Citizen:
An Aspect of the Role in Realizing Davidic Citizenship

David's prayer does not directly reveal an aspect of the role in realizing Davidic citizenship; instead, it repeatedly refers to Nathan's oracle (וַתְּדַבֵּר [you have spoken (v. 17)]; לְהֹדִיעַ אֶת־כָּל־הַגְּדֻלּוֹת [to make know all these great things (v. 19)]; הַדָּבָר אֲשֶׁר דִּבַּרְתָּ [the word that you have spoken (v. 23)]; גָּלִיתָ אֶת־אֹזֶן עַבְדְּךָ [you have revealed to the ear of your servant (v. 25)]). Thus, it is necessary to investigate Nathan's oracle to reveal a particular aspect of Davidic citizenship. God's word in Nathan's oracle reveals interrelation between the kingdom and the temple, and this relation hints at a fundamental aspect of the audience's realization of the Davidic citizenship: the security or perpetuity of the kingdom is related to the construction of the temple.[102]

Two Houses

God's promise to David involves an agenda for establishing two houses: the temple and the dynasty of the Davidic line (וּבַיִת יִבְנֶה־לְּךָ יְהוָה [Yhwh will build a house for you (v. 10)]; הוּא יִבְנֶה־לִּי בָיִת וְכֹנַנְתִּי אֶת־כִּסְאוֹ עַד־עוֹלָם [He shall build a house for me and I will be establishing his throne forever (v. 12)]). This agenda exhibits the relationship between these two houses and hints at how the perpetuity or security of Davidic kingdom can be achieved.[103] The reviewing of God's deeds/promises in Israel's history and

---

102. Even though views among scholars concerning the nature of the Davidic kingdom vary, in Nathan's oracle, the principle aspect in which the audience can become citizens is fundamentally revealed, regardless of the types or shapes of the kingdom or timing of the actualization of the kingdom. Here the meaning of the nature of the Davidic kingdom follows Boda's terms: shape of the fulfillment (i.e., David or community), timing (i.e., future or present), and effect (i.e., cataclysmic or continuity) (Boda, "Gazing through the Cloud of Incense," in Evans and Williams, *Chronicling the Chronicler*, 217).

103. Scholars have recognized the Davidic dynasty's role in relation to the temple. Riley says, "The Chronicler's interest in the Davidic dynasty can therefore be seen as more concerned with the role of the dynasty in relation to the Temple than with the dynasty's unending rule over Israel.... For the Chronicler, the centre of the covenant

the projection of his plan for two houses are given in a historical-sequential arrangement (vv. 9–14).[104] The table below presents the overview of Nathan's oracle in reflection of that particular arrangement.

---

with David is not formed by the dynastic promise, but by the task of temple-building, and the fulfillment of the covenant is to be sought in the completed Temple rather than in an unending Davidic rule" (Riley, *King and Cultus*, 75). Although Riley's expression of an unending Davidic rule must be evaluated carefully, his view on the relationship between the temple and the Davidic dynasty is correct. See also Mason, *Preaching the Tradition*, 32; Kelly, *Retribution and Eschatology*, 158.

104. Although Knoppers does not use the particular term historical-sequential, his view on Nathan's oracle systematically integrates various themes (i.e., social, martial, and political factors) in a sequential manner (Knoppers, "Nathan's Oracle," 104, 108).

Verse	Text	Status of Dynasty	Remark
9	וְשַׂמְתִּי מָקוֹם לְעַמִּי יִשְׂרָאֵל וּנְטַעְתִּיהוּ וְשָׁכַן תַּחְתָּיו ("I [Yhwh] will appoint a place for my people Israel and plant them and dwell)"[105]	Not yet established in the promise	Reminding of God's promise to Moses
10a	וּלְמִיָּמִים אֲשֶׁר צִוִּיתִי שֹׁפְטִים עַל־עַמִּי יִשְׂרָאֵל וְהִכְנַעְתִּי אֶת־כָּל־אוֹיְבֶיךָ (from the days that I appointed judges of my people Israel and I have humbled all your enemies)	Not yet established in the promise	Recalling of God's protection during the days of judges
10b	וָאַגִּד לָךְ וּבַיִת יִבְנֶה־לְּךָ יְהוָה (and I declare[106] to you Yhwh will build a house[107] for you)	Promise of establishment is given to David (initial)	Security or perpetuity of the dynasty is not yet guaranteed in the promise
11b	וַהֲקִימוֹתִי אֶת־זַרְעֲךָ אַחֲרֶיךָ אֲשֶׁר יִהְיֶה מִבָּנֶיךָ וַהֲכִינוֹתִי אֶת־מַלְכוּתוֹ (I will raise up your descendants after you, who shall be one[108] of your own sons, and I will establish his kingdom)	Promise of establishment is expanded to the descendants of David (developed)	Security or perpetuity of the dynasty is not yet guaranteed in the promise

105. This particular expression is similar to Exod 15:17 and Ps 80:9: תְּבִאֵמוֹ וְתִטָּעֵמוֹ בְּהַר נַחֲלָתְךָ מָכוֹן לְשִׁבְתְּךָ (You will bring and plant them on the mountain of your inheritance, the place to dwell [Exod 15:17]); גֶּפֶן מִמִּצְרַיִם תַּסִּיעַ תְּגָרֵשׁ גּוֹיִם וַתִּטָּעֶהָ (You brought a vine out of Egypt and drove out nations and planted it [Ps 80:9]). Although there is no verbatim, 1 Chr 17:9 alludes to Deut 11:23–24, which says, וְהוֹרִישׁ יְהוָה אֶת־כָּל־הַגּוֹיִם הָאֵלֶּה מִלִּפְנֵיכֶם וִירִשְׁתֶּם גּוֹיִם גְּדֹלִים וַעֲצֻמִים מִכֶּם כָּל־הַמָּקוֹם אֲשֶׁר תִּדְרֹךְ כַּף־רַגְלְכֶם בּוֹ לָכֶם יִהְיֶה מִן־הַמִּדְבָּר וְהַלְּבָנוֹן מִן־הַנָּהָר נְהַר־פְּרָת וְעַד (And Yhwh will drive out all these nations before you, and you will dispossess greater and mightier nations than yourselves. Every place on which the sole of your foot treads shall be yours. Your territory shall be from the wilderness to the Lebanon and from the river, the river Euphrates, to the western sea).

106. Note that the LXX writes αὐξήσω σε (I will increase you), so that it understands that God would make David a greater figure.

107. The word בַּיִת (house) most likely refers to dynasty. David is the second king of Israel, already enthroned in 1 Chr 11:3. For a detailed discussion and further reference for semantic study of בַּיִת, see Lynch, "Davidic Covenant," in MacDonald, *Covenant and Election*," 172–73.

108. Note that the MT does not provide a word for *one*. Most English translations (ESV, NASB, NET, NIV, NLT, NRS, TNK, CSB) add this word, so they read, "one of your . . ." From the immediate context (vv. 12–14), it is not arbitrary to understand that Nathan refers to one of David's sons, who is Solomon. Verses 12–14 specifically refer to one of his descendants by using extensive singular grammatical markers (e.g.,

Verse	Text	Status of Dynasty	Remark
12	הוּא יִבְנֶה־לִּי בָיִת וְכֹנַנְתִּי אֶת־כִּסְאוֹ עַד־עוֹלָם (He will build a house for me and I will establish his throne forever).	Promise of eternal dynasty is given and is effective for David's descendants	First appearance of the temple construction in the oracle
14	וְהַעֲמַדְתִּיהוּ בְּבֵיתִי וּבְמַלְכוּתִי עַד־הָעוֹלָם וְכִסְאוֹ יִהְיֶה נָכוֹן עַד־עוֹלָם (but I will confirm him in my house and in my kingdom forever, and his throne will be established forever)	Promise of eternal dynasty is reaffirmed	Defining the nature of the kingdom (theocracy)[109]

Table. Historical-Sequential Projection of Nathan's Oracle

In Nathan's oracle, God's promise develops sequentially. Initially, it does not specify any particular person or place (v. 12). Then, it appoints David (לְךָ [for you (v. 10b)]) and affirms that his kingdom would be established; yet there are no words referring to the security of his monarchy. The effectiveness of the promise gets expanded[110] and specified to his

---

מַלְכוּתוֹ [his kingdom (v. 11b)]; אֶת־כִּסְאוֹ [his throne (v. 12)]; לוֹ [to him (v. 13)]; מֵעִמּוֹ [with him (v. 13)]; וְכִסְאוֹ [his throne (v. 14)]). See also 2 Chr 6:9b: כִּי בִנְךָ הַיּוֹצֵא מֵחֲלָצֶיךָ הוּא־יִבְנֶה הַבַּיִת לִשְׁמִי (but your son who shall come from your loins will build the house for my name).

109. This book defines theocracy as the kingdom ruled by God through earthly kings. Thus, Israel is the kingdom of Yhwh. Dyck dedicates his monograph to this particular subject in Chronicles (Dyck, *Theocratic Ideology*). See Rudolph, "Zur Theologie des Chronisten," 285; Nel, "Davidic Covenant"; Raison, "From Theocracy to Kingdom." See also Kelly: "Although 'theocracy' is often used interchangeably for 'hierocracy', the rule of cultic personnel, the Chronicler has a quite different understanding of how the divine kingship is exercised. The theocracy in Chronicles is really the union of two interests that have their origin in the Davidic covenant, the dynasty and the temple. Together these institutions are the principal expressions of Yahweh's kingdom" (Kelly, *Retribution and Eschatology*, 156).

110. Here, expanded does not mean that there are two separated promises to David and to his descendants. In other words, there are not two promises but, instead, two aspects of one promise. God does not promise David that God will establish a kingdom for David and then separately give words of security to David's descendants. Instead, there are two aspects under one umbrella. In terms of the words of security or eternity for David's descendants, the Chronicler is careful to point out that Solomon is the one who would build the temple and that the confirmation of the eternity is related to Solomon's given task. In v. 12, God promises that Solomon's throne would be forever (אֶת־כִּסְאוֹ [his throne], third person masculine singular suffix). This expression occurs again in v. 14 (וְכִסְאוֹ), and in this case, the Chronicler adds it instead of

descendants (אֶת־זַרְעֲךָ אַחֲרֶיךָ [your descendants [v. 11]), thus confirming the security of the kingdom (vv. 12–14).

In verses 12–14, the Chronicler is careful to define the relationship between the house of David and the house of God. God will establish Solomon's kingdom (אֶת־מַלְכוּתוֹ [his kingdom (v. 11)]), and Solomon will build the temple (הוּא יִבְנֶה־לִּי בָיִת [he shall build the house for me (v. 12)]). Then, the following phrase says וְכֹנַנְתִּי אֶת־כִּסְאוֹ עַד־עוֹלָם (Then, I will establish his throne forever [v. 12]); thus, verses 11–12 present the idea that the completion of the temple is closely related to the security of the throne.[111] Verses 13–14 carry a father-son analogy (אֲנִי אֶהְיֶה־לּוֹ לְאָב וְהוּא יִהְיֶה־לִּי לְבֵן [I will be a father for him, and he will be a son for me (v. 13)]), include the word חֶסֶד (hesed [v. 13]), and reaffirm the eternality of the dynasty by repeating the word עוֹלָם (forever [v. 14]).[112]

Overall, the Davidic promise in 1 Chronicles 17 reveals that God has chosen Solomon as the temple builder, and through the completion of the task, Solomon's kingdom would be secure. The text conveys the

---

כִּסְאֶךָ (your [David's] throne [2 Sam 7:16]). Thus, the Chronicler intends to delineate between God's plan and his assigning of different duties to David and Solomon. This agenda becomes clear in the following chapters, 1 Chr 18—2 Chr 7, which describe David as a preparer of the temple and Solomon as a temple builder.

111. *Waw*-consecutive in וְכֹנַנְתִּי (v. 12) translated as "then." It establishes a sequential (i.e., cause-effect) relationship.

112. Jarick, *First Chronicles*, 117. For a detailed study on the origin of the father-son analogy, see Knoppers, *First Chronicles 10–29*, 670–71.

Williamson once noted that "one of the few points about which all commentators on Chronicles are agreed is that the Temple was of central significance to its author" (Williamson, "Temple in the Books," 15). When considering the number of chapters dedicated to the temple and related stories (i.e., the preparation, transportation of the ark, construction, dedication, and preservation), Williamson rightly sees the significance of the temple in the book of Chronicles. Scholars have shown various interests in relation to the temple. For instance, Dillard's literary analysis of the Solomon narrative is classic. It would not be an exaggeration to say that everyone who discusses the literary structure of the temple construction or Solomon narrative refers to Dillard's literary analysis, for instance, Kalimi, *Reshaping*, 224. See Dillard, "Literary Structure," 90. Hahn sees the temple as a new tabernacle and a new creation (Hahn, *Kingdom of God*, 114). Cudworth focuses on war in Chronicles in relation to Solomon and his temple (Cudworth, *War in Chronicles*). Selman discuss the temple in light of the city of Jerusalem (Selman, "Jerusalem in Chronicles," in Wenham and Hess, *Zion*, 43–56). Tiňo is interested in the relationship between kingship and the temple (Tiňo, *King and Temple*). Braun says the central theme of the book of Chronicles is the temple (Braun, "Message of Chronicles"). Stafford attempts to explain the temple in relation to eschatology (Stafford, "Temple? What Temple?").

message that the establishment and eternality of the Davidic dynasty and the temple construction are closely related.[113]

David, a Faithful Supplicant

Chronicles characterizes King David as a faithful supplicant who serves as a model figure for the members of the post-exilic community. The text reveals that David clearly recognizes the object of prayer. David calls on God's name ten times during his prayer (i.e., vocative).[114] He does not superficially or mystically call on God's name, but as a monotheistic believer, he puts faith in the expectation that God would certainly fulfill his promise. Chronicles portrays David as he who exhibits his faith by replacing David's word יְבֹרַךְ (shall be blessed [2 Sam 7:29]) with בֵּרַכְתָּ (you have blessed [1 Chr 17:27]) in his final affirmation of God's promise.[115] This change can characterize David as the one who believes either that God's promise has already been fulfilled or that it is currently being actualized.[116]

One may raise a question, then: why does David pray for something he has already received?[117] This type of question could be meaningful to the post-exilic community since they may ask a similar question: why do we have to pray for the revival of the Davidic kingdom, if God has already promised its perpetuity to David and his descendants? Knoppers answers,

> Nathan grants the king everything he wished for—and much, much more—but he delays the date for the implementation of

---

113. One may raise a question concerning a situation after the completion of the temple (i.e., why is there no tangible kingdom in the post-exilic days?). For this discussion, see "Citizens of the Davidic Kingdom" in ch. 4.

114. יְהוָה אֱלֹהִים (Yhwh, God [v. 16]); אֱלֹהִים (God [v. 17]); יְהוָה אֱלֹהִים (Yhwh God [v. 17]); יְהוָה (Yhwh [v. 18, 19, 20, 23, 26, 27]); אֱלֹהַי (my God [v. 25]).

115. Compare the following two verses: 2 Sam 7:29 reads, כִּי־אַתָּה אֲדֹנָי יְהוִה דִּבַּרְתָּ וּמִבִּרְכָתְךָ יְבֹרַךְ בֵּית־עַבְדְּךָ לְעוֹלָם פ (for you the Lord Yhwh have spoken and with your blessing the house of your servant shall be blessed), whereas 1 Chr 17:27 says, כִּי־אַתָּה יְהוָה בֵּרַכְתָּ וּמְבֹרָךְ לְעוֹלָם פ (for you Yhwh, you have blessed and it is blessed forever).

116. Beentjes correctly sees that, "Whereas this latter verse [2 Sam 7:29] has been modelled as a *supplication* for blessing in the future, 1 Chr 17:27 should be characterized as a *panegyric* establishing that God's blessing on the House of David has already been realized" (Beentjes, *Tradition and Transformation*, 44).

117. David utters, כִּי אַתָּה אֱלֹהַי גָּלִיתָ אֶת־אֹזֶן עַבְדְּךָ לִבְנוֹת לוֹ בָּיִת עַל־כֵּן מָצָא עַבְדְּךָ לְהִתְפַּלֵּל לְפָנֶיךָ (for you, my God, have revealed to your servant to build a house for him, therefore your servant has found courage/strength to pray before you [1 Chr 17:25]). For the translation of found courage, see Clines, "מצא," in *DCH*, 434–42.

most of these promises until the reign of David's heir. Given the postponement, a royal prayer is appropriate both as a forum for thanksgiving and as a petition for future fulfillment (v. 25) . . . . If David's heir did not succeed him, most of the other divine assurances would become irrelevant. In the context of postmonarchic Judah, a time in which the splendor of the Davidic dynasty was a thing of the past, David's petitions may well have taken on additional significance, functioning as a prayer for a new realization of the divine promises.[118]

The post-exilic community was not in an essentially different context from David's circumstances. Similar to David, who wished that God would actualize his dynastic promises in David's future, the post-exilic community desires and prays for God to remember and fulfill his promises in their days. In this regard, the members of the community become active supplicants with a firm faith in God's promise by following the model, David.

Conclusion

The prayer in 1 Chronicles 17 takes a unique position among the other recorded prayers in Chronicles as it specially presents God's dynastic promises to David. In response to Nathan's prophecy, the Chronicler characterizes David as one who has faith in God's establishment and securing of the dynasty. The prayer exhibits that the completion of the temple construction is a critical element for the establishment of the kingdom. In addition, the prayer portrays David as an exemplary figure, who exhibits a solid monotheistic belief with the heart of a servant and prays with a deep faith in God's fulfillment of his dynastic promise. Overall, the Chronicler's characterization of David in the prayer speaks to the audience that in their desiring for the coming or revival of the Davidic kingdom, they too should pray in faith and hold to a solid monotheistic belief—just like David.

---

118. Knoppers, *First Chronicles 10–29*, 687.

First Chronicles 29:10–19: David's Final Prayer

Introduction

First Chronicles 29:10–19 is the last recorded prayer of David in Chronicles. The prayer does not appear in Chronicles' *Vorlage* (Sam-Kgs) but it is Chronicles' *Sondergut*;[119] thus, it is probable that the prayer may exhibit the Chronicler's own concern for the post-exilic community as he incorporates David's prayer into writing Israel's historiography. Chronicles provides the prayer at the transitionary period of the kingship from David to Solomon (chs. 28–29) during the final days of David's reign.[120] David's foremost concern is the readiness of Solomon and the people to accomplish the task of the temple's construction. David remembers God's promise and appoints Solomon as the temple builder before the leaders of Israel (28:2–8). David encourages Solomon to fulfill the given task (דַּע אֶת־אֱלֹהֵי אָבִיךָ וְעָבְדֵהוּ בְּלֵב שָׁלֵם) [understand the God of your father and serve with all your heart (v. 8)]; חֲזַק וַעֲשֵׂה [be strong and do it (v. 9)]). David provides Solomon a blueprint of the temple construction (vv. 11–21) and summons all the assembly of Israel (29:1) as he announces his efforts of offering resources to God (vv. 2–5). This example leads the other leaders of Israel and the people to offer willingly their resources for the temple construction (vv. 6–9) with great joy (שִׂמְחָה גְדוֹלָה [v. 9]).

The prayer (vv. 10–21) also reflects David's projection of the preparation process. David's prayer exhibits his praise (vv. 10–12), appreciation (vv. 13–16), and petition (vv. 17–19) toward God.[121] These elements in prayer are based on David's recognition of God's greatness, especially regarding God's generous provision (vv. 12–17) of the temple construction and David's continual hope for God's guidance in finishing the task (vv. 18–19). In light of this context, the prayer's particular function in shaping

---

119. For a list of Chronicles' *Sondergut*, see Beentjes, "Psalms and Prayers in the Book of Chronicles," in Becking and Peels, eds., *Psalms and Prayers*, 10.

120. Williamson, *First and Second Chronicles*, 178–89; Japhet, *First and Second Chronicles*, 482–83; R. Klein, *First Chronicles*, 517–18; Knoppers, *First Chronicles 10–29*, 917–19.

121. Hill understands the prayer as having three sections: doxology (29:10-12), thanksgiving (29:13-16), and supplication (29:17-19) (Hill, *First and Second Chronicles*, 349–50). Other scholars have divided this prayer in other ways. Throntveit delineates the prayer by a change of subject: you, Yhwh, and we (see vv. 10b-12, 13-17, 18-19) (Throntveit, *Significance*, 120). Ahn basically follows Throntveit's delineation (Ahn, *Persuasive Portrayal*, 201). Klein also discerns three sections: vv. 10b-12, 13-17, and 18-19 (R. Klein, *First Chronicles*, 532).

Israel's identity is to motivate the members of the community to realize the characteristics of monotheistic believers.

Israel's Supreme God over the Universe

David's words of praise and thanksgiving toward God reflect the king's recognition of Israel's special relationship with their God and his supremacy over the world.[122] As the audience of the prayer joins in David's prayer, the prayer is then able to motivate them to become active monotheistic believers.[123] First, David acknowledges God as the object of his prayer. In the initial act of calling upon God, the king refers to God as Yhwh (יְהוָה) and God of Israel (אֱלֹהֵי יִשְׂרָאֵל), and he tries to remind God of Israel's special relationship with him (1 Chr 29:10). Similar expressions are repeated throughout the prayer (אֱלֹהֵינוּ [our God (vv. 13, 16)]; אֱלֹהָי [my God (v. 17)]; יְהוָה אֱלֹהֵי אַבְרָהָם יִצְחָק וְיִשְׂרָאֵל [Yhwh, God of Abraham, Isaac, and Israel (v. 18)]). The notion of God as Israel's own deity (vv. 10, 18) occurs at the opening and the closing of the prayer; thus, the prayer begins and ends its messages (i.e., praising, thanksgiving, and petition) by recognizing Israel's special relationship with their unique God.[124]

Second, David acknowledges God's sovereignty over the universe. This notion is demonstrated by the following: ownership, kingship, and

122. Throntveit summarizes the theme of the prayer as follows: "The prayers employ portions of the lament or entire laments to repeatedly make one point: the contrast between Yahweh's power and might and the weakness and dependence of his people" (Throntveit, *Significance*, 120).

123. Ahn argues that the prayer, including other prayers in Chronicles, can be defined as a genre of deliberative rhetoric. He adopts this idea from Kennedy, who understands ancient rhetorical strategy in three ways: judicial or forensic rhetoric, deliberative rhetoric, and epideictic rhetoric. The purpose of deliberative rhetoric is to impact the audience's decision-making process concerning their future (Ahn, "Rhetorical Study," 111; Kennedy, *New Testament Interpretation*, 36).

124. Japhet likewise notices David's manner of calling upon God as establishing a more solid and personal relationship between God and the people. "In two small details the opening words deviate from the common formula: (a) The blessing is not addressed, as is more usual, in the third person (cf. Ps. 41.14; 72.19; 89.53, etc.); rather, a second person invocation is inserted: 'Blessed art thou, the Lord' etc. (elsewhere only in Ps. 119.12)—a change which immediately determines the disposition of all that follows. (b) To the title 'the God of Israel' is added 'our Father', thus defining 'Israel' not as the people in general, but as their common forefather Jacob/Israel. This allusion brings to mind the more personal relationship between God and the people's forefathers, thus setting the tone for the blessing and supplication on the people's behalf, culminating in v. 18" (Japhet, *First and Second Chronicles*, 509).

benefaction. The literary structure below (v. 11) reveals the emphatic points of the given message.

לְךָ֣ יְהוָ֔ה[a]
הַגְּדֻלָּ֧ה
וְהַגְּבוּרָ֛ה
וְהַתִּפְאֶ֖רֶת
וְהַנֵּ֣צַח
וְהַה֑וֹד
כִּי־כֹ֖ל בַּשָּׁמַ֣יִם וּבָאָ֑רֶץ
לְךָ֣ יְהוָ֔ה[b]
הַמַּמְלָכָ֔ה
וְהַמִּתְנַשֵּׂ֖א לְכֹ֥ל ׀ לְרֹֽאשׁ

The verse can be divided into two subsections (a and b). The two clauses begin with לְךָ (belong to you, or to you), thus creating rhetorical force (*anaphora*).[125] The first לְךָ clause depicts God's ownership by listing הַגְּדֻלָּה וְהַגְּבוּרָה וְהַתִּפְאֶרֶת וְהַנֵּצַח וְהַהוֹד (greatness, power, beauty, glory, and majesty [v. 11a]; *accumulation*). The Chronicler provides these words in parallel to one another in order to address God as the one who receives very great exaltation.[126] The use of the definite article ה functions to "elevate a position of uniqueness," so it expresses the superlative qualities that God possesses,[127] culminating in proclamation that God possesses everything in the heaven and the earth (כִּי־כֹל בַּשָּׁמַיִם וּבָאָרֶץ).[128]

God not only possesses things or qualities in the universe but also rules over them. The second clause also begins with לְךָ and reads יְהוָה הַמַּמְלָכָה (Yhwh, belongs kingship) and וְהַמִּתְנַשֵּׂא לְכֹל לְרֹאשׁ (you shall be exalted over all as head [v. 11b]). In the first subsection (11a), the כִּי clause

---

125. Bullinger, *Figures of Speech*, 199.

126. Japhet, *First and Second Chronicles*, 509; Ahn, *Persuasive Portrayal*, 202–3. As Lynch notes, it is not easy to figure out the Chronicler's intention of employing each quality. Yet, the rhetorical effect is more clearly revealed when each attribute is used in a cumulative way to emphasize God's greatness (Lynch, *Monotheism and Institution*, 218).

127. Waltke and O'Connor, *Introduction to Biblical Hebrew*, §13.6a; 14.5c. Lynch's grammatical observation agrees with this book concerning the understanding of the Chronicler's intention: "Verse 11a employs the definite article —ה to mark each attribute, though the article lack antecedents (cf. 1 Chr 17:19). Like the noun כל, repeated ten times in this prayer, —ה is a marker of totality and thus underscores Yhwh's total possession of supreme qualities" (Lynch, *Monotheism and Institution*, 218).

128. כִּי as casual.

emphasizes the totality of God's possession (*merism*),¹²⁹ while the second subsection (11b) involves וְהַמִּתְנַשֵּׂא (be exalted [hithpael participle form of נשׂא]), which is the only verbal root in the verse, so it accentuates God's divine governance.

Verse 12 reconfirms God's possession of supreme qualities (וְהָעֹשֶׁר וְהַכָּבוֹד מִלְּפָנֶיךָ [riches and honor come from you])¹³⁰ and his ruling power (וְאַתָּה מוֹשֵׁל בַּכֹּל [you rule over all]). Particularly, later in Chronicles' historiography, King Jehoshaphat reiterates אַתָּה מוֹשֵׁל בְּכֹל (2 Chr 20:6), which is a verbatim record, when he encounters a national crisis (v. 1). Jehoshaphat adopts David's prayer as a model, demonstrating his monotheistic belief as he supplicates God to deliver him and his people (vv. 6–12). The two kings' exemplary acts are able to motivate the readers, so that they exhibit the same characteristics of monotheistic believers.¹³¹

David's prayer appreciates that God is the provider of all the resources for the temple construction. Verse 12 describes God as the benefactor (וּבְיָדְךָ כֹּחַ וּגְבוּרָה וּבְיָדְךָ לְגַדֵּל וּלְחַזֵּק לַכֹּל [in your hand, there are strength and might, and in your hand it is to make great and to give strength to all]). The notion of God as the benefactor is presented through the expression וּבְיָדְךָ (his hand [x2]), which often represents God's generous provision for his people in Chronicles.

Following David's Outward and Inward Expressions

David's prayer attests to certain aspects of monotheistic believers. The first section of the prayer (vv. 10–12) exhibits David's initial praising of God (בָּרוּךְ אַתָּה יְהוָה אֱלֹהֵי יִשְׂרָאֵל אָבִינוּ מֵעוֹלָם וְעַד־עוֹלָם [blessed are you, Yhwh, God of Israel, our father, from everlasting and to everlasting (v. 10)]) and sets the ground for his appeal (i.e., the supplicants' recognition of God's supremacy). Now, the second section (vv. 13–19) switches its focus from God's supremacy to monotheistic believers' outward and inward expressions.¹³²

---

129. For *merism*, see Bullinger, *Figures of Speech*, 435.

130. מִן for source (Williams, *Williams' Hebrew Syntax*, §322).

131. Knoppers, *First Chronicles 10–29*, 953.

132. Verse 13 begins with עַתָּה and repeats אֱלֹהֵינוּ (our God) and words of praise (וּדִים אֲנַחְנוּ לָךְ וּמְהַלְלִים לְשֵׁם תִּפְאַרְתֶּךָ [we give thanks and praise your glorious name]).

Believers' Outward Expression: Offerings

The literary structure below (vv. 14–16) forms a core of this second section (vv. 13–17) and particularly emphasizes the theme of monotheistic believers' offering.[133]

וְכִי מִי אֲנִי וּמִי עַמִּי ᵃ
כִּי־נַעְצֹר כֹּחַ לְהִתְנַדֵּב כָּזֹאת ᵇ
כִּי־מִמְּךָ הַכֹּל ᶜ
וּמִיָּדְךָ ᵈ
נָתַנּוּ לָךְ ᵉ
כִּי־גֵרִים אֲנַחְנוּ לְפָנֶיךָ וְתוֹשָׁבִים כְּכָל־אֲבֹתֵינוּ ᵃ′
כַּצֵּל יָמֵינוּ עַל־הָאָרֶץ וְאֵין מִקְוֶה ᵇ′
יְהוָה אֱלֹהֵינוּ כֹּל הֶהָמוֹן הַזֶּה ᶜ′
אֲשֶׁר הֲכִינֹנוּ לִבְנוֹת־לְךָ בַיִת לְשֵׁם קָדְשֶׁךָ ᵉ′
מִיָּדְךָ הִיא וּלְךָ הַכֹּל ᵈ′

The literary analysis exhibits a parallel structure (abc-a′b′c′) with a transposition (de-e′d′) at the end.[134] The structure begins with David's rhetorical question, asking about his and the people's identity (a). In recognition of Israel's unique God (אֱלֹהֵינוּ [our God (v. 13)]), the question expresses David's humility by stating a self-abasing rhetorical question.[135] Verse 15 includes answers to the question by identifying Israel as כִּי־גֵרִים אֲנַחְנוּ לְפָנֶיךָ וְתוֹשָׁבִים (strangers and sojourners [29:15; a′]). It is not clear to whom strangers and sojourners refers; it could be Abraham, Isaac, and Israel in light of the context (v. 18). Yet, when considering the text's expression of כְּכָל־אֲבֹתֵינוּ (like all of our forefathers), it most likely alludes to the entirety of Israel's history; thus, it points out the transience of Israel (v. 15) in contrast to the eternal existence of God (v. 10).[136] Then, the following clause (b) of David's question describes Israel as having ability

---

133. Kalimi simply notes that vv. 14–16 form a chiastic structure, but his observation is implausible and needs further explanation, since the structure shows complexity. He only makes a connection between "for all things come from" (v. 14) and "and is all your own" (v. 16), and he also sees a parallel between "from your hand it comes" (v. 14) and "and of your hand have we given to you" (v. 16) as the central elements (Kalimi, *Reshaping*, 221).

134. See Walsh's explanation of a structure of transposition (Walsh, *Style and Structure*, 111–12).

135. For a self-abasing rhetorical question, see Moshavi, "What Can I Say?," 95–96; Moshavi, "Can a Positive Rhetorical Question," 254.

136. Estes, "Metaphorical Sojourning," 538.

(כִּי־נַעְצֹר כֹּחַ [v. 14]).¹³⁷ David's words of humility are particularly related to his and people's current ability, which originates from God, to offer the resources (כִּי־נַעְצֹר כֹּחַ לְהִתְנַדֵּב כָּזֹאת [that we should be able to offer willingly like this (v. 14)]).¹³⁸ The paired clause (b´) reads כַּצֵּל יָמֵינוּ עַל־הָאָרֶץ וְאֵין מִקְוֶה (like shadow on the days of the earth, there is no hope [v. 15]). The word מִקְוֶה occurs only four times in the MT (Jer 14:8; 17:13; Ezra 10:2; 1 Chr 29:15). It conveys that Yhwh alone is Israel's hope in the context of Israel's turmoil (Jer 14:8; 17:13; see 17:17) and that in Israel's repentance, obeying God's commandment and renewing the covenant will bring them hope (Ezra 10:2–3).¹³⁹ In addition, the word צֵל (shadow [v. 15]) refers to human life as transitory in nature (see Job 8:9; 14:1–2; Pss 102:12 [Eng. v. 11]; 144:4; Eccl 6:12), so it recalls the finiteness of human beings in contrast to the supremacy of God (vv. 11–12).¹⁴⁰ Thus, in light of clause b, clause b´ exhibits that the people of Israel, as finite beings, have no ability without God (i.e., helplessness). Clauses c and c´ share the word כֹּל and recognize the resources that they have or currently offer (כִּי־מִמְּךָ הַכֹּל [everything comes from you (v. 14)]; כָּל הֶהָמוֹן הַזֶּה [all this abundance (v. 16)]). Now clauses d and d´ both confess that the resources are from God's hands (וּמִיָּדְךָ [and it is from your hand (v. 14)]; מִיָּדְךָ הִיא (it is from your hand [v. 16]). Lastly, clauses e-e´ describe Israel's act of offering (אֲשֶׁר הֲכִינֹנוּ לִבְנוֹת־לְךָ נָתַנּוּ לָךְ [we have given to you (v. 14)]);

---

137. Klein notices that כח עצר is often observed in Late Biblical Hebrew, which can be translated as "have enough strength." It is synonym of יכל in Chronicles and Daniel (R. Klein, *First Chronicles*, 538).

138. Based on the near context, כָּזֹאת (like this) presumably refers to the resources that David provides (vv. 2–5) and to the offerings of the leaders (vv. 6–8) and the people to God (v. 9).

Note that כֹּחַ וּגְבוּרָה (strength and power) belong to God (1 Chr 29:12).

139. The English translations of מִקְוֶה exhibit variety. The ESV and JPS translate this word as abiding, whereas the NAS, NIV, NKJ, NRS, and this book translate the word as hope. It seems that those who support the former interpret this word in light of the context (e.g., sojourners and strangers have no land) (Wallenstein, "Lexical Material," 214). This interpretation should support the notion that Israel is dependent on God, and without him, there is no hope. In Lev 25:23, God says, "For the land is mine; for you [Israel] are strangers and sojourners with me." For Israel, having no land, there is no hope, since those who do not have ownership should serve others as slaves or bondservants in order to live. In light of Lev 25:23, then, 1 Chr 29:15 indicates that without land, there is no hope but God (Tuell, *First and Second Chronicles*, 111). On the contrary, one could understand this word as hope, that the references to sojourners and strangers cover the entirety of Israel's history and that those terms reflect the nature of Israel's reality (i.e., without God, there is no hope).

140. Schwab, "צֵל," in *TDOT*, 12:372–83.

בַּיִת לְשֵׁם קָדְשֶׁךָ [that we have provided for building a house for you, for your glorious name (v. 16)]).

The transposition of d′ and e′ in the literary structure draws readers' attention and underscores the act of offering. Israel's offering originates from God's hands (d-d′) and should be returned to God (e-e′). The preceding act of offering (e) describes Israel's act in a broad or general sense, but the following act of offering (e′) clarifies their action in more detail, explaining the purpose and intention of their offering to God: to build the house of Yhwh for his name. This effect does not appear in other pairs in the structure. The text simply raises a question (a) and answers it (a′); or, each element of pairs symmetrically responds to the other without any further developed notion.[141] In sum, the literary structure of verses 14–16 motivates the members of the community to express their monotheistic belief in admission of God's ownership, ruling authority over all resources, and supreme qualities (vv. 10–12) and in offering what originally belongs to God (vv. 14–16).[142]

Believers' Inward Expression: True Heart

The last section of the prayer (vv. 17–19) reveals that in Israel's act of offering, the heart of a giver is a significant matter. God certainly discerns the heart of a giver (אַתָּה בֹּחֵן לֵבָב [you (Yhwh) test the heart (1 Chr 29:17)]; see Jer 11:20; 17:10; 20:12),[143] and David's heart demonstrates what the appropriate attitude of a giver should be. The particular characteristics or deeds that David exhibits in his act of offering are מֵישָׁרִים (integrity), יֹשֶׁר (uprightness), נדב (to offer willingly), and שִׂמְחָה (joy). Then, David's interest is specifically directed to the temple builder, Solomon (v. 19), and various characteristics culminate in the temple builder's characteristic, wholeheartedness (29:19; see 28:9; 29:9).[144] These elements of attitude

---

141. Each element essentially carries the following notions: (1) b: Israel has ability; b′: Israel is helpless; (2) c-c′: Israel has resources; and (3) d-d′: resources are from God.

142. Hooker, *First and Second Chronicles*, 114; Roth, "Characteristics of Joyful Giving."

143. The word בחן appears only here in Chronicles, and the similar expression concerning God's interest in heart occurs in 1 Chr 28:9 (כָּל־לְבָבוֹת דּוֹרֵשׁ [he (Yhwh) searches every heart]) (Knoppers, *First Chronicles 10–29*, 954).

144. Verse 19 begins with וְלִשְׁלֹמֹה (also, to Solomon), so David's words of prayer should be understood in light of vv. 17–19, where its major theme is the heart of giver. See also 2 Chr 1:18—2:17 (Eng. 2:1–16), which describes Solomon's preparation (i.e.,

should indwell and be maintained in every heart of the people of Israel as well as the readers of the prayer.

The prayer informs readers that the manifestation of such an inward attitude is possible only through divine assistance (שָׁמְרָה־זֹּאת לְעוֹלָם לְיֵצֶר מַחְשְׁבוֹת לְבַב עַמֶּךָ וְהָכֵן לְבָבָם אֵלֶיךָ [keep this forever in the intent of the thoughts of the heart of your people, and fix their heart toward you (29:18)]; וְלִשְׁלֹמֹה בְנִי תֵּן לֵבָב שָׁלֵם (also to Solomon, my son, give wholehearted heart).[145] The expression לְיֵצֶר מַחְשְׁבוֹת (the intent of the thoughts) is rare, since the combination of יֵצֶר and מַחֲשָׁבָה only occurs three times in the MT (i.e., Gen 6:5; 1 Chr 28:9; 29:18). The human heart, once judged as evil before God,[146] can be preserved in a right manner with divine assistance and can even be pleasing to God (וּמֵישָׁרִים תִּרְצֶה [you are pleased with integrity (v. 17)]). This overall observation implies, then, that when Israel makes an offering, they should recognize God's sovereignty and ask that God would touch their hearts, enabling them to serve and give offerings. If they do so, then they exemplify the characteristics of monotheistic believers. David's words to Solomon well illustrate this point. Only if God grants (תֵּן [v. 19]) Solomon wholeheartedness would the king then be able to keep (לִשְׁמוֹר [so that he keeps (v. 19)])[147] all the commandments, testimonies, and statues; therefore, he could accomplish the given task (מִצְוֹתֶיךָ עֵדְוֹתֶיךָ וְחֻקֶּיךָ וְלַעֲשׂוֹת הַכֹּל וְלִבְנוֹת הַבִּירָה אֲשֶׁר־הֲכִינוֹתִי [v. 19]).

Conclusion

David's final words of prayer portray the king as an exemplary figure of a monotheistic believer. In David's preparation of the temple construction (esp. the act of offering), the king recognizes his God as Israel's unique divine being, who holds the highest qualities in the universe and rules over them. God is the provider of all resources, which are sufficient to accomplish the divinely given task. The prayer also points out that even the

---

act of giving) for the temple construction.

145. R. Klein, "Last Words of David," 23.

146. Genesis 6:5 reads, וַיַּרְא יְהוָה כִּי רַבָּה רָעַת הָאָדָם בָּאָרֶץ וְכָל־יֵצֶר מַחְשְׁבֹת לִבּוֹ רַק רַע כָּל־הַיּוֹם (Yhwh saw that the wickedness of man was great on the land, and every intent of the thoughts of one's heart was only evil all the time). See also Gen 8:21 (Selman, *First Chronicles*, 271).

147. וְלִבְנוֹת: infinitive construct as purpose (Waltke and O'Connor, *Introduction to Biblical Hebrew*, §36.2.3d).

heart of a giver should be prepared by divine assistance. Overall, in shaping the characteristics of a monotheistic believer, the prayer motivates the audience to become monotheistic believers, who, as givers, admit that God is the origin of resources and the motivator of a giver's heart.

Second Chronicles 6:14–42: Solomon's Prayer

Introduction

Second Chronicles 6:14–42, widely renowned as Solomon's prayer, appears in the midst of the temple dedication (2 Chr 5–7). The account of Solomon (2 Chr 1–9) is dedicated to describing Solomon's building project, the temple,[148] and scholars have noticed that the temple dedication narrative is the climax of Solomon's story.[149] The significance of Solomon's prayer in the temple dedication narrative is to contribute to conveying the Chronicler's intended message.[150] Particularly, it can meaningfully function to shape the post-exilic community members' identity, since the text portrays the way the king perceives the role and nature of the first temple. As the members confront their own second temple, the prayer is able to persuade them to accept the same understanding of the role and nature of the temple.

In this regard, Solomon's prayer describes supplicants as those who repent of their sins. Also, the text portrays Solomon as a monotheistic believer who understands the temple as the place that displays God's pre-eminence and uniqueness. Lastly, through the completion of the temple construction, the text characterizes Solomon as appealing to his hope for the fulfillment of the Davidic promise. Thus, the prayer encourages the post-exilic audience to be active supplicants (i.e., penitents) of their special and supreme God in hope of the fulfillment of the Davidic promise (i.e., the revival of the Davidic kingdom).

---

148. McKenzie, *First-Second Chronicles*, 227.

149. See several literary analyses of narratives concerning the account of Solomon: Dillard, "Literary Structure," 90; Duke, *Persuasive Appeal*, 64–65; Johnstone, *Chronicles and Exodus*, 290–91.

150. Boda, *Return to Me*, 139; Mariottini, "Prayer in First–Second Chronicles," in Camp and Longman, *Praying with Ancient Israel*, 152.

Solomon's Appeal to God: Israel as Active Supplicants

Solomon's prayer describes the king as an active supplicant. The text characterizes the king as a model, and this portrayal could persuade the audience to imitate this king. The king's practice of prayer in outward conduct and speech vividly visualize the king as the petitioner. First, concerning the scene of Solomon's prayer to God, the text says וַיִּבְרַךְ עַל־בִּרְכָּיו נֶגֶד כָּל־קְהַל יִשְׂרָאֵל וַיִּפְרֹשׂ כַּפָּיו הַשָּׁמָיְמָה (he knelt on his knees before the assembly of Israel and spread out his hands toward heaven [2 Chr 6:13]). This visualization is unique in Chronicles: the expression ברך (to kneel down [v. 13]) or וַיִּפְרֹשׂ כַּפָּיו (to reach out his hands [v. 13; see v. 12]) occurs only here.[151]

Second, the major topic of Solomon's prayer is the act of prayer. The Chronicler's particular interest in the prayer is presented by Solomon's usage of the words פלל (to pray) and תְּפִלָּה (prayer). Many times, Solomon mentions the words prayer or to pray (vv. 20, 21, 24, 26, 29, 32, 34, 38).[152] The content of the prayer also assumes the situations in which an Israelite is praying (i.e., repenting) to God. The prayer describes several distressing situations among the Israelites (vv. 22–40) and assumes that people will resolve their difficulties (i.e., receive God's forgiveness) through prayer.

Third, the king certainly desires that when he and his people pray, God would listen and respond to their prayers. Solomon exhibits his desire that Yhwh regard the prayer of supplicants by specifying God's expected act of response to the prayer. Solomon requests for Yhwh to turn his attention to (פנה)[153] supplicants so that he may listen to (לִשְׁמֹעַ) their prayers (v. 19). The king repeats his request (שמע) two times in the following verses (vv. 20–21). At the end of Solomon's prayer, the king's appeal for God's response reappears. Similar to verse 19, verse 40 specifies the supplicants' desired response from God by portraying God's

---

151. Werline says, "In their [the people's] petitions and in their posture, the people imitate Solomon, for they can also 'stretch out their hands" toward the place where YHWH's name dwells . . . . In speech and in body the king and the people become united" (Werline, "Prayer, Politics, and Power," 13).

152. The word פלל (to pray) occurs fourteen times in the book of Chronicles. Interestingly, seven of these occurrences are found in Solomon's prayer. See 1 Chr 17:25; 2 Chr 6:19, 20, 21, 24, 32, 34, 38; 7:1, 14; 30:18; 32:20, 24; 33:13. Similarly, תְּפִלָּה (prayer) occurs eleven times, and all these instances appear at the beginning of Solomon's prayer. See 2 Chr 6:19 (x2), 20, 29, 35, 40; 7:12, 15; 30:27; 33:18, 19.

153. Köhler et al., "פנה," in *HALOT*, 937–38.

act: וְאָזְנֶיךָ קַשֻּׁבוֹת לִתְפִלַּת הַמָּקוֹם הַזֶּה (your ears attentive to the prayer of this place). Solomon's request of God's answering (שמע) the supplicants' prayer appears relatedly throughout different situations in which Solomon assumes that people pray (vv. 23, 25, 27, 30, 33, 35, 39). Thus, Solomon hopes that the prayer would not be an echo in the air but would receive God's answer.

God's response to Solomon's prayer (2 Chr 7:13–16) can function significantly in shaping the Israelites as active supplicants in two ways relating to the effectiveness of prayer.[154] First, God communicates with Solomon. In other words, God's act of response confirms that he hears Solomon's prayer. God speaks to Solomon, saying, שָׁמַעְתִּי אֶת־תְּפִלָּתֶךָ (I have heard your prayer [v. 12]) and וְאָזְנַי קַשֻּׁבוֹת לִתְפִלַּת הַמָּקוֹם הַזֶּה (now my ears will be attentive to prayer offered in this place [v. 15]), which repeats almost verbatim what Solomon says (6:40). Second, God interacts with what Solomon asks for (i.e., the content of prayer). In Solomon's prayer regarding the distressing situations, the king's concern fully lies with the people (עַם) of Israel (vv. 21, 24–27, 29, 34, 39), except the one situation regarding foreigners (נָכְרִי [v. 32]). Second Chronicles 7:13–15 specifically focuses on the people (עַמִּי [my people]) and provides God's specific answer to what Solomon asks for in his prayer. Therefore, the audience of the prayer witnesses the scene that God not only responds to the king's prayer but also confirms what Solomon prays for: God answers people's prayers.[155] In sum, the characterization of the king's behavior and speech in light of Chronicles' *Sondergut* motivate the audience to become active supplicants.

Supplicants Who Ask God's Forgiveness[156]

Solomon's prayer conveys a particular aspect of supplicants: repentance. First, the text notes that the purpose of Solomon's prayer is to request

---

154. The Chronicler uniquely adds God's response to Solomon's prayer in 2 Chr 7:13–16 (*Sondergut*) to Chronicles' *Vorlage*. Second Chronicles 7:1–22 shows similarity to 1 Kgs 8:62—9:9, yet 2 Chr 7:1–11 is expanded, and 2 Chr 7:13–16 is a new unit inserted by the Chronicler (Endres et al., *Chronicles and Its Synoptic Parallels*, 183; Japhet, *Ideology of the Book*, 65).

155. The text does not specify a preposition: לִתְפִלַּת הַמָּקוֹם הַזֶּה (2 Chr 7:15). Most English translations (ESV, JPS, NAS, NIV, NKJ) accept "in this place," but TNK takes "from this place."

156. This section is adapted from K. Kim, "Chronicler's View of Forgiveness."

God's forgiveness when an Israelite repents. Solomon's prayer can be divided as follows: introduction (vv. 14–21) with two subsections (vv. 14–17, 18–21), petitions for seven different situations (vv. 22–39), and conclusion (vv. 40–42).[157] In the very last phrase of the introduction (vv. 14–21), the text articulates forgiveness as the purpose of Solomon's prayer: תִּשְׁמַע מִמְּקוֹם שִׁבְתְּךָ מִן־הַשָּׁמַיִם וְשָׁמַעְתָּ וְסָלָחְתָּ (you hear from your dwelling place, heaven, when you hear, you forgive [v. 21]). Solomon concludes his prayer with a decisive tone, saying, וְסָלַחְתָּ (you forgive).[158]

Second, Solomon's prayer presents several distressing situations in which an Israelite may ask for God's forgiveness. Those situations can result from sin; out of the seven situations mentioned, five originate, either explicitly or implicitly, from human actions (i.e., sin).[159] Verses 24–25 specifically mention when people sin before God (וְאִם־יִנָּגֵף עַמְּךָ יִשְׂרָאֵל לִפְנֵי אוֹיֵב כִּי יֶחֶטְאוּ־לָךְ [if your people Israel defeat before the enemy for they sin against you (v. 24)], and the next situation (vv. 26–27) also concerns sinning against God (כִּי יֶחֶטְאוּ־לָךְ [for they sin against you (v. 26)]; וְסָלַחְתָּ לְחַטַּאת עֲבָדֶיךָ וְעַמְּךָ [forgive sins of your servants and your people (v. 27)]). The situation in verses 28–31 does not use the word sin; but the unique words דֶּבֶר, שִׁדָּפוֹן, וְיֵרָקוֹן and אַרְבֶּה (plague, blight, and mildew [v. 28]) recall Deuteronomy 28:20–36, where the people are judged because of their disobedience to God.[160] Hence, disasters and diseases in verse 28 imply that people would receive these judgments because of

---

157. The literary delineation basically agrees with Selman's observation with slight modification: "(i) request for continuing fulfillment of the Davidic covenant (vv. 14–17); (ii) basic principles of intercession (vv. 18–21); (iii) situations in which prayer might be offered (vv. 22–40); (iv) request for God's continuing presence and power (vv. 41–42)" (Selman, *Second Chronicles*, 326).

Although E. Talstra's observation on the syntactical structure of the seven petitions focuses on Solomon's prayer in Kings, his study can still be applied to Chronicles (Talstra, *Solomon's Prayer*, 102):

Case: conj. + imperf. or prep. + inf.
Continuation: a few times perf. + ו (often התפלל)
Petition: second pers. (ו + pron. + imperf. or perf. + ו) שמע
Continuation: perf. + ו.

158. Boda, *First-Second Chronicles*, 261.

159. Boda, *First-Second Chronicles*, 272. Forgiveness refers to God's restoration. Solomon understands forgiveness as restoration, such as "bringing people back to the land" (6:25), "raining on the land" (6:27), "walking in your ways" (6:31), and "healing of the land" (7:14). Repentance refers to the rejection of sins and seeking God. The act of repentance can be expressed in several ways in 7:14: to humble oneself, to seek God's face, or to turn from one's evil way.

160. Particularly for דֶּבֶר, see Deut 28:21. See also Deut 28:22 for שִׁדָּפוֹן and יֵרָקוֹן.

their sin.[161] The following situation (vv. 32–33) does not describe any distressing occasion or sinful action, but here, Solomon prays for non-Israelites. Solomon's prayer in verse 32 extends the efficacy of prayer to foreigners (אֶל־הַנָּכְרִי [v. 32]).[162] Solomon asks God that for whatever foreigners might pray, he would hear them and act according to their prayers (וְעָשִׂיתָ כְּכֹל אֲשֶׁר־יִקְרָא אֵלֶיךָ הַנָּכְרִי) so that non-Israelites can also repent (i.e., pray) for their forgiveness.[163] The tone of verse 36 is striking since Solomon conclusively and confidently states, כִּי אֵין אָדָם אֲשֶׁר לֹא־יֶחֱטָא (there is no one who does not sin), in verses 36–39. This statement would have been striking to the Chronicler's audience, because this situation not only demonstrates one of the possible sinful occasions, but is true to the experience of the Jews during the exile.[164] Therefore, although two situations show exceptions (6:22–23; 34–35),[165] the remaining five situations assume the situations in which people pray and repent so that they may ask for God's forgiveness.

Third, concerning the aspect of the supplicants (i.e., petitioners), Solomon's prayer highlights several critical actions of repentance. In the prayer, the Chronicler hints at what these actions are. The Chronicler writes וְשָׁבוּ (turn again [vv. 24, 37]), מֵחַטָּאתָם יְשׁוּבוּן (turn from their sin [v. 26]), and וְשָׁבוּ אֵלֶיךָ בְּכָל־לִבָּם וּבְכָל־נַפְשָׁם (turn to you with all their mind and heart [v. 38]).[166] In sum, the purpose of Solomon's prayer, the

---

161. For the discussion on sin (disobedience) and calamity, see Botica, "'When Heaven Is Shut Up,'" 115.

162. See Isa 56:7, which says, כִּי בֵיתִי בֵּית־תְּפִלָּה יִקָּרֵא לְכָל־הָעַמִּים (for my house shall be called a house of prayer for *all people* [italics added]).

163. Myers says, "It is significant that no condition is laid upon the foreigner; he is neither required to confess his faith nor to confess his sins, though both may be implied by an attraction to Yahweh" (Myers, *Second Chronicles*, 33).

164. Japhet writes, "repentance is described again and again in every possible way" (Japhet, *First and Second Chronicles*, 599).

165. These two cases concern God's judgment (וְשָׁפַטְתָּ [you judge (v. 23)]) on an oath made by a man at the altar and Israel's engaging in war.

166. One may argue that the Chronicler simply adopts the notion of the acts of repentance in Solomon's prayer from his *Vorlage* in 1 Kgs 8, but the Chronicler's addition of 7:14 describes the act of repentance and corroborates that in order to receive forgiveness, people need both prayer and repentance. The analyzed structure of v. 14 shows how the Chronicler views the four words: פלל (to pray), תְּפִלָּה (prayer), כנע (to humble), בקש (to seek), and שוב (to turn away).

וְאִם־אֲשַׁלַּח דֶּבֶר בְּעַמִּי
וְיִכָּנְעוּ עַמִּי
אֲשֶׁר נִקְרָא־שְׁמִי עֲלֵיהֶם

situations that the prayer assumes, and the required acts of supplicants together emphasize that Israelites need to be active petitioners who ask God's forgiveness in the midst of their sinful acts.

God's Preeminence and Uniqueness

Solomon's words of prayer confirm that Yhwh is Israel's special God and praise God's supremacy over the world. This king's acknowledgement ought to be the same confession for the post-exilic community so that they become monotheistic believers like Solomon. Concerning Yhwh as Israel's special deity, there are several textual markers that exhibit Solomon's perception of the relationship between God and Israel. First, at the very beginning of his prayer, Solomon lays the foundation of his prayer by calling upon Yhwh: יְהוָה אֱלֹהֵי יִשְׂרָאֵל (Yhwh, God of Israel [v. 14]). Solomon is not praying to any other god but Yhwh, who keeps covenant and shows his *ḥesed* to his servants (לַעֲבָדֶיךָ [v. 14; plural]). Solomon grounds his appeal upon God's covenant keeping faithfulness and mercy toward his own people.[167] Second, Solomon keeps referring to Israel as God's own people. The text says either עַמְּךָ יִשְׂרָאֵל (your people Israel [vv. 24, 25, 27, 29, 32, 33]) or simply עַמְּךָ (your people [vv. 34, 39]). Third, one should not miss that the text distinguishes between Israel and foreigners.

וְיִתְפַּלְלוּ
וִיבַקְשׁוּ פָנַי
וְיָשֻׁבוּ מִדַּרְכֵיהֶם הָרָעִים
וַאֲנִי אֶשְׁמַע מִן־הַשָּׁמַיִם
וְאֶסְלַח לְחַטָּאתָם
וְאֶרְפָּא אֶת־אַרְצָם

The structure shows (7:13b–14) God's action mainly in first person singular verbs and the human response in third person plural verbs. Human actions (to pray, to humble themselves, to seek before God, and to turn away from their evil way) come as a response to God's judgment and lead to God's forgiveness (וְאֶסְלַח לְחַטָּאתָם) and restoration (וְאֶרְפָּא אֶת־אַרְצָם). The literary structure shows that to humble, to pray, to seek God, and to turn away stand parallel to one another. Thus, the Chronicler suggests that if people pray (i.e., repent), God will forgive them (2 Chr 6; 7:14–16). For turn away, see 2 Chr 30:6, 9; 36:13. See Fabry, "שׁוּב," in *TDOT*, 12:461–522.

Also notable is the rapidly increasing frequency of the words פלל (to pray), תְּפִלָּה (prayer), and כנע (to humble) from chs. 6–7 in relation to the context of repentance. For פלל (to pray) and תְּפִלָּה (prayer), see 76n152. The word כנע (to humble) appears one time in 1 Chr, but it does not mean "humble" but "subdue." See also 2 Chr 7:14; 12:6, 7, 12; 13:18; 28:19; 30:11; 32:26; 33:12, 19, 23(x2); 34:27(x2); 36:12.

167. See Deut 7:9, 12.

It does not simply list God's people or foreigners but clarifies that foreigners do not belong to God (וְגַם אֶל־הַנָּכְרִי אֲשֶׁר לֹא מֵעַמְּךָ יִשְׂרָאֵל הוּא [v. 32]).

Concerning God's supremacy, Solomon's words straightforwardly proclaim the idea that אֵין־כָּמוֹךָ אֱלֹהִים בַּשָּׁמַיִם וּבָאָרֶץ (there is none like you [God] in heaven or on earth [6:14]; see Deut 3:24; 4:39). Solomon's words here allude to his father's prayer: אֵין כָּמוֹךָ וְאֵין אֱלֹהִים זוּלָתֶךָ (there is none like you and there is no other God except you [1 Chr 17:20]). The audience witnesses that at the moment of receiving the task of temple building, the father (i.e., David) proclaims God's supremacy, while the son reaffirms the same idea at the moment of the completion of temple building. Solomon further adds הִנֵּה שָׁמַיִם וּשְׁמֵי הַשָּׁמַיִם לֹא יְכַלְכְּלוּךָ (behold, the heaven, even the highest heaven cannot contain you [2 Chr 6:18]). In most contexts in which כול occurs in the MT, the word usually conveys the notion of God's incomparability vis-à-vis creatures (1 Kgs 8:27; 2 Chr 2:5; 6:18; see Isa 40:12; Joel 2:11; Mal 3:2).[168] In sum, the post-exilic community witnesses the two model figures (i.e., David [1 Chr 17] and Solomon [2 Chr 6]) affirm God's supremacy over the world, which could stimulate the post-exilic community's monotheistic belief.

God of Israel's Preeminence and the Nature of the Temple[169]

Solomon's prayer portrays an aspect of the monotheistic believer in relation to the nature of the temple. Solomon's prayer recognizes that the temple represents God's uniqueness and preeminence over the world; thus, the post-exilic audience as monotheistic believers could find God's preeminence and uniqueness through their recognition of the nature of the temple. This acknowledgement, however, is not an easy process, since the nature of the temple is complex. On the one hand, Solomon affirms God's incomparability vis-à-vis the temple (אַף כִּי־הַבַּיִת הַזֶּה אֲשֶׁר בָּנִיתִי [how much less this house that I built (2 Chr 6:18; see 2:4–5 [Eng. vv. 5–6])]). Yet, on the other hand, Chronicles raises the quality of the temple to the paramount level by indicating that the temple bears God's name (6:33; 20:8) and receives God's attention (לִהְיוֹת עֵינֶיךָ פְתֻחוֹת אֶל־הַבַּיִת הַזֶּה יוֹמָם וָלַיְלָה [that your eyes oversee this house *day and night* (6:20 [italics added]). Lynch attempts to break the tension by explaining the nature of the temple portrayed in Chronicles: "The Chronicler must turn

---

168. Baumann, "כול," in *TDOT*, 7:85–89.
169. This section is adapted from K. Kim, "Chronicler's View of Forgiveness."

to the past in order to construct an argument concerning the location and nature of divine supremacy in the present, and to cast his vision for a society unified around the Temple—the visible connection between past, present, and future."[170] The Chronicler utilizes the institutions (i.e., the temple, the priesthood, and the Davidic king) to make them participate and express God's divinity, in order to urge people to recognize and align themselves with God's preeminence.[171] Thus, the temple reflects God's preeminence and uniqueness.[172]

Second Chronicles 6:32–33 provides an example of how people possibly perceive God's uniqueness through their prayer in relation to the temple. The prayer assumes the situation that foreigners pray toward the temple (וְהִתְפַּלְלוּ אֶל־הַבַּיִת הַזֶּה [v. 32]). Solomon prays that God would respond to foreigners, in order for them to know (וְלָדַעַת)[173] God, for the temple bears God's name (כִּי־שִׁמְךָ נִקְרָא עַל־הַבַּיִת הַזֶּה אֲשֶׁר בָּנִיתִי [v. 33]), and like the people of Israel (כְּעַמְּךָ יִשְׂרָאֵל), for them to fear God (וּלְיִרְאָה אֹתְךָ [v. 33]). In other words, a part of the function of the temple is to manifest God's uniqueness. Likewise, when the audience prays toward the temple and receives God's answer, they would realize God's uniqueness and preeminence, a process which may shape them to be active monotheistic believers.

Solomon's Hope of Davidic Dynasty

Solomon's prayer hopes for the fulfillment of God's promise to David (2 Chr 6:12–42; esp. vv. 14–17, 40–42; see 4–11), and as the audience joins in the prayer, this king's desire for the Davidic dynasty is able to encourage the post-exilic community to be Davidic citizens. First, verses 14–17 particularly appeal to God's fulfillment of the Davidic promise. Solomon

---

170. Lynch, *Monotheism and Institutions*, 18.

171. Institutions are not identical to God since they only participate in his divinity; but they are "categorically apart from any other cult" because of God's preeminence compared to other gods (Lynch, *Monotheism and Institutions*, 73).

172. Lynch uses some different words when he describes the particularity of the temple in relation to God. For instance, the temple reflects, participates in, shares in, manifests, creates impressions of, is iconic of, is a signpost of, is a vehicle of/for, or evidences God's deity. The temple's sharing in divine uniqueness does not threaten God's own uniqueness. Lynch explains that the Chronicler was struggling to preserve God's uniqueness; he suggests that the Chronicler develops the iconic function of the temple. For further discussion, see Lynch, *Monotheism and Institutions*, 72–136.

173. לְ as purpose.

claims that God would keep the promise that he made with David (וְעַתָּה יְהוָה אֱלֹהֵי יִשְׂרָאֵל שְׁמֹר לְעַבְדְּךָ דָוִיד אָבִי אֵת אֲשֶׁר דִּבַּרְתָּ לּוֹ [now, Yhwh, God of Israel, keep what you said to your servant, my father David (6:16)]). Solomon specifically requests security or eternality of the Davidic dynasty. Solomon realizes that God's promise has been fulfilled (6:10, 15),[174] but it is a partial realization, from Solomon's standpoint.[175] The absolute effectiveness or fulfillment of God's promise, which includes the everlasting establishment of the dynasty, depends upon Solomon's obeying God's law and finishing the temple (1 Chr 17:4–14, 23–24; 22:9–12; 28:6–10).[176]

174. וָאָקוּם תַּחַת דָּוִיד אָבִי וָאֵשֵׁב עַל־כִּסֵּא יִשְׂרָאֵל כַּאֲשֶׁר דִּבֶּר יְהוָה (for I have risen in the place of my father David and sit on the throne of Israel, as Yhwh promised [2 Chr 6:10]).

175. Hill, *First and Second Chronicles*, 392.

176. This statement does not mean that the Davidic promise is a conditional covenant in its nature. This book sees that when God gave his promise to David, the unconditional nature of the covenant had already been revealed. The way this book understands it is that although Solomon's construction of the temple is critical element for the eternity of the kingdom, when God foretold his plan, God had already known that Solomon would build the temple (1 Chr 22:9–10).

Scholars have given different opinions on the nature of the Davidic covenant. For instance, 1 Chr 17:13 shows a striking difference from Chronicles' *Vorlage* (2 Sam 7:14). It omits אֲשֶׁר בְּהַעֲוֹתוֹ וְהֹכַחְתִּיו בְּשֵׁבֶט אֲנָשִׁים וּבְנִגְעֵי בְּנֵי אָדָם (when he commits iniquity, I will correct him with the rod of men and the strokes of the sons of men). This omission shows the enhanced presentation of eternality of the Davidic covenant (Knoppers, *First Chronicles 10–29*, 671; Selman, *First Chronicles*, 187–88). Jonker, rather, focuses on the Chronicler's characterization of Solomon. He believes that it is omitted to emphasize Solomon's blamelessness (Jonker, *First and Second Chronicles*, 125–26). A difficulty still arises, because there are occurrences where the Chronicler repeats a seemingly conditional nature of the covenant, such as 1 Chr 28:8–9 and 2 Chr 7:19–22. In this regard, Lynch well summarizes Williamson's view: "While the Davidic covenant was conditional, its conditionality was predicated on Solomon's completion of the Temple and his complete obedience to the law (1 Chr 29.19). On fulfillment of these conditions, Yhwh establishes Solomon's house 'in perpetuity' (1 Chr 17:11b–12; 22.9–10; 28.5–10; 2 Chr 7.17–18)" (Lynch, "Davidic Covenant," in MacDonald, *Covenant and Election*, 180–81). See also Williamson, "Eschatology in Chronicles." Similarly, Kelly says, "The two 'houses' are, in fact, mutually related: Solomon's obedience in building the temple is understood as the means through which the covenant is accepted and confirmed, and henceforth the dynastic promise is presented as established and unconditional" (Kelly, *Retribution and Eschatology*, 156). These ideas comply with this book's previous presentation on the nature of the covenant: there are two aspects under one covenant. Therefore, Solomon's mission is critical to activate the effectiveness of kingdom security, and the audience confirms that Solomon certainly completed his mission in the Chronicler's historiography. So, there is reason to believe that God's unconditional promise is still in effect in the days of the post-exilic community. For the Chronicler's portrayal of Solomon as a perfect temple

Now, Solomon insists that his mission is completed; thus, he is able to request that God would fulfill the promise. In order to increase the certainty of the promise, Solomon reminds God of the divine promise (לֹא־ יִכָּרֵת לְךָ אִישׁ מִלְּפָנַי יוֹשֵׁב עַל־כִּסֵּא יִשְׂרָאֵל [you shall not lack a man to sit on the throne of Israel (2 Chr 6:16)]) and requests again God's confirmation of his promise (יֵאָמֵן דְּבָרְךָ אֲשֶׁר דִּבַּרְתָּ לְעַבְדְּךָ לְדָוִיד [let your word be confirmed, which you have spoken to your servant David (v. 17)]).[177]

Second, although Solomon's enumeration of seven distressing situations in the main body of the prayer (6:22–39) alludes to covenant curses (Deut 28:15–60; see Lev 26:14–15),[178] the prayer's focus on the theme of prayer and God's forgiveness creates a whole different theological agenda: when people repent, God forgives and delivers his people.[179] This simple principle, in fact, is astonishing when considering the final situation (2 Chr 6:36–39) in relation to the hope of the Davidic dynasty. Various situations culminate in the situation of Israel's exile. It is the worst-case scenario that the nation may confront.[180] Solomon declares כִּי יֶחֶטְאוּ־לָךְ כִּי אֵין אָדָם אֲשֶׁר לֹא־יֶחֱטָא (for when they sin against you, since there is no man who does not sin [v. 36]; see Eccl 7:20). What this declaration implies then is that Solomon assumes that the exile (i.e., the loss of the land) is inevitable.[181] How-

---

builder, see Braun, "Solomon."

177. Williamson, *First and Second Chronicles*, 219.
Verse 17 begins with וְעַתָּה, which this book translates as "therefore." In other words, the argument Solomon develops in vv. 14–17 is as follows: first, Solomon appeals to the characteristic of God, who keeps his covenant (v. 14); second, the king requests that God would keep the promises by reminding God of the promise he made to David; third, since God requires Solomon's obedience to the law, וְעַתָּה (v. 17) constructs a cause-effect relationship between vv. 16 and 17. Therefore, the logical flow established between the two verses indicates that Solomon insists upon his completion of the task and obedience of the law, and consequently, he requests that God keeps his covenant.
Sailhamer raises the following question: "Solomon has already said that God's word to David has been fulfilled (6:10). Why should he now ask that His word be established? That comment by Solomon reveals that even he saw that the Lord's working in his own kingdom was not the end of the promise to David. Even Solomon acknowledged that more was to be expected from God's promise to David" (Sailhamer, *First and Second Chronicles*, 77).

178. For a detailed connection between the seven situations and the covenant curses in Torah, see Selman, *Second Chronicles*, 328–30. See also B. Long, *First Kings*, 103.

179. Boda writes, "Throughout the prayer in 2 Chronicles 6 divine disciplines are designed to prompt a penitential response" (Boda, *Return to Me*, 139).

180. Sailhamer, *First and Second Chronicles*, 76; Selman, *Second Chronicles*, 330.

181. Klein observes, "since sin is inevitable, exile seems almost inevitable as well" (R. Klein, *Second Chronicles*, 97). See also Ben Zvi, *History, Literature and Theology*, 201.

ever, the king does not give up hope; instead, he prays for God's deliverance of his people. This model king's prayer for the hope of God's intervention in a desperate situation (וְעָשִׂיתָ מִשְׁפָּטָם וְסָלַחְתָּ לְעַמְּךָ [6:39]) can bring about the same hope for the post-exilic community: God does not abandon his people, so the effectiveness of God's promise (i.e., eternality or security of the dynasty) is not nullified through the exile.

Third, the conclusion of the prayer (6:40–42) deviates from its *Vorlage* (i.e., 1 Kgs 8:50–53) but echoes Psalm 132:8–10, and these particular verses can contribute to motivate the audience to hope to become Davidic citizens.[182] Although it is difficult to identify the exact date of the psalm,[183] it is most likely the Chronicler who congruently adopts the portion (vv. 8–10) and replaces the ending of the prayer from Chronicles' *Vorlage*.[184] Thus, it is necessary to investigate the intention of the Chronicler in relation to the message of Psalm 132.

The significance of Psalm 132 from the standpoint of the role of Davidic citizenship is that it focuses on the motif of Zion as God's dwelling place and gives attention to David as God's anointed one who receives God's promise.[185] Although the most straightforward divine confirmation

---

182. Concerning the theme of the Davidic promise, a few scholars have argued that these particular verses convey the Chronicler's hope of the actualization of Davidic promise. In his analysis of Ps 132, Barbiero insists that the theological thrust of the psalm is close to Chronicles, and he sees that the author of psalm hopes for the restoration of the Davidic throne (Barbiero, "Psalm 132," 258). See also Berlin, "Psalm 132," in Yonah et al., *Marbeh Ḥokmah*, 65–72; O'Kennedy, "Twee Weergawes."

183. The date of Ps 132 is obscure. Mays and Berlin see it is written in the post-exilic period (Mays, *Psalms Interpretation*, 411–12; Berlin, "Psalm 132," in Yonah et al., *Marbeh Ḥokmah*, 66). However, Davidson regards its date as the pre-exilic (Davidson, *Validity of Worship*, 428). Dahood considers it dates around the tenth-century BCE (Dahood, *Psalms Two: 51–100*, 241). Zenger does not specify the particular period but extends its period from the time of Solomon into the Maccabean period (Hossfeld and Zenger, *Psalms Three*, 458). Widmer suggests the possibility that the psalm's origin is in the pre-exilic period but that its final form is completed in the post-exilic period (Widmer, *Message of Psalms*, 471). Goldingay points out the unanimous nature of the subject: "An interchange over the date of Ps. 132 at the end of the twentieth century showed that the world of scholarship has made no progress over the question whether the psalm belongs to the early monarchy or postexilic period" (Goldingay, *Psalms*, 544).

184. Barbiero says, "It is also clear that the passage in Chronicles depends on that in Psalm 132 because, according to the Chronicler's narrative, the ark had already been placed in the Temple (see 2 Chr 5:2–10). Psalm 132 is, therefore, anterior to the Chronicler's history even if it shares the same spirit, as demonstrated by the frequent parallels" (Barbiero, "Psalm 132," 246).

185. Mays, *Psalms*, 409; Kraus, *Psalms 60–150*, 476; Tournay, *Seeing and Hearing God*, 208; Waltner, *Psalms*, 632; DeClaissé-Walford et al., *Book of Psalms*, 933; Cezula,

of the Davidic promise is given in verse 11, the Chronicler's interest lies in verses 8–10.[186] The historical situation of verses 6–10 in Psalm 132 is suitable for the Chronicler's purpose concerning the historical situation of 2 Chronicles 5 and 6 (esp. the conclusion of Solomon's prayer). The setting of the psalm is related to 2 Samuel 6 (cf. 1 Chr 13, 15), which describes David's search and transference of the ark to Jerusalem.[187] Thus, the psalm's setting may be pertinent to the historical context of 2 Chronicles 5 and 6, where the ark takes its final journey and settles in the temple, where Solomon prays to God to dwell with it (אַתָּה וַאֲרוֹן עֻזֶּךָ [you and the ark of your strength (6:41)]).

Also, in Psalm 132:1–10, the ground of the psalmist's persuasion is linked to God's remembrance of David's deed (v. 1). God regards David's past events (vv. 2–10), and in response to David's vow and deeds, God reveals his future plan for David (לֹא־יָשׁוּב מִמֶּנָּה [he *will* not turn back (v. 11; italics added)]) and Zion (זֹאת־מְנוּחָתִי עֲדֵי־עַד [this is my resting place forever (v. 14)]).[188] In other words, in the psalm, the transition takes place from recording past events (vv. 1–10) to describing the hope of the future (vv. 11–18). Barbiero understands this transition as follows: "the evocation of the past . . . is thus transformed into a prayer for the future."[189]

"Chronicler as Biblical Paradigm," 277.

An overview of the psalm is as follows. The psalm begins with a petition to God to remember David's hardship that he experienced in his life (132:1). David vowed to God that he would search for the ark (vv. 2–5) and was able to find it (vv. 6–7). Verses 8–10 invite Yhwh to come to his resting place (v. 8) and offer a prayer for God's active deeds for his priests, saints, and anointed ones (vv. 9–10). Verses 11–18 begin with Yhwh's oath to David (נִשְׁבַּע־יְהוָה לְדָוִד [Yhwh swore to David), promising his eternal dynasty (vv. 11–12) and continuing to God's election of Zion (v. 13) as the eternal place (v. 14). The section ends with God's promise of salvation for his people (vv. 15–17).

186. The placement of vv. 8–10 in the psalm is not easy to understand, since scholars disagree over the major divisions of the psalm. In other words, scholars have disagreed on the end of the first section, between vv. 9 and 10. There is no consensus regarding the division of the psalm. Fretheim views the psalm as divided into two sections (vv. 1–9 and 10–18), whereas Zenger and DeClaissé believe the psalm consists of vv. 1–10 and 11–18. This book argues that the latter division of the section makes more sense. See Fretheim, "Psalm 132," 289; Hossfeld and Zenger, *Psalms Three*, 458; DeClaissé-Walford et al., *Book of Psalms*, 934–35.

187. Hossfeld and Zenger, *Psalms Three*, 457, 459, 461; Ross, *Commentary*, 270–71; Fretheim, "Psalm 132," 294–96.

188. For several literary structures that exhibit how David's oath and Yhwh's oath work symmetrically in the psalm, see Hossfeld and Zenger, *Psalms Three*, 460; DeClaissé-Walford et al., *Book of Psalms*, 933; Ross, *Commentary*, 731–32.

189. Barbiero, "Psalm 132," 258.

Then, the Chronicler's rhetorical strategy of adopting the portion (vv. 8–10) from the first half section of the psalm (i.e., past events) is that, like the psalmist, Solomon depends upon David's deeds in the past and expects God's affirmation of the Davidic promise given in Psalm 132.[190] This connection might be the reason why Solomon reiterates verses 8–10 almost verbatim. Solomon finds the legitimacy of his hope of Davidic promise in David's deeds.[191]

However, Chronicles produces an escalated rhetorical impetus as the book adopts Psalm 132:8–10 in the context of the temple dedication. When considering the placement of the ark, the journey of the ark has not finished until it finds its ultimate place. In this regard, Solomon accomplishes his task of the transference of the ark (2 Chr 22:19; 28:11–19, esp. v. 18) into its final place (2 Chr 5:1–10), a process initiated by David in order to find a place of everlasting rest for the ark (Ps 132:2–5, 14). The summoning of the people, the reverence for the dignity of the ark (v. 7), and the significance of the God's resting place (v. 8) all culminate in the temple dedication. All-Israel gathers (כָּל־קְהַל יִשְׂרָאֵל [all assembly of Israel (2 Chr 6:3)]) in Jerusalem and offers unsurpassed worship and sacrifice (5:11–14; 7:1–10).[192] Also, the word מְנוּחָה (resting place [Ps 132:8]) is accentuated in Chronicles (נוֹחַ [2 Chr 6:41]) because the word coheres with a characteristic of Solomon, conveying the notion that Solomon as a man of peace/rest built the resting place of Yhwh.[193] Therefore,

---

190. Concerning לְחַסְדֵי דָוִיד עַבְדֶּךָ in 2 Chr 6:42, scholars have disagreed on how to understand the nature of the genitive. Williamson believes it is an objective genitive (i.e., *ḥesed* done to David), but Japhet and Dillard insist that it is a subjective genitive (i.e., the *ḥesed* of David). Klein does not choose between the two positions; instead, he insists that in either case, God is obligated to keep his promise to David (R. Klein, *Second Chronicles*, 99–100) See also Williamson, *First and Second Chronicles*, 220–21. This book is inclined toward Japhet and Dillard's view, since the word *ḥesed* is given in a plural form; thus, it most likely refers to David's deeds (i.e., subjective genitive) in connection with the theme of Ps 132. For a detailed discussion, see Japhet, *First and Second Chronicles*, 604–5; Dillard, *Second Chronicles*, 51–52.

191. What Solomon desires is clear: God would listen to the prayer offered in the temple (וְאָזְנֶיךָ קַשֻּׁבוֹת לִתְפִלַּת הַמָּקוֹם הַזֶּה [your ears be attentive to the prayer offered in this place (v. 40)]), which certainly includes the king's petition for the Davidic dynasty (vv. 14–16). Also note that the past events in Ps 132:1–10 begin with David (v. 1) and end with David (v. 10). Solomon's prayer begins with reference to the Davidic promise (2 Chr 6:14–16) and concludes with the name of David (v. 42).

192. See Wenham's explanation on numbers in 2 Chr 7:5, where the Chronicler emphasizes the greatness of sacrifice in the temple dedication (Wenham, "Large Numbers," 49).

193. The characterization of David and Solomon in Chronicles has received

in Chronicles' context, Solomon not only relies upon David's past deeds and God's response to that event but also appeals to God for his current accomplishment of the divine task. The ark is finally in the temple, its intended perpetual resting place. Therefore, the conclusion of the prayer strongly hopes for God's affirmation of the Davidic promise.

Conclusion

Solomon's prayer in 2 Chronicles 6:14–42 portrays the king as a supplicant who holds a monotheistic belief and hopes for the fulfillment of the Davidic promise. Not only does the text describe Solomon as a model supplicant for the audience, but also the content of the king's prayer hopes for Israel to become active supplicants. Regarding the aspect of a supplicant, the prayer demonstrates supplicants who repent of their sins in order to receive God's forgiveness. Also, Israelites should become monotheistic believers as they realize the nature of the temple, since it symbolizes Yhwh as the unique and preeminent deity. Lastly, Solomon's prayer hopes for the fulfillment of the Davidic promise. Solomon desires that in his completion of the task of the temple construction, God ought to keep the promise he gave to David. Overall, the prayer contributes to shaping the identity of the post-exilic community: active supplicants who hold monotheistic belief and await the Davidic dynasty.

Second Chronicles 14:10: Asa's Prayer

Introduction

The prayer of Asa in 2 Chronicles 14:10 (Eng. v. 11) appears in the midst of King Asa's battle against the Cushite army. The account of Asa's battle follows the king's successful religious reformation (vv. 1–6 [Eng. vv. 2–7]) and his achievement of military strength (v. 7 [Eng. v. 8]). Interestingly, right after this positive portrayal of Asa's reign (vv. 1–7 [Eng. vv. 2–8]), especially the king's military growth, the Chronicler reports that Asa encounters Zerah's outnumbering legion. The battle story continues, conveying that

---

scholarly interest. In Chronicles, David is portrayed as a man of war, but Solomon is portrayed as a man of peace (1 Chr 22:9) (Jonker, "Chronicler's Portrayal of Solomon," 655–62).

Asa prays to God for his intervention and concluding that the king's prayer brings about God's deliverance of Judah from an imminent threat.

In Chronicles' *Vorlage* (1 Kgs 15:9–24), most stories of Asa appear in a compressed manner, and even Asa's prayer is absent; thus, it is reasonable to assume that the Chronicler intends to convey a certain message to the post-exilic community through his detailed report of Asa's reign.[194] Dillard suggests a reason for such an amplified report in relation to the Chronicler's eagerness to explain retribution theology within the entire regime of King Asa (chs. 14–16).[195] Yet this book is particularly interested in the period of Asa's early reign (i.e., the battle against the Cushites), which includes the king's recorded prayer. From the standpoint of shaping Israelite identity, this book asks the following questions: (1) what does Asa do when confronted with a national crisis; and (2) what is the king's perception of God in dealing with his difficulty. The following argument will posit that the text portrays King Asa as a supplicant who maintains monotheistic belief in Yhwh, since almighty God is capable of delivering his people from their enemy. As the post-exilic community joins Asa's prayer and communicates with the text, it motivates them to become active supplicants to God and monotheistic believers.

Asa Cries Out to Yhwh

The story of King Asa's battle against the Cushites is able to persuade the audience of Chronicles to become active supplicants. First, the king prays to his God amid a national crisis. This king's act of prayer is an exemplary model of conduct as other figures in Chronicles repeat the act in similar situations (i.e., war [2 Chr 13:14; 20:6–12; 32:20–23]).

Second, King Asa not only prays for God's deliverance, but he also receives what he asks for from God; his prayer illustrates the effectiveness of prayer. Out of seven verses (2 Chr 14:8–14 [Eng. vv. 9–15]) in the battle scene, the Chronicler assigns five verses (vv. 10–14 [Eng. vv. 11–15]) to describe the act of prayer and the victory that Asa and Judah receive from God. Thus, the text's focus is not on creating a scary mood through the battle scene but on depicting the image of a God who cares

---

194. Merrill counts verses in Kings and Chronicles. The former devotes fifteen verses to recounting of Asa's story, but the latter includes forty-eight verses (Merrill, *Commentary*, 398).

195. Dillard, "Reign of Asa," 208–11.

about the prayers of his people. In God's response to Asa's prayer, the very first report by the Chronicler is וַיִּגֹּף יְהוָה אֶת־הַכּוּשִׁים (Yhwh struck the Cushites [v. 11 (Eng. v. 10)]). This report creates the impression that when people pray to God during a difficult situation, God willingly and immediately steps into that situation and delivers his people.

Third, Asa's prayer reflects the principle established in Solomon's prayer (2 Chr 6:34–35). Asa prays to God for deliverance as Solomon exemplified in his prayer—that is, in cases of a war, the people could pray to God.[196] Later, Jehoshaphat's prayer also reflects this principle; thus, Chronicles conveys the message that the same principle is still in effect in the post-exilic days. Overall, Asa's prayer and God's response create sufficient rhetorical impetus to shape members of the post-exilic community as active supplicants.

Trust in Yhwh, the Savior

Asa's act of prayer in a difficult situation exhibits the king's perception of his God. Asa believes that Yhwh is the unique and supreme God; thus, he is able to deliver Judah from their enemy. This king's belief characterizes him as a monotheistic believer. Asa perceives God as a unique divine being, Yhwh, for himself and Judah. First, the Chronicler informs readers of Asa's perception by indicating Yhwh as the king's God (יִקְרָא אָסָא אֶל־יְהוָה אֱלֹהָיו [Asa cried out to Yhwh, *his* God (2 Chr 14:10 [Eng. v. 11])]; italics added). Second, Asa's words of prayer agree with the Chronicler by uttering יְהוָה (Yhwh) three times in the prayer. In this short prayer, Asa is eagerly looking for his God, Yhwh, to intervene in this national crisis (עָזְרֵנוּ יְהוָה אֱלֹהֵינוּ [help us, Yhwh, our God (v. 10 [Eng. v. 11])]). Third, Asa establishes the notion that attacking Judah is defiance against Yhwh. At the end of the prayer, Asa appeals to God, saying, יְהוָה אֱלֹהֵינוּ אַתָּה אַל־יַעְצֹר עִמְּךָ אֱנוֹשׁ (Yhwh, our God, let no man prevail against you [v. 10 (Eng. v. 11)]). Asa perceives that the threat is not simply against Judah but is a hostile act against God. Thus, Asa's prayer establishes the notion that Judah stands on Yhwh's side, and Judah's God answers his people's prayers as their unique deity (vv. 11–12 [Eng. vv. 12–13]).

Asa further understands Yhwh as the supreme divine being who is incomparable to any other. The king says, יְהוָה אֵין־עִמְּךָ לַעְזוֹר בֵּין רַב לְאֵין כֹּחַ

---

196. Pratt, *First and Second Chronicles*, 418; Barber, *Second Chronicles*, 115; Hill, *First and Second Chronicles*, 470.

(Yhwh, there is no one beside you to help between mighty and weak).[197] One should understand the intention of this phrase in the given context. The word רַב (many) refers to Asa's enemy in relation to the word הָמוֹן (multitude; i.e., the Cushites), and לְאֵין כֹּחַ relates to Judah's weak status.[198] Thus, the prayer exhibits Asa's belief that there is no one upon whom he can rely except Yhwh, who has the ability to deliver weak Judah from its strong enemy.

Asa's Perception of God

The prayer of Asa in the battle story reveals a certain aspect of the king's monotheistic belief to readers. Based on the acknowledgement of God's uniqueness and supremacy, Asa's prayer, believing in the God of omnipotence, exhibits his solid dependence on Yhwh, the savior.[199] First, the text's portrayal of the mighty God appears throughout the king's prayer and the scene of victory.[200] The prayer begins with a statement of incomparability (אֵין־עִמְּךָ לַעְזוֹר בֵּין רַב לְאֵין כֹּחַ [there is no one beside you to help between mighty and weak (v. 10 [Eng. v. 11])]), and the text continues to describe God as a mighty warrior (וַיִּגֹּף יְהוָה אֶת־הַכּוּשִׁים [Yhwh struck the Cushites (v. 11 [Eng. v. 12])]; כִּי־נִשְׁבְּרוּ לִפְנֵי־יְהוָה [for they were destroyed before Yhwh (v. 12 [Eng. v. 13])]; כִּי־הָיָה פַחַד־יְהוָה עֲלֵיהֶם [fear of Yhwh was over them (v. 13 [Eng. v. 14])]).[201]

Second, the text demonstrates that Asa relies upon (שָׁעַן) Yhwh (2 Chr 14:10 [Eng. v. 11]). In Chronicles, the verb שָׁעַן (to rely upon) appears five times, and all usages occur in Asa's narrative (13:18; 14:10 [Eng. v. 11]; 16:7 [x2], 8). The Chronicler uses the verb to exhibit that a man relies upon either Yhwh (2 Chr 13:18; 14:10; 16:8; see Prov 3:5)

---

197. The syntax of the given phrase is difficult to understand. It literally reads, "Yhwh, there is none with you to help, between many and lack of strength."

198. Japhet, *First and Second Chronicles*, 711; Williamson, *First and Second Chronicles*, 265. For לְאֵין, see Williams, *Williams' Hebrew Syntax*, §411. לְאֵין as a privative particle (i.e., lack of something).

199. Scholars have noticed that the major theme of the battle scene is to present God's omnipotence. See Japhet, *First and Second Chronicles*, 711; Barber, *Second Chronicles*, 115.

200. Selman defines the theme of the battle story as Yahweh's war (Selman, *Second Chronicles*, 408). Merrill introduces the holy war motif (Merrill, *Commentary*, 402–3).

201. DeVries, *First and Second Chronicles*, 298–99; Pratt, *First and Second Chronicles*, 417.

or human forces (2 Chr 16:7), and the result of the decision evidently follows that the former earns victory and blessing (13:18–21; 14:10–14 [Eng. vv. 11–15]; see Isa 10:20–23), but the latter receives God's punishment (2 Chr 16:8–9, 12).[202]

The object being relied upon (i.e., Yhwh) is highlighted by placing כִּי־עָלֶיךָ (for to you) before the verb (שען); this word placement thus exhibits that Asa notices Yhwh as the origin of help. The texts also put וּבְשִׁמְךָ (in your name) before the verb (בוא) at the beginning of the phrase (וּבְשִׁמְךָ בָאנוּ עַל־הֶהָמוֹן הַזֶּה יְהוָה [2 Chr 14:10 (Eng. v. 11)]). These constructions emphasize the act of relying upon Yhwh.[203] Klein writes, "The first clause is a faith statement (cf. 2 Chr 13:18), while the second affirms the faith that Judah's power lies in Yahweh and implies that Yahweh's reputation or name is at stake."[204] Overall, these two inverted constructions persuade God to intervene in the situation, since the battle now becomes God's affair as well.

Third, Asa's direct request for divine help (עָזְרֵנוּ יְהוָה אֱלֹהֵינוּ [help us, Yhwh, our God (2 Chr 14:10 [Eng. v. 11])]) portrays the king's act of relying upon God. Asa's request for God's help is rational, since in this imminent crisis, Asa perceives that God is Israel's God, Yhwh (יְהוָה אֱלֹהֵינוּ אַתָּה [Yhwh, you are our God (2 Chr 14:10 [Eng. v. 11])]), and in that circumstance, God is incomparable to any other for delivering Judah (אֵין־עִמְּךָ לַעְזֹר [there is no one to help except you]).[205] Thus, the word עזר (to help) conveys the essence of Asa's monotheistic belief (i.e., God as the incomparable warrior). In other words, having the perspective of God as supreme and unique, a supplicant is able to confidently ask God for help based on his reliance upon God.[206]

---

202. Dahmen, "שען," in *TDOT*, 15:352–56. For a detailed discussion on the theme of relying upon God in Chronicles, see Knoppers, "Yhwh Is Not with Israel."

203. Asa's prayer can be delineated by the prayer's use of יְהוָה : (1) calling on Yhwh at the beginning, (2) יְהוָה, an imperative followed by the second calling of Yhwh (עָזְרֵנוּ יְהוָה), and (3) the last calling of Yhwh (יְהוָה). DeVries understands the literary structure of prayer similarly: (1) "description of Yahweh (incomparability statement)," (2) "cry for help and appeal," and (3) "challenge to self-demonstration" (DeVries, *First and Second Chronicles*, 298). See also Japhet, *First and Second Chronicles*, 711. In other words, עָזְרֵנוּ יְהוָה אֱלֹהֵינוּ כִּי־וּבְשִׁמְךָ בָאנוּ עַל־הֶהָמוֹן הַזֶּה does not stand separately from עָלֶיךָ נִשְׁעַנּוּ, but together they form the second Yhwh line.

204. R. Klein, *Second Chronicles*, 219–20.

205. כִּי as "because" in עָזְרֵנוּ יְהוָה אֱלֹהֵינוּ כִּי־עָלֶיךָ נִשְׁעַנּוּ וּבְשִׁמְךָ בָאנוּ עַל־הֶהָמוֹן הַזֶּה. The verb עזר is employed twice (once in the imperative form) in Asa's prayer.

206. Wilcock, *Message of Chronicles*, 181.

Particularly, one should not overlook the phonological word-play between עזר (לַעְזוֹר; cf. עָזְרֵנוּ) and עצר (יַעְצֹר), since the two words produce similar sounds. Asa's request for God's help (עזר) concludes with his declaration that no human power should stand against God (אַל־יַעְצֹר עִמְּךָ אֱנוֹשׁ). This last phrase of the prayer is difficult to understand, yet, as Japhet suggests, the verb יַעְצֹר is most likely an elliptical representation of כּוֹחַ יַעְצֹר; thus, the fuller meaning of this verb includes a man's strength (כּוֹחַ).[207] In light of this observation, then, the preposition עִם in אַל־יַעְצֹר עִמְּךָ אֱנוֹשׁ should mean "against."[208] Ultimately, Asa's request for God's help relates to Yhwh's reputation, since it recognizes God's omnipotence vis-à-vis human weakness (אֱנוֹשׁ).[209] In sum, the aspect of Asa's monotheistic belief in the prayer and its context is that King Asa is a model figure who relies upon the almighty God as savior amid a national crisis.

Reliance upon Only God

The prayer and its related context do not simply convey the theological message that Israel should rely upon God but that they should rely only upon God.[210] The Chronicler's intention here is revealed when one focuses on his reference to the number of military personnel. Asa has 580,000 military personnel (14:7 [Eng. v. 8]), whereas Judah's enemy possesses 1,000,000 personnel and 300 chariots (v. 8 [Eng. v. 9]).[211] Therefore, the

207. Literally, "no man prevails by one's strength."

208. Japhet, *First and Second Chronicles*, 711.

209. אֱנוֹשׁ seems to represent the nature of human weakness (i.e., mortal) when considering the Chronicler's emphasis on God as omnipotent. See R. Klein, *Second Chronicles*, 220; Selman, *Second Chronicles*, 408; Hooker, *First and Second Chronicles*, 188; Myers, *Second Chronicles*, 83, 85.

210. The Chronicler's purpose does not simply lie in reporting bare facts but in conveying a theological message (Myers, *Second Chronicles*, 85). Boda also believes that this battle story is designed to convey the Chronicler's particular message. He particularly focuses on the structure of prayer, understanding it as a common form of a sermon/prayer in Chronicles: doctrine, application, exhortation (Boda, *First-Second Chronicles*, 305–6).

211. Syriac (𐊈) and Arabic (𐊀) Scriptures changed the number 300 to 300,000. The smaller size in the MT (also in the LXX) could be understood figuratively, since Zerah comes with 1,000,000 soldiers (Hognesius, *Text of 2 Chronicles 1–16*, 160). Japhet identifies the Chronicler's work here as a schematic-theological interpretation (Japhet, *First and Second Chronicles*, 710).

The identification of Zerah is not this book's primary task. For an introduction to different views on the person of Zerah, see R. Klein, *Second Chronicles*, 217–19.

text grants its readers a chance to compare both camps, conveying that Judah's enemy outnumbers her and that no option remains for Asa except prayer, since his military strength has become useless. Then, one may ask the following question: why has the text assigned space to describe Asa's faithfulness (2 Chr 14:2–7) and the crisis which eventually confirms his feebleness? The Chronicler places Judah's crisis (v. 8 [Eng. v. 9]) right after Asa's faithful act before Yhwh (vv. 1–7 [Eng. vv. 2–8]). The Chronicler does not explain the reasons for the faithful king's confrontation with war or for comparing the military strength of two camps. Scholars have conjectured various reasons for the war: it could be that God is testing the faithful king[212] or that the Chronicler wants to communicate to his readers that even God's faithful people can suffer in their lives.[213] Either view does not harm Chronicles' intention to communicate the theological message to the post-exilic audience, because the emphasis of the king's war lies not on the justification of the war but on the response of suffering people. The Chronicler's addition of Asa's military strength to its *Vorlage* is one illustration that conveys the Chronicler's theological emphasis. Asa, who had 580,000 military personnel, has experienced the evaporation of his strength before numerous Cushite troops.[214] For the Yehud community, there was no form of a nation, let alone 580,000 soldiers.[215] Therefore, the intended message to the post-exilic audience is that it does not matter whether the community has any sort of ability (e.g., military strength) in dealing with its own vulnerable status. Instead, it is important that when the community faces a crisis, even without knowing the causes of suffering, its members should still depend solely upon their omnipotent Yhwh (2 Chr 15:2, 12–15).[216]

---

212. Johnstone argues that the text writes of only 300 chariots and it does not mention any of cavalry (cf. 1200 chariots and 60,000 cavalries in 1 Chr 12:3), because Asa's battle is essentially God's test for the king (Johnstone, *First and Second Chronicles*, 2:63–64). Hooker also sees the battle as God's test (Hooker, *First and Second Chronicles*, 187).

213. Selman, *Second Chronicles*, 407–8. A righteous king who suffers is not unique in Chronicles. Jehoshaphat and Hezekiah also have wars during their respective reigns (2 Chr 20:1–34; 32:1–23).

214. Sanchez, "Royal Limitation," 168–73.

215. According to Ben Zvi, "the population of the Achaemenid Jerusalem was only about 6 percent of late monarchic Jerusalem" (Ben Zvi, "Urban Center," in Mirau et al., *Urbanism in Antiquity*, 196).

216. Jonker, *First and Second Chronicles*, 223.

Recorded Prayers in Chronicles 95

Conclusion

Asa's prayer is able to persuade the post-exilic community to become monotheistic believers who pray to God during difficult circumstances. In coming forth to the battle, King Asa's military strength vanishes before the immense number of enemy forces. Asa's prayer for God's help in this exigent situation and God's response to the prayer are able to motivate the community to be active supplicants. Asa, as a monotheistic believer, persuades God that the war relates to God's reputation, revealing God's omnipotence over mortal beings; thus, when the audience joins in the king's prayer, the prayer encourages the members to rely upon God in dealing with their vulnerable circumstances. The Chronicler's portrayal of Asa particularly exhibits an aspect of monotheistic belief. The Chronicler characterizes King Asa who relies solely upon God, because Yhwh is Judah's God and is the mighty warrior who fights against the enemies of his people.

Second Chronicles 20:5-13: Jehoshaphat's Prayer

Introduction

Jehoshaphat prays to Yhwh (2 Chr 20:5-13) in the midst of Judah's confrontation of her enemies (i.e., the Moabites, Ammonites, and Meunites [v. 1]) at the battle scene. The prayer and the battle scene (ch. 20) do not appear in Chronicles' *Vorlage*,[217] and they have received scholarly attention, because they contribute to shaping Chronicles' theological and ideological axis.[218]

---

217. In fact, the account of this king's reign in Chronicles is much longer than Kings' account (1 Kgs 22:1-55 [Eng. vv. 1-50]), and especially 2 Chr 19:1—20:31 has been considered to be the Chronicler's unique report (i.e., *Sondergut*) of the latter period of Jehoshaphat's reign (R. Klein, *Second Chronicles*, 282). For a comparison between Kings and Chronicles, see Pratt, *First and Second Chronicles*, 439. For a discussion about the Chronicler's use of sources, see Japhet, *First and Second Chronicles*, 784-85; Jonker, "Was the Chronicler More Deuteronomic," 185-97.

218. E.g., Selman even insists that the Jehoshaphat's account (esp. 2 Chr 20) is "outstanding not only in Chronicles but also in the whole Bible" (Selman, *Second Chronicles*, 420). Kleinig shows interest in Jehoshaphat's account concerning the public worship during the warfare (Kleinig, *Lord's Song*, 170-81). Beentjes suggests Jehoshaphat's prayer as an example of the Chronicler's employment of inner biblical interpretation (Beentjes, "Tradition and Transformation"). Scholars also have argued that the theme of holy war in Jehoshaphat's battle well represents divine activity in

The recorded prayer of Jehoshaphat and its close context have a significant function in shaping Israelite identity in Chronicles. In light of the Chronicler's report of Jehoshaphat's overall reign (chs. 17–20), especially the two battles stories in chapters 18 and 20, the particular intention carried by the battle report of Jehoshaphat (i.e., ch. 20) is to characterize an appropriate outward conduct and inward attitude of the king and the people, so that they can overcome a national crisis.[219] The Chronicler criticizes King Jehoshaphat's reliance on Ahab, king of Israel, in the battle against Aram at Ramoth-Gilead (18:1–34; 19:2); but, the author positively portrays Jehoshaphat's dependence upon God in the king's later battle against the coalition (20:1–30; esp. v. 20; see 22:9).[220] In light of this broader observation on Jehoshaphat's reign, Jehoshaphat's prayer and God's response to the prayer (i.e., the oracle of the prophet Jahaziel [20:13–17] and the report of victory [vv. 22–30], illustrating the effectiveness of prayer) encourage the audience of the book to become active supplicants who maintain a monotheistic belief amid a national crisis. There are two unique aspects of Jehoshaphat's prayer from the perspective of a supplicant: (1) the prayer characterizes Jehoshaphat as a prototypical supplicant who transforms a past prayer into his own prayer; thus, the audience could observe the king's interpretation and application of the past prayer, which would encourage them to apply other model prayers in Chronicles to their contemporary context; (2) the prayer particularly emphasizes the significance of public prayer (i.e., the act of praying together) with faith in Yhwh. Concerning the aspect of monotheistic believers, in recognition of God's supremacy and uniqueness, the members of the post-exilic community should rely upon God in expecting divine justice for their situation.

Chronicles. See Pratt, *First and Second Chronicles*, 24, 342; Thompson, *First, Second Chronicles*, 295; R. Klein, *Second Chronicles*, 291; Hooker, *First and Second Chronicles*, 21; Boda, *First-Second Chronicles*, 330. DeVries particularly insists that the holy war in Chronicles exhibits the development of the ideology of holy war in the OT Scriptures (DeVries, "Temporal Terms," 103–5). Lynch and Tiňo observe the Chronicler's emphasis on the role of Levites in Jehoshaphat's battle account (Lynch, *Monotheism and Institution*, 176–77; Tiňo, *King and Temple*, 60–61).

219. Boda, *First-Second Chronicles*, 328–39; McKenzie, *First-Second Chronicles*, 294.

220. Williamson, *First and Second Chronicles*, 278; Thompson, *First, Second Chronicles*, 292.

Jehoshaphat:
The Prototypical Supplicant for the Post-Exilic Community

King Jehoshaphat's act of prayer can be model behavior for the audience of Chronicles. The text motivates the audience to become active supplicants in various ways. First, the text characterizes the king and the people as active supplicants. When Jehoshaphat receives the report of a threat toward Judah (20:2), he sets his face to seek Yhwh and calls for a fast throughout all Judah (וַיִּתֵּן יְהוֹשָׁפָט אֶת־פָּנָיו לִדְרוֹשׁ לַיהוָה וַיִּקְרָא־צוֹם עַל־כָּל־יְהוּדָה [v. 3]). The act of seeking Yhwh is religious behavior in which one searches for God's help,[221] and particularly in this context, the act of prayer (i.e., intercession) is implied.[222] Not only does the king pray, but also the people of Judah respond to the king's summons and join in the prayer (לְבַקֵּשׁ אֶת־יְהוָה [to seek Yhwh (v. 4)]; וַיַּעֲמֹד יְהוֹשָׁפָט בִּקְהַל יְהוּדָה וִירוּשָׁלִַם [Jehoshaphat stands in the assembly of Judah and Jerusalem (v. 5)]).[223] The act of fasting also occurs when people cry out for God's assistance, and it exhibits the people's self-abasement before God in dealing with their crisis.[224]

Second, the text shows that the prayer is effective for the audience on two levels. First, the king's prayer receives God's response (vv. 14–17) and brings about a positive result, the victory against Judah's enemies (vv. 20–30);[225] thus, the audience learns that God responds to Jehoshaphat's prayer.

Second, there is an escalated rhetorical impact in that the audience witnesses that not only Jehoshaphat's prayer receives God's answer, but Solomon's prayer also is still in effect. Jehoshaphat's words of prayer, particularly verses 8–9, strongly allude to 2 Chronicles 6:28–30 and God's response to Solomon (7:13–16).[226] As the members of the post-exilic community

---

221. Williamson, *First and Second Chronicles*, 295; Japhet, *First and Second Chronicles*, 787; Selman, *Second Chronicles*, 424; Jonker, *First and Second Chronicles*, 230.

222. This book has argued for the motif of seeking Yhwh in the discussion of the prayer of 1 Chr 16. Yet note that, concerning 1 Chr 16, this book discusses this motif in relation to the role of worshipers.

223. Levin observes, "Jehoshaphat's speech to the assembly gathered 'before the new court' [2 Chr 20:5] of the Temple is usually classified as a prayer" (Levin, *Chronicles*, 153).

224. Stolz, "צום," in *TLOT*, 1066–67. See Judg 20:26–27.

225. Levin evaluates God's response as immediate response, and Hill even refers to it as the perfect answer (Levin, *Chronicles*, 155; Hill, *First and Second Chronicles*, 490).

226. Boda, *First-Second Chronicles*, 229; Japhet, *First and Second Chronicles*, 790.

observe the report of Jehoshaphat's victory, the text conveys the message to the audience that God has not forgotten the promise made to Solomon (i.e., he would respond to prayers offered toward the temple [7:13–16]); thus, the community still expects that God listens to their prayers.

Past Prayer as a Model

Jehoshaphat's prayer exhibits a few aspects of a supplicant. First, it is not obligatory that the members of the community adopt the forefathers' prayers verbatim when they join those past prayers; instead, they could apply the principles of past prayers to their contemporary circumstances. In this regard, Jehoshaphat's prayer plays a significant role in establishing the argument of this book, since King Jehoshaphat's act of prayer, as the model prayer, exhibits the manner in which the post-exilic community possibly adopts, interprets, and applies their forefathers' prayers in Chronicles. For instance, in Solomon's prayer, the distressing situations are assumed because of the Israelites' possible sinful acts (2 Chr 6:28). However, in Jehoshaphat's prayer, the text does not imply any sinful action on the part of the king or the people of Israel.[227] Thus, even though the situation Jehoshaphat confronts is identical to what Solomon assumed in his prayer (כִּי־יָצַר־לוֹ אוֹיְבָיו בְּאֶרֶץ שְׁעָרָיו [if their enemy besieges them in the land at their gate (v. 28; see 20:2)]), technically, it seems that Solomon's prayer is not applicable to Jehoshaphat's present circumstances, since Solomon clearly asks for God's forgiveness (וְסָלַחְתָּ [2 Chr 6:30]) for the Israelites in his prayer at the temple dedication. Yet, although a discrepancy exists between the two kings' prayers, Jehoshaphat's prayer still adopts the core principle that both Solomon's prayer and God's response have established: in a distresssing situation, the people can pray for God's help.[228] In the narrative, Jehoshaphat achieves victory through God's intervention in the situation (2 Chr 20:22–23, 27–29); thus, the

---

227. It seems that the battle in ch. 20 does not imply any kind of sinful act on Jehoshaphat's part (Johnstone, *First and Second Chronicles*, 2:98). Chapter 19 positively portrays Jehoshaphat's reformation all over the territory (19:4), and ch. 20 grammatically and syntactically follows the events recorded in ch. 19 (וַיְהִי אַחֲרֵיכֵן [then, after this; *waw*-consecutive (20:1)]). Williamson does not clearly indicate that Jehoshaphat's sin is the origin of the battle, but he implies that Jehoshaphat's sin might be involved in this incident. He writes that proclaiming a fast is "a symbol of earnest *repentance*" (Williamson, *First and Second Chronicles*, 295; italics added). Boda sees Jehoshaphat's act of seeking Yhwh (20:4) as evidence of his repentance (Boda, *Return to Me*, 143).

228. See 2 Chr 6:29–30; 7:14; 20:9.

king's prayer affirms that the principle which Jehoshaphat adopts from Solomon's prayer is still in effect.

In addition, Solomon describes the people's acts with words of כָּל־תְּפִלָּה כָל־תְּחִנָּה (prayer and supplication [6:29]), but Jehoshaphat utters וְנִזְעַק (we will cry out [20:9]). One may argue that the act of crying out could be just a different way of referring to the act of prayer, but the text suggests that when observing what Jehoshaphat has learned from the battle at Ramoth-Gilead, the king's word choice could be more than a synonym. By overcoming a life-threatening moment, Jehoshaphat has learned that when he cries out to God (וַיִּזְעַק [18:31]), he earns God's help (וַיהוָה עֲזָרוֹ [v. 31]). Thus, as Jehoshaphat faces a new threat (20:2), the king applies what he has learned from his previous battle to his current circumstances.[229]

Furthermore, as Boda notes, Jehoshaphat's modification of Solomon's prayer also appears in the king's generalization or appropriation of Solomon's prayer.[230] In Solomon's prayer, the subject of the act of prayer is given in third person marks (לְכָל־הָאָדָם וּלְכֹל עַמְּךָ [by any man or by all your people (2 Chr 6:29)]). However, Jehoshaphat's prayer indicates that those who pray to God are not any man or all your people but we (נַעַמְדָה לִפְנֵי הַבַּיִת הַזֶּה [we stand before this house (20:9)]; וְנִזְעַק אֵלֶיךָ [we cry out to you (v.9)]). Thus, in Jehoshaphat's utterance of the third person plural, Solomon's prayer truly becomes Jehoshaphat's and the people's own prayer. This text's appropriation opens a door to the post-exilic community, in that the members of the community also adopt past prayers from Chronicles and transform them to their own prayers.

The king's reference to Abraham (לְזֶרַע אַבְרָהָם אֹהַבְךָ לְעוֹלָם [to the descendant of Abraham, your beloved, forever [20:7]) could remind the audience of the phrase אֲשֶׁר כָּרַת אֶת־אַבְרָהָם (the covenant he [God] made with Abraham [1 Chr 16:16]).[231] In the past prayer during David's transference of the ark (1 Chr 16), the reference to the name Abraham

---

229. Note that in Kings, although the text writes וַיִּזְעַק (he [Jehoshaphat] cried out [2 Kgs 22:32]), it does not report that Yhwh helped, as in Chronicles (2 Chr 18:31). Therefore, in Chronicles, the text more clearly establishes the notion that when "the king cried out, God helped him" (B. Kim, "We Do not Know," 91).

230. Boda understands Jehoshaphat's modification as the king's democratization of Solomon's prayer (Boda, *First-Second Chronicles*, 329). See also Japhet, *First and Second Chronicles*, 790.

231. The word Abraham appears eight times in Chronicles (1 Chr 1:27, 28, 32, 34; 16:16; 29:18; 2 Chr 20:7; 30:6), yet only these two verses imply God's promise to Abraham.

and the call for the remembrance of God's past act in promising the land (16:18) to this patriarch contribute to constructing the notion of God's special relation with his people, Israel (זִכְרוּ לְעוֹלָם בְּרִיתוֹ [remember his covenant forever (1 Chr 16:15)]). Yet, in Jehoshaphat's prayer, the king brings God's promise with Abraham into his particular war context, exclaiming that the land, which God had given to Abraham, is in danger of being extorted by foreign nations (20:7, 11). The king's intention of this contextualization of the past prayer is affirmed when considering that the expression לְזֶרַע אַבְרָהָם אֹהַבְךָ לְעוֹלָם (to the descendant of Abraham, your beloved, forever [20:7]) alludes to Isaiah 41:8 (אֲשֶׁר בְּחַרְתִּיךָ זֶרַע אַבְרָהָם אֹהֲבִי [that I have chosen the descendant of Abraham, my beloved]). The literary context of Isaiah 41:8 assures God's people of his salvific plan for them from their adversaries;[232] thus, based on the past prayer (1 Chr 16) and the prophetic words of Isaiah, Jehoshaphat hopes for deliverance by Israel's special God.

Therefore, Jehoshaphat's prayer constructs a new theological system on top of the foundational principles embedded in the past prayers.[233] The king retrieves core doctrines of the past prayers and applies them to his present circumstances. The king not only adopts the past prayers but also modifies them with his own theological doctrine, so that he could transform the past prayers into his and the people's own prayer. The text provides a way for the post-exilic community to construct their own prayer based on the theological principles they have learned from the prayers in Chronicles.

The Power of Communal Prayer

The second way that Jehoshaphat's prayer exhibits the aspect of a supplicant is that supplicants should pray together during a national calamity

---

232. Thompson, *First, Second Chronicles*, 293. Concerning Isa 41:8, Oswalt comments, "*My friend* (lit. 'my lover' or 'my beloved') suggests that election is not an austere, judicial act but is rooted and grounded in love, both the love of God for the chosen and the love of the chosen for God. Thus, as those particularly chosen to serve God, offspring of his unique friend (2 Chr 20:7; Jas. 2:23), they have nothing to fear (John 15:14–15)" (Oswalt, *Book of Isaiah*, 90; italics in original).

233. Beentjes similarly observes, "These biblical texts (2 Chr 20:6–13, 14–17, 20), however, have not been adopted in a merely mechanical way, but have been transformed into a new literary and theological setting" (Beentjes, "Tradition and Transformation," 260).

(i.e., public prayer).²³⁴ When King Jehoshaphat calls for a fast (20:3), the people of Judah gather themselves together (וַיִּקָּבְצוּ יְהוּדָה [v. 4]). The text notes that the people come from all the cities of Judah (מִכָּל־עָרֵי יְהוּדָה [v. 4]), and the supplicants even include the men's wives and children (גַּם־טַפָּם נְשֵׁיהֶם וּבְנֵיהֶם [v. 14]). In addition, the first person plural pronoun or mark appears throughout the prayer (אֲבֹתֵינוּ [our father (v. 6)]; אֱלֹהֵינוּ [our God (v. 7)]; נַעֲמְדָה [we stand (v. 9)]; וְנִזְעַק [we cry out (v. 9)]; עָלֵינוּ [to us (v. 11)]; הוֹרַשְׁתָּנוּ [you have given us to possess (v. 11)]); thus, King Jehoshaphat's prayer reveals that the king is not the only one who prays; instead, he represents all the supplicants of the people who participate in the public prayer. The text immediately reports God's response (vv. 14–17) to the prayer as well as Judah's victory (vv. 22–30); thus, it affirms the effectiveness of public prayer to the audience. Overall, the prayer exhibits the power of community prayer. During a national crisis, the community should gather themselves and offer prayers to God.

Israel's Unique and Mighty God amid Warfare

Jehoshaphat's prayer exhorts the audience of Chronicles to believe that God is the unique and supreme deity throughout the history of Israel and that he is capable of defeating Israel's enemy. Concerning Yhwh as Israel's special deity, the king repeatedly avows his faith in Israel's relationship with God (יְהוָה אֱלֹהֵי אֲבֹתֵינוּ [Yhwh, God of our father (v. 6)]; אֱלֹהֵינוּ [our God (vv. 7, 12)]; עַמְּךָ יִשְׂרָאֵל [your people of Israel (v. 7)]; לְזֶרַע אַבְרָהָם אֹהַבְךָ לְעוֹלָם [to the descendant of Abraham, your beloved, forever (v. 7)]).

In addition, the king acknowledges that Israel has enjoyed many years of relationship with God, even from the days of Abraham and the exodus event (vv. 7, 10–11).²³⁵ The king acknowledges that God has granted the land to the descendants of Abraham (v. 7) and guided his people during their journey in the wilderness (v. 10; see Deut 2:1–22).²³⁶ Particularly, the king asserts Israel's special relationship with God by claiming Israel's right of יְרֻשָּׁה (inheritance [v. 11]). Pratt observes:

---

234. Pratt, *First and Second Chronicles*, 465; Hill, *First and Second Chronicles*, 490; R. Klein, *Second Chronicles*, 284.

235. The Chronicler has a tendency of not mentioning Egypt or the exodus event. For a discussion on the Chronicler's deviation from this tendency, see Japhet, *First and Second Chronicles*, 791–92.

236. Beentjes, *Tradition and Transformation*, 261–62.

The terminology of inheritance is derived from Mosaic legal language which indicated a permanent bestowal of land from God (see Lev. 25:23–24; Deut. 11:8–12; 1 Kgs. 21:3; 1 Chr. 28:8). As Israel's King, God gave the land of Canaan to his people in perpetuity.[237]

Further, King Jehoshaphat claims that not only had Israel received the land, but also they built the temple in that land for God's name's sake (vv. 7–8), and God has promised that he would deliver his people who pray toward the temple (v. 9; see 6:12–42). Thus, the land (i.e., inheritance) and the temple are visual testimonies of Israel's special relationship with God.

Moreover, God proclaims that the battle is not Judah's but Yhwh's. God stands on Judah's side (וַיהוָה עִמָּכֶם [Yhwh is with you (v. 17)]) and encourages his people (אַל־תִּירְאוּ וְאַל־תֵּחַתּוּ [do not be afraid and dismayed (vv. 15, 17)], referring to the effectiveness of prayer). Judah does not need to fight (לֹא לָכֶם לְהִלָּחֵם בָּזֹאת [you will not need to fight in this battle [v. 17]), because God himself will defeat Judah's enemy (כִּי לֹא לָכֶם הַמִּלְחָמָה כִּי לֵאלֹהִים [for the battle is not yours but God's [v. 17]) and bring salvation (וּרְאוּ אֶת־יְשׁוּעַת יְהוָה עִמָּכֶם [see the salvation, Yhwh with you (v. 17; see vv. 22–30)]).[238] In sum, both Jehoshaphat's prayer and God's response to the king's appeal exhibit that Israel has a special relationship with God.

Regarding Yhwh as Israel's supreme deity over their adversaries, Jehoshaphat relates God's supremacy to his divine location and ruling authority. He raises a rhetorical question: הֲלֹא אַתָּה־הוּא אֱלֹהִים בַּשָּׁמַיִם (are you not God in the heaven? [v. 6]). The heaven as God's place in Chronicles appears in various passages (2 Chr 6:21, 23, 25, 27, 30, 33, 35, 39;

---

237. Pratt, *First and Second Chronicles*, 469; Selman, *Second Chronicles*, 425. See Num 20:14–21; Deut 2:1–19; Judg 11:14–18.

238. Second Chronicles 20:17 shows a high similarity to Exod 14:13 and Isa 41:10. God's words of confirmation in v. 17 are not simply Chronicles' own theological construct but are repeatedly given to the people of Israel; thus, the text reassures the post-exilic community of what they have learned from Scripture. See Exod 14:13 and Isa 41:10.

Regarding the similarity between 2 Chr 20:17 and Exod 4:13, Beentjes says, "Both 2 Chr and Exod 14 display a similar narrative structure. In both texts, a situation of distress is found, caused by a hostile attack. This brings about a lament by people, which is answered by an encouraging speech and clear instructions about how to react. From a distance, Israel is therefore a witness of the enemy's defeat at the hand of God. From this parallel structure, one can draw no other conclusion than that the frame of 2 Chr 20 is determined to a high degree by Exod 14" (Beentjes, "Tradition and Transformation," 265).

7:14; 18:18; 30:27; 36:23)[239] and portrays the following images concerning God: (1) the God of justice (6:23, 30) listens to the people's prayers, forgives their sins (vv. 21, 25, 35, 39; 30:27), and receives awe from both Israel and foreigners (v. 33); (2) God has the ability to restore the life of the people (i.e., bringing the people back to the land [v. 25]; granting rain on the land [v. 27; see 7:14]); (3) God sits on the throne at the center of the host of heaven (18:18); and (4) God has the ability to grant all the kingdoms of the earth to whomever he pleases (36:23). Thus, the notion of God of the heaven denotes that God is supreme (18:18; 36:23) and is capable of intervening in human affairs (2 Chr 6:21, 25, 27, 33, 35, 39; 30:27). In Jehoshaphat's words, the reference to God in the heaven, together with the notion of God's earthly reign (וְאַתָּה מוֹשֵׁל בְּכֹל מַמְלְכוֹת הַגּוֹיִם וּבְיָדְךָ כֹּחַ וּגְבוּרָה וְאֵין עִמְּךָ לְהִתְיַצֵּב [you rule over all the kingdoms of the nations; power and might are in your hand, and no one can withstand you (20:6)]) confirms God's preeminence over the world.

Furthermore, verse 6 reminds the post-exilic audience of God's cosmic reign and possession of supreme qualities in the prayers of David/ the Levites (1 Chr 16:21; 29:11).[240] As Lynch notes, the notion concerning God's supremacy over the cosmos in David's prayer (i.e., heaven and earth [1 Chr 29:11], a merism) is modified in Jehoshaphat's prayer (i.e., heaven and all the kingdom of the nations [2 Chr 20:6]) in a more "religious-political" manner that better fits into Judah's current circumstances.[241] Thus, the prayer particularly addresses that God is supreme and has the power to defeat Judah's adversaries.

Another way that the prayer exhibits the supremacy of God is by reporting Jehoshaphat's victory in the near context of the prayer (illustrating the effectiveness of prayer). This report affirms that the king's belief in God's mighty strength is valid (2 Chr 20:20–30). In Jehoshaphat's battle

---

239. The word heaven appears in Chronicles as follows: 1 Chr 16:26, 31; 21:16, 26; 27:23; 29:11; 2 Chr 2:5 [x3], 11; 6:13, 14, 18 [x3], 21, 23, 25–27, 30, 33, 35, 39; 7:1, 13–14; 18:18; 20:6; 28:9; 30:27; 32:20; 33:3, 5; 36:23.

240. Johnston, *First and Second Chronicles*, 2:96.

כִּי as asseverative (Williams, *Williams' Hebrew Syntax*, §449).

First Chronicles 16:21 reads, יִשְׂמְחוּ הַשָּׁמַיִם וְתָגֵל הָאָרֶץ וְיֹאמְרוּ בַגּוֹיִם יְהוָה מָלָךְ (Let the heaven be glad, and the let the earth rejoice, and the let them say among the nations, 'Yhwh reigns'). See also 1 Chr 29:11, which reads, לְךָ יְהוָה הַגְּדֻלָּה וְהַגְּבוּרָה וְהַתִּפְאֶרֶת וְהַנֵּצַח וְהַהוֹד כִּי־כֹל בַּשָּׁמַיִם וּבָאָרֶץ (belong to you, Yhwh, greatness, power, beauty, glory, and the majesty surely everything in the heaven and earth belongs to you).

241. Lynch, *Monotheism and Institution*, 178.

account, scholars have observed that the motif of holy war is evident.²⁴² There are several elements in identifying the motif of holy war in this story. Setting ambushes (מְאָרְבִים [v. 22]) is a typical strategy of holy war (Josh 8:2, 7, 12, 14, 19, 21; Jer 51:12; 2 Chr 13:13).²⁴³ Levitical music on the battlefield is another feature of holy war (2 Chr 20:19, 21; see Josh 6:4–20; Judg 7:18–20; 2 Chr 13:11–12). In addition, the shortcoming of Israel's military strength compared to its enemies (20:12; see Josh 11:4) is apparent,²⁴⁴ yet no single enemy combatant (v. 24; see Josh 8:24) survives the war.²⁴⁵

The codified principles of holy war (Deut 20:1–20) reveal God's intention to vanquish Israel's adversaries: כִּי יְהוָה אֱלֹהֵיכֶם הַהֹלֵךְ עִמָּכֶם לְהִלָּחֵם לָכֶם עִם־אֹיְבֵיכֶם לְהוֹשִׁיעַ אֶתְכֶם (for Yhwh, God, is he who goes with you to fight for you against your enemies, to give you the victory [v. 4]),²⁴⁶ and God certainly carries out his intentions through the battle (2 Chr 20:22–23). God's holy war brings about victory for Judah and produces dread (פַּחַד [v. 29; cf, 17:10]) in Judah's enemies; thus, the holy war motif eventually reveals God's supreme power over the nations.²⁴⁷

Monotheistic Believers Expect God to Be Just

In Jehoshaphat's prayer, the king expects God to be just, and the king's expectation can become the audience's hope for God to bring about justice in their contemporary circumstances.²⁴⁸ Jehoshaphat understands the

---

242. The holy war motif in Chronicles is not unique. See other passages in Chronicles: 2 Chr 13:3–21; 14:7–13 (Eng. vv. 8–14); 25:5–13 (DeVries, *First and Second Chronicles*, 434; Dillards, *Second Chronicles*, 161).
This book uses the terms battle and war interchangeably.

243. Thompson, *First, Second Chronicles*, 295.

244. Dillards, *Second Chronicles*, 157.

245. R. Klein, *Second Chronicles*, 283.

246. Stuart, *Exodus*, 395–97.

247. Thus, there has been a suggestion that the term "Yhwh war" is a better and more appropriate expression than "holy war." However, this book perceives no difference between the two terms, since the former focuses on the act (i.e., battle), while the latter focuses on the purpose (i.e., holy). See Thistlethwaite, "'You May Enjoy," 67.

248. Justice is the one of the major themes in Jehoshaphat's account. For instance, the meaning of Jehoshaphat's name is "Yhwh has judged," and the Chronicler particularly dedicates ch. 19 to reporting Jehoshaphat's judicial reform. See Pratt, *First and Second Chronicles*, 47; Hicks, *First and Second Chronicles*, 377. Dillard specifically focuses on the theme of retribution (Dillard, "Chronicler's Jehoshaphat").

characteristics of God: just, impartial, and honest (כִּי־אֵין עִם־יְהוָה אֱלֹהֵינוּ עַוְלָה וּמַשֹּׂא פָנִים וּמִקַּח־שֹׁחַד [for there is no injustice with Yhwh, our God, or partiality or taking bribes (2 Chr 19:7)]); the king also perceives that these elements are benchmarks for divine judgment (וְעַתָּה יְהִי פַחַד־יְהוָה עֲלֵיכֶם שִׁמְרוּ וַעֲשׂוּ [now then let the fear of Yhwh be upon you; be very careful what you do (v. 7)]).[249] From Jehoshaphat's perspective on God's nature, then, it is unjust for Judah to be invaded by enemies. During the events surrounding the exodus, Israel spared their enemies (i.e., Ammon, Moab, and Mt. Seir; see Deut: 2:2–22) at God's command, but now, those enemies invade Judah. Verses 10 and 11 imply that Judah's current crisis (v. 11) is not an abrupt development but, instead, relates to their past history (v. 10).[250] Thus, Jehoshaphat complaints of unfairness and asks God to judge his enemies: הֲלֹא תִשְׁפָּט־בָּם (will you not judge them? [2 Chr 20:12]).[251] The king's petition for God's justice is not simply based on the obedience of Judah's forefathers to God's instruction; the king also asserts that the coalition encroaches upon the inheritance that God has bestowed upon Israel (v. 11). Hence, the king tries to engage God in Judah's warfare and demands divine justice.[252] Jehoshaphat's argument is theologically meaningful. As McKenzie states, "By jeopardizing Israel's existence in the land given to it by Yahweh, the invaders threaten to reverse Yahweh's divine plan and challenge his universal sovereignty."[253] Then, for the post-exilic community that has lived as a vulnerable community surrounded by foreign powers, Jehoshaphat's argument could be meaningful in shaping their view, as monotheistic believers, of God as the God of justice. The divine justice that the audience could expect from God would be that the unique and supreme God is expected to secure the inheritance that he has bestowed upon his special people and to protect them from Persian power.[254]

249. Johnston, *First and Second Chronicles*, 2:93. Judges should fear Yhwh since God is just, impartial, and honest. Any violation of these values is considered disobedience to God's law (Deut 16:19).

250. R. Klein, *Second Chronicles*, 288.

251. Japhet, *First and Second Chronicles*, 788.

252. Johnston, *First-Second Chronicles*, 2:99; Japhet, *First and Second Chronicles*, 788; Good, "Just War," 393. Certainly, God involves himself in the war and declares that it is his war (2 Chr 20:15).

253. McKenzie, *First-Second Chronicles*, 295. The land is God's permanent bestowal; thus, forfeiture of it violates God's sovereign plan.

254. One may raise a question regarding the implication of the prayer for the Yehud community, since there was no heavy warfare in the post-exilic era. For a detailed

Conclusion

Jehoshaphat's recorded prayer exhibits the role of an active supplicant and a monotheistic believer. Amid a national crisis, Jehoshaphat and the people of Judah cry out for God's help. Yhwh is their unique God, who exercises divine supremacy over Israel's enemies. Chronicles reports Judah's miraculous victory through a sacred war, and God's response to Jehoshaphat's prayer and his faith in Israel's unique and supreme Yhwh could sufficiently persuade the members of the post-exilic community to perceive their roles as supplicants and monotheistic believers.

Jehoshaphat's prayer also conveys certain aspects of a supplicant and a monotheistic believer. Concerning the former, Jehoshaphat's prayer portrays the king as a model supplicant who adopts his past prayers (e.g., David and Solomon) and transforms them into his own prayer that is appropriate to Judah's imminent crisis. Thus, the king's manner of transformation becomes a hermeneutical illustration. In this regard, the audience of Chronicles may also cultivate past prayers in light of their own circumstances. In addition, Jehoshaphat prays together with all the people of Judah; thus, the prayer singles out the significance of public prayer.

Concerning the latter, Jehoshaphat perceives that God is unique to Israel and supreme over Judah's foes. The text depicts the king as expecting God to be just. The king addresses the invasion of Judah's territory as a direct defiance against Yhwh, implying that God himself should defeat Judah's adversaries. In this regard, if the post-exilic community felt threatened, they could desire for the same God, the God of justice, to come and protect the community under the Persian rulers.

Second Chronicles 30:18–20: Hezekiah's Prayer

Introduction

The last recorded prayer in Chronicles (i.e., Hezekiah's prayer [2 Chr 30:18–20]) is embedded in the stories of King Hezekiah (chs. 29–32). Chapters 29 to 31 describe how Hezekiah purifies and restores Israel's worship. These chapters do not appear in Chronicles' *Vorlage*;[255] hence,

---

discussion, see "Citizens of the Davidic Kingdom" in ch. 4.

255. The chapters' main themes would be as follows: (1) Hezekiah purifies the temple (2 Chr 29:1–19), (2) Hezekiah's renewal of the Passover (30:1–27), and (3) Hezekiah's nationwide purification (31:1–21) (Levin, *Chronicles*, 285–326).

it is probable that they convey the Chronicler's intended message to the post-exilic community.[256]

Hezekiah's prayer appears in the middle of the story of Hezekiah's reformation of Israel's worship and ceremony of the Passover, and it describes the king's eagerness to accomplish successful worship. The message of the prayer reflects a specific concern that arises from this process (i.e., the renewal of the Passover). Therefore, the research on this prayer will also require an investigation about its context.[257]

During the Passover, there were many participants in Jerusalem (2 Chr 30:13), since people not only gathered from the southern territory (i.e., Judah) but also from the northern territory, including the aliens (גֵּר) who dwelled in Israel and Judah (v. 25). According to the law of Moses, the participants were required to be consecrated (v. 16; see Exod 12:43–51), but many, especially Ephraim, Manasseh, Issachar, and Zebulun, had not purified themselves (2 Chr 30:18). In this situation, Hezekiah intercedes for them by praying that God would forgive (יְכַפֵּר [atone (v. 19)]) their uncleanness, the result of which eventually leads to the successful Passover with all participants.

In light of this context, Hezekiah's prayer exhibits the Chronicler's particular concerns about (1) the renewal of proper worship, (2) the reminder of Israel's relationship with Yhwh, and (3) the revival of the Davidic kingdom. Therefore, Hezekiah's prayer is able to encourage the post-exilic community, who have recognized their Davidic citizenship, to be active worshipers and supplicants as the community witnesses King Hezekiah's eagerness to seek all-Israel's worship toward their special God.

---

256. The Chronicler's particular interest in this king should not be dismissed. As Williamson indicates, the Chronicler assigns more space to write Hezekiah's story than those of David or Solomon themselves (Williamson, *First and Second Chronicles*, 350). Myer observes, "The Chronicler reflects only eighteen verses of Kings; the other material is his own (approximately 100 verses)" (Myers, *First Chronicles*, lxi).

257. Unlike Jabez's prayer in 1 Chr 4:9–10, reading Hezekiah's prayer alone does not provide a full view of the reason the king offers such prayer. Therefore, the interpretation of the prayer requires an investigation of Hezekiah's characterization and a historical and exegetical, literary, or rhetorical analysis on the context of the prayer. For instance, the following questions are important. For what reason does the king want to receive God's forgiveness (יְכַפֵּר [v. 30])? What is the king's ultimate goal that he wants to achieve through the prayer? If one is not attentive to these types of questions, he or she may not be able to understand the penetrating theme of Hezekiah's story.

Hezekiah as a Model Figure for Israel's Enthusiastic Worship

The prayer and its context demonstrate King Hezekiah's passion for the worship of Yhwh, and this exemplary act can motivate the audience of the book to become worshipers like the king. First, the prayer and its near context use particular terms that relate to Israel's proper procedure of the cult. In light of this observation, it is reasonable to believe that this given prayer's direct concern is the worship of Yhwh (i.e., the cult).[258] In Hezekiah's prayer, the king's particular language in his request is יְכַפֵּר (to atone [2 Chr 30:18]).[259] The prayer's near context (2 Chr 30:17–19) provides several other sacrifice-related terms or expressions, such as consecration (לֹא־הִתְקַדָּשׁוּ [they have not consecrated (v. 17)]), cleansing (לֹא הִטֶּהָרוּ [they did not cleanse (v. 18)]; וְלֹא כְּטָהֳרַת הַקֹּדֶשׁ [not according to purification of the sanctuary (v. 19)]), and atonement (יְהוָה הַטּוֹב יְכַפֵּר בְּעַד [the good Yhwh may atone for them (v. 18)]).

Second, the Chronicler's characterization of King Hezekiah in the prayer and its context reveals the king's effort for successful worship (i.e., the reformation of Israel's religion, esp. the Passover). Hezekiah's prayer could exhibit the king's ardor for worship, since neither the northern people nor the Levites or priests ask for God's forgiveness (יְכַפֵּר [2 Chr 30:18]), but the king intercedes with God on behalf of the people (עֲלֵיהֶם) in dealing with the issue of uncleanness.[260]

Hezekiah narratives (chs. 29–31) collaborate with the prayer to characterize Hezekiah as the reformer of Israel's worship.[261] Hezekiah takes a principal role in the process of reformation. He diagnoses Israel's sin (מְעַלוּ [act unfaithfully (29:6)]) and initiates a cure by commanding (עַתָּה הִתְקַדְּשׁוּ וְקַדְּשׁוּ אֶת־בֵּית יְהוָה) [consecrate yourselves and the house of

---

258. For atonement, see some examples from the Scriptures: Lev 1:4; 4:20, 26, 31, 35; 5:6, 10, 13, 16, 18, 26; 6:23; 7:7; 8:15, 34. For consecration, see Lev 6:11, 20; 8:10, 11, 12, 15, 30; 16:19; 1 Chr 6:49; 15:14; 23:13. Concerning cleansing, see Lev 11:32; 12:7, 8; 13:6, 17, 23, 28, 34, 37, 58; 16:9, 30; Num 8:6, 7, 15, 21; 19:12, 19; 31:23, 24; 2 Chr 29:15, 16, 18; 34:3, 5, 8.

259. Hezekiah requests God's intervention "because there was neither sufficient number of priests who had consecrated themselves" (כִּי הַכֹּהֲנִים לֹא־הִתְקַדָּשׁוּ [2 Chr 30:3]) nor enough time (כִּי לֹא יָכְלוּ לַעֲשֹׂתוֹ בָּעֵת הַהִיא [they could not at that time—the second month (v. 3)]). Levites try to consecrate unpurified people (v. 17), but there are still many who remain who are not able to be cleansed.

260. For עֲלֵיהֶם, see Waltke and O'Connor, *Introduction to Biblical Hebrew*, §11.2.13c.

261. See Shaver, "Hezekiah is not the innovator but reformer" of Israel's religion (Shaver, *Torah and Chronicler's History Work*, 132).

the Lord (v. 5)]) and encouraging (בְּנַי עַתָּה אַל־תִּשָּׁלוּ [do not be neglected (v. 11)]; see 30:22) Levites to be consecrated.[262] Hezekiah also supervises (וַיָּבוֹאוּ פְנִימָה אֶל־חִזְקִיָּהוּ הַמֶּלֶךְ וַיֹּאמְרוּ [they went to King Hezekiah and reported (29:19)]) the Levites to clean the altar of burnt offering and the temple (v. 18). When the altar and the temple are prepared for sacrifice, Hezekiah again proactively takes the lead in order for all the participants to offer successful worship of Yhwh.[263]

Worshiping Yhwh by Following Hezekiah's Path

Hezekiah's prayer and its context portray unique aspects of worship or worshipers: (1) public worship and (2) a sacrificial ritual. First, one of the prominent themes in Hezekiah's narrative is all-Israel (כָּל־יִשְׂרָאֵל; i.e., the unity of the community or togetherness).[264] Hezekiah's prayer also reflects this theme as the king tries to purify the northern people (2 Chr 30:18–19); thus, the Passover could be the worship of both northern and southern people. Second, Hezekiah's worship involves a sacrificial ritual. Hezekiah's worship is neither mystic nor unorganized; rather, it essentially maintains Israel's conventional cultic procedure.[265] As stated above, a part of the reason that Hezekiah offers the prayer is to successfully

---

262. Understanding the imperative as Hezekiah's will, wish, or desire. In this sense, the imperative is the king's encouragement. See Joüon, *A Grammar of Biblical Hebrew*, §1140.

263. The text is careful in this characterization, as it says of Hezekiah, וַיַּשְׁכֵּם יְחִזְקִיָּהוּ הַמֶּלֶךְ (the king woke up early [29:20]), לְכָל־יִשְׂרָאֵל אָמַר הַמֶּלֶךְ (the king commanded to all-Israel {v. 24]), וַיַּעֲמֵד אֶת־הַלְוִיִּם בֵּית יְהוָה (he [Hezekiah] stationed Levites in the temple [v. 25]), וַיֹּאמֶר חִזְקִיָּהוּ (Hezekiah commanded [v. 27]), וַיֹּאמֶר יְחִזְקִיָּהוּ הַמֶּלֶךְ וְהַשָּׂרִים (Hezekiah and officials commanded [v. 30]). See also 30:1, 5.

264. See "Celebrating the Passover Together (30:1–27; 35:17–19)" in Jonker, *Defining All-Israel*, 186–90.

Note that the theme of all-Israel is one of the significant motifs in the book of Chronicles. The Chronicler uses this phrase a total of twenty-two times in the book (1 Chr 11:1, 10; 12:39; 13:5; 14:8; 15:3; 18:14; 19:17; 21:5; 28:4, 8; 29:23, 25, 26; 2 Chr 9:30; 10:1, 16; 11:3; 18:16; 29:24; 30:1; 31:1). For further discussion concerning this particular motif, refer to Jonker's monograph above.

265. See Jonker, where he agrees with Japhet and says, "With regard to content, Japhet (1993, 1044–1045) remarks that Hezekiah's Passover is portrayed as 'an *ad hoc* undertaking' of which the main purpose was 'to provide a cultic-religious framework for the integration of the people of the North into the Jerusalem cult'" (Jonker, *Reflections of King Josiah*, 50–51).

accomplish the Passover. In sum, the Chronicler portrays the king as one who pursues public worship, that is a sacrificial ritual.

A related context of the prayer well corroborates Hezekiah's passion for united worship and a sacrificial ritual. For instance, in Hezekiah's preparation of the Passover, the king sends out a letter to all-Israel (30:5–12).[266] In Hezekiah's words of invitation, the king says, בְּנֵי יִשְׂרָאֵל שׁוּבוּ אֶל־יְהוָה אֱלֹהֵי אַבְרָהָם יִצְחָק וְיִשְׂרָאֵל (sons of Israel, return to the Lord God of Abraham, Isaac, and Israel [v. 6]). This particular designation for Yhwh in Chronicles occurs only here and in David's prayer (1 Chr 29:18) and may show the king's embracing heart toward the northern people by the recollection of their ancestral root, which Judah and Israel share.[267] Therefore, the text is dedicated to showing Hezekiah's desire and prudence in worshiping Yhwh with people from both northern and southern areas.[268]

Regarding a sacrificial ritual, the Chronicler repeatedly points out the proper manner of Israel's worship (i.e., cult) throughout chapters 29–31. For instance, the text describes the king's observance of the particular roles of Levites and priests (29:12–19). It also shows that the preparation procedure reflects what the law indicates (30:22–24; see 35:1; Lev 4:26;

---

266. The text reports this incident with the expression מִבְּאֵר־שֶׁבַע וְעַד־דָּן (from Beersheba to Dan [v. 5]), which idiomatically refers to the entire territory of both the northern and southern areas of Israel. See also 1 Sam 3:20; 2 Sam 3:10; 17:11; 24:2, 15; 1 Kgs 5:5 (Eng. 4:25); 1 Chr 21:2. Chronicles also specifically notes the recipients of the king's message with names of tribes such as Ephraim, Manasseh, Zebulun (30:10), Asher (v. 11), and Issachar (v. 18).

267. Jonker's observation is incorrect, since this particular designation occurs in 1 Chr 29:18 as well (יְהוָה אֱלֹהֵי אַבְרָהָם יִצְחָק וְיִשְׂרָאֵל). However, his understanding of Hezekiah's embracing of both southern and northern people is still meaningful for this book: "This designation [the Lord God of Abraham, Isaac, and Israel] for Yahweh occurs only here in Chronicles, and the Chronicler hereby not only relates Hezekiah's Passover to the ancestral era before the existence of the monarchy, but also includes both southern and northern tradition" (Jonker, *Defining All-Israel*, 187).

268. Concerning this theme of united worship, the Chronicler's usage of the expression כָּל־הַקָּהָל (all-congregation) should receive attention as well (2 Chr 30:2, 4, 23; see 1 Chr 29:10, 20; 23:3). The Chronicler confirms the nationwide response to Hezekiah's invitation of all-Israel in 30:13. He writes קָהָל לָרֹב מְאֹד (a very great congregation), a particular phrase that alludes to קָהָל גָּדוֹל מְאֹד (a very great congregation) in 2 Chr 7:8. The two expressions essentially share the same sense; so, the text is trying to recall the audience of Solomon's worship among all-Israel (וְכֹל בְּנֵי יִשְׂרָאֵל [all sons of Israel (2 Chr 7:3)]). Hee-Hak Lee's analysis on 30:23–25 well explains how the literary structure reflects the theme of all-congregation (i.e., all-Israel). The passage shows that Hezekiah's hope of the united worship is successful even at the second celebration (2 Chr 30:23–25). The Chronicler provides a meaningful report in 30:25 regarding the groups that belong to this congregation. See H. Lee, "Studies on the Meanings," 17–19.

8:15). During Hezekiah's worship, following the rules of the law and offering a proper form of sacrifice is still taken seriously (2 Chr 30:15–16, 24).[269] The text further comments on the necessity of keeping the law in Israel's worship in a direct note (כִּי לֹא לָרֹב עָשׂוּ כַּכָּתוּב [for they had not kept in large numbers what is written (30:5)]; כְּמִשְׁפָּטָם כְּתוֹרַת מֹשֶׁה [according to the law of Moses (v. 16)]; בְּלֹא כַכָּתוּב [contrary to what was written (v. 18)]). Overall, the post-exilic community witnesses that their forefathers are to keep the law in their reformation and their offering of sacrifices.

Hezekiah, the Supplicant

The Chronicler's portrayal of King Hezekiah can motivate the post-exilic community to become active supplicants. The most effective impetus of this identity formation would rise from where the text writes God's answer to Hezekiah's prayer (30:20; i.e., effectiveness of prayer). The Chronicler does not stop at stating that God simply responds to the prayer; instead, he further reports that God actually heals the people (וַיִּרְפָּא אֶת־הָעָם [v. 20]). This additional information shows that God is in action when a supplicant prays (e.g., 1 Chr 4:9–10; 2 Chr 14:12; 20:22–23; 32:24; 33:13). In Chronicles, the particular verb "to heal" occurs only in 2 Chronicles 7:14 and 30:20, especially in the context of a direct communication (e.g., prayer or dream) with Yhwh. God, as the healer, promises to answer the supplicant's prayer in Solomon's dream (2 Chr 7:14). One may argue that God would heal only the land, not the people, based on God's particular promise to Solomon (v. 14). However, even though such could be the case, the portrayed image of God as the healer in response to the supplicant's prayer does not change between the two passages (i.e., 2 Chr 7:14; 30:20). Therefore, this verb (to heal) in 2 Chronicles 30:20 can still remind readers of God's promise to Solomon (2 Chr 7:14).

Effectiveness of Prayer in an Abnormal Circumstance

The distinctiveness of Hezekiah's prayer lies in the situation that Hezekiah and his people encounter. The stories of Hezekiah's reformation and renewal of ceremony (i.e., chs. 29–31) repeatedly emphasize people's

---

269. See also 2 Chr 31:4, where Hezekiah orders the people of Israel to serve the priests and Levites according to the law of the Yhwh (בְּתוֹרַת יְהוָה); see 1 Chr 28:7–8; 29:19; 2 Chr 33:8.

obligation to the law or the regulations of sacrifice; but, in Hezekiah's prayer, the king seems to violate what he is supposed to keep. The king clearly notices that there are participants who have not cleansed themselves (וְלֹא כְּטָהֳרַת הַקֹּדֶשׁ [not according to purification of sanctuary (30:19)]), but he does not attempt to purify them according to the law. Instead, he prays for their atonement (יְכַפֵּר [v. 18]), and, surprisingly, God answers his prayer (v. 20).

Hezekiah's prayer does not mean that the prayer has more power to transform a certain circumstance or is a better way of communicating with God than the law. Chronicles does not present either element as superior to the other. Second Chronicles 31:21 is part of the concluding verses (vv. 20–21) of chapters 29–31 (i.e., Hezekiah's reformation and ceremony); it summarizes Chronicles' theological principle in what proper service appears to be.[270] When comparing this passage to Hezekiah's prayer, the prayer seems to give the impression that even though people fail to keep the law, if supplicants seek Yhwh, then they will receive God's answer. However, the literary structure of 31:21 detailed below conveys something different. At a glance, this verse shares the same root of the verb לִדְרֹשׁ (to seek [31:21]) with a word from Hezekiah's prayer (לִדְרוֹשׁ [30:19]), and it seems to signify the act of seeking Yhwh by adding בְּכָל־לְבָבוֹ (with all his heart). But one should not miss what this passage emphasizes; there should be a balance among elements in what is וַיַּעַשׂ הַטּוֹב וְהַיָּשָׁר וְהָאֱמֶת לִפְנֵי יְהוָה אֱלֹהָיו (good, righteous, and faithful before God [31:20]).[271]

וּבְכָל־מַעֲשֶׂה[a]
אֲשֶׁר־הֵחֵל
בַּעֲבוֹדַת בֵּית־הָאֱלֹהִים[b]
וּבַתּוֹרָה[c]
וּבַמִּצְוָה[d]
לִדְרֹשׁ לֵאלֹהָיו בְּכָל־לְבָבוֹ עָשָׂה[e]
וְהִצְלִיחַ[f]

270. Williamson, *First and Second Chronicles*, 377–78.

271. Hezekiah's reformation of Israel's religion and renewal of ceremony is certainly good, righteous, and faithful work before God. Verses 20–21 conclude the narratives of chs. 29–31. Verse 20 begins וַיַּעַשׂ כָּזֹאת יְחִזְקִיָּהוּ (thus, Hezekiah did all this). The demonstrative pronoun (this) refers to what Hezekiah has done throughout the reformation and the ceremony. The main verb (וַיַּעַשׂ) of this pronoun appears again in the second half of this verse (וַיַּעַשׂ [v. 20b]). Verse 21 begins with מַעֲשֶׂה (a noun form of the verb וַיַּעַשׂ). In other words, the particular work or deed (מַעֲשֶׂה) in v. 21 probably refers to Hezekiah's reformation and renewal of ceremony.

Hezekiah as a model figure shows that in doing God's work (a), the person is required not only to seek God (e) but also to serve in the temple (b), with the law (c) and the commandment (d), so that the person could prosper (f). The Chronicler locates the list of items (i.e., b, c, d) in parallel form in order to emphasize the necessity of them.[272]

Thus, one should not understand the relationship between the prayer and the law to reflect a competing mode. Hezekiah's prayer shows the Chronicler's rhetorical strategy, indicating the effectiveness of the prayer to the post-exilic community in an abnormal circumstance. Ben Zvi's observation on the theological complexity in Chronicles provides a clue for resolving the tension between the effectiveness of the prayer and the obligation to the law and ordinances.[273] He points out that in Chronicles, there can be an exception to so-called dogmatic theology (e.g., retribution theology) for a rhetorical purpose.[274] In other words, each account can emphasize a certain theological teaching. This type of presentation does not contradict Chronicles' general presentation of a certain teaching, since the audience can find a balance between different emphases throughout their interaction with the book.[275] As mentioned above, in Hezekiah's prayer and the related texts (i.e., chs. 29–31), the

---

272. Bullinger, *Figures of Speech*, 351.

273. Ben Zvi's particular interest lies in so-called retribution theology. He observes that in Chronicles this retribution theology does not operate as a universal rule (Ben Zvi, "Sense of Proportion").

274. Ben Zvi says, "The fact that accounts illustrating an individually assessed correspondence between actions and deeds vastly outnumber those standing in contradiction or tension with this principle does *not* necessarily point to the Chronicler's adherence to a certain 'dogmatic' theology nor should it lead to a scholarly construction of a list of 'inconsistencies.' This situation is better explained in terms of the historical and rhetorical circumstances of the Chronicler. One may assume that there was much more need to persuade the audience of the existence of a certain coherence of actions and effects rather than to demonstrate that it may fail" (Ben Zvi, "Sense of Proportion," 46; italics in original).

275. Ben Zvi continues: "In sum, whereas the persuasive social function of the individual accounts in Chronicles may explain their *seemingly* unequivocal, universal claims, the cumulative effect of the implications or implicatures of the different accounts provided the community with an interpretative and qualifying key to understand their true message. The community may have read and learned separate accounts and may have abstracted from them theological or ideological lessons, but eventually the community read and learned the entire book, and lessons were integrated and reinterpreted according to the emerging pattern, a pattern in which a sense of proportion and balance was much at the forefront" (Ben Zvi, "Sense of Proportion," 47; italics in original).

Chronicler does not undermine people's obligation to the law and ordinances; rather, in light of this emphasis, the effectiveness of prayer is further highlighted.

In sum, Hezekiah's prayer conveys the Chronicler's desire to teach the effectiveness of prayer to the post-exilic community in an abnormal circumstance. The people are still obligated to follow the law and ordinances in general, and Yhwh will still listen and respond to their prayers when they seek him with all their heart (2 Chr 30:19; 31:21; 33:13).

Hezekiah's Good Yhwh: God of the Fathers

Hezekiah's prayer portrays the king as a monotheistic believer. The Chronicler emphasizes the object of the prayer with several different references (הָאֱלֹהִים יְהוָה הַטּוֹב [Yhwh, who is good (30:18)]; אֱלֹהֵי אֲבוֹתָיו [God, Yhwh, God of his fathers (v. 19)]). The expression יְהוָה הַטּוֹב (Yhwh, who is good; appellation of God, Yhwh + definite article the + adjective good) occurs only here in the MT, except for 1 Chronicles 19:13. This combination may exhibit the Chronicler's particular emphasis on the good nature of God to the audience.[276] The phrase recalls the community's special relationship with God, that he is the one whom they worship and to whom belong (1 Chr 16:34; 2 Chr 5:13; 7:3; see Ezra 3:11; Pss 34:8; 100:5; 106:1; 107:1; 118:1; 118:29; 135:3; 136:1; Jer 33:11).[277]

The latter epithet אֱלֹהֵי אֲבוֹתָיו (God of the fathers; lit. God of his fathers) is not rare in Chronicles, as it appears twenty-seven times in Chronicles.[278] Scholars show no consensus on this particular epithet, so it is not easy to determine why the king mentions the ancestors in his prayer.[279] However, this phrase can still remind the audience of their

---

276. But, 1 Chr 19:13 says וַיהוָה הַטּוֹב בְּעֵינָיו יַעֲשֶׂה. It seems that many English translations (e.g., ESV, JPS, NAS, NIV, NKJ, NRS, TNK) follow what the LXX understands (καὶ κύριος τὸ ἀγαθὸν ἐν ὀφθαλμοῖς αὐτοῦ ποιήσει [and the Lord shall do what is good in his eyes]).

277. See also Pss 52:11; 54:8, where they say that God's name is good.

278. This epithet involves the reference of "God of your/their/his/our fathers"; see 1 Chr 5:25; 12:18; 29:18, 20; 2 Chr 7:22; 11:16; 13:12, 18; 14:3 (Eng. v. 4); 15:12; 19:4; 20:6, 33; 21:10; 24:18, 24; 28:6, 9, 25; 29:5; 30:7, 19, 22; 33:12; 34:32, 33; 36:15 (Japhet, *Ideology of the Book*, 11).

279. Japhet writes that the epithet "emphasizes the continuity of the relationship between the Lord and His people and may be seen as a transitional stage to the later usage, commonly found in the liturgy, 'our God and God of our father'" (Japhet, *Ideology of the Book*, 15). Von Rad rather sees that this expression is simply Chronicles'

special relationship to God. In Chronicles, when the epithet "God of his/our/their/your fathers" is given in a particular text, the images of God projected in that context appear in several ways. First, God is pictured as the object of worship or sacrifice. This case occurs in two ways: (1) a king or the people of Israel should properly serve God, but they fail to do it (1 Chr 5:25; 2 Chr 20:33; 24:18, 24 [see vv. 23–27]; 28:6, 9, 25; 30:7; 36:15); and (2) a king or the people of Israel successfully worships, serves God, or offers a proper sacrifice, which leads to a positive result (2 Chr 11:16; 13:11–12; 15:12; 29:5; 30:19, 22; 33:12). Second, God is portrayed as the direct object of praise by Israel (1 Chr 29:20). Third, God is the object of Israel's prayer (2 Chr 13:18; see v. 14). Fourth, God is Israel's judge (1 Chr 12:17–18; 2 Chr 19:4 [see v. 7]). Fifth, God is the one who makes the covenant with Israel (2 Chr 21:10 [see vv. 7–10]; 34:32–33; see Exod 3:6; Deut 1:31; 8:5; 14:1–2; 32:6; Isa 1:2; Hos 11:1; Ps 2:7). Sixth, God is the one who gives the law or reminds his people of it, and the king and people of Israel are required to keep it (1 Chr 29:18; 2 Chr 7:22; 14:4). Seventh, God is the ruler of the kingdom of nations (2 Chr 20:6) from the perspective of Israel's king (i.e., Jehoshaphat). Throughout the Chronicler's historiography, the epithet "God of the fathers" appears in different contexts, yet the portrayed God is always special, who relates to his people in various ways.

Hope of a United Kingdom

Hezekiah's prayer portrays Hezekiah as an ideal king; thus, it is able to motivate the post-exilic community to hope for a Davidic king and his kingdom. In doing so, they may become citizens of the Davidic kingdom.[280]

---

dependence on Deuteronomy (von Rad, *Geschichtsbild des chronistischen Werkes*, 7). Cudworth further investigates this expression and reveals that this epithet conveys a specific referent. The epithet can function to remind Yhwh of his promise to Israel's ancestors. In Hezekiah's case, Cudworth tries to compare and contrast King Ahaz and King Hezekiah. Ahaz's idolatry and forsaking of the God of the fathers (2 Chr 28:6, 9) weaken his position in the land as he encounters a series of threats (i.e., Aram, Israel, Edom, Philistia, and Assyria); but Hezekiah's reformation and calling of on the God of their fathers brings about a positive result. Hezekiah is able to unite people and worship the Lord in the land (Cudworth, "God of the Fathers"). Hahn thinks that the theme of God of the fathers refers to divine election in connection with Abraham. His analysis fn this epithet seems to loosely connect to the particular context of Chronicles (Hahn, *Kingdom of God*, 27).

280. Concerning Hezekiah as an ideal king, scholars have identified the king as the

In the prayer, the king is active in resolving the issue of uncleanness among the people (לֹא הִטֶּהָרוּ [they had not purified themselves (2 Chr 30:18)]). The prayer exhibits the king's willingness and enthusiasm for all-Israel's successful worship by embracing the people of Israel (i.e., Ephraim, Manasseh, Issachar, and Zebulun [v. 18]). Hezekiah's call for all-Israel to worship and the people's response[281] to the king's summons recall Israel's ideal kings, David and Solomon. Similar to Hezekiah, David

second David and/or Solomon. For those who see Hezekiah as the second David, see DeVries, "Moses and David"; Mosis, *Untersuchungen*, 189; Moriarty, "Chronicler's Account," 401. For those who insist on Hezekiah as the second Solomon, see Williamson, *Israel in Books of Chronicles*, 119–25; Edelman, "Hezekiah's Alleged Cultic Centralization," 399; Hill, *First and Second Chronicles*, 579. Some scholars believe that Hezekiah is both the second David and Solomon. See Johnstone, *First and Second Chronicles*, 2:188; Graham, "Setting the Heart to Seek God," in McKenzie et al., *Worship and the Hebrew Bible*, 131; Throntveit, "Relationship of Hezekiah to David and Solomon," in Knoppers et al., *Chronicler as Theologian*, 103–21.

Throntveit summarizes the reasons for Hezekiah being seen as the second David: Hezekiah's righteousness according to David (2 Chr 29:2) and Hezekiah's deliverance Jerusalem from Sennacherib (2 Chr 32:1–23) as compared to David's deliverance of Israel from Philistines (1 Chr 14). Throntveit also compares the matters of the storerooms between Hezekiah and David (1 Chr 9:6; 26:22; 28:12; 2 Chr 31:11–14). People show one heart (לב אחד [1 Chr 12.29 (Eng. v. 38); 2 Chr 30:12]) toward their kings. The text refers to the God of Abraham, Isaac, and Israel (1 Chr 29:18; 2 Chr 30:6); and there are encouragement formulae in 1 Chr 22:13; 2 Chr 32:7 (Throntveit, "Relationship of Hezekiah to David and Solomon," in Knoppers et al., *Chronicler as Theologian*, 108–13).

Concerning the connection between Hezekiah and Solomon, see Graham, who provides seven possible connections. First, Hezekiah brought great joy to Jerusalem, which had not been observed since the days of Solomon (2 Chr 30:26). Second, both Solomon and Hezekiah summoned all-Israel to the ceremony, and the two festivals lasted for two weeks. Third, Hezekiah's words of promises concerning divine mercy and salvation (2 Chr 30:6–9) resonated with Solomon's prayer at the temple (2 Chr 6:24–25; see vv. 36–39) and God's affirmation (7:12b–15). Fourth, both kings were concerned for foreigners (2 Chr 6:32–33; 30:24). Fifth, both kings offered intercessory prayers (2 Chr 6; 30:18–19). Sixth, there was great joy in both ceremonies (2 Chr 5:13; 7:6, 10; 30:21–23, 26). Seventh, in both ceremonies, a great number of sacrifices and provisions were made (2 Chr 5:6; 7:1, 4–5; 30:15–16, 22, 24) (Graham, "Setting the Heart to Seek God," in McKenzie et al., *Worship and the Hebrew Bible*, 132–33).

Japhet disagrees with identifying Hezekiah as a second David or Solomon. Hezekiah's story is not designed to demonstrate a certain type, whether or not he resembles another figure. Japhet argues instead that Hezekiah should be understood according to "the lively particulars of his person, deeds and historical circumstances" (Japhet, *First and Second Chronicles*, 998).

281. Although some of the northern people did not respond amiably to Hezekiah's invitation to the Passover (2 Chr 30:10), other people from the north humbled themselves (נִכְנְעוּ [v. 11]).

and Solomon had a passion for successful worship and ruled over all-Israel (1 Chr 11:1–3; 28:4–5; 29:22). David receives the spotlight as the foremost figure in implementing and operating Israel's cult (1 Chr 13–16; 23–27), and Solomon also has significant status as being the temple builder (2 Chr 1–7) among Israel's kings.[282]

King Hezekiah's calling of the northern tribes (2 Chr 30:5–9) and his embracing of them in the prayer (vv. 18–19) could imply that Hezekiah's authority extends to the northern territory or people (2 Chr 31:1, 6).[283] In Chronicles, the concept of all-Israel connotes a united group of tribes from both the north and the south.[284] This phrase frequently occurs during the reigns of David and Solomon; in the period of the monarchy's division, the Chronicler uses this expression only three times.[285] In this regard, Hezekiah is the only king who successfully summons the people of Israel and Judah after David and Solomon. In sum, the Chronicler's characterization of Hezekiah as an ideal king in the prayer could motivate the post-exilic community to hope for successful worship again under a Davidic king's reign.

Conclusion

Hezekiah's prayer reveals several roles or characteristics of Israel's identity. The text portrays King Hezekiah as one who is eager to worship (i.e., the Passover) with all-Israel. In addition, Hezekiah's prayer exhibits that God listens and responds to a supplicant's prayer, even when a supplicant

---

282. For David as the cult founder, see DeVries, "Moses and David." Williamson notes that the climax of Chronicles' history is Solomon's temple dedication (Williamson, "Temple in the Books," 15). See also Braun, "Message of Chronicles."

As the second David and/or Solomon, Hezekiah reestablishes Israel's religion and refocuses on the temple worship. These high similarities between Hezekiah and the idealized kings can confer credibility to Hezekiah as a model figure, a sincere worshiper. See Duke, *Persuasive Appeal*, 54, 66; Throntveit, "Idealization of," in Handy, *Age of Solomon*, 411–27; Pratt, *First and Second Chronicles*, 281–83; McConville, "First Chronicles 28:9"; Jones, *First and Second Chronicles*, 48.

283. See וַיְנַתְּצוּ אֶת־הַבָּמוֹת וְאֶת־הַמִּזְבְּחֹת מִכָּל־יְהוּדָה וּבִנְיָמִן וּבְאֶפְרַיִם וּמְנַשֶּׁה (they destroyed the high places and the altars throughout all Judah, Benjamin, and in Ephraim and Manasseh [2 Chr 30:1]).

284. Thompson, *First, Second Chronicles*, 34.

285. During David and Solomon's reign: 1 Chr 11:1, 10; 12:39; 13:5; 14:8; 15:3; 18:14; 19:17; 21:5; 28:4, 8; 29:23, 25, 26; 2 Chr 9:30. In the times of Israel's division before Hezekiah's reign: 2 Chr 10:1, 16; 11:3; 18:16.

prays in an abnormal situation (e.g., violation of a proper/required procedure). Also, Hezekiah's prayer reveals the king's perception of God, who is good and special to Israel, God of the fathers. Lastly, the prayer and its context characterize Hezekiah as an ideal king, the second David/Solomon, who successfully embraces both northern and southern tribes. Therefore, the text can persuade the post-exilic community to hope to see all-Israel gather together and offer sacrifices and prayers to their good God, the God of their fathers, under the reign of a Davidic king.

— *Chapter Four* —

Tracing Israelite Identity in Its Sociohistorical Context

in the Post-Exilic Biblical Literature

Introduction

THIS CHAPTER TRACES THE roles and characteristics portrayed in the recorded prayers in chapter 3 within the sociohistorical context of the post-exilic community. Chapter 3 has revealed that Chronicles desires the members of the post-exilic community to be a worshiping, praying, and monotheistic believing community that consists of Davidic citizens. Also, each prayer portrays aspects of roles or characteristics in its given context. Yet, a question remains as to how the identity (i.e., roles or characteristics) portrayed in Chronicles (i.e., literary historical context; in this regard, Israel's pre-exilic history) relates to the post-exilic community in its sociohistorical setting. Therefore, chapter 4 broadens its scope of research beyond the literary world of Chronicles and examines the implications of the roles and characteristics in the sociohistorical situation of the post-exilic community during the Persian era.[1]

Tracing Israelite identity in the Achaemenid imperial context (circa 550–330 BCE) can reveal the sociohistorical reality of the Yehud community, since it suggests the community's surrounding dynamics. It is

---

1. In other words, Chronicles does not directly speak about the sociohistorical reality of the post-exilic community, since Chronicles is essentially the record of Israel's pre-exilic history. Thus one needs to ask: why did the Chronicler portray certain roles or characteristics for the post-exilic community members?

probable that without the empire's colony-friendly stance, the identity formation process in the Yehud community would be intermittent and dull. Therefore, two tasks are necessary. First, it is essential to investigate any possible external influences upon the members of community. In this regard, the Achaemenid imperial policies and ideology receive attention. Second, as the post-exilic community relates to the Persian world (i.e., external influences), one could conjecture that there were internal voices (i.e., biblical literature) reacting against the imperial policies or ideology; thus, this presumption requires that one listen to the post-exilic community's inner voice.[2] In other words, this particular point relates to revealing the implication of the portrayed identity (i.e., roles or characteristics) in Chronicles in the post-exilic community's sociohistorical setting. For instance, two questions would be as follows: why does the Chronicler vocalize that community members should become worshipers, supplicants, or monotheistic believers who maintain Davidic citizenship in the Persian context? What is the implication of having particular aspects of suggested roles or characteristics?

The Post-Exilic Biblical Literature and Its Testimony

After a brief presentation of the Achaemenid imperial policies and ideology and the empire's relation to roles or characteristics portrayed in Chronicles, this book will focus on the internal responses of the post-exilic community to the imperial policies. Specifically, this book undertakes this task based on literary evidence (e.g., Ezra-Nehemiah, Chronicles).[3]

---

2. Concerning the post-exilic social, religious, cultural, political, and historical realities, scholars have investigated both the internal and external causes with different emphases. For instance, Wellhausen focuses on the internal dynamics. He is particularly interested in Israel's institutionalized religion (Wellhausen, *Prolegomena*; Knight, "Wellhausen and the Interpretation," 26). However, Martin Noth emphasizes the external factor, particularly the Persian policy (Noth, *History of Israel*, 304–18).

3. Non-literary evidence, such as archaeological artifacts or inscriptions, may provide a fragment for reconstructing the sociohistorical reality of the Yehud community. Yet they do not provide a conclusive portrait of the community but only assist in reconstructing the sociohistorical reality of the society. For instance, Ziony Zevit and Israel Finkelstein have argued against each other concerning the exile returnees and their settlement in the land. Zevit tends to focus on the literary evidence, but Finkenstein insists on the reliability of archeological records. See Zevit, "Is There an Archaeological Case"; Finkelstein, "Persian Period Jerusalem and Yehud." For the nature of archeological discipline, see Dever, *What Did Biblical Writers Know*, 53–95 (esp. 62–64).

The literary evidence could embrace various issues in the lives of the people, represent their behavior patterns, and portray the thoughts and interrelationships among the people in the community;[4] thus, literature can function to mirror and testify about social and historical realities. In this regard, literature in the Second Temple period under the Persian Empire could reveal the sociohistorical reality of the Yehud community.[5]

In fact, scholars have delved into various literatures either written (e.g., Ezra-Nehemiah, Chronicles) or authorized (e.g., Torah) during the Persian period in order to understand the lives of Yehud community members.[6] Likewise, this book understands that the literary evidence and the scholarly discussion concerning it could provide reliable information to reconstruct the sociohistorical reality of the lives of Yehud community members.

This book will primarily, but not exclusively, examine various post-exilic biblical texts.[7] One may argue that the biblical literature does not project an objective/actual historical situation of the community, since the texts reflect the theological/ideological perspectives of the biblical authors. Such an argument does not, however, preclude biblical literature (esp. Ezra-Nehemiah, Chronicles) from having historical value; in fact, biblical literature could be useful, since it may underscore particular sociohistorical,cultural, and religious concerns within the community.[8]

---

4. Albrecht, "Relationship of Literature," 426–27; Baumbach et al., *Literature and Values*, 6.

5. Jon L. Berquist recognizes the significant role of the literature: "Overtime, I developed a conviction: literature and history are both human productions, and the people who lived historical life in ancient Israel were the same ones who wrote the first versions of today's biblical texts. Of course, it is not that easy—often an elite minority produced the texts, and so a text reflects the social relationships of its origins" (Berquist, *Judaism in Persia's Shadow*, iv). Hamilton also points out, "Sources related to Jewish identity during the Achaemenid period are mostly literary" (Hamilton, "Who Was a Jew," 103).

6. Ramírez Kidd, *Alterity and Identity*; Watts, *Persia and Torah*; K. Lee, *Authority and Authorization*; Knoppers and Levinson, *Pentateuch as Torah*; Jonker, *Historiography and Identity*; Jonker, *Defining All-Israel*; Becking, *Ezra, Nehemiah, and Construction*; Tiemeyer, *Ezra-Nehemiah*; Durant, *Ezra Pound*; Beyerle, *Book of Daniel*.

7. E.g., Ezra, Nehemiah, and other post-exilic psalms and prophetic literature.
Note that it is beyond this book's task to investigate the extensive and enumerated research on the many literary sources. Thus this section will focus instead on depicting an overall picture of the post-exilic community.

8. Bautch, "Function of Covenant," in Boda and Redditt, *Unity and Disunity*, 9; Jonker, "Chronicles in an (Un)changing World," 275.

Thus, from the standpoint of this book's interest in theological and ideological presentation of Chronicles concerning identity formation within the Yehud community, various theological or ideological reports of the biblical texts may reflect a vector or aspect of identity formation within the community. Ultimately, these reports could provide an opportunity for this book to discern the similarities and differences between aspects of roles or characteristics as portrayed in Chronicles and other biblical literature.

However, one should notice that the result of this research may reflect only a fraction of the lives of the Yehud community members. Two limitations produce uncertainty vis-à-vis the reconstruction of the sociohistorical portrait. First, although the period is not completely blank, essentially, there is no sufficient source for investigating the sociohistorical realities during the Persian period. In addition, the scholarly emphasis on the Persian period was relatively less compared to the emphasis on the pre-monarchy or pre-exilic periods; because of these reasons, the Persian period has been termed the dark age or silver age at best.[9] Second, the biblical literature is meaningful material from the standpoint that it speaks for the inner voice of the community, but may not represent the entire concern or belief system of the various groups in the community.[10] Therefore, these limitations obstruct one from making a conclusive statement as to whether actual identity formation took place in every member of the Yehud community in accordance with the Chronicler's desire.

Overall, based on the methodological considerations presented above, chapter 4 endeavors to detect traces of identity formation in the Yehud community specifically—in line with Chronicles' emphases—traces which related to the roles of supplicant, worshiper, and Davidic citizen and the characteristics of monotheistics believers. Even though the textual evidence may not provide certainty concerning the community's identity formation, the biblical literature and the related scholarly discussion will provide a fair amount of material to suggest, at the very least, what attempts took place among the members of the Yehud community.

---

9. Berquist, "Approaching Yehud," in Berquist, *Approaching Yehud*, 1.
For recent developments in Persian historiography, see Jonker's summarization and references in "Chronicles in an (Un)changing World," 269–74.

10. Since it is highly hypothetical to discern or pinpoint a particular literary text that officially represents and reflects the voice of the majority of community members, this second limitation is confined not only to the biblical literature.

Achaemenid Imperial Influence: Policy and Its Ideology (539–332 BCE)

When Cyrus of Persia conquered Babylon (539 BCE), the provinces in the Ancient Near East admitted that a new era had arrived.[11] The Persian Empire promulgated several new policies and its ideology, which permeated the lives of the colonized people under its power.[12] In general overview, the Persian Empire saw itself as one structured body which unites different nations,[13] and the newly promulgated policy reflected this empire's ideology and its relation to the nations under its supervision. Kyung-jin Min categorizes the policy according to eight imperial mechanisms: (1) migration and grouping, (2) commercialization, (3) militarization, (4) realization, (5) appointment of pro-Persian governors, (6) codification of law, (7) support for the construction of temples, and (8) rituals.[14] Although all these policy elements, essentially, were implemented among subordinate nations for the empire's self-benefit (e.g., taxation), some of these elements directly affected the process of the Yehud community's identity reconstruction after the exile.[15] In particular, migration and grouping, appointment of a pro-Persian governor, support for the construction of a temple, and allowance of the local religious

---

11. Grabbe, *Introduction to Second Temple Judaism*, 3.

12. The term ideology is not limited to ideology formed by the Persians. Jonker says, "Since the Persian Empire was a conglomerate of diverse ethnic and cultural groups, it is difficult to define some influence from this period as uniquely 'Persian'" (Jonker, "Chronicles in an [Un]changing World," 278). Thus, this term refers to ideology which affects the Yehud community under the Persian empire.

13. Wöhrle, "Abraham amidst the Nations," in Knoppers and Bautch, *Covenant in Persian Period*, 32.

14. For a detailed explanation on each policy, see Min, *Levitical Authorship*, 93–97. Here is a brief summary of each policy: (1) migration and grouping—moving populations to peripheries; deportees return to their lands; (2) commercialization—commercial activities among countries under the Persian oversight; (3) militarization—authorization of local troops for the fortification of their territory but obligated to serve the Persian power and defend the Persian imperial border; (4) realization—process of developing the rural area/country side to increase tribute sources; (5) appointment of pro-Persian governors—appointment of the Persian friendly leadership; (6) codification of law—allowing each colony's own legal tradition under the Persian supervision; (7) support for the construction of temples—approval of construction of the temples for taxation; (8) rituals—granting each community's rituals to impel positive attitude toward the Persian policy.

15. Jonker, "Chronicles in an (Un)changing World," 277.

rituals could be directly related to the Yehud community's identity formation from the perspective of this current research.

First, the Achaemenid empire approved deportees to return their homeland. The exile returnees comprised one of the major populations of the Yehud community (Ezra 1:5–11; 2:1–2; 5:14–16; 7:1—8:36; Neh 7:5–72), who were a part of the Chronicler's target audience and whom the Chronicler expected to actualize the desired roles and characteristics as portrayed in Chronicles. The demographic composition in the Yehud community was not simple, since it included various groups of people (i.e., returnees from the exile, remained inhabitants of Judah [e.g., Ezek 11:15], and foreigners [e.g., Neh 3:5; 5:17]).[16] Thus, this policy could provide an opportunity for the members of community to contemplate the true meaning of community membership (e.g., Ezra 9–10).[17] Specifically, the rebuilt temple was the major reason for the return of priestly and Levitical groups and other temple-related personnel, and Jerusalem maintained its status as a cultic center.[18] The Chronicler is highly interested in the status and roles of Levites in the community. In addition, in terms of shaping Israel's identity, he emphasizes the notion of all-Israel's worship (2 Chr 30:1–27).[19] Likewise, the people also could have a chance to ponder their membership from the perspective of all-Israel as God's people (כָּל־יִשְׂרָאֵל [Ezra 6:17; 8:35; Neh 13:26; Mal 3:22 (Eng. 4:4)]). In sum, as the returnees had come back to their home soil and revived their community, they were able to contemplate their united identity and role.

Second, the empire allowed its subject people to reestablish or maintain their religious institutions within the framework of the empire. This allowance does not mean that the subject people received full tolerance, since the people had to communicate with the empire under control of the bureaucracy or the imperial army; yet, the subordinate nations

---

16. For further discussion on demographic notes on the post-exilic Judah, see Weinberg, *Citizen–Temple Community*, 34–48. See also recent discussion on the archaeological analysis regarding returnees' settlement: Finkelstein, "Archaeology and List of Returnees"; Finkelstein, "Persian Period Jerusalem and Yehud"; Zevit, "Is There an Archaeological Case."

17. Berquist, "Constructions of Identity," 53–66. See also Hamilton, "Who Was a Jew."

18. Lipschitz, "Achaemenid Imperial Policy," in Lipschitz and Manfred, *Judah and Judeans in Persian Period*, 33.

19. Jonker's monograph is particularly dedicated to this subject. See Jonker, *Defining All-Israel*.

certainly had enough autonomy to entertain their customs.[20] Under these circumstances, the Yehud community received an opportunity to revive their religious roles as they reconstructed the temple (Ezra 3–6), fortified Jerusalem (Neh 3–4), and preserved and practiced the codified law (i.e., Mosaic law; see Ezra 3:2; Neh 8) and the rituals.[21]

These attempts to revive Israel's religious institutions closely relate to the current discussion of shaping Israel's identity (esp. worshipers, monotheistic believers, and supplicants) because Chronicles' portrayal of Israel's identity through prayers emphasizes petitioners' perspectives on God or their practice of Israel's cult. For instance, the Chronicler portrays that supplicants should pray, either individually or together, to the omnipotent and just God with faith in their difficult situation, and they should pray for God's forgiveness when they sin, since God listens and forgives the penitential prayers. In Israel's practice of worship and belief, the supplicants should perceive God as the unique and supreme divinity who deserves worshipers' offerings.[22]

Particularly, upon the rebuilding of the second temple, the Yehud community could raise a question regarding the reason or nature of the existence of the temple in relation to the Persian influence. The Chronicler

20. Bright, *History of Israel*, 362.

21. Stern's archaeological survey suggests that the areas that Jews inhabited might have had good momentum in reviving their religious identity. He observes that before the Babylonians destroyed the Judeans and other nations in Palestine (e.g., Geshur; the Phoenicians; the Samaritans; the late Philistines: Ashdod, Ashkelon, Gaza, and Ekron; the Ammonites; the Moabites; the Edomites), they maintained their own unique religious identity. The exact situation is difficult to reveal regarding each country's cult during the Babylonian period, since the Babylonians literally wiped out almost all of their enemies; thus, this period is known as a vacuum. When the Persian era came, archaeological evidence hints that many of the nations' unique religious characteristics became vague and exhibited a mixture of one another. However, this situation could be an exception for the Yehud community, since archaeologists failed to identify particular evidence that Jews had lost their own characteristics of religion in their region. This does not mean that Jews' religious purity or characteristics were identical to their pre-exilic status, but it still could suggest that Jews were in a better, or at least different, situation in terms of shaping their religious identity (i.e., roles or characteristics) (Stern, "Religious Revolution" in Lipschitz and Manfred, *Judah and Judeans in Persian Period*, 199–204).

22. I.e., praying in a difficult situation (1 Chr 4:9–10; 2 Chr 14:10 [Eng. 11]; 20:5–13); praying in faith (1 Chr 4:9–10; 17:16–27); praying for God's forgiveness (2 Chr 6:14–42); public prayer (2 Chr 20:5–13); God as omnipotent (2 Chr 14:10 [Eng. 11]); God of justice (2 Chr 20:5–13); God as unique for Israel and supreme divinity (1 Chr 4:9–10; 16:8–36; 17:16–27; 29:10–19; 2 Chr 6:14–42; 14:10 [Eng. 11]; 20:5–13; 30:18–19); God who deserves offerings (1 Chr 16:8–36; 29:10–19).

portrays the nature of the temple by reminding the audience of God's preeminence and uniqueness and emphasizes the role of the temple servants (i.e., the Levites) so that they would continue to serve their role as worshipers (i.e., singers and instrumentalists) in Israel's sacrificial rituals (1 Chr 16:8–36; 2 Chr 30:18–19). But, the implication of this Chronicler's portrayal of the temple needs to be revealed more deeply than on the sociohistorical level. Overall, as the Achaemenid empire allowed the subordinate nations to revive or maintain their own religious practices, this policy could provide an opportunity for the Yehud community to speculate on their identity, especially focusing on Israel's religion.

Third, the geopolitical reality that the Yehud community faced as a Persian colony was a critical element for defining Israelites' political identity, especially from the perspective of Davidic citizenship in Chronicles (1 Chr 17:16–27; 2 Chr 6:14–42; 30:18–19). Since they were a colony, it is a reasonable conjecture that there were both internal and external (i.e., imperial) influences within the community's development of their identity.

Regarding the external influence of the empire, it does not seem that there was a dramatic or harsh wave upon the community. Initially, the province where the Yehud community was located did not receive the empire's primary attention, since the empire's governmental, military, and economic concern centered on the Mediterranean coast. The Persians wanted to stabilize the coastal area and promoted trades through maritime means. The Achaemenids built their forts and administrative hubs, where their primary concern lay, and developed those areas as urban centers. The Achaemenid empire's interest in the hill country (e.g., the Yehud or Samaria province) was relatively less. This does not mean that the empire exclusively abandoned this province from its sight; Nehemiah's reports attest to the empire's more direct intervention (Neh 2:4–8) authorizing the fortification of Jerusalem in the middle of the fifth century.[23] But, essentially, the Achaemenid empire's political influence in

---

23. Scholars have shown different opinions regarding the Persian Empire's interest in the Yehud community and its surrounding province. For instance, it could be that the Persian Empire wanted to stabilize the area from various revolts (e.g., Egypt), it simply tried to induce the loyalty of its subordinate nations, or it attempted to expand its territory in the middle of the fifth century (Lipschitz, "Achaemenid Imperial Policy," in Lipschitz and Manfred, *Judah and the Judeans in the Persian Period*, 36–40).

the Yehud community seems relatively late or less than other provinces where the empire primarily gave its attention.[24]

Berquist points out that internal dynamics could be a driving factor for the Yehud community's understanding of their political identity. He says,

> It was possible for external causes to be completely determinative of Yehud's life. Yet, Yehud also was heir to traditions that shaped its character. Although Persia controlled Yehud, Yehud was still only a colony, with some degree of *political* self-determination, even if Persia limited its options severely. Yehud formed its own society, complete with internally determined goals, activities, norms, and values, as well as conflicts .... Yehud experienced its *political* establishment through the activity of Persia's imperial expansion and administration, but the community maintained and transformed itself through the dynamics of internal social formation.[25]

In fact, biblical texts exhibit internal voices (i.e., the people's political response or the authors' desire) in reaction to their colonized status under the Persian power. For instance, Chronicles emphasizes the actualization of the Davidic promises and kingdom (e.g., 1 Chr 17:1–27; 2 Chr 6:14–42). Nehemiah's public prayer (Neh 9:37–38) seems to show people's negative perspective against imperial monarchy.[26] In short, no matter how the people expressed their desire, it was natural for the members of the community to respond to their surrounding political situation. Overall, the geopolitical situation of the Persian Empire and the internal dynamics of the Yehud community could promote some degree of self-determination on the Yehud community's political identity and provided the community members an opportunity to contemplate the current and future shape of their community.

---

24. Nehemiah 13:16 hints that when Nehemiah arrived at Jerusalem, local authority had already been established (Edelman, "Tyrian Trade in Yehud under Artaxerxes I," in Lipschitz and Manfred, *Judah and Judeans in the Persian Period*, 207).

Lipschitz concludes, "In spite of attempts to repopulate the city, the poor archaeological remains in Jerusalem (at least in the narrow area of the city of David) show us that, even after the city wall had been rebuilt, the actual demographic and architectural situation in the city did not change dramatically. In fact, Jerusalem did not become a real urban center until the Hellenistic Period" (Lipschitz, "Achaemenid Imperial Policy," in Lipschitz and Manfred, *Judah and Judeans in Persian Period*, 40).

25. Berquist, *Judaism in Persia's Shadow*, 10; italics added.

26. Janzen, "Yahwistic Appropriation," 839.

However, one should not misunderstand the possession of self-determination as meaning that the Yehud community maintained a full and independent governing system outside the imperial power, since the Achaemenid empire governed its territory through a strategic administrative system. The empire selected authorities whose primary concern was establishing loyalty to the imperial government (i.e., pro-Persian governors),[27] and Persia controlled its territories through appointed governors. As long as appointees were cooperative and loyal to the central power, the empire tolerated local cultures, religion, and some level of decision-making processes within the local administrative agenda.[28] Biblical literature attests that local governors were involved in the important affairs of the Yehud community (see פֶּחָה [Ezra 5:14, 16; 6:7; Neh 5:14–17; 12:26; Hag 1:1, 14; 2:2, 21]). It seems that they sometimes communicated even with the highest authority at the center of the imperial power to deal with local administrative matters (e.g., Ezra 5:13–17; Neh 2:1–8).

Thus, one should not dismiss the pro-Persian governor policy in the imperial context vis-à-vis the Chronicler's desire to actualize the role of Davidic citizenship in the Yehud community. Did he really hope for a tangible kingdom? This type of question requires an investigation of the nature of the Chronicler's desire regarding the Davidic kingdom. For even if the Yehud community had a certain level of self-determination, such partial autonomy does not suggest that it might have been easy for them to reestablish a monarchy similar to their pre-exilic status. The Persians were harsh against rebellions within their territories and actively stopped them (e.g., Egypt, Babylon). In quelling rebellions, the Persians particularly destroyed the symbols of the target groups (e.g., their temple). Cataldo writes,

---

27. Cataldo, *Theocratic Yehud*, 33–66.
    In this regard, scholars disagree as to whether the Yehud community enjoyed their internal autonomy or not. For instance, Briant believes that there was much autonomy in the Yehud community, whereas Fried insists the opposite—that there were not really any means to run their own governing system (e.g., "no assemblies or lay bodies to advise the governor or Sanhedrins") (Briant, *From Cyrus to Alexander,* 487–88; Fried, *Priest and Great King,* 233).

28. Cataldo understands the definition of a self-governing system as follows: "If by 'self-governing' one means local bodies that wholly controlled their provinces, then the answer seems to be negative. If one intends instead to show that the imperial government allowed local individuals to sit in the position of provincial government, as well as district and sub/half-district governments, then one might answer in the affirmative" (Cataldo, *Theocratic Yehud,* 45).

While temples appear to have been permitted as symbols of religious and social identity, the Persian authorities monitored them. The destruction of temples in response to rebellions suggests that the imperial government only permitted local cults as long as the province remained loyal.[29]

This given situation therefore suggests that the reestablishment of the Davidic kingdom was not a subject or idea that could be casually circulated among the members of the Yehud community. The Chronicler's hope concerning Davidic citizenship should be understood in light of the Persian administrative strategy toward its subordinated provinces.

Tracing Israelite Identity in Its Sociohistorical Context

Monotheistic Believing Community

The reality that the post-exilic community had lost their monarchy and was a small province under the Persian Empire suggests that there was no longer a center around which the community members could unify themselves. Accordingly, the Yehud community's religion received increased attention and gained higher importance as the center for unifying the community members.[30] In line with this situation, Chronicles persuades the post-exilic community to gather around and be devoted to Israel's religious institutions (e.g., the temple and priesthood) so that those institutions would eventually reveal Yhwh's distinctiveness (e.g., 1 Chr 22:5).[31]

From the perspective of a monotheistic believing community, then, Yhwh's distinctiveness can be revealed through the people's perception of their God; hence, the post-exilic community needed to correctly perceive their deity.[32] As the community experienced the tumultuous period (i.e., the exile), the problems the people faced had included not only

---

29. Cataldo, *Theocratic Yehud*, 36.

30. Berquist, *Judaism in Persia's Shadow*, 147.
For a summary of archaeological observations regarding the Yehud community's religious practices, see Lynch, *Monotheism and Institutions*, 54–56.
In this regard, Weinberg insists that the Yehud community developed a theocratic-like structure or a theocratic state for its governing system (Weinberg, *Citizen-Temple Community*, 407).

31. Lynch, *Monotheism and Institutions*, 262.

32. Hoffman, "Concept of 'Other Gods,'" in Hoffman et al., *Politics and Theopolitics*, 74–75.

religious matters but also social and economic issues. The community was experiencing dynamic changes throughout all aspects of their lives. In this circumstance, foreign nations specifically questioned the existence of their God, Yhwh, and mocked God's divinity (Pss 79:10; 115:2); thus, the community needed to respond to the question concerning Yhwh's dignity.[33]

However, the challenge that the Yehud community faced was not simple, since the people were continually influenced by Persian ideology. There was an influx of the Persians into the community, and this physical contact could have brought continual cultural-religious impact upon the community.[34] Particularly, this influence could have been a potential threat to Yahwistic believers, since there was a certain level of theological affinity between religions of the Yahwistic believers and the Persians.[35] For instance, history as a deity's field to accomplish the divine will is similar in the biblical and Persian views.[36] Also, for Zoroastrianism, purity laws took a significant position in the Persians' religious practices.[37] Similarly, the purification of the community became a critical matter for maintaining their

---

33. Collins, "Cognitive Dissonance and Eschatological Violence," in MacDonald and Brown, *Monotheism in Late Prophetic*, 203.

34. Various pieces of archaeological evidence (e.g., dog burials at Ashkelon, Achaemenid style of names in papyri, Achaemenid style of a vase and a bronze throne leg, Samarian coins) support the notion that the Persians possibly inhabited the Palestine area throughout the Persian period (Silverman, *Persepolis and Jerusalem*, 86–88, 90). According to Knoppers, the Persians' inhabitation of Yehud is not conclusive, but, as he points out, the interaction between Samaria and the Yehud community was in progress; thus there was an inflow of the Persians and their ideology into Yehud (Knoppers, "Revisiting the Samarian Questions," in Lipschitz and Manfred, *Judah and Judeans in Persian Period*, 278–79). Janzen insists that the Persians resided in the province of Yehud for trade with Greek and other areas, based on discoveries of Attic pottery, Greek coins, Rhodian glass vessels, etc. (Janzen, *Witch-Hunts, Purity*, 142).

35. Silverman indicates, "If there were no similarities or potentials for rapprochement, interaction could have remained solely superficial or only have occurred in negative ways. What is more important, there are several categories of theological and sociological affinities between the Judaeans and the Persians which increase the likelihood that Persian ideas could be seen in a favorable light or viewed as latent within Judaism itself" (Silverman, *Persepolis and Jerusalem*, 92).

36. The history of Israel and Judah demonstrates that God has revealed his power by punishing his people (i.e., exile) and foreign nations (e.g., Jer 46–51) and by remembering his people (i.e., returning to the land). Similarly, the Persians believed that history had its particular purpose in demonstrating that Ahura Mazda, as their only god, defeats Angra Mianyu (i.e., destructive spirit in the belief system of Zoroastrianism) (Silverman, *Persepolis and Jerusalem*, 95).

37. Silverman, *Persepolis and Jerusalem*, 95–96.

worship practices and everyday lives (e.g., Ezra 9:10–12; Neh 13:1–3).[38] In addition, both the biblical tradition and Zoroastrianism showed interest in divine wisdom. In the Persian religion, the Persians referred to their god Ahura Mazda as the Wise Lord,[39] while in the biblical tradition, for instance, the Chronicler notes that wisdom—which makes it possible for Solomon to build the temple and Huram-abi to support this king—originated from Yhwh (2 Chr 1:7–17; 2:11–12).[40]

The above observation does not attest that the belief system in the post-exilic community adopted the Persian religion's ideology or vice versa. Instead, since the post-exilic community was consistently communicating with their neighboring religious-cultural influences, the sharing of similarities could prove advantageous for the Chronicler trying to communicate effectively with his audience. In other words, the post-exilic community could perceive the message of the Chronicler without resistance, since the Chronicler tried to communicate with the audience based on the way the community perceived its surrounding influences. Yet, there could be a possible threat to the shaping of Israel's identity if the distinctiveness of Yhwh and Israel's religion was not revealed to the audience.

In this regard, the community needed to maintain the correct perception of divinity, especially understanding their Yhwh as the unique and supreme deity, with other gods as idols in their religious belief system (e.g., 1 Chr 4:9–10; 16:8–36; 17:16–27; 29:10–19; 2 Chr 6:14–42; 14:10 [Eng. v. 11]; 20:5–13; 30:18–19; Ezra 1:2; 4:3; 5:11; 6:21; 7:27; Neh 4:8 [Eng. v. 14]; 6:16; 9:7–8, 32).[41]

On the one hand, therefore, Chronicles and other biblical literature endeavor to persuade the post-exilic community to believe that they are

---

38. Olyan, "Purity Ideology in Ezra-Nehemiah."

39. Silverman, *Persepolis and Jerusalem*, 96.

40. For an analysis concerning Huram-abi's wisdom, see Lynch, *Monotheism and Institutions*, 123–24; Dillard, *Second Chronicles*, 4–5.

41. Granerød says, "In general, the deity YHWH (or YHW as the name was spelled in Elephantine), was the chief god of Judaeans, regardless of whether they lived in the province of Judah or in diaspora communities like the one in Elephantine .... The religious system we may call Yahwism—the main characteristic of which was that the deity YHWH (or as he was called in Elephantine: YHW/YHH) was worshipped as the most important god—had many dimensions" (Granerød, *Dimensions of Yahwism*, 324). Kratz indicates, "Biblical tradition provides a multifaceted but definite answer: a Judean shall regard himself as part and representative of 'Israel,' the people whom God once chose and who sinned against their God and were punished severely by him" (Kratz, "Judean Ambassadors," in Lipschitz et al., *Judah and Judeans in Achaemenid Period*, 439).

in direct continuity with their past. For the Yehud community, the people lost the Davidic kingdom, and God's promise concerning the perpetuity of the Davidic kingdom seemed as though it might have been nullified. In this situation, the prayers in Chronicles note that the members of the community could hope for God's activity, since they were God's chosen people with whom Yhwh had made a covenant (e.g., the Abrahamic covenant [1 Chr 16:16–18; 2 Chr 20:7]) since the ancient days.[42] Similar to Chronicles, the writers of other biblical literature remind the members of the Yehud community of Israel's special relationship with God by recalling Israel's history and emphasizing the covenant made between God and Israel.[43] Various texts report a long history of Israel regarding Yhwh's making a perpetual promise with the patriarchs, granting lands as their inheritance (בְּרִית עוֹלָם [Ps 105:9–11]; see 1 Chr 16:15–17; Neh 9:7–8; Pss 106:45; 135:12; 136:21), delivering his people through the exodus event and from exile (Ezra 1:5–8, 11; 6:19–22),[44] and making Israel his special

---

42. See also this book's explanation on the notion of "Hezekiah's Good Yhwh" in ch. 3.

43. Taking account of Israel's history is not uncommon in late biblical historiography, since the post-exilic community tried to understand its identity and reconfirm continuity with the pre-exilic era by reviewing their history (Japhet, *From the Rivers of Babylon*, 397).
  Merrill correctly points out, "Fundamental to Israel's faith was the recognition and recollection that Yhwh was Israel's God" (Merrill, "Remembering," 32).

44. Ezra-Nehemiah highlights the exodus event to shape theology of the book. Ezra-Nehemiah portrays the deportees returning to their homeland as the protagonists of the second exodus. They are genealogically connected to pre-exilic Israel (Ezra 2:1–70; 8:1–20). For the returnees, then, the exodus event was not simply a past event to remind them of God's intervention to the forefathers' lives; instead, in their contemporary situation, the events of their exile and their journey back to the land became their own exodus. Therefore, Ezra-Nehemiah assures the post-exilic community that the community members still stand in line with pre-exilic Israel, and the community could attest to God's special concern for his people.
  Williamson notes, "The purpose of this typological pattern is to encourage the readers to interpret the return as an act of God's grace that can be compared in its significance with the very birth of the nation of Israel itself.... Yet typology opens the eye of faith to the hand of God behind the historical process, inviting an appreciation of his action in bringing his people to a point of rebirth no less wonderful than that which had been accomplished in the deliverance of Israel from the slavery of Egypt" (Williamson, *Ezra, Nehemiah*, 20). In addition to a typological pattern for establishing the continuity, Williamson points out the institutional connection between the post-exilic community and the pre-exilic Israel. He argues that the tangible point of contact between pre- and post-exilic era is the temple (Williamson, *Ezra and Nehemiah*, 82–83). Also, Tollefson and Williamson suggest that the intention of genealogical purity in the community is because genealogy connects the post-exilic community

possession (יִשְׂרָאֵל לִסְגֻלָּתוֹ [Ps 135:4]). For the post-exilic people who had returned to God's promised land, their historical reality of living in the land could have encouraged them to be able still to rely upon the covenant God of their patriarchs and to identify themselves as God's special people.[45]

On the other hand, the post-exilic community also needed to perceive Yhwh as their supreme deity over the universe. Thus, various texts are attentive to emphasize Yhwh's activity in the universe. This notion is one of the theological paradigms which was formulated and became evident through the Israelites' turbulent period of warring against foreign nations as well as their forced migration. During this period, the Israelites witnessed that Yhwh used the nations that surrounded them as his instrument to punish his people (e.g., Isa 7:17; 10:5–6; Hab 1:2–11),[46] and they eventually returned to their home soil by the hand of a foreign king (i.e., Cyrus). All these historical observations led the people to give more attention to Yhwh's sovereignty as extending over the world (e.g., 2 Chr 16:9; 20:6; Ezra 1:2; Jer 10:7; Nah 1:1—3:19; Zeph 2:4–15; Zech 1:9; Dan 2:37; 4:17; Ps 47:8–9).[47] However, although Israelites had returned to the land, since they were still subordinated to the Persian Empire, the question remains: is Yhwh supreme over even the Persian power?[48]

---

to their land, ancestors, cultures and gods to the past. See Tollefson and Williamson, "Nehemiah as Cultural Revitalization," 55.

Japhet explains that Ezra-Nehemiah understands the past event as being rooted in the Yehud community's present circumstances. The particular concept of history presented in the book is based on a cause-and-effect relationship (Japhet, *From the Rivers of Babylon*, 368).

Chronicles tends to diminish the significance of the exodus event with regard to Israel's settlement in the land, and it portrays Israel's possession of the land as though it were continuous throughout their history. In other words, the Chronicler portrays Israel's early history as though the people had never been slaves in Egypt (i.e., the people of Israel as autochthonous to the land) (Japhet, *From the Rivers of Babylon*, 38–52).

45. Gosse, therefore, observes that some post-exilic biblical literatures substitute the Davidic covenant with the Abrahamic covenant (e.g., Pss 89; 105–6) (Gosse, *David and Abraham*, 26–27).

46. Ben Zvi, "Total Exile, Empty Land," in Ben Zvi and Levin, *Concept of Exile*, 163.

47. Y. Kim, "포로기와 포로기 이후의 신학사상 [Theological Paradigms during the Exilic and the Post-Exilic Period]," 33–50; Von Rad, *Old Testament Theology*, 112–13.

Here, sovereignty means Yhwh's ruling authority over the universe (e.g., 1 Chr 29:11–12; Ps 47:2; Isa 2:4; Jer 10:7; Zech 14:9) and his possession of all things (e.g., 1 Chr 29:14; Ps 24:1–2).

48. Throntveit introduces similar questions that possibly arose from the community: "Has God sent them [the Israelites] into exile, or has the gods of Babylon been victorious? Were they still the chosen people, or had God abandoned them? . . . Was

The Chronicles and other biblical literature could answer this question, and the various theological responses to the question that arose from the community could have helped them in reacting against their given circumstances under the Persian Empire. The Chronicler's history endeavors to portray Yhwh as the incomparable deity who is above other gods in the universe (1 Chr 16:23–33; 29:11–12; 2 Chr 6:14). Other biblical literature agrees with the Chronicler's view on God's supremacy over the universe. Ezra-Nehemiah and prophetic literature well persuade the community to perceive Yhwh's universal ruling authority, even if they live under external imperial powers. God opens the door for the returning of the deportees and the building of the temple (Ezra 1:1–4) through Cyrus. God is the creator and sustainer of the universe (Neh 9:6) who appoints and protects Nehemiah to accomplish the task of fortifying the city of Jerusalem (2:5) through a foreign king (i.e., Artaxerxes [2:8, 18]).[49] Even this foreign king recognizes the God of heaven and provides whatever Ezra requires (Ezra 7:6, 21, 23).[50] The prophet Haggai also confirms God's universal ruling authority (Hag 2:6–7; see Mal 1:5, 11), particularly focusing on God's possession of monetary resources. The prophet encourages them to see that resources, which are transferred from other nations for the temple construction (v. 7), originally belong to God (v. 8), not to the nations (see 1 Chr 29:12, 16). Several psalms, which are considered to have originated during the post-exilic period (e.g., Pss 105–6, 135–36), also attest to God's ruling authority over the universe. Although Israel went through

---

God able to deliver them? Was God will to deliver them? Would God remember the promises to Abraham and David?" (Throntveit, *Ezra-Nehemiah*, 10).

49. Note that prayer in Neh 9 repeatedly uses first person plural pronouns (e.g., vv. 16, 32 [x7], 33 [x2], 34 [x4], 36 [x3], 37 [x5], 38 [x4]). Thus, one may assume that the participants of the prayer agree with the particular view of God conveyed in v. 6.

50. God's sovereignty over the universe can be revealed through the biblical writers' use of the phrase אֱלֹהֵי הַשָּׁמַיִם (God of the heaven [Gen 24:3, 7; 2 Chr 36:23; Ezra 1:2; Neh 1:4, 5; 2:4, 20; Jonah 1:9]), אֱלָהּ שְׁמַיָּא (Dan 2:18, 19). Breneman points out that the Persians commonly spoke the phrase "God of heaven," and as the books of Ezra-Nehemiah and Daniel exhibit, the Persian kings even utter this expression (Breneman, *Ezra, Nehemiah, Esther*, 171). Olley explains that "the religious practices of the Persian rulers would be well-known by biblical writers in the Persian period. Nevertheless, they feel free to affirm, without criticism, the beliefs of the emperors in the Supreme Being, especially when linked with freedom for and support of worship of Yahweh in Jerusalem" (Olley, "God of Heaven," 78). These statements, then, imply that even if the highest ruler might not be a true believer in Israel's God (e.g., Artaxerxes says "your God" [Ezra 7:17]), the writers wanted to express that Israel's God, Yhwh, ruled over the universe through foreign kings (Rata, *Ezra and Nehemiah*, 18).

terrifying days (i.e., the exile), God delivered them (106:46) from other nations. Other nations worship idols which are handmade and powerless, and worshipers of idols exhibit the same incompetency (Ps 135:15–18), but God is the creator and sustainer (135:5–9, 25), who maintains his position above other gods (וַאֲדֹנֵינוּ מִכָּל־אֱלֹהִים [v. 5]), and he has particularly exhibited his mighty power over foreign kings (vv. 17–20, 23–24).

This notion of Yhwh's sovereignty over the universe can be meaningful for the post-exilic community, since it could encourage the vulnerable Yehud community when they interact with their surrounding imperial influences. The Yehud community did not have political independence, and they suffered economically by oppressive foreign governors (Neh 5:15).[51] In this situation, the Chronicler imparts that the sovereign and just God is omnipotent and mighty, possesses supreme qualities (i.e., he is rich and honorable), rules over the universe, and thus has the ability to deliver his people (1 Chr 16:35; 17:21; 29:11–12; 2 Chr 14:11–14 [Eng. vv. 12–15]; 20:22–23). Hence, the Chronicler encourages the community to depend solely upon Yhwh (2 Chr 14:10 [Eng. v. 11])[52] and to expect and witness what the God of justice would fulfill, when they feel any threat surrounding them (2 Chr 20:14–15).[53]

In sum, Chronicles and other post-exilic literature overall convey the message that there is no God except Yhwh, and other gods are only idols. Yhwh is their unique God, who made the covenant from their past, and he is the supreme divine who displays his sovereignty over the universe. Therefore, the post-exilic community could rely upon Yhwh in their vulnerable situation.

Worshiping Community

The members of the Yehud community as monotheistic believers should recognize Yhwh as their supreme and unique deity, and this distinguishing feature of God could be revealed through the temple, its service personnel, and service participants.[54] In this regard, the Yehud community needs

51. Yamauchi, *Persian and the Bible*, 278; Schoville, *Ezra-Nehemiah*, 180.

52. See Knoppers, "Yhwh Is Not with Israel."

53. This does not mean that the post-exilic community should engage in a battle against the Persian Empire. For a discussion regarding the Chronicler's agenda toward post-exilic community's political/military action, see "Citizens of the Davidic Kingdom" in this chapter.

54. As Solomon's prayer presents, the temple can represent Yhwh's uniqueness and

to be identified as a worshiping community. Participation in worship (i.e., sacrificial ritual [e.g., 2 Chr 29–30, 35), or the proper operation of the temple, is one of the foremost concerns in Chronicles' history, and through this history, the text conveys the message that worshiping Yhwh excludes worshiping idols. By carefully modifying his *Vorlage*, the Chronicler portrays that, when kings or people worship God, no act of worshiping idols takes place.[55] The Israelites have to choose to worship either Yhwh or idols, and this distinction should be made, since Yhwh is a divinity incomparable to other gods.[56] This observation thus implies that in their recognition of Yhwh as their supreme and unique divine being, the post-exilic community should participate in Israel's cult as a worshiping community.

Ezra-Nehemiah also exhibits great interest in shaping the post-exilic community as a worshiping people. The narratives of Ezra-Nehemiah revolve around the issues of the temple, the temple-city (i.e., Jerusalem), and the community's proper worship.[57] Ezra-Nehemiah points out that worship is the community's proper response to divine provision (Ezra 6:13–22). Thus, the themes in Ezra-Nehemiah are various issues concerning the religious revitalization of the community. Reading and listening

---

preeminence (Lynch, *Monotheism and Institutions*, 262).

55. See Lynch's various illustrations on this message (Lynch, *Monotheism and Institutions*, 77–78).

56. Lynch, *Monotheism and Institutions*, 76–102.

57. Ezra begins with Cyrus's decree of commanding the construction of the Jerusalem temple. Then, Ezra reports various affairs in relation to the community's attempt to construct the temple (chs. 1–6), followed by Ezra's taking care of the temple supplies and his implementation and imposition of the Torah to the community (chs. 7–10). Nehemiah also begins with a royal authorization (i.e., Artaxerxes [Neh 1:1—2:10]), deals with issues regarding the fortification of Jerusalem (2:11—7:73), and assigns a large portion of his writing to describe religious reformation (chs. 8–13).
Williamson suggests that the strategic literary structure of the Ezra-Nehemiah narrative consists of four sections (Ezra 1–6; 7–10; Neh 1–7; 8–13), and the sections repeat a pattern of divine-initiated journey, opposition to the task, and successful completion of the task, followed by the closing celebration (e.g., the Passover). Yet, Williamson argues that after the celebration is reported at the end of first section (Ezra 6:13–22), all other celebration is postpone, in order to highlight the climactic celebration (12:27–43) in the overall story-line (Williamson, *Ezra, Nehemiah*, xlix–1). Eskenazi similarly gives attention to the progressive nature of the narrative: Ezra-Nehemiah sets the object of the task (Ezra 1:1–4), then exhibits the advancement of the task (Ezra 1:5–Neh 7:72), and closes the story by reporting the success of the task (8:1—13:31) (Eskenazi, "Structure of Ezra-Nehemiah," 652). These literary strategies signify that the theme of worship is that successful completion of the divine plan (Ezra 1:1–4; Neh 2:1–10) results in the celebration of God.

to God's words (Neh 8:1–11), praying and repenting of their sins (Ezra 8:21–23; 9:1–15; Neh 1:4; 9:1–38), celebrating the Feast of Tabernacles and the Passover (Ezra 3:4: 6:19), enumerating the temple service personnel (Neh 12:1–26), and dedicating the walls (Neh 12:27–43) well illustrate the community's efforts toward religious revitalization.[58] The book of Haggai also emphasizes the theme of worship in relation to the temple construction. People had recognized that the temple needed to be rebuilt, but, instead, they built their own houses (Hag 1:2, 9). Hence, the prophet encouraged the people to rebuild the temple and thus witness God's glory again (Hag 2:6–9). Zechariah calls for the people's responsibility in their relationship with Yhwh and encourages them by promising the restoration of Jerusalem (Zech 7–8). In sum, although post-exilic literature may highlight different aspects of worship and related practices, overall, they attest that the community had continual discourse regarding its religious restoration and worship service during the post-exilic era.

Revitalizing and maintaining proper worship in the post-exilic community seems to be a natural and healthy effort of the community in response to their surrounding circumstances. At the scene of the desolation, the first temple was ruined by foreign powers, and the leaders were taken captive; so, the Israelites lamented over the destruction of their nation (Jer 41:4–6; Ps 137). Those deported to Babylon (Jer 52:28–30) were allowed to assemble in order to live, people were able to gather to hear the word of God through a prophet (Ezek 33:30–32), and some demonstrated their continual faith to Yhwh (Dan 3). But still, there was no temple, no functioning priests, and no festivals. The institutions for worshiping Yhwh no longer existed.[59] People who lived outside of the Yehud province (e.g., Elephantine) even developed improper worship by incorporating syncretism into their practices.[60] But, the situation changed

---

58. Hess, *Old Testament*, 369.

59. Ross, *Recalling the Hope of Glory*, 347–49; Knoppers, "Construction," 19.

60. Merrill, *Kingdom of Priests*, 498–99. Judeans in Elephantine left some Aramaic papyri that originated from the fifth-century BCE, and these texts represent their syncretism. The people interacted with the native pantheon paradigm, which includes the gods of Anat-Yahu, Bethel, Anat-Bethel, Eshem, Eshem-Bethel, Herem, and Herem-Bethel (Anderson, *Monotheism and Yahweh's Appropriation*, 32–33; Cowley, *Aramaic Papyri*). Hamilton suggests possible syncretism in Elephantine, but he also points out a necessity of further study: "It is interesting that the total amount of money was divided among Yahweh, Eshembethel, and Anathbethel, the last two apparently being manifestations of the Aramaean god Bethen (cf. Bresciani-Kamil 4). . . . Interpreting this fact has generally revolved around the question of Jewish syncretism. It is difficult to

when Cyrus allowed deportees to return home and rebuild the temple. There was a river of joy among the people (Ps 126), and they believed that the construction of the temple was the fulfillment of God's promise of restoration (Jer 25:11–12; 29:10; see Ezek 40:1—43:12). People regained their symbol of religion (i.e., the temple).

Yet, since there had been a seventy-year void in religious practices, and since they had also started a new and different structure of the community from the pre-exilic monarchy, some in the post-exilic community addressed the subject of reinvigorating the proper practice of worship in their given sociohistorical context (Chronicles, Ezra-Nehemiah, Haggai, Zechariah).[61] The reality is that the Yehud community was failing its cult.[62] Even if the temple became the center of the community and served as a location for ritual practices, various activities took place in and around the temple. For instance, one of the rooms in the temple was diverted for Tobiah's use (Neh 13:4–5), and because of this incident, the temple became a place of conflict among a leadership group (vv. 8–9).

From the empire's administrative perspective, the temple was an important source of taxation. It was where highly educated personnel gathered and cooperated with the empire's administrative direction. Specifically, with the removal of the monarchy system, the priests started gaining more power to steer the community, and they misused their authority concerning the temple and its proper worship practice.[63] Under

---

deny that the Jewish community sought to contribute to the worship of Eshembethel and Anathbethel. At the same time, it begs the question to describe this contribution as syncretism: one can speak of syncretism only if the elements syncretized are known, and Elephantine Judaism is not a known datum. Therefore, one should try to seek an explanation for the worship of Yahweh and other deities by some other means" (Hamilton, "Who Was a Jew," 110).

61. Plöger, *Theocracy*, 43; Hess, *Old Testament*, 364.
62. Ristau, "Reading and Rereading Josiah," 242.
63. See below (pp. 143–45), for an example of the priests' misuse of their authority. See also Berquist, *Judaism in Persia's Shadow*, 147; and Silverman, who says, "Pre-exilic Judaean (and Israelite) society had a triad of authority sources: the king, the priests, and the prophets. The prophets largely functioned as mirrors of the *status quo*, both upholding and critiquing the institutions of cult and monarchy. Scribes would have had a mostly administrative and relatively minor role. Following the restoration, Yehud's authority structure was altered from this paradigm. While executive power first devolved upon a local Persian governor, probably even the Davidic scion, the ultimate authority was 850 miles away. This had the effect of increasing the authority of the Persian-supported priests ... as well as those with expertise in handling the imperial administration–scribes" (Silverman, *Persepolis and Jerusalem*, 17–18).

these circumstances, a series of deportees continually returned to Jerusalem (Ezra 1–2; 7–8), and inhabitants who lived outside of Jerusalem gathered around the temple (Neh 8:13–18; 11:1–3, 25–36) in order to worship Yhwh.[64] Thus, this historical reality drew people's attention to the temple and Jerusalem, but the Yehud community certainly did not reflect the ideal worship practice that had been offered by David, Solomon, Hezekiah, or Josiah.[65]

In this regard, therefore, Chronicles exhibits its concerns with regard to the manners of the worshipers or the worshiping community. The Chronicler persuades the post-exilic community to realize the chief purpose of the act of worship or worshipers. Prayers in Chronicles call for worshipers to exhibit appropriate outward and inward attitudes. The primary aim of Israel's worship should be to pursue the manifestation of God's presence (1 Chr 16:7–11) through their outward expressions (e.g., Levitical music [1 Chr 16:4–11]; see 6:17 [Eng. v. 32]; 24:1–19; 25:1, 6; 2 Chr 30:22) and their wholehearted pursuit of Yhwh.

Particularly, the primary aim of worship and its achievement (i.e., the manifestation of God's presence) is articulated by emphasizing the functionality of Israel's institutions (i.e., the temple, priesthood, and kingship) in its sociohistorical context. In other words, the temple service personnel should properly serve in their duties[66] given through David (1 Chr 16:4–6; 23:1—27:24; esp. 2 Chr 8:14–15; 35:4) and Moses (2 Chr 29:1—30:27; 35:1–19 esp. 29:15; 30:16; 31:4; 35:6) and should recognize the temple as a place of sacrifice (7:12), to which Yhwh is attentive (vv. 13–16).[67] Also, in the operation of Israel's worship, Chronicles acknowledges the Davidic kings' major role in establishing Israel's cult (i.e., David [1 Chr 16:4–6; 28:1—29:9; 2 Chr 29:25–28), building the first temple (i.e., Solomon [2 Chr 2–7]), maintaining the temple

---

64. Knowles, *Centrality Practiced*, 86, 90. For archaeological observation concerning the resident sites around Jerusalem, see Janzen, *Witch-Hunts, Purity*, 102–5.

65. Ristau, "Reading and Rereading Josiah," 242.
Scholars have shown different views concerning Josiah as an ideal model for the audience. Some scholars directly compare Josiah to David or Solomon, evaluating Josiah as the exemplary figure in the history of Israel. See Blenkinsopp, "Remembering Josiah," in Ben Zvi and Edelman, *Remembering Biblical Figures*, 243; Ristau, "Reading and Rereading Josiah," 222–24; Nel, "Theopolitics," 428–29.

66. Nurmela, *Levites*, 166.

67. For instance, the temple should not serve the empire's taxation purposes. For the Chronicler's polemic against the empire's taxation through the temple, see Evans, "Function of Chronicler's Temple Despoliation."

service,[68] and reforming the sacrificial ritual (i.e., Hezekiah [29–30] and Josiah [35:1–19]).[69]

---

68. Various kings should maintain the proper manner of worship, otherwise they receive judgment accordingly. Some exemplary kings in Chronicles are as follows: first, when Azariah approaches King Asa and urges the king to seek Yhwh (2 Chr 15:1–7), the king listens and repairs the altar. This restoration leads to the people's joyful sacrifice (vv. 11–15) and God-given security. However, the Chronicler also reports Asa's failure to maintain the temple. The king attempts to make a treaty with Ben-Hadad, the king of Aram, by offering him of a bribe of treasure taken from the temple (16:2). The Chronicler makes clear that Asa's deed is unfaithful to God, as the Chronicler deliberately conveys a warning from the prophet Hanani (16:7–10)—which does not appear in Chronicles' *Vorlage*—and further reports King Asa's death with a negative evaluation (v. 12; cf. 1 Kgs 15:23). Second, when King Joash, along with the priest Jehoiada, desires to restore the temple (2 Chr 24:4), he collects money from Judah and Jerusalem (vv. 5–10) and restores it (vv. 12–13). However, when Jehoiada dies, the king and the people abandon the temple (v. 18) and eventually confront the army of Aram, which results in Aram's killing all the leaders of Judah and plundering the land (v. 23). Third, the Chronicler reports the unfaithfulness of Ahaz (2 Chr 28:22). The king insults the temple (v. 24), which provokes God's anger (v. 25). The Chronicler reports in a short but critical manner that the result of the king's unfaithfulness was the downfall of him and all-Israel (v. 23). Fourth, in Hezekiah's narrative, the Chronicler contrasts Hezekiah and Ahaz. Hezekiah repairs the doors of the temple (v. 3) and commands the restoration of the temple (v. 5). He evaluates Israel's forefathers by indicating their failure of to seek Yhwh (v. 6). The expression "our fathers" and the reference to their unfaithfulness (v. 6) most likely refer to the days and deeds of Ahaz in light of the final report that Hezekiah receives concerning the temple restoration (v. 19). Hezekiah, who walks the opposite path of Ahaz, is able to reunite the northern and southern peoples during his Passover celebration, an event which once again paints a picture of one united monarchy (i.e., the reigns of David and Solomon). Fifth and finally, Josiah is also dedicated to the repair and restoration of the temple (34:8–13). Josiah's particular efforts make possible the discovery of the book of the Law (v. 15). Through this incident, Josiah humbles himself and repents before God (v. 27), an act that postpones God's judgment upon Judah (v. 28). Josiah then summons all the people in the land (34:29–33)—just like Hezekiah did in his restoration of Israel's worship (30:1–12). Josiah gathers all the elders in Judah and Jerusalem (34:29) together with "all the men of Judah, inhabitants of Jerusalem, the priests, the Levites, and all the people, young and old" (v. 30), and then he reads the Law in their hearing and renews the covenant (v. 31). Chronicles reveals that King Josiah's reformation is a nationwide task (v. 33) and that the following ceremony of the Passover is very successful. The Chronicler comments that Josiah's Passover is the best one, among all the kings in Israel, since the days of Samuel (35:18). Overall, all of Josiah's successes begin with his desire for temple reformation, which certainly involves the maintenance of the temple. Like Hezekiah, Josiah is able to reunite the kingdom again.

69. The Chronicler portrays Hezekiah as a second David/Solomon who is a model worshiper for the audience; see "Hezekiah's Prayer" in ch. 3.

In terms of the temple service personnel's functionality, the Chronicler discusses a few aspects.[70] He appoints the specific roles of the Levites (1 Chr 23–27) and intends to restrict the authority of the high priests by conveying the message that they are subordinate to the regulations ordained by David (2 Chr 8:14–15; 35:2, 4, 10).[71] In order to maintain proper cultic activities in the post-exilic era, the Chronicler needed to confirm the organization of the Levitical groups and emphasize Levitical responsibility. The Chronicler's view toward this group is not identical to that of Ezra-Nehemiah (e.g., three musical families of Asaph, Jeduthun, and Heman [1 Chr 25; see Ezra 2:41; Neh 11:17, 22]; musicians and gatekeepers [1 Chr 23–27; see Ezra 10:23–24; Neh 7:43–45; 10:28; 11:15–19]).[72] This difference could have originated from the reality that the two texts do not share the same dynamic of the community, because they might not reflect the exact same historical time frame. Therefore, this difference could imply the historical reality that the Levitical groups experienced continual changes (e.g., expansion)[73] or that the two texts differently understood the roles or boundaries of the Levite groups, so they simply recorded the Levites according to their own perspectives.[74] In any

---

70. Knoppers also gives attention to the functionality of chosen institutions. He argues that God has chosen the Levites (בחר) with purpose. In other words, Yhwh's election of the Levites does not simply lies in divine preference but in Yhwh's purposeful intention. Knoppers further emphasizes the responsibility of elected institutions: "Divine election and covenant carry inherent responsibilities. People are chosen for a purpose. If the Levites, even though they are divinely chosen, do not fulfill their responsibilities or are not allowed to do so, deleterious consequences may follow" (Knoppers, "Judah, Levi, David, Solomon," in MacDonald, *Covenant and Election*, 164).

71. This does not mean that the Chronicler disregards the critical roles of the priest in the temple service. Yet, the Chronicler certainly alleviates the authority of the priest. For instance, unlike Num 3:6; 8:26; 18:2, where the text appoints the Levites to serve (שרת) the Aaronides, in Chronicles, the Levites stand "at the side of the sons of Aaron" (לְיַד־בְּנֵי אַהֲרֹן) (Knoppers, "Hierodules, Priests, or Janitors," 51–55, 68–69). For the translation of 1 Chr 23:28, see Knoppers, "Hierodules, Priests, or Janitors," 59n39. Scholars have disagreed with the Chronicler's view regarding the Levites and the priests. Some argue that the Chronicler's attitude toward the Levites is positive (pro-Levite) and some insist the opposite (pro-priest). For the former, see Williamson, *First and Second Chronicles*, 28–31; Min, *Levitical Authorship*, 66–70; Welch, *Post-Exilic Judaism*, 172–84; DeVries, *First and Second Chronicles*, 191–96. For the latter view, see Mosis, *Untersuchungen*, 44–45; Willi, *Chronik als Auslegung*, 195–204.

72. Selman, *First Chronicles*, 229–30.

73. Selman, *First Chronicles*, 230.

74. Yeong Seon Kim's monograph is dedicated to tracing the function of the Levites in Chronicles. Kim argues that the Chronicler does not describe the roles of the

case, considering the substantial responsibilities with which this group of people are charged (e.g., musical activities in the cult [1 Chr 16:4–6]; service in various temple affairs [1 Chr 22:24–32]; supervising of temple service [2 Chr 34:12]) in the cultic-centered community),[75] it is presumed that the Chronicler needed to clarify and emphasize their function.

In terms of the restriction of the priesthood authority and emphasis on their proper function, the priests' submission to Davidic kingship does not mean that the priests are departing from the law given through Moses, since Israel's cult certainly pursues sacrificial ritual. Yet, in Chronicles, David is portrayed as the foremost figure in establishing and operating Israel's cult. He specifies the roles of the Levites and plans the temple construction, and through David's endeavors, worship of Yhwh was able to reach its climax.[76] The priest had been able to access knowledge of Torah, and he was capable of applying it to the lives of Israelites. Yet, especially in the post-exilic era, the lack of a competing source of authority,[77] which could restrain the priestly power, opened a door for the priests to regulate the community and its members with increased power.[78] In other words, they had the authority to determine the purity status (i.e., clean or unclean) of the members in the temple-centralized locus, which was a critical mark to enter a sacrificial ritual; thus, their practice of authority could create discrimination among different social groups or strata (i.e., insiders and outsiders).[79] Although the community

---

Levites; instead, he prescribes his expected roles of the Levites in the sociohistorical context of the Persian era (Y. S. Kim, *Temple Administration*).

75. Pratt, *First and Second Chronicles*, 675.

76. Scholars do not exhibit an identical view on this subject. DeVries understands David, together with Moses, as the ultimate founder of Israel's cult (DeVries, "Moses and David," 639). Some see David simply as the second Moses or the second founder of Israel's cult. In this view, David is a follower of Moses (Zucker, "Downplaying the Davidic Dynasty," 189–90). See also Joo, who agrees with the Chronicler's downplaying of David (Joo, "Past No Longer Present"). Note that, still, this view does not overlook David's significant role in Israel's religion.

77. E.g., there was no longer a king in the post-exilic era.

78. Watts even says, "The priests thus disguised their role in the arguments of their times by hiding behind God and Moses and casting their speeches in the distant past" (Watts, "Torah as the Rhetoric of Priesthood," in Knoppers and Levinson, *Pentateuch as Torah*, 321).

79. In addition to the religious aspect, Hamilton observes the boundaries and core of Jewish communities in social and economic diversity: "Judean Jews were socially and economically diverse and increasingly dominant in their region. The Elephantine community was apparently egalitarian, while that in Judea was more stratified"

had preserved the law for a long time, in a new social context—a mixture of Yahwistic and non-Yahwistic believers (e.g., the Persians)—the priests' increased power allowed them to easily produce distinctions among social groups as they applied the law to the community. This then implies that through the community's approval of the priestly authority, the priests could establish a so-called religious-juridical hierarchy system, and by the priestly authority, there was the potential that the Yahwistic worshipers could be expelled from their groups at any moment.[80] In addition, the priests were in close contact with the political leaders of Yehud, and it seems that the two elite groups shared a certain level of their authority. For instance, Governor Nehemiah removed Tobiah and his goods from the temple and intervened in affairs related to the temple by ordering the purification of one of the rooms in the temple. This incident initially occurred when the priest Eliashib contacted this neighboring governor and provided residence (Neh 13:4–9). Thus, it is presumed that this priest had a certain level of relationship with this politician. Berquist indicates, "Priests considered themselves to have the power to house politicians, and politicians thought themselves capable of determining the actions of priests within the Temple."[81] In the restoration of the post-exilic community's worship practices, this tendency could have been a hindrance to restoring the ideal worship that was established and rendered during the pre-exilic era. In this regard, the Chronicler warned the post-exilic high priests against regulating outside their sphere of authority and reminded them of their proper function by indicating the prescribed roles ordained and specified by Moses and David (2 Chr 8:14–15).[82]

The Chronicler reveals his intention to signify the temple as the place of sacrificial ritual through his emphasis on all-Israel's participation in Israel's cult (2 Chr 29–30), and this focus could reflect the geo-political/religious reality that the Yehud community faced. The Chronicler portrays the northern tribes positively and addresses that both the

---

(Hamilton, "Who Was a Jew," 112).

80. Berquist, *Judaism in Persia's Shadow*, 150–51. Watts also agrees, saying, "In post-exilic Judea, a Pentateuch containing supposedly thousand-year-old divine revelations to Moses about how to build and service God's sanctuary fulfilled the same purpose. The priest would have used the Pentateuch to guarantee the accuracy of their ritual practices and buttress their authority to adjudicate ambiguous cases" (Watts, "Scripturalization," 6).

81. Berquist, *Judaism in Persia's Shadow*, 153.

82. Williamson, *First and Second Chronicles*, 29.

northern and southern tribes share a common heritage and identity (2 Chr 28:8–15).[83] He overtly conveys the notion that all-Israel includes the northern tribes through the Hezekiah narrative (2 Chr 29–30).[84] During the Persian period, then, Hezekiah's summoning of the northern tribes could be interpreted as a calling of the Samarians, who had already established their own temple at Mt. Gerizim, to join in the sacrificial ritual at the Jerusalem temple.[85] From the Chronicler's perspective, the post-exilic community's sacrificial ritual should be offered at the temple in Jerusalem,[86] but the reality was that the Samarians offered their own

83. Both share a similar social structure, such as "a tribal organization, a group assembly, Yahwistic prophets, etc." For instance, the prophet Oded speaks of אֱלֹהֵי־אֲבוֹתֵיכֶם (the God of your [northerners] father [2 Chr 28:9]). See, also 2 Chr 13:10–12. Abijah's speech exhibits the Chronicler's perspective toward the northern people. Abijah persuades the northern people not to rebel against Yhwh. True worshipers are those who maintain their faith in Yhwh (McKenzie, *First-Second Chronicles*, 51). See 2 Chr 34:1—35:19, which describes Josiah's reformation and includes northern and southern parties (Knoppers, *Jews and Samaritans*, 80, 97).

84. A subject of all-Israel from the perspectives of the membership in the community has been one of the debatable issues among Chronicles and Ezra-Nehemiah scholarship. Yet, since this book focuses on the concept of all-Israel from the perspective of functionality (particularly the assigned role of the temple), this book does not delve into the membership issue. Briefly, the Chronicler's understanding of all-Israel is reflected in 2 Chr 30:25, which includes members of the northern and southern tribes and the foreigners who inhabited the territories of Judah and Israel. Jonker's monograph specifically contributes to this subject. For further scholarly discussion on this subject and references regarding Chronicles, see Jonker, *All-Israel*, 28–60. In Ezra-Nehemiah, the membership issue, or the community identity, is quite complicated in relation to Ezra 9–10 and Neh 13, the intermarriage or holy seed issue in the community. For various references for the scholarly discussion, see 1n1. For a discussion on mixed marriages in Chronicles in relation to Ezra-Nehemiah, see Williamson, *Israel in Books of Chronicles*, 60–61.

85. For a discussion on the emergence of the temple (e.g., time period) at Mt. Gerizim, see Magen, "Dating of the First Phase," in Lipschitz et al., *Judah and Judeans in Fourth Century B.C.E.*, 157–76.

86. The Chronicler emphasizes the theme of the centralization of Israel's cult. Chronicles reports the existence of two recognized cultic sites in the days of David and Solomon (e.g., Jerusalem [1 Chr 6:17 (Eng. v. 32)] and Gibeon [2 Chr 1:3]). Yet, the Chronicler portrays the site at Gibeon as a legitimate sacrificial place (e.g., 1 Chr 16:37–43; esp. v. 40), whereas the site at Jerusalem is described as the place where mainly musical performance is offered to Yhwh (1 Chr 6:16–17 [Eng. vv. 31–32]; 16:4, 37). First Chronicles 16:2 writes of David's burnt offering and fellowship offerings; but, at Jerusalem, it seems that there were not regular offerings as in Gibeon (see תָּמִיד [1 Chr 16:40]). After Solomon completes the temple construction, the sacrificial site at Gibeon no longer appears; instead, Chronicles reports sacrifices at the temple. In addition, various high places (בָּמָה) in Chronicles receive a negative evaluation (e.g.,

sacrifices to Yhwh.⁸⁷ Therefore, the emergence of a Samarian community and, especially, its functioning as the site of sacrificial ritual could be an issue, from the Chronicler's perspective.⁸⁸ In terms of the function of the Jerusalem temple, it is particularly designated (i.e., וּבָחַרְתִּי [I have chosen]) as the house of sacrifice by Yhwh (2 Chr 7:12).⁸⁹ Thus, the Chronicler's message may reflect his desire for the post-exilic community to perceive the function of the temple accordingly and offer ritual sacrifice correctly and in Jerusalem.⁹⁰

Ezra-Nehemiah also features its own emphasis on the aspect of worshiper or worship. It highlights that worshiping God is closely related to the people's obedience to the law of and traditions associated with Moses (Ezra 6:18; Neh 8:6). Since there was a two-generation void in sacrificial ritual after the destruction of the first temple, the community could raise questions regarding ritual legitimacy.⁹¹ In this regard, the law from Israel's past could certainly play the role of a compass for the community concerning their revitalization of worship. In fact, an attempt to revitalize sacrificial ritual through the law was not the first, for, in the days of Josiah, the people had already experienced a renewal of sacrificial worship (2 Kgs 22:3—23:27; 2 Chr 35:1–19).

The Yehud people believed that the law did not originate with Moses but Yhwh (Neh 8:14); therefore, it was critical to keep the law in order to

---

2 Chr 21:11; 28:25; 33:19) (Japhet, *Ideology of the Book*, 177–82). See Ps 132:13–14.

87. Archaeological discoveries reveal that at Mt. Gerizim, Samarians offered their sacrificial offering to Yhwh according to Lev 1–6. Hundreds of bones have been excavated, including one to three years of sheep, goat, cattle, and pigeons (Hjelm, "Mt. Gerizim and Samaritans," in Mor and Reiterer, *Samaritans*, 28). See also Knoppers, "Judah, Levi, David, Solomon," in MacDonald, *Covenant and Election*, 143–44.

88. Knoppers writes, "If Yahwistic communities could be found in both Yehud and Samaria during the Persian and Hellenistic periods and if each of these communities had its own Yahwistic sanctuary, it is likely that the religious relations between those two communities were an issue for at least some members of their elites" (Knoppers, "Mt. Gerizim and Mt. Zion," 325).

89. This notion is quite evident when comparing the temple from the perspective of the house of prayer. People could pray at/in (בְּ) or toward (אֶל) the temple (2 Chr 6:20–39; see פָּנֶה [20:5]) even from a distant place (2 Chr 6:34), but the sacrifice should be offered only at the designated temple (Lynch, *Monotheism and Institution*, 120).

90. Williamson, *First and Second Chronicles*, 30.

91. Watts suggests a few questions that possibly arose in the community: "How does one know if one is doing it right? How can priests be sure that their tradition of performance is correct? How can participants know that the priests are competent?" (Watts, "Ritual Legitimacy," 405).

offer proper worship to Yhwh. After reading the law of Moses, Ezra called Yhwh their great God (הָאֱלֹהִים הַגָּדוֹל [v. 6]) and people exhibited their natural response to this act by worshiping Yhwh (vv. 1–6, 9–12).[92] This response implies that worship may be characterized by the reading of the law. The reason the law should be central for worship is that in Ezra-Nehemiah, worship is construed as a holy activity (Neh 13:22) offered by the sanctified people of Yhwh (Ezra 8:28; 9:2) in the holy place (Neh 11:1, 18). In light of this understanding, properly keeping a given form of worship (i.e., sacrifices) was important. Thus, various daily (Ezra 3:1–3) and seasonal sacrifices (i.e., the Feast of Booths [3:4–6]; the Passover [6:19–22]) were offered, and people needed to learn the statutes and ordinances (חֹק וּמִשְׁפָּט [7:10]).[93] The law served as a guide for the people to keep the sacred day of Yhwh (Neh 8:7–8, 10–11).[94] It could have also functioned as a safeguard when the community encountered any illegitimate form of worship (Ezra 4:1–3).[95] The prophet Malachi similarly points out the importance of keeping the law. He condemns corrupted priests (Mal 1:6—2:9) and calls for repentance and the restoration of proper worship (3:1–6). He particularly indicates the priests' failure to learn the law and teach it to the people.[96]

Overall, both Chronicles and other biblical literature (i.e., Ezra-Nehemiah and Malachi) are eager for the restoration of proper worship in the post-exilic community. Ezra-Nehemiah and Malachi particularly emphasize that the law should be located at the center of the people's lives and should encourage them to live by it in the shaping of their worshiping community. The Chronicler also admits the significant role of the law in Israel's cult; yet, in the rehabilitation of Israel's worship, Chronicles specifically emphasizes the proper functioning of the temple and its service personnel, with all-Israel's participation under an ideal Davidic king's supervision.

92. Rata, *Ezra and Nehemiah*, 17, 23.
93. Steinmann, *Ezra and Nehemiah*, 78–82.
94. McCarthy, "Covenant and Law," 35.
95. For instance, the people had a conflict with those who claimed to be Yahwistic worshipers (i.e., the enemies of Judah and Benjamins [Ezra 4:1–3]), and these enemies probably exhibited aspects of syncretism in their worship of Yhwh (see 2 Kgs 17:24–41). The text does not write of the people's interaction with the law in this particular situation, but when the people faced the syncretistic Yahwists, the law could have helped the Yehud community pursue proper worship (Steinmann, *Ezra and Nehemiah*, 100).
96. Ross, *Recalling the Hope of Glory*, 351.

Citizens of the Davidic Kingdom

A difficult question remains: if the Yehud community should worship under the supervision of an ideal Davidic king, then what does this notion imply without having a tangible monarchy system during the post-exilic era? This book has already revealed in chapter 3 that prayers in Chronicles deliver hope for the revival of the Davidic kingdom;[97] yet, the nature or particular characteristics of the kingdom should still be discussed. Scholars have presented a few views concerning the shape of the kingdom and the timing of its actualization. Two major opinions are at hand. On the one hand, some insist that the Chronicler desired the viable reestablishment of the Davidic kingdom. On the other hand, some scholars believe that the Chronicler conveyed the message that the community should supersede the kingdom or that the Davidic promise would be fulfilled through the community.[98] In terms of the timing of the actualization of

---

97. This book has particularly revealed the relationship between the Davidic kingdom and the temple (i.e., two houses). The temple and Israel's institutions do not replace the kingdom, but the Davidic kingdom (or kings) is responsible for maintaining the temple. See also Hwang, *Hope for the Restoration*, 203.

In addition to the recorded prayers, Chronicles' genealogy and narratives corroborate the delivery of hope for the revival of the kingdom. In its genealogy, the tribe of Judah and the line of David serve as a focal point (1 Chr 3:17–24). David's speech to Solomon (1 Chr 22, 28, 29) confirms the Davidic promise (1 Chr 17). Boda sees David's speech as essentially a rehearsal of his 1 Chr 17 speech (Boda, *First-Second Chronicles*, 182). In David's speech, the text carries a conditional aspect of the divine promise. See 83n176 for a detailed discussion of the nature of the promise. In its *Vorlage*, the Chronicler replaces Judah (2 Kgs 8:19) with house of David (2 Chr 21:7). King Abijah's speech in 2 Chr 13:5 shows the Chronicler's favor in Davidic kingship. Also, when the Chronicler refers to a divine promise to David and his descendants, it seems that he carefully and intentionally chooses the word covenant. For instance, 1 Kgs 9:5 says, כַּאֲשֶׁר דִּבַּרְתִּי עַל־דָּוִד (as I spoke to David), but 2 Chr 7:18 says, כַּאֲשֶׁר כָּרַתִּי לְדָוִיד (as I made covenant with David). Similarly, 2 Kgs 8:19 says, אֶת־יְהוּדָה לְמַעַן דָּוִד עַבְדּוֹ (Judah for the sake of David his servant), but 2 Chr 21:7 says, אֶת־בֵּית דָּוִיד לְמַעַן הַבְּרִית אֲשֶׁר כָּרַת לְדָוִיד (the house of David for the sake of the covenant that I made with David).

Knoppers focuses on בחר and argues that the Chronicler strategically uses this word to portray theocracy. God chose David and Solomon, and through Davidic kings, Yhwh rules over Israel (Knoppers, "Judah, Levi, David, Solomon," in MacDonald, *Covenant and Election*, 139–68).

98. Boda's observation provides a list of works on the subject of the Davidic kingdom or covenant in Chronicles until the year 2009. The following list refers to those who support the view that the Chronicler desired the reestablishment of the Davidic kingdom: Butler, "Forgotten Passage"; Cross, Reconstruction of Judean Restoration"; Freedman, "Chronicler's Purpose"; Horbury, *Jewish Messianism*; Jarick, *First*

the kingdom, scholars often agree that the Chronicler presents his hope for the Davidic kingdom/kinship. Yet, they either integrate Israel's history into a present realization (or inaugurated realization; i.e., the final fulfillment is yet to come) of the Davidic kingdom/kingship,[99] or they relate the status of the kingdom to a distant future-oriented agenda.[100] However, in

---

Chronicles; Kaufmann, "Messianic Idea"; Laato, *Star Is Rising*; McKenzie, *First and Second Chronicles*; Newsome, "Toward a New Understanding"; North, "Theology of the Chronicler"; Selman, *First Chronicles*; Willi, *Chronik als Auslegung*.

The following list exhibits some scholars who believe that the dynastic promise in Chronicles is fulfilled in/through the community: Ackroyd, "Chronicler as Exegete"; Baltzer, "Ende des Staates Juda," in Rendtorff and Koch, *Studien zur Theologie der Alttestamentilchen*, 33–43; Braun, *First Chronicles*; Coggins, *First and Second Books*; Dumbrell, "Purpose of the Books"; Goldingay, "Chronicler as Theologian"; Kellermann, *Messias und Gesetz*; Mason, *Preaching the Tradition*; Murray, "Dynasty, People, and Future"; Mosis, *Untersuchungen*; Plöger, *Theocracy and Eschatology*; Rudolph, *Chronikbücher*; Riley, *King and Cultus*; Schniedwind, "Prophets and Prophecy," in Graham et al., *Chronicler as Historian*, 215–45.

A few noticeable contributions should be added to the category of Boda's list, such as Hwang, *Hope for the Restoration*, and Janzen, *Chronicles and Politics*.

99. For the present realization, see Newsome, "Toward a New Understanding": Ackroyd, "History and Theology"; Throntveit, "Was the Chronicler a Spin Doctor"; Selman, *First Chronicles*.

100. For the future agenda or nonroyalistic view, see Dumbrell, "Purpose of the Books"; Stinespring, "Eschatology in Chronicles"; DeVries, "Moses and David."

Since there is a gap between the sociohistorical and literary historical reality, some scholars have suggested an eschatological approach to the actualization of the Davidic kingdom and its connection with the hope of the coming messiah. In other words, the Davidic kings and their kingdom are idealized; thus, the Chronicler's presentation of the ideal Davidic kingship does not seem to play well with the post-exilic era. See Kaufmann, "Messianic Idea"; North, "Theology of the Chronicler," 369; Selman, *First Chronicles*, 224. However, Japhet points out, "All those who argue that Chronicles is an eschatological text arrive at their conclusion in the same way—by inference. They base their interpretations on the book's structure and hypothetical divisions, on its selection of material from its sources, on literary allusions and verbal associations ... the book of Chronicles does not contain a single reference to the end of days or direct expression of eschatological yearnings" (Japhet, *Ideology of the Book*, 388). In addition, scholars have used the term eschatology without a consensus concerning its meaning. In a narrow sense, it deals with a catastrophic end-time event, whereas in a broad sense, it carries the expectation of a better situation in a future time (i.e., status quo). Specifically, regarding the latter case, scholars are divided into two groups concerning the presentation of this future hope: messianic or royalistic (Hwang, *Hope for the Restoration*, 19). Thus, regarding the Chronicler's future hope of the Davidic kingdom, this book avoids using the term eschatology; instead, it employs the phrase "the Chronicler's royalistic hope."

Also, from this book's methodological approach, the portrayed Davidic kings are idealized but at the same time instrumentalized. In other words, they are a model

light of the Chronicler's presentation of the Davidic kingdom, one does not necessarily need to choose one position or the other. Furthermore, even the timing of the actualization and shape of the kingdom may not be what the Chronicler is primarily aiming to demonstrate in reporting Israel's history. From the perspective of shaping the identity of the community, it seems instead that the Chronicler's interest lies in the role of the audience as they desire a better political shape of the community. In other words, what does the post-exilic community fulfill in order to bring about the future Davidic kingdom?

When considering the circumstance in the post-exilic era, it does not seem that the Chronicler expects to persuade his audience to bring about a political cataclysm. As stated previously, the Achaemenid empire was harsh against any rebellious movements in its colonial provinces. Since the empire selected a pro-Persian governor or leadership, it is unlikely that the Chronicler attempted to persuade the elite groups to undertake radical rebellious action to actualize the Davidic kingdom.[101] Instead, the probable situation which the Chronicler encountered was that the leadership (i.e., the priests) tried to solidify the grounding of their authority in a given sociohistorical situation, and the Chronicler responded to them by warning against the misbehavior of leadership (e.g., the priests).

In fact, the Chronicler persuades the audience to refrain from activism, especially military contest. Jehoshaphat's prayer and its narrative convey the notion of being a witness rather than having activism. The prayer portrays the king's and the people's acts of relying upon God (2 Chr 20:3, 4, 20); yet, it further describes the nature of this act in the community's desire for God's intervention in their suffering. God does not require Judah to fight; instead, he urges them to not be afraid (vv. 15, 17) and to stand and see the salvation of Yhwh (v. 17).[102] The text's report of Judah's victory indicates that warfare is entirely secured by God alone. Hence, this practical instruction could speak to the audience of the post-exilic community. It does not seem that the post-exilic community should undertake heavy warfare with neighboring powers, but

---

for the audience. They utilize persuasion to encourage the audience to bring about the desired future (Ristau, "Reading and Rereading Josiah," 224; Jonker, *Reflections of King Josiah*, 33).

101. Janzen, *Chronicles and Politics*, 3.

102. Williamson notes, "Deliverance is eagerly awaited, but it must be entirely of God's own doing, unaided by human contrivance" (Williamson, *First and Second Chronicles*, 297).

the Chronicler conveys the message that, even if there is warfare, they should await God's intervention without (military) activism in their current circumstances (v. 20).

Another question then follows: what should the community do while they await Yhwh's intervention?[103] The Chronicler suggests that the audience should become worshipers.[104] The battle scene describes all of Judah's acts of worship and emphasizes the role of the Levitical music in the battle (esp. in the holy war). The function of worship could signify that the act of worshiping Yhwh is one of the major elements of the holy war.[105] But, as Kleinig insists, the Levitical music invokes God's presence in that, if the Israelites' proper worship performance is accompanied by prayer, then God would be present among the Israelites and fight for them. Therefore, the performance of worship becomes Judah's own warfare, since the performance invites the warrior (i.e., Yhwh), who brings about triumph for the people of God.[106] Thus, the core principle of this sacred battle story is that the members of the community are expected to fulfill the role of worshipers of Yhwh. The post-exilic community might not have been engaged in a fatal battle like Jehoshaphat had, but the act

---

103. Although the members of the post-exilic community should await God's intervention in their circumstances in dealing with neighboring powers, this patient disposition does not mean that they maintain a form of quietism or pacificism (Knoppers, "Jerusalem at War in Chronicles," in Wenham and Hess, *Zion*, 74; Knoppers, "Of Rewritten Bibles," 84). The Chronicler writes various accounts of warfare, and his interest here in military matters does not comply with such ideologies (i.e., quietism or pacificism). For a detailed list of wars and battles in Chronicles, see Beentjes, "War Narratives," 589–90.

104. Jehoshaphat and all the people of Judah and Jerusalem respond to Jahaziel's prophecy by worshiping God (לְהִשְׁתַּחֲוֹת לַיהוָה [v. 18]). The text particularly highlights the Levites by recording their act of praising Yhwh (לְהַלֵּל לַיהוָה אֱלֹהֵי יִשְׂרָאֵל [v. 19]) along with their names (Kohathites and Korahites [v. 19]). Further, the next morning, the Levites march before the army and praise Yhwh (v. 21), then God's mighty strike comes upon Judah's enemies when the Levites begin to shout and praise (וּבְעֵת הֵחֵלּוּ בְרִנָּה וּתְהִלָּה [v. 22]). וּבְעֵת: lit. "at the time when" (Köhler et al., "עֵת," in *HALOT*, 899–901).

105. See "Israel's Unique and Mighty God amid Warfare" in ch. 3.

106. Kleinig, *Lord's Song*, 171–72. The proper outward and inward manners of worship aim to manifest the presence of God (see 1 Chr 16 in ch. 3 of this book). In this regard, Lynch suggests that Chronicles describes the singers (the Levites [v. 21]) as a "musical vanguard, announcing Yhwh's presence in battle" (i.e., iconic role) (Lynch, *Monotheism and Institution*, 177). See also Kleinig, *Lord's Song*, 172, 174, 179.

of worship could still serve as the vulnerable community's armament as they interact with their neighboring powers.[107]

The above observation does not mean that the Chronicler tries to find the community's new identity only in a "religious-cultic realm."[108] As this book previously explained, the community identity could be constructed by the sum of roles or characteristics.[109] Therefore, it rather implies the multiple roles of the community in their pursuit of the Chronicler's desired community. In other words, the Chronicler's desired community identity is not achieved until the members of the community acquire the Davidic citizenship in a tangible monarchy system. In the meantime, the confronted task for the community is to function in their role of worshipers while maintaining their monotheistic belief. Particularly, in the actualization of the Davidic citizenship, the Chronicler portrays an aspect of Davidic citizenship in close relation to the status of the temple (i.e., as Davidic temple citizens [1 Chr 17]). Nathan's oracle reveals that the perpetuality of the Davidic kingdom is secured upon Solomon's completion of the temple.[110]

However, the post-exilic community presumably needed to interpret Nathan's oracle in order to apply it to their sociohistorical reality. What tasks would the people need to actualize after the completion of the temple construction in order to attain or maintain their citizenship? From the community's observation, even after the completion of the second temple, it might not seem possible for the Davidic kingdom to arise again under the Persian Empire. In addition, the security or eternality of the dynasty is essentially given not to the days of David but to those of his offspring,[111] and the audience witnesses that even after the suc-

---

107. Dillard explains the purpose of the reformulation of the holy war motif in Chronicles. He argues that the story is eschatological/apocalyptic from the post-exilic community's point of view (Dillard, *Second Chronicles*, 158). Yet, as Knoppers indicates, this narrative does not resemble those literary genres (Knoppers, "Jerusalem at War," 74).

108. For instance, a scholar like Jonker primarily focuses on religious-cultic identity based on direct speeches that appear in 2 Chr 10–36. He does not totally ignore the political-ethnic aspect; yet, in terms of the shaping of identity, this category does not constitute Israel's identity. In other words, Jonker understands religious-cultic identity in a political-ethnic context (Jonker, "Who Constitutes Society," 718).

109. See ch. 1.

110. See "Davidic Temple Citizen" (David's prayer) in ch. 3.

111. 1 Chr 17:4; 22:10; 28:4, 7; 2 Chr 21:7. Concerning 1 Chr 28:4, McKenzie understands forever to refer to David's own lifetime (McKenzie, *Covenant*, 75).

cessful completion of the first temple, Israel and Judah experienced continuous national crises (e.g., 2 Chr 12:1–12; 14:9–15; 20:1–34; 32:1–21).[112] Therefore, God's promise about the security or eternality of the Davidic kingdom only upon the construction of the temple could be a problem, since Chronicles has revealed to the community that the completion of the temple construction itself does not guarantee the security or perpetuity of the dynasty. The Chronicler's history implies that the temple construction can be a prerequisite for the security or eternality of the dynasty, but the former is not the guarantee of the latter. Therefore, in the Chronicler's historiography, after the completion of the temple construction, the maintenance of the temple and the temple service become a critical element concerning the security or eternality of the kingdom.

In this regard, the Chronicler's final evaluation of Israel's history merits attention (2 Chr 36:17–21). In Judah's demise, the temple is devastated at the hands of Babylonians (v. 17), and God's promise concerning the eternality of the kingdom is seemingly broken, since there is no tangible monarchy in power.[113] Yet, through the mouth of Cyrus, the Chronicler conveys that in Israel's restoration, the temple should be rebuilt (v. 23).[114] Interestingly, the Chronicler stops writing at the scene where Cyrus decrees the rebuilding of the temple (v. 22), and the author does not clearly indicate the next task for the returned exilic people. But this lack of detail does not mean that the Chronicler is not interested in the task of the community who live in the days of the post-construction

---

112. The observations vis-à-vis the kings (i.e., Asa, Joash, Ahaz, Hezekiah, and Josiah) affirm that the maintenance of the temple affects the security of the kingdom. When the king and people repair and maintain the proper function of the temple, the kingdom receives peace and joy from God. The opposite, however, is also possible: when the people insult God's house, they often encounter a national crisis.

This book does not limit the concept of the maintenance of the temple to building repair only. Although it is certainly a major task for the maintenance of the temple, often in Chronicles the repair of the Temple reflects the proper relationship between the people and Yhwh (e.g., the people seeking Yhwh).

113. Merrill, "Chronicler," 402.

114. Selman observes that the expression לִבְנוֹת־לוֹ בַיִת (to build a house for him [2 Chr 36:23]) echoes "the central theme of Davidic covenant." He continues, "Cyrus of course is thinking only of the house in *Jerusalem*, but in the Chronicler's thought this phrase is inevitably connected with both houses of the Davidic covenant, the dynasty as well as the temple. In the end, therefore, the end is also a fresh start. God's promises continue through the exile, on through his own generation and into the future" (Selman, *Second Chronicles*, 572). See Hahn, who also makes a connection between 2 Chr 36 and 1 Chr 17 and Jeremiah's prophecy (Hahn, *Kingdom of God*, 187).

of the second temple. The open-ended nature of the book could produce a rhetorical effect that guides the audience back to the reports of the lives of the people of Israel who lived in the post-construction of the first temple (i.e., the post-Solomonic era). In other words, at the end of the book, the audience living with the second temple could have inquired about their own roles and characteristics. But, since the Chronicler does not answer this question at a superficial level, the audience would have attempted to seek the answer from the lives of their forefathers in the first temple era. Therefore, this ending functions to motivate the community to follow the model figures (e.g., Hezekiah, Josiah, and the people of Israel in those days) who faithfully served the temple of Yhwh and experienced the successful unification of the kingdom (e.g., 2 Chr 30:6, 11; 31:25; 34:9, 21, 33; 35:18) after the completion of the first temple.[115] In sum, while the Yehud community awaits God's sovereign providence in the actualization

---

115. Some scholars insist that since there is no direct affirmation of the Davidic covenant in the scene of Judah's demise, there is no longer a hope of the Davidic monarchy in Chronicles. Riley argues that with Judah's end, the role of Davidic dynasty transferred to the cult (Riley, *King and Cultus*, 201). Wilcock is quite confident of this historical reality: "I certainly do not think he is hoping for a restoration of the monarchy in the old style." Instead, Wilcock focuses on the relationship between God and his people presented in Chronicles: "Though the old-style kingdom and priesthood have vanished, they are being taught by the Chronicler the inner principles which David's throne and Solomon's temple stood for. They know that where the God-to-man and man-to-God relationships are right, there the true Israel will always be, from now till the end of time" (Wilcock, *Message of Chronicles*, 286). Boda understands that the exile does not mean the total vanishing of the kingdom; instead, the exile's purpose is the purification of the land. Boda points out that the optimistic presentation of the Chronicler's portrayal of Israel's future creates a new hope for the "beginning of the *nation*" (Boda, *First-Second Chronicles*, 429; italics added). See also Murray, who insists that the ending of Chronicler does not foster the Davidic kingdom (Murray, "Dynasty, People, and Future").

However, Japhet's description to the end of Chronicles is similar to this book's view: "Dans les Chroniques, par contraste, la première phrase du décret de Cyrus constitue la fin du récit. Le décret de Cyrus est en effet présenté dans les Chroniques comme le début d'un changement mais il n'est pas suivi d'un accomplissement.... La conception globale de l'histoire du Chroniste vise l'avenir, où Israël réalisera sa vraie destinée. C'est une croyance dans la renaissance concréte d'Israël, en termes politiques et terrestres, dans un cadre strictement historique. Le modèle de cette renaissance est l'époque de David et Salomon c'est-à-dire la plus vaste expansion d'Israël en tant que peuple et pays, l'indépendance politique et le royaume davidique. La garantie pour la réalisation de cet avenir est ce que le Chroniste essaye de décrier avec tant d'efforts: l'image positive de la providence de Dieu. Son gouvernement par la justice et la compassion doit mener à la renaissance prochaine d'Israël, dans toute sa gloire" (Japhet, "Historiographie Post-Exilique" in Pury et al., *Israël construit son histoire*, 145).

of the Davidic kingdom, they should maintain the proper functionality of their religious institutions (i.e., the role of worshipers). In this way, the community members may contribute to a potential future revival of the kingdom.

While they pursue the proper functioning of their given roles, then, what is the probable way in which the post-exilic community understands their status quo, especially concerning the shape of the kingdom? From the perspective of the post-exilic community, without a monarchy, their hope of restoration of the Davidic kingdom is dependent on the way the community perceives God's promise.[116] In other words, the post-exilic community members are able to hope for the restoration of the Davidic kingdom only after they have faith in Yhwh's eternal promise given to David and Solomon and maintain their perspective in Yhwh's capability (i.e., God's supremacy), which is sufficient to fulfill his promise. Therefore, they could raise a question: is God's promise still effective?

Although the Chronicler consistently conveys the unconditionality of the Davidic promise, he also sporadically presents its conditionality. Various scholars attempt to explain this tension in Chronicles.[117] Hwang, however, introduces the concept of lacuna. He explains that the Chronicler relates the conditional nature of the promise to the perpetuity of the Davidic kingdom, because the existence of the kingdom temporarily ceases when the kingdom does not meet a certain condition. Namely, the nature of the divine promise is essentially unconditional, but the conditional nature of the promise serves the purpose of training or punishment for the Israelites.[118] In this regard, concerning the status quo of the com-

---

116. Hwang, *Hope of the Restoration*, 7–8.

117. See 83n176 for scholarly dialogue concerning the relationship between the conditionality and unconditionality of the promise in Chronicles.

118. Hwang, *Hope of the Restoration*, 206. Hwang explains, "The Chronicler believes in and hopes for a restoration of the Davidic dynasty after the period of God's discipline is finished. Another illustration for this complementary relationship is the reign of Athaliah, the only non-Davidic ruler in the history of Judah, and Joash's restoration of the Davidic line. Although the Davidic line ceased for six years during Athaliah's reign, this pause did not mean an annulment of the Davidic covenant" (Hwang, "Coexistence of Unconditionality," 242).

See p. 244 of the same article, where Hwang indicates that the coexistence of the conditional and unconditional promises is not rare in the ANE documents. For example, a treaty between Hattušiliš III (or Tudhalyaš IV) and Ulmi-Tešup of Dattaša or a royal decree by Tudhaliyaš IV and Puduhepa to the sons of Šahurunuwaš in Hittite documents exhibit both conditionality and unconditionality. See also Weinfeld, *Deuteronomy and Deuteronomy School*, 78–79; Weinfeld, "Covenant of Grant," 189–90.

munity under the Persian governance, the Chronicler explains that God's promise regarding the Davidic kingdom is not annulled, but its existence temporarily ceased. Thus, the Chronicler persuades his audience that, in the meantime, the members of the community should fulfill their roles or exhibit characteristics properly until the revival of the kingdom comes.

Even though various biblical writings also articulate the hope of restoration in the post-exilic community, a comparison of Chronicles to other literature suggests that it would not be an exaggeration to state that Chronicles is the book that most explicitly addresses the restoration of the Davidic kingdom, especially in a literal sense. Other biblical works generally understand the restoration of the Davidic dynasty in a perspective somewhat distinct from Chronicles, because they presumably reflect the vulnerable political milieu of the Yehud community as the Persia empire's small province.

Scholars have generally recognized the absence of Davidic hope from Ezra-Nehemiah,[119] although a few scholars still argue that Davidic hope is not fully subdued in Ezra-Nehemiah.[120] Ulrich insists that Ezra-Nehemiah uses the name David strategically to convey messianic hope. He understands that Ezra-Nehemiah is associated with Jeremiah's royal hope (Jer 23:5–6; 33:15–16; see Ezra 1:1), and the writer of Ezra-Nehemiah presents hope by placing the name David in major narrative units; thus, the post-exilic community continually associates with the figure of David and his teaching (Ezra 3:10; 8:20; Neh 12:24, 45).[121] However, Ulrich's view still does not provide a clear picture of the future Davidic kingdom.[122] Goswell notices the repeated appearance of the name David,

---

The Chronicler conveys the message that there could be a second chance for errant Israelites (e.g., 1 Chr 21:1–30; 2 Chr 12:5–12; 19:1–11; 25:5–13; 33:10–17) (Knoppers, "Images of David").

119. Japhet "Sheshbazzar and Zerubbabel," 76; Williamson, *First and Second Chronicles*, 9–10; Eskenazi, *In an Age of Prose*, 33–36; Karrer-Grube, "Scrutinizing the Conceptual Unity," in Boda and Redditt, *Unity and Disunity*, 155–59.

120. The name David appears eleven times in Ezra-Nehemiah (Ezra 3:10, 8:2, 20; Neh 3:15, 16; 12:24. 36, 37 [x2], 45, 46).

121. Ulrich says, "The reference in Ezra 3:10 ties David to the reconstruction of the temple. The reference in Ezra 8:20 links David with Ezra's teaching ministry that prepared people to worship at the temple. The references to David in Neh 3:15–16 and 12:24–40 occur in the context of rebuilding the wall and celebrating its completion" (Ulrich, "David in Ezra-Nehemiah," 61).

122. Ulrich admits this by saying, "The writer of Ezra-Nehemiah mentions David's name in an eschatologically neutral way" (Ulrich, "David in Ezra-Nehemiah," 49; italics added).

but he believes that there is no hope for the revival of Davidic rule in Ezra-Nehemiah; instead, David is only honored and remembered in the community through Israel's cultic practice and the appellation of the city of Jerusalem (i.e., city of David).[123]

The ending of the book of Haggai encourages the audience with an affirmation of Yhwh's plan in destroying the foreign kingdoms and selecting Zerubbabel (Hag 2:22–23). Scholars have suggested different views regarding the nature of God's promise in relation to Zerubbabel. Redditt argues that the prophet Haggai projects the hope of a literal restoration of the Davidic kingdom through this governor (פַּחַת [Hag 1:1]),[124] for he was the grandson of Jehoiachin (1 Chr 3:17–19; Matt 1:12), the royal scion.[125] On the other hand, Merrill insists that this oracle portrays the revival of the messianic king within an eschatological perspective.[126] At the end of the prophecy, Zerubbabel is no longer called a governor but a servant (עַבְדִּי [2:23]); thus, the text blurs the image of a future king, and, instead, this person serves as a prototype of a coming messiah, who is a political procurator or vice-regent of the true king, Yhwh. Therefore, Zerubbabel, a visible Davidic successor, could serve the book's rhetorical purpose of persuading the post-exilic community that the fulfillment of the divine promise of revival is in view.[127]

---

123. Goswell, "Absence of Davidic Hope."

124. Redditt links the final oracle of Haggai to Zech 4:6–10 and 6:9–15. He argues that in Zechariah, Zerubbabel is charged with rebuilding the temple (Zech 4:6–10), but he suddenly disappears in the text, and his responsibility of the rebuilding the temple is transferred to Joshua (6:9–15). Redditt believes there is some reason that Zerubbabel disappears from the Yehud community; thus, he is no longer able to carry any political assignment as implied in Haggai. Redditt argues that this is the reason the latter part of Zechariah (chs. 9–14) does not portray earthly kingship but instead portrays Yhwh as the king (Redditt, "Prophecy and the Monarchy").

125. In the discussion of the Yehud community's political landscape, Zerubbabel has been one of the major subjects of scholarly interest. Various biblical traditions (Chronicles, Ezra-Nehemiah, Haggai, and Zechariah) attest to the existence of this historic Davidic figure, yet his mysterious disappearance from the text only adds difficulty to the discussion. For a scholarly discussion on this particular person, see Schreinder, "Zerubbabel, Persia."

126. Haggai's prophecy involves several characteristics of eschatological literature (e.g., בַּיּוֹם הַהוּא [see Isa 2:11, 17, 20; 3:7, 18; Amos 8:3, 9 Hos 2:18, 21]) (Merrill, *Haggai, Zechariah, Malachi*, 56–57).

127. Merrill, *Haggai, Zechariah, Malachi*, 137. Boda similarly understands Zerubbabel, as a "symbol of hope for the community of God" (Boda, *Haggai, Zechariah*, 160).

The book of Zechariah exhibits interest in the restoration of leadership (Zech 3–4). It also speculates about the reinstatement of the Davidic line, in a view toward restoration (Zech 9:9–10; 12:10–12). Yet the prophecy does not present the hope of restoration as far as regaining political power in its sociohistorical context. Instead, it expects the coming kingdom in a messianic-eschatological view.[128] In this kingdom, Yhwh is the king over the earth (14:9) who renews his relationship with Israel (8:8; 13:9). He even extends his restoration to all nations (2:11; 8:20–23; 9:7, 10; 14:16–21).[129]

Malachi considers the notion of the covenant in a serious manner (i.e., the Levitical covenant [Mal 2:8], the covenant of the fathers [2:10], the covenant of marriage [2:14]), yet the Davidic covenant does not play a significant role in the prophecy. Instead, Malachi shares a similar view with Zechariah, in that Yhwh is the great king over the nations (1:14). In preparation for Yhwh's coming (2:17—3:6), Malachi informs readers of the emergence of a messenger sent by Yhwh (מַלְאָכִי [my messenger]; מַלְאַךְ הַבְּרִית [messenger of the covenant]; 3:1); yet, the text does not explicitly reveal the identity of the messenger. It could be Malachi himself,[130] or, if one follows the interpretation of the New Testament tradition (Matt 11:10; see Mark 1:2), then it could be John the Baptist. In any case, the text hardly implies that this figure is the one who leads the literal political restoration of the Davidic kingdom in the Persian context.

Overall, post-exilic historiography and prophecy do not seem to portray a royalistic restoration of the kingdom. Instead, they desire the future kingdom of Yhwh in a cataclysmic way or portray David as the one who set the standard for Israel's cult and deserves the community's remembrance. In this regard, Chronicles conveys the hope for the royalistic revival of the Davidic kingdom in a manner distinct from other biblical literature.

In addition, Chronicles' focal point may not lie in demonstrating the shaping and timing of the future kingdom. Instead, the book is interested in the manner in which the future kingdom is actualized. Thus, the post-exilic community should properly fulfill the desired roles and characteristics of the community in order to bring about the Davidic kingdom.

---

128. G. Klein, *Zechariah*, 69–73; Boda, *Exploring Zechariah*, 93. For Zechariah's messianic prediction, see Zech 9:9–11; 10:2; 13:7; 14:1–19.

129. Boda, *Haggai, Zechariah*, 47.

130. The pronunciation of מַלְאָכִי (my messenger) is similar to that of the name Malachi (Merrill, *Haggai, Zechariah, Malachi*, 371).

Praying Community

The practice of prayer and sociohistorical milieu are closely related to each other, since the practice of prayer is often regarded as a response to history. Although this practice was not a newly rising movement in the Persian period in light of the history of Israel's religious practice,[131] the post-exilic literature reflects the community's great interest in it. For instance, Chronicles includes many more recorded and reported prayers than its *Vorlage*.[132] The prayers reported in other literature (e.g., Ezra-Nehemiah and Daniel) are elaborate in their length and reflection of theological speculation and historical reality.[133] As the community has survived through the Persian period and then enters into the Hellenistic period, prayer receives increased attention and becomes a central feature of religious practice. Gillmayr-Bucher and Häusl indicate:

> During that time [the post-exilic period], a transformation took place: from short, individual prayers to longer theological and historical reflections, ritualized recitations, instructions reciting normative values and commandments, confirmations of hope, prophecy, and penitential prayers.[134]

In light of this reflection, it is not far-fetched to presume that prayers in Chronicles and other biblical literature echo the contemporary issues in their community. In other words, the act of prayer was one of the ways in which the community members understood their painful experience

---

131. Reif, "Place of Prayer," in Reif and Egger-Wenzel, *Ancient Jewish Prayers*, 2.

132. Matlock provides a list of recorded and reported prayers in Chronicles, and they exhibit Chronicles' great interest in prayer. He does not provide his definition of recorded prayer, and according to his classification, it seems that his definition differs from this book's view. Yet, his classification and enumeration of many prayers in Chronicles still prove that the Chronicler has greater interest in prayer than the author of Sam-Kgs (Matlock, "Rhetorically and Ideologically Shaping the Narrative," in Gillmayr-Bucher and Häusl, *Prayers and the Construction*, 13–14).

133. Newman, *Praying by the Book*, 1; Gillmayr-Bucher and Häusl, "Introduction," in Gillmayr-Bucher and Häusl, *Prayers and Construction*, 1.

134. Gillmayr-Bucher and Häusl, "Introduction," in Gillmayr-Bucher and Häusl, *Prayers and Construction*, 1. See also Wagner, "Strukturen des Gebets." This book does not agree with everything in this work (e.g., dating or interpretation of psalms). However, Wagner's work reveals aspects of the transformation of prayer/the psalms in the post-exilic era.

(i.e., the exile) and resolved their difficult situations as a vulnerable community under the Persian Empire.[135]

In chapter 3, this book has already revealed that in Chronicles, the text portrays supplicants, both individuals and communal, who seek God during their difficult situation in faith. Other biblical literature also exhibits various prayer practices in the post-exilic community.[136] In Ezra-Nehemiah, similar to the prayers of Jabez, Asa, and Jehoshaphat in Chronicles, the historical reports affirm that people understand the power of prayer during difficult situations. When Ezra comes back to Jerusalem (Ezra 7:6), he and his people are in need of military protection (8:22). But Ezra refuses Artaxerxes's offer of an escort and, instead, seeks God's help. When Nehemiah hears the heartbreaking news concerning the remnants

---

135. O'Kennedy, "Prayer in the Post-Exilic," 9.

136. The practice of prayer held a significant position in the lives of the members of the post-exilic community. Prayer was one of the major practices that the people could not leave out of their daily lives. Although the origin of a customary time-fixed prayer is uncertain, many psalms allude to the act of prayer being a daily matter that permeated the people's lives. For instance, people could offer a prayer in the morning (Pss 5:3; 30:6; 57:9; 88:14; 90:14; 92:3; 119:147; 143:8) as well as at night (Pss 6:7; 16:7; 17:15; 27:8; 42:8; 59:15; 63:7; 77:7; 92:3; 119:62, 148; 130:6; 143:8) (Penner, *Patterns of Daily Prayer*, 49–51). For the post-exilic situation in relation to the practice of the psalms, see G. Wilson, *Psalms*, 28. Also, Nehemiah's prayer exhibits his practice of prayer in the morning and at night (Neh 1:6).

Significantly, several biblical historiographies report instances of prayer practices in the post-exilic era (Ezra 9:6–15; Neh 1:4–11; 9:5–37; Dan 9:3–19). Although there is no recorded prayer, the references to prayers are also given in the post-exilic prophetic literature (Zech 7:13; 8:20–23; 10:1, 6; 12:10; 13:9; 14:16–17; Mal 1:9). For references to prayers, various terms are used, such as קרא (to call [Zech 7:13]), שאל (to ask [Zech 10:1]), תַּחֲנוּן (supplication [Zech 12:10]), חוה (to worship [Zech 14:10]), חנן (ask favor [Zech 7:2; 8:21; 22; Mal 1:9]) (O'Kennedy, "Prayer in the Post-Exilic," 7–9).

Some other apocryphal literatures or non-MT manuscripts attest to the act of prayer continuing to be cultivated in the Yehud province as well as other sectarian communities throughout the Persian Empire and later in the Hellenistic period (e.g., priestly prayer in *m. Tamid* 5.1; Qumran texts [4Q502–509, 512; 1QS1:16—2:26; 11QPsaZion; 1QM13:1—14:15; 1QSb; 11QBer; 4Q380-381; 11QPsa, b, f; 1QHa; 4QHa,b; 4QTLevia; 4Q372 1]; the prayer of Azariah in LXX Dan 3:25–45). The following are some brief introductions to each text: 4Q503—evening and morning benediction; 4Q504-506—liturgy for the days of the week; 4Q507–509—Sabbath songs; 1QS 1:16—2:26—annual covenant ceremony; 4Q502—marriage ceremony; 4Q512—purification ceremony; 11QPsaZion—eschatological prayer; 1QM13:1—14:15—for use during a final war; 1QSb; 11QBer—eschatological blessing; 4Q380-381; 11QPsa, b, f—collections of psalms; 1QHa; 4QHa,b—Hodayot hymns ("individual thanksgiving hymns"); 4QTLevia; 4Q372 1—prose prayer (Chazon, "Prayers from Qumran," 267–68).

who survived the exile, he prays and fasts on behalf of the Jews who are suffering from great trouble and shame in Jerusalem (Neh 1:5–11). When Sanballat and Tobiah the Ammonite interfere with the Jews' project of rebuilding the wall, Nehemiah prays to God for his help (8:1–6). Also, the text exhibits that, in the act of prayer, supplicants recognize the importance of maintaining faith in God's promise or covenant. In Chronicles, David and Solomon pray with faith in God's promise. They rely upon a characteristic of God: that he keeps his promise (1 Chr 17:16–27 [esp. vv. 17, 23, 25]; 2 Chr 6:14–17). Nehemiah also believes that God listens to the prayers of the servants who fear him and that God keeps his covenant to his people (Neh 1:5–11; see Ezra 10:3).[137] Public or communal prayer was one of the aspects of prayer that the Yehud community practiced. When Ezra is praying and confessing sins before the house of God (Ezra 9:1–15), the people join his prayer, and they all weep together (10:1).[138]

The above observations attest that the post-exilic community actively prayed in their religious practice. However, a question still remains regarding the peculiarity of the act of prayer during the Second Temple period. What elements create the distinctiveness of prayer practices particularly during this period? Three major elements are highlighted in light of Chronicles' portrayal of the act of prayer: 1) the temple as the locus of prayer, 2) penitential prayer, and 3) the past prayer as a model.

First, the rebuilt temple in the Persian era was recognized as the center of cultic activity, and the community's religious life revolved around the Temple.[139] The Chronicler associates the function of the temple with the act of prayer by reporting Solomon's prayer (2 Chr 6:12–42). In Solomon's prayer, the temple is uniquely portrayed as the locus of prayer in/at/toward which people could pray (6:20, 21, 24, 26, 29, 32, 34, 38).[140] In

---

137. The difference remains that the Davidic promise is a major grounding for appeals to God in the prayers of David and Solomon, whereas it is the Mosaic covenant that serves as the major grounding for Nehemiah's prayer (v. 8). Yet all the prayers significantly recognize the role of covenant within the prayers themselves.

138. The public prayer in Ezra's circumstances is different from Jehoshaphat's prayer in Chronicles. Unlike Jehoshaphat, Ezra and his people confess their sins, and they are not in a war situation. However, Ezra's prayer portrays the aspect of public prayer. Ezra's prayer, like Jehoshaphat's (2 Chr 20:13), includes men, women, and even children (Ezra 10:1).

139. See "Monotheistic Believing Community" in this chapter.

140. Several scholars have suggested different opinions regarding the notion of praying toward/at/in the temple. David Frankel suggests the idea of a portal, conduit, or magnet. He asserts that when people pray to the temple, it attracts their prayers

fact, this perception concerning the temple as the place of prayer continued throughout the post-exilic period until 70 CE, especially in the area of Palestine.[141] However, a difficulty arises as the Chronicler creates a discrepancy by associating petitioners' prayer not with the temple but with either heaven or God (2 Chr 30:27; 32:20, 24; 33:12, 13, 18). In Chronicles, after Solomon's prayer is offered, only King Jehoshaphat prays to/in the temple in the Chronicler's history (2 Chr 20:9).

In this regard, on the one hand, the Chronicler associates the temple with God's presence and dwelling place (2 Chr 6:2) in various ways.[142] The temple bears God's name (1 Chr 22:7, 8, 10; 22:19; 28:3; 29:16; 2

---

and transfers them to heaven. However, this is not convincing, because if there is no temple, then there is no portal. In fact, Frankel's critical mistake is that he ignores the non-existence of the temple during the exile (Frankel, *Land of Canaan*, 165–66).

Japhet similarly refers to the temple as a medium; however, she does not reconcile the tension but, rather, gives more effort to explaining the different aspects of God's location (i.e., temple and heaven) (Japhet, *Ideology of the Book*, 47–67). In her commentary, Japhet also uses the term portal as a means by "which prayer finds its way to God" (Japhet, *First and Second Chronicles*, 593).

Pratt examines various royal prayers (i.e., David, Solomon, Rehoboam, Asa, Abijah, Jehoshaphat, Hezekiah, and Manasseh) and insists that Solomon's prayer compels the audience to recall that the temple was central to their lives. Pratt explains that these royal prayers are the Chronicler's program (i.e., rhetorical strategy) used to invite the post-exilic community to the task of temple reconstruction. Pratt explains that the Chronicler believed that the Temple reconstruction would bring God's blessings (as they manifested in the past) once again; so, he attempts to remind the community of thetTemple and its necessity in order to see God's blessing and the glorious kingdom. According to Pratt, the people know they can still pray to God, and he can hear from heaven. However, Pratt's words are not fully satisfactory, for he writes, "What was the way of forgiveness and restoration? The Chronicler's response was straightforward. The example of Manasseh makes it clear that restoration can occur only through effective prayers offered toward the Temple." It seems that this particular estimation contradicts his overall research. The Scriptures do not even record that Manasseh prayed to the temple (2 Chr 33:12–13) (Pratt, "Royal Prayer," 245–72, 332–67).

141. As the synagogue emerges as an important locus for religious practice outside of Palestine, the diaspora synagogue serves as a center for Jewish worship and prayer (Rief, *Judaism and Hebrew Prayer*, 46, 72–75). However, people generally conceived of Jerusalem as the place of the prayer (e.g., Jdt 4:9–15; 2 Macc 1:21–30; 3:15; Luke 1:10; 2:37; 18:10).

It is apparent that the function of the temple was not limited to the practices in the temple, and the Chronicler makes clear that the temple is the place for sacrifice (e.g., 2 Chr 7:12); yet even the act of sacrificing at the temple could involve the act of prayer (6:12–42; 7:1–10).

142. This section is adapted from K. Kim, "Chronicler's View of Forgiveness."

Chr 1:18; 2:3; 6:20; 33, 38; 20:8).[143] The glory of God is in the temple (e.g., 5:13, 14; 7:3 [cloud]), and the cloud often signifies God's presence with his people.[144] Also, Joash and the people forsake the house of Yhwh and worship idols (24:18–20), and the Chronicler equates this act with forsaking God himself.

On the other hand, God does not always dwell in the temple. The Chronicler mentions several times that God hears from heaven (2 Chr 6:21, 23, 25) and dwells in it (6:30, 33, 39; 30:27).[145] God's answer to Solo-

---

143. Jehoshaphat's prayer in 2 Chr 20:8 speaks of the name of God being in the temple (וַיִּבְנוּ לְךָ בָּהּ מִקְדָּשׁ לְשִׁמְךָ [I have built for you in it the sanctuary for your name]). This expression is similar to the Davidic expression in 1 Chr 22:7: לִבְנוֹת בַּיִת לְשֵׁם יְהוָה אֱלֹהָי (to build the house for the name of my God). Japhet aptly explains the Chronicler's use of God's name and presence with the temple, saying, "When the context concerns the building of the Temple, God's 'name' is used . . . as an expression of divine presence" (Japhet, *Ideology of the Book*, 56). Cf. Hahn, *Kingdom of God*, 111.

144. The picture of the temple dedication recalls the dedication of the tabernacle in Exod 40. For further discussion, see W. Maier, "Divine Presence," 81.

145. See also Deut 26:15 and Isa 63:15. The issue of God's placement becomes more complicated when considering 2 Chr 2:5 (Eng. v. 6) and 6:18. In 2 Chr 2:5, the Chronicler writes that heaven and the highest heaven cannot contain God (הַשָּׁמַיִם וּשְׁמֵי הַשָּׁמַיִם לֹא יְכַלְכְּלֻהוּ). Similarly, in 2 Chr 6:18, the Chronicler writes that if heaven and the highest heaven cannot contain God, how much less his temple (הִנֵּה שָׁמַיִם וּשְׁמֵי הַשָּׁמַיִם לֹא יְכַלְכְּלוּךָ אַף כִּי־הַבַּיִת הַזֶּה אֲשֶׁר בָּנִיתִי). The Chronicler says that neither heaven nor the temple can contain God. The expressions of hearing from heaven and the idea of God being uncontainable imply God's omnipresence (2 Chr 2:5; 6:18; 16:9; Jer 23:24; Ps 139:7–10). A. W. Tozer explains God's omnipresence as follows: "God is near to everywhere, everyone and everything." He argues that if God is everywhere, God has no border or size (Tozer, *Attributes of God*, 117–20). Luco J. van den Brom also views omnipresence in a similar way as referring to God as a "spaceless being" (Van den Brom, *Divine Presence*, 169). Lynch explains the Chronicler's monotheism and compares God and other gods, pointing out that other gods are inferior to God because they take on spatial and geographical dimensions (Lynch, *Monotheism and Institutions*, 73). Understanding God to be a deity limited by space is contrary to Jewish thought (Hooker, *First and Second Chronicles*, 144). Therefore, when the Chronicler mentions that God is hearing from heaven, he is symbolizing the idea that there is no actual distance between people and God. When people pray, God shows his immediate response to their prayers (see 2 Chr 32:21, 24; 33:13), since the eyes of God watch the whole earth (כִּי יְהוָה עֵינָיו מְשֹׁטְטוֹת בְּכָל־הָאָרֶץ [2 Chr 16:9]). The polel participle שׁוט with God as subject occurs only in 2 Chr 16:9 and Zech 4:10, and it symbolizes God's dominion and transcendence over the world (Rudolph, *Chronikbücher*, 249; Waschke, "שׁוט," in *TDOT*, 14:528–32). Japhet believes that 2 Chr 16:9 could be a quotation of Zech 4:10. The two verses contain almost the same expression (עֵינֵי יְהוָה הֵמָּה מְשׁוֹטְטִים בְּכָל־הָאָרֶץ) (Japhet, *First and Second Chronicles*, 735). Klein says, "'Eyes' refer anthropomorphically to the Lord . . . God's transcendence and sovereignty" (G. Klein, *Zechariah*, 163). Japhet explains, "The increase in distance is only physical; there is no

mon's prayer (7:16) confirms that the temple is not the dwelling place of God but is the place of divine oversight. Thus, one cannot establish the notion that the temple is God's spatial location.

One needs to understand this discrepancy regarding the Chronicler's rhetorical strategy. This strategy could have been designed to ensure the audience of the certainty of God's willful response to the prayers of supplicants.[146] Based on the discussion above, when the people of Israel pray, no matter where they are located, God listens and forgives their sins. God's presence is not limited only to the temple. But, having maintained the notion of praying toward/at/in the temple, the supplicants could pray to God with an increased certainty of his response, because God promises that he will watch the temple and be attentive to any prayers that are offered in/at/toward the temple (2 Chr 7:15; see 6:40). Although many historical records in Chronicles provide examples of God's answering a supplicant's prayer (e.g., Asa, Jehoshaphat, Hezekiah, Manasseh), Solomon's prayer conveys a much stronger rhetorical impetus regarding the certainty of God's response, since the prayer directly introduces the manner of communication between God and the people via the temple.[147] Then, for the post-exilic audience, the temple is the real and visible locus that testifies to God's manifestation of his presence, that God still listens to their prayers and answers them.

Second, the development of penitential prayer as a particular form of religious practice is another observable phenomenon during the post-exilic era.[148] As the community attempted to restore and maintain their

---

disruption of the spiritual link or the experience of divine presence." Thus, one should not misunderstand heaven as a spatial realm (Japhet, *Ideology of the Book*, 67).

146. Ackroyd explains that the early post-exilic people began to develop the idea of the temple as a symbol of the presence of God. He says, "It is the outward sign of that manifestation of divine presence and power which is essential for any kind of reorganization or establishment of the common life . . . . The essential basis of thought about the Temple is that of the mediation of divine life and power at the will of the deity himself." Ackroyd insists that this concept is expanded to the idea of the holy city or the holy land. The concept is further developed in the New Testament: "These lines of thought are elaborated in the understanding of Jesus himself as the Temple, as that place in which God chooses to manifest himself and in which, therefore, his power and presence are made known and operative" (Ackroyd, *Chronicler in His Age*, 245–46).

147. In this regard, Hill refers to the Temple as "the symbolic focal point of God's interest in and care for humanity" (Hill, *First and Second Chronicles*, 394).

148. Scholarly research or debate on penitential prayer in the Second Temple period is not abundant. For the history of scholarly research as well as the current research status on this issue, see Boda et al., *Origins of Penitential Prayer*.

community, there was struggling within the people to turn to Yhwh (Neh 1:9; 9:26), seek Yhwh (Ezra 6:21; see Dan 9:13), and properly serve Yhwh (Neh 9:35).[149] The biblical tradition reports that in the post-exilic community's dealing with sins or uncleanness, specific behavioral changes were required, and people executed those requirements (Ezra 6:21; 10:2, 11; Neh 1:9; 8:9–12, 14–18; 9:35; see Dan 4:27; 9:5–6, 10–11, 13, 24). This exhibits, therefore, that repentance was a critical issue in the community.[150]

In Chronicles, Solomon's prayer exhibits a particular interest in people repenting of their sins before God.[151] This prayer does not simply assume that people are praying to Yhwh but specifies particular circumstances in which people repented of their sins. Further, Solomon's prayer is not the only prayer describing the circumstance of offering penitential prayer, but the Chronicler actually showcases more cases of repentance (1 Chr 21:8; 2 Chr 33:10). The Chronicler explicitly calls for practical application in people's repentance by suggesting several typical actions or characteristics, such as turning from evil ways (6:26; 7:14) with humility (7:14; 12:6–7, 12; 28:19; 30:11; 33:12, 19, 23; 34:27–28; 36:12), restoring the temple and temple worship (2 Chr 29:11–19; 30:1–4; 33:15), or confessing sins (1 Chr 21:8, 17; 2 Chr 6:37). In addition, the Chronicler conveys the message that repentance is often related to God's disciplinary intention (e.g., pestilence [1 Chr 21]; covenant curses [2 Chr 6–7];[152] for-

---

For the definition of penitential prayer, see Rodney A. Werline, who says, "Penitential prayer is a direct address to God in which an individual, group, or an individual on behalf of a group confesses sins and petitions for forgiveness as an act of repentance" (Werline, "Defining Penitential prayer," in Boda et al., *Origins of Penitential Prayer*, xv). In terms of penitential prayer as a particular form or a literary genre, Bautch identifies five features make this prayer unique: functional efficacy—prayer effects God's forgiveness of sin; communal dimension—even individual repentance is offered in solidarity with the moral failure of the community; structuring convention—"self-conscious use of literary convention relating to lament form"; ceremonial context—"the prayer is associated with a cultic context, but the context was not reducible to the cult"; and intertextual character—religious thought from earlier texts or generations is rearticulated (Bautch, *Development in Genre*, 1–6).

149. See some of penitential prayers offered in the post-exilic days: Ezra 9; Neh 1, 9; Dan 9; see also Ps 106.

150. Boda, *Return to Me*, 132.

151. See the section "Supplicants Who Ask God's Forgiveness" (Solomon's prayer) in ch. 3. This book has already articulated that the particular aspect of supplicants from Solomon's prayer is those who repent of their sins before Yhwh.

152. For covenant curses, see "Solomon's Hope of Davidic Dynasty" (Solomon's prayer) in ch. 3.

eign forces [33:11–12]) toward his people. Thus, prophetic warnings often prompt repentance (1 Chr 21; 2 Chr 12:1, 5; 16:7–10; 18:12–27; 19:3; 24:19–20; 33:18; 34:22–28), and through divine discipline, the people repent of their sins or uncleanness and experience God's forgiveness (2 Chr 6:21, 25, 27, 30, 37; 7:14; see Ezra 9; Neh 1, 9; Dan 9; Ps 106) and his healing of the land or people (7:14; 30:20).[153] Thus, the Chronicler's message could effectively motivate the post-exilic audience to consistently repent when they sin in their lives or when any type of uncleanness arises in their sacrifice.[154] Through penitential prayer, accompanied by proper behavior, the community would hope for divine intervention in their lives and experience the restoration of the community (see Ezra 9:12; Neh 9:17, 28, 31–33).[155]

Third, the Chronicler illustrates Jehoshaphat and his prayer as a model and conveys the messages that the post-exilic community could adopt a past prayer and transform it into their own prayer.[156] Although this contextualization of the past prayer is more often observed in the Hellenistic period (e.g., Jdt 9; 3 Macc 2), in line with the development of the genre of prayer, this phenomenon was not exceptional during the Persian period as well (e.g., Neh 9). Newman particularly defines the post-exilic prayers' reuse of past Scriptures as scripturalization,[157] and argues that

---

153. Boda, *Return to Me*, 144.

The expression וְאֶרְפָּא אֶת־אַרְצָם (I will heal their land (2 Chr 7:14)]) is an enigma, for it appears only here in Chronicles. The verb רפא as to heal appears in 2 Chr 7:14; 16:12 (cf. physician); 22:6; 30:20. The noun מַרְפֵּא appears in 2 Chr 21:18; 36:16. There is no verse related to the land except 2 Chr 7:14. In other instances, the word רפא relates to the land (Exod 15:26; Deut 29:22) (Taylor, "Application of 2 Chronicles 7:13–15," 151). One could associate this expression with some type of literal restoration of the land. Or, as Klein gives attention to Jeremiah's prophecy, it could be God's healing of the people (הִנְנִי מַעֲלֶה־לָּהּ אֲרֻכָה וּמַרְפֵּא וּרְפָאתִים ["Behold, I will bring it healing and cure, and I will heal them and bringing back of the people and security" (Jer 33:6)]) (R. Klein, *Second Chronicles*, 112).

154. This means that prayer neither replaces a sacrifice nor has more power than sacrifice. See "Hezekiah, the Supplicant" in ch. 3.

155. See 78n159 of this book for the essential nature of forgiveness conveyed by Solomon's prayer.

156. See "Past Prayer as a Model" (Jehoshaphat's prayer) in ch. 3.

157. Newman does not limit the category or form of the source of prayer only to past prayer but includes biblical scriptures more in general. Also, she admits that the term Scripture could be anachronistic when applying it to the post-exilic era, yet she argues that in this period, the post-exilic people have already recognized some authoritative texts (e.g., Torah). Thus she defines this term as "the collection of texts that would eventually become the Jewish and part of the Christian Bible" (Newman,

the development of the genre of prayer does not result only in a fixed or patterned form of prayer. Instead, the development could also exhibit the so-called "free-form phenomenon" by supplicants' employment of different literary features (e.g., biblical citation, nuanced allusion).[158] Newman differentiates this phenomenon from the inner-biblical interpretation[159] and explains it as follows:

> The reuse of scripture does not necessarily entail the presumed author's *conscious* interpretation of scripture. My use of the term "scripturalization" is broad enough to include at times clear references to biblical stories or incidents that may contain no biblical references to biblical stories or incidents that may contain no biblical reference other than an identifiable personal or place name. It also includes instances in which the author seemed to be using biblical wording without regard to its source, but simply to provide a biblical "ring" to the composition.[160]

According to her understanding of the source (i.e., a biblical ring), the prayers by notable figures in the history (e.g., Jabez, David, Solomon, Asa, Jehoshaphat, Hezekiah) could certainly be the source of the postexilic community's prayers.[161] The Chronicler consistently idealizes those supplicants and instrumentalizes them as model supplicants for the

---

Praying by the Book, 11).

158. Newman, *Praying by the Book*, 15–16, 240–41.

159. Fishbane, *Biblical Interpretation*. Kugel and Greer, *Early Biblical Interpretation*.

160. Newman, *Praying by the Book*, 13–14. Newman also writes, "The few examples (1 Kgs 8:23–53; Jdt 9:2–14; 3 Macc 2:2–20) treated here are just the tip of the iceberg of a widespread trend in prayers of the Second Temple period. What appear as brief reference to the past and earlier traditions in a handful of pre-exilic prayers gradually becomes an unself-conscious use of scriptural words, phrases, and interpretation." Newman sees that the process of redaction took place in the prayer of 1 Kgs, especially concerning the section after v. 40 to the end of the prayer; thus Solomon's prayer is appropriated to those who lived in the days of the exile and the returned people. However, it is not necessary to follow this view; instead, it is probable that Solomon assumes the worst-case scenario regarding Israel's destiny (see p. 84 of this book). Newman indicates that other passages could indicate this phenomenon, such as 2 Sam 7:18–29; 2 Kgs 19:15–19; Jonah 2:2–11 (Eng. vv. 1–10); 4:2–3; however, these passages should be examined in accordance with one's view regarding the dates of the text (Newman, "Scripturalization of Prayer," in Kugel, *Prayers That Cite Scripture*, 23–24).

161. On Chronicles' use of authoritative resources, see Ben Zvi and Edelman, *What Was Authoritative*. Especially, Ben Zvi's article "One Size Does Not Fit All: Observations on the Different Ways That Chronicles Dealt with the Authoritative Literature of Its Time" in this collection of essays explains the Chronicler's use of Sam-Kgs.

audience. In this regard, the Chronicler's use of Jehoshaphat's prayer is a good illustration to use to communicate with the post-exilic audience. Jehoshaphat does not adopt Solomon's prayer verbatim but alludes to the content of Solomon's prayer and the prophecy of Isaiah. Thus, his prayer illustrates an example of a transformation of the past prayer in a prayer relevant to the king's historical context. By observing this feature, the post-exilic community could pray like those historic supplicants, and through their own prayer, they could expect success similar to what the exemplary supplicants achieved (e.g., receiving God's deliverance and forgiveness [e.g., 1 Chr 4:9; 2 Chr 14:10, 20:5–13; 30:18–20; 33:12–13)]), and they could manifest their praise of God with thanksgiving (e.g., 1 Chr 16:8–36; 17:16–27; 29:10–19; 2 Chr 6:12–42; 7:1–10).

Overall, biblical literature (e.g., Ezra 9; Neh 1, 9) attests to the post-exilic community's practice of prayer. Chronicles also exhibits various prayer practices through model supplicants in Israel's history. This book has observed three highlighted concepts in Chronicles' shaping of the post-exilic community into praying community. The community could pray toward/at/in the temple, which Yhwh oversees and where Yhwh's presence manifests. Also, in their effort concerning the restoration of the community, they are encouraged to repent if they sin. Finally, they could transform past prayers into their own contextualized prayers in order to experience Yhwh's intervention into their lives. In these ways, the community could become an active praying community.

— *Chapter Five* —

Conclusion

The fundamental conclusion of this book is that the recorded prayers in Chronicles function to persuade the post-exilic community to actualize the Chronicler's desired community identity. The Chronicler portrays his ideal future Israel as the liturgical community that consists of the citizens of the revived Davidic kingdom who maintain the roles of praying and worshiping and the characteristic of monotheistic belief.

For the members of the post-exilic community, Babylonian exile and Persian governance raised vital questions concerning their status quo and prompted them to search for their identity. The post-exilic community's circumstances were certainly not identical to its past, and the exile created a discontinuity between their past and the present. In this regard, the community retrieved their past records and examined themselves in light of them. Furthermore, the past records allowed them to see future possibilities that could help them to overcome the gap between the past and present.

Chronicles was able to serve this purpose of bridging the past and the present and illuminating the future of the community. Specifically, the recorded prayers as the Chronicler's strategic literary artifacts assist the audience of the post-exilic community to reflect on its past experience in light of other historical narratives in the book. The prayers also persuade them to perceive and internalize the Chronicler's desired roles or characteristics in dealing with their current situation under Persian control and influence. Thus, the members of the community could eventually actualize the ideal community identity envisioned by the Chronicler.

Chapter 1 laid out the background of this study. Specifically, it provided the notion of identity that this book understands. This study did not aim to reveal the identity of individuals in the community but instead focused on community identity as a whole, which consists of multiple roles or characteristics of its members.

In chapter 2, this book argued for the recorded prayers' unique rhetorical effect in Chronicles. Prayer could invite the audience to join in a supplicant's prayer in Chronicles; then, the participants could transform the recorded prayer into their own prayer that is relevant to their present life setting. Further, this book revealed the relationship between the rhetorical effect of prayer and the identity formation process. Prayers in Chronicles contain the post-exilic community's past memories and hope for God's intervention in their lives for a better future. This feature means that the participants of prayer are able to pray to the same Yhwh of their past, the One who promised to answer the supplicants' prayer. In this regard, the Chronicler instrumentalized various supplicants in Chronicles as exemplary models for the participants (i.e., his audience). Hence, the participants adopt the prayers of the historical figures and ultimately interpret the contents of those prayers in order to apply them to their own circumstances. The recorded prayers and their surrounding stories collaborate to motivate the post-exilic participants to manifest an appropriate attitude in order to bring about a better future; thus, the participants could fulfill or maintain the Chronicler's desired roles or characteristics.

Chapter 3 rendered a major task for this book. It undertook literary and rhetorical analysis of eight recorded prayers in Chronicles (1 Chr 4:9–10; 16:8–36; 17:16–27; 29:10–19; 2 Chr 6:12–38; 14:10 [Eng. v. 11]; 20:5–12; 30:18–20). Since Chronicles' primary aim is not to shape the identity of the post-exilic audience but to report Israel's history, prayers do not systemically portray roles or characteristics. Each prayer highlights different roles or characteristics in its unique literary context, and these features could be revealed as the audience interacts with each prayer and its context. In this regard, this book was able to conclude that through recorded prayers, the portrayed roles or characteristics are prayer, monotheistic belief, worship, and Davidic citizenship. This book further argued for the aspects of different roles or characteristics.

First, supplicants should distinctively recognize Yhwh as the object of prayer and maintain faith, believing that Yhwh is the only deity upon whom they could rely, since he has the power, strength, and wealth to deliver supplicants from their difficult situations (1 Chr 4:9–10; 17:16–27;

14:11 [Eng. v. 10]; 2 Chr 20:5–12). Chronicles also underlines that supplicants should repent and ask Yhwh for his forgiveness when they sin (2 Chr 6:12–38) and highlights the power of communal prayer (20:5–12). Chronicles even conveys the message that prayer has the power to transform supplicants' circumstances into improved ones, even if the better situation is actualized in an abnormal way in the supplicants' perception (30:18–20).

Second, this book revealed that the recorded prayers in Chronicles contribute to shaping the post-exilic audience into monotheistic believers. In shaping this characteristic, Chronicles revolves around two pillars: Yhwh's uniqueness to Israel and his supremacy over the universe. Israel is Yhwh's chosen people, who have had a long and covenantal relationship with their unique God (1 Chr 16:8–36; 2 Chr 6:14–42; 14:10 [Eng. v. 11]; 20:5–12; 30:18–20), and Yhwh is the sovereign deity, who maintains his incomparable position to other deities (1 Chr 17:16–27; 2 Chr 6:14–42) and deserves the universal recognition of his supremacy (1 Chr 16:8–36; 29:10–19; 2 Chr 6:14–42; 14:10 [Eng. v. 11]; 20:5–12). Thus, monotheistic believers should manifest their belief that Yhwh still remembers his people and is able to exhibit his salvific deeds for the post-exilic audience (1 Chr 16:6–36; 17:16–27; 2 Chr 14:10 [Eng. v. 11]; 20:5–12), and they need to respond to their special God in the appropriate manner (1 Chr 29:10–19). One way that the audience finds Yhwh's uniqueness and supremacy is through their recognition of the nature and function of the temple (2 Chr 6:14–42).

Third, the recorded prayers motivate the post-exilic audience to become a worshiping community. Although the Chronicler elucidates the distinctive roles of the priests and Levites (1 Chr 23–27), through the recorded prayers and its related context, he essentially considers all-Israel's role as worshipers (2 Chr 30:18–20; see 20:13–30). The worshipers should manifest the appropriate inward and outward attitudes; thus, they could manifest Yhwh's presence among worshipers and in the universe (1 Chr 16:6–36). Chronicles limits the form of worship particularly to sacrificial ritual and provides a model worshiper, the Davidic king Hezekiah, whom the post-exilic audience could follow (2 Chr 30:18–20).

Fourth, three recorded prayers are specifically devoted to motivating the post-exilic audience to desire the attainment of the Davidic citizenship (1 Chr 17:16–27; 2 Chr 6:14–42; 30:18–20). David's prayer—in line with Nathan's oracle (1 Chr 17:3–15)—is the strongest affirmation of the Davidic dynasty, since it involves God's direct verbal revelation through the prophet. This passage particularly reveals the close relationship between the temple construction and the perpetuity of the Davidic dynasty. Solomon's prayer (2 Chr 6:14–42) affirms this relationship again as the king asks God to keep his promise concerning the everlasting Davidic kingdom at the scene of the temple's completed construction and dedication. Furthermore, the Davidic king Hezekiah demonstrates his authority over the northern and southern territories in his successful temple worship, even after the monarchy is divided (30:18–20). All these prayers, therefore, together conclusively persuade the post-exilic audience to be dedicated to temple-related duties.

Chapter 4 attempted to trace community identity in the sociohistorical context of Yehud. This book examined the implications of the roles and characteristics, portrayed in the Chronicler's literary historical matrix, in light of the reality that members of the Yehud community lived under the Persian Empire's influence and control. For this investigation, this study specifically delved into the biblical literature, since it is a relevant resource for listening to the inner voice of the community and revealing Chronicles' unique message in comparison to other biblical literature.

This chapter revealed that the roles and characteristics portrayed in chapter 3 were indeed ongoing subjects in the community's conversation regarding the process of its restoration. The implications of pursuing the roles and characteristics in the post-exilic community can be summarized in the following ways from the perspective of Chronicles. For the characteristic of monotheistic belief, it is imperative for the vulnerable Yehud community to rely upon their unique Yhwh, who is the supreme divinity, as they interact with the ruling foreign power. As the worshiping community, the people of Yehud should be eager to restore their worship practices, and Chronicles particularly emphasizes the proper functionality of the religious institutions in their restoration efforts. In terms of the actualization of Davidic citizenship, the Yehud community should await a royalistic revival of the Davidic dynasty without any enterprise of cataclysmic upheaval; meanwhile, the community should fulfill the roles or exhibit the characteristics portrayed in Chronicles. As the praying community, the members of the community must give their attention to the temple, since it receives God's special attention. In the practice of prayer, they could transform the past prayers into their own prayer in hope of God's intervention. In addition, they are encouraged to continually repent of their sins in order to bring about the restoration of their community.

The convergence of the results of this book is the Jerusalem temple with the temple service. Since the Yehud community had no tangible political structure under Persian rule, the temple played a major role in the process of their community identity formation. Namely, the roles and characteristics of the community could be heavily identified in relation to the nature and function of the Jerusalem temple and to the community's practice of temple-related duties. In this regard, the sum of the portrayed roles and characteristics in Chronicles indicates that the post-exilic community should be identified as a liturgical community.

Through the recorded prayers, the Chronicler shapes the post-exilic audience as monotheistic believers by reminding them of their unique relationship with Yhwh and persuading them that Israel's powerful God of the past still manifests himself in their present lives under Persian rule. This distinctive perception concerning Yhwh's unique relationship with his people and his supremacy over the universe is closely associated with the act of worship and prayer. Concerning the former (i.e., Yhwh's unique relationship with his people), Israel's acts of worship and prayer are rooted in a covenantal relationship. Israel's belief in Yhwh is neither an advent *ex nihilo* nor the Chronicler's invented oeuvre; rather, it is based on Israel's long-established relationship with God, which holds Israelites responsible for worshiping and praying to Yhwh (1 Chr 15:25–28; 16:15–16; 17:22; 28:8–9; 29:18–19; 2 Chr 6:11, 14; 34:29—35:6). Concerning the latter (i.e., Yhwh's supremacy over the universe), the emanation of monotheistic belief becomes possible through the community's participation in the temple service and duties, which conform their perception of the quality of the temple, since it, as Yhwh's primary locus in the earthly realm, manifests his supremacy over the world. In other words, the cultivation of the perspective of Yhwh's uniqueness and supremacy among the community members could provide a foundation for their practice of prayer and worship, namely, that their monotheistic belief embodies the object of prayer and worship. Therefore, having been surrounded by polytheistic believers in the Persian era, the post-exilic monotheistic community should be the worshiping and praying community by participating in temple worship and praying toward/at/in the temple, the place of Yhwh's oversight.

The post-exilic community's participation in temple worship could be characterized as a public and sacrificial ritual. The Chronicler envisions that all-Israel is accountable to worship Yhwh (1 Chr 16:36; 2 Chr 11:6–7; 15:9–15) and that the institutions (e.g., the temple, priests, and

Levites) in particular play significant roles in the performance of the worship service. Thus, Israel's worship is not a form of individual piety or private meditation.

However, one should not misconstrue Israel's demonstration of faith as remaining in the formality of the religious process. Chronicles formulates the core of worship as lying in the manifestation of worshipers' inner status, namely, wholeheartedness. The community's temple worship involves both an appropriate inner heart and sacrificial performance. Similarly, the Israelites' act of prayer in Chronicles involves each supplicant's personal interaction with Yhwh. Although each supplicant's perception concerning the essential characteristics of Yhwh exhibits a similar manner—that is, Yhwh is the special and supreme divinity—the way each supplicant articulates his prayer is unique, since each supplicant's circumstances are not identical. Therefore, the Chronicler's encouragement for the post-exilic community to pray toward/at/in the temple should not be understood as limited only to a particular patterned or fixed prescription for the practice of prayer. The act of prayer certainly reflects the inner status or attitude of the supplicants. Like Jabez, Asa, and Jehoshaphat, the community could address their difficult circumstances to Yhwh. Similar to David, the community could have faith in God's promise with a humble heart. Like Solomon's prayer, the community boldly requires Yhwh to fulfill his promises. Resembling Jehoshaphat's prayer, the community is allowed to freely express their words in prayer by employing past prayers. In sum, having maintained an unequivocal perception of Yhwh's characteristics, the post-exilic community could become a liturgical community by actualizing the cooperative application of both inner attitudes and outer performance in temple worship and the act of prayer.

However, the above-described liturgical community is not yet an ideal liturgical community from the perspective of the Chronicler's shaping of the post-exilic community's identity. The Chronicler conveys the message that the future Israel should maintain Davidic citizenship, and this citizenship can be attained as the community continually devotes itself to the temple service and duties until the days of the Davidic kingdom's revival. This feature implies then that the Chronicler does not abandon his hope for the future Israel as a political entity. However, even the fundamental characteristic of the future Israel is still defined by the community's religious practices—namely, praying, worshiping, and being a monotheistic believing community—thus, as the post-exilic community attains Davidic citizenship, it ultimately becomes an ideal liturgical community.

The two key subjects of this book are recorded prayers in Chronicles and the identity formation of the post-exilic community. In previous chapters, this book revealed that scholars have been interested in these subjects in recent decades; yet, integrated research in both fields is not abundant. In that respect, the particular contribution of this book can be summarized in two aspects. In terms of the post-exilic community's identity, this study focused primarily on the Chronicler's literary and rhetorical portrayal of identity. The recent scholarly trend in employing various sociological methodologies often alleviates or ignores the authorial intention of the literature and, instead, seeks to understand how the literature functions in each sociological methodology's matrix. Because of the nature of the research subject (i.e., identity formation), this study did not completely overlook the sociological landscape, and it attempted to communicate with other scholarly approaches. However, this book primarily undertook exegetical, literary, and rhetorical analysis in order to discover the process of the identity formation from the perspective of the Chronicler's intent. This particular task could contribute to the study of Chronicles and the post-exilic community's identity formation process, because the essence of this methodology helps contemporary readers listen to one of the authoritative inner voices of the community.

In terms of the recorded prayers in Chronicles, scholars have delved into the genre of prayer, and some have exhibited their interest particularly in the reported and recorded prayers in Chronicles. In this regard, this study's dedication to recorded prayer in Chronicles is nothing new. However, this study has made a contribution to the field by revealing the unique rhetorical effect of the recorded prayer. The rhetorical features of recorded prayer are distinct from forms of direct speech, the genre of narrative, or even reported prayer, since recorded prayer can invite and persuade the audience of Chronicles to transform their behavior in order to fulfill the Chronicler's desired roles and characteristics. In this regard, this study, in comparison to previous studies, has been able to bestow increased rhetorical power to recorded prayer and establish a substantial connection between the function of recorded prayer and identity formation.

Concerning the results of this study, two further study points could be pursued: a synchronic approach to the process of identity formation in the post-exilic community and a diachronic tracing of the post-exilic community's identity. Concerning the former, future research may need to investigate recorded prayers in other biblical and non-biblical literature in relation to identity formation (e.g., do they portray similar roles or characteristics to Chronicles, or how does recorded prayer function in other literature). In chapter 4, this study provided an overview of the roles or characteristics presented in other biblical literature. Yet, because of the scope of this research, the study in that chapter was not comprehensive, especially concerning the recorded prayers in other literature. In regard to the latter, future research will need to trace the post-exilic people's perception of their identity and their manifestation of it over time. This research would be a critical task, because the external dynamic changes as time passes (e.g., from the Persian to the Hellenistic and Roman period) and, specifically, as the second temple is destroyed, and thus the central locus of identity vanishes.

Bibliography

Ackroyd, Peter R. "The Chronicler as Exegete." *JSOT* 2 (1977) 2–32.
———. *The Chronicler in His Age*. JSOTSup 101. Sheffield, UK: JSOT, 1991.
———. "History and Theology in the Writings of the Chronicler." *CTM* 38, no. 8 (1967) 501–15.
Ahn, Suk-il. *The Persuasive Portrayal of David and Solomon in Chronicles: A Rhetorical Analysis of the Speeches and Prayers in the David-Solomon Narrative*. McMaster Biblical Studies. Eugene, OR: Pickwick, 2018.
———. "A Rhetorical Study of David's Speech and Prayer in 1 Chr 28–29." *KEOTS* 12 (217) 89–130.
Albrecht, Milton C. "The Relationship of Literature and Society." *AJS* 59, no. 5 (1954) 425–36.
Alexander, T. Desmond, and Brian S. Rosner, eds. *NDBT*. Downers Grove, IL: InterVarsity, 2000.
Allen, Leslie C. *Psalms: 101–150*. WBC 21. Rev. ed. Waco, TX: Word, 2002.
Amar, Itzhak. "The Twofold Literary Structure of the Chronistic David Narrative (1 Chr 11–29)." *SJOT* 30, no. 2 (2016) 261–79.
Anderson, James S. *Monotheism and Yahweh's Appropriation of Baal*. LHBOTS 617. London: T&T Clark, 2015.
Arndt, William, et al. *BDAG*. Chicago: University of Chicago Press, 2000.
Avioz, Michael. "Nathan's Prophecy in 2 Sam 7 and in 1 Chr 17: Text, Context, and Meaning." *ZAW* 116, no. 4 (2004) 542–54.
Balentine, Samuel E. *Prayer in the Hebrew Bible: The Drama of Divine-Human Dialogue*. OBT. Minneapolis: Fortress, 1993.
———. "Prayers for Justice in the Old Testament: Theodicy and Theology." *CBQ* 51, no. 4 (1989) 597–616.
Balz, Horst Robert, and Gerhard Schneider. *EDNT*. Grand Rapids: Eerdmans, 1990.
Barbiero, Gianni. "Psalm 132: A Prayer of 'Solomon.'" *CBQ* 75, no. 2 (2013) 239–58.
Bar-Efrat, Shimon. *Narrative Art in the Bible*. Edinburgh: T&T Clark, 2004.
Barrick, W. B., and John R. Spencer, eds. *In the Shelter of Elyon: Essays on Ancient Palestinian Life and Literature in Honor of G. W. Ahlström*. JSOTSup 31. Sheffield, UK: Sheffield Academic, 1984.
Baumbach, Sibylle, et al., eds. *Literature and Values: Literature as a Medium for Representing, Disseminating and Constructing Norms and Values*. Trier, Germ.: Wissenschaftlicher, 2009.

Bautch, Richard J. *Development in Genre between Post-Exilic Penitential Prayer and the Psalms of Communal Lament.* SBL Academia Biblica 7. Leiden, Neth.: Brill, 2003.

Becking, Bob. *Ezra, Nehemiah, and the Construction of Early Jewish Identity.* FAT 80. Tübingen, Germ.: Mohr Siebeck, 2011.

Becking, Bob, and Eric Peels, eds. *Psalms and Prayers: Papers Read at the Joint Meeting of the Society for Old Testament Study and Het Oud Testamentisch Werkgezelschap in Nederland en België, Apeldoorn August 2006.* OTS 55. Leiden, Neth.: Brill, 2007.

Beentjes, Pancratius C. "Tradition and Transformation: Aspects of Innerbiblical Interpretation in 2 Chronicles 20." *Biblica* 74, no. 2 (1993) 258–68.

———. *Tradition and Transformation in the Book of Chronicles.* Leiden, Neth.: Brill, 2008.

———. "War Narratives in the Book of Chronicles: A New Proposal in Respect of their Function." *SBLHS* 59, no. 3 (2003) 587–96.

Begg, Christopher T. "Seeking Yahweh and the Purpose of Chronicles." *Louvain Studies* 9, no. 2 (1982) 128–41.

Ben Zvi, Ehud. "The Book of Chronicles: Another Look." *SR* 31, no. 3–4 (2002) 261–81.

———. *History, Literature and Theology in the Book of Chronicles.* Oakville, CT: Equinox, 2006.

———. "In Conversation and Appreciation of the Recent Commentaries by Steven L. McKenzie and Gary N. Knoppers." *JHS* 5, no. 20 (2005) 21–45.

———. "A Sense of Proportion: An Aspect of the Theology of the Chronicler." *SJOT* 9, no. 1 (1995) 37–51.

———, ed. *Utopia and Dystopia in Prophetic Literature.* PFES 92. Göttingen, Germ.: Vandenhoeck & Ruprecht, 2006.

Ben Zvi, Ehud, and Christoph Levin, eds. *The Concept of Exile in Ancient Israel and Its Historical Context.* New York: Walter de Gruyter, 2010.

Ben Zvi, Ehud, and Diana V. Edelman, eds. *Imagining the Other and Constructing Israelite Identity in the Early Second Temple Period.* LHBOTS 456. New York: T&T Clark, 2014.

———. *Leadership, Social Memory, and Judean Discourse in the Fifth-Second Centuries BCE.* Worlds of the Ancient Near East and Mediterranean. Sheffield, UK: Equinox, 2016.

———. *Memory and the City in Ancient Israel.* Winona Lake, IN: Eisenbrauns, 2014.

———. *Remembering Biblical Figures in the Late Persian and Early Hellenistic Periods: Social Memory and Imagination.* Oxford: Oxford University Press, 2013.

———. *What Was Authoritative for Chronicles?* Winona Lake, IN: Eisenbrauns, 2011.

Berquist, Jon L., ed. *Approaching Yehud: New Approaches to the Study of the Persian Period.* SemeiaSt 50. Atlanta SBL, 2007.

———. *Judaism in Persia's Shadow: A Social and Historical Approach.* Minneapolis: Fortress, 1995.

Beyerle, Stefan. *The Book of Daniel and Its Social Setting.* VTSup 83. Leiden, Neth.: Brill, 2001.

Black, David Alan, and David S. Dockery, eds. *Interpreting the New Testament: Essays on Methods and Issues.* Nashville: Broadman & Holman, 2001.

Boda, Mark J. "Encountering an Alternative Reality: Schweitzer and the Utopian Turn." *JHS* 9, no. 11 (2009) 4–9.

———. *Exploring Zechariah: The Development of Zechariah and Its Role within the Twelve.* ANEM 16. Atlanta: SBL, 2017.

———. *First–Second Chronicles*. Edited by Philp W. Comfort. CBC 5a. Carol Stream, IL: Tyndale, 2010.
———. *Haggai, Zechariah*. NIVAC. Grand Rapids: Zondervan, 2004.
———. *Return to Me: A Biblical Theology of Repentance*. Downers Grove, IL: InterVarsity, 2015.
Boda, Mark J., and Iain W. Provan, eds. *Let Us Go Up to Zion: Essays in Honour of H. G. M. Williamson on the Occasion of His Sixty-Fifth Birthday*. VTSup 153. Leiden, Neth.: Brill, 2012.
Boda, Mark J., and Paul L. Redditt, eds. *Unity and Disunity in Ezra-Nehemiah Redaction, Rhetoric, and Reade*. HBM 17. Sheffield, UK: Sheffield Phoenix, 2008.
Boda, Mark J., et al., eds. *The Development of Penitential Prayer in Second Temple Judaism*. Vol. 2 of *Seeking the Favor of God*. EJL 22. Atlanta: SBL, 2006.
———. *The Origins of Penitential Prayer in Second Temple Judaism*. Vol. 1 of *Seeking the Favor of God*. EJL 21. Atlanta: SBL, 2006.
Boer, Roland T., ed. *Jameson and Jeroboam*. SemeiaSt. Atlanta: Scholars, 1996.
———. "Utopia, Dystopia and Uchronia in Chronicles." *JHS* 9, no. 11 (2009) 10–14.
Bosman, Jan Petrus. "Social Identity in Nahum: A Theological-Ethical Enquiry." PhD diss., University of Stellenbosch, 2005.
Botica, Aurelian. "'When Heaven Is Shut Up': Ancient Near Eastern Backgrounds to the Concept of Natural Calamity." *Perichoresis* 4, no. 1 (2006) 95–115.
Botterweck, G. Johannes, et al., eds. Translated by John T. Willis et al. *TDOT*. Grand Rapids: Eerdmans, 1977–2012.
Bowen, Nancy R., et al., eds. *A God So Near: Essays on Old Testament Theology in Honor of Patrick D. Miller*. Winona Lake, IN: Eisenbrauns, 2003.
Braun, Roddy L. *First Chronicles*. WBC 14. Dallas: Word, 1986.
———. "Message of Chronicles: Rally 'Round the Temple." *CTM* 42, no. 8 (1971) 502–14.
———. "Solomon, the Chosen Temple Builder: The Significance of 1 Chronicles 22, 28, and 29 for the Theology of Chronicles." *JBL* 95, no. 4 (1976): 581–90.
Breneman, Mervin. *Ezra, Nehemiah, Esther*. NAC 10. Nashville: Broadman & Holman, 1993.
Brettler, Marc Zvi. *The Creation of History in Ancient Israel*. London: Routledge, 2003.
Briant, Pierre. *From Cyrus to Alexander: A History of the Persian Empire*. Winona Lake, IN: Eisenbrauns, 2002.
Bright, John. *A History of Israel*. 4th ed. Westminster Aids to the Study of the Scriptures. Louisville, KY: Westminster John Knox, 2000.
Broyles, Craig C. *Psalms*. UBC. Grand Rapids: Baker Academic, 1999.
Bullinger, E. W. *Figures of Speech Used in the Bible*. New York: Cosimo Classics, 2012.
Burke, Kenneth. *The Rhetoric of Religion: Studies in Logology*. Boston: Beacon, 1961.
Butler, Trent C. "A Forgotten Passage from a Forgotten Era (1 Chr. XVI 8–36)." *VT* 28, no. 2 (1978) 142–50.
Camp, Phillip G., and Tremper Longman III, eds. *Praying with Ancient Israel: Exploring the Theology of Prayer in the Old Testament*. Abilene, TX: Abilene Christian University Press, 2015.
Cataldo, Jeremiah W. *A Theocratic Yehud?: Issues of Government in a Persian Province*. LHBOTS 498. New York: T&T Clark, 2009.

Cezula, Ntozakhe Simon. "The Chronicler as a Biblical Paradigm for a Theology of Reconstruction in Africa: An Exploration of 2 Chronicles 6:32." *OTE* 29, no. 2 (2016) 277–96.

Chazon, Esther. "Prayers from Qumran and Their Historical Implications." *DSD* 1 (1994) 265–84.

Clayton, J. Nathan. "Symbol, Service, and Song: The Levites of 1 Chronicles 10–29 in Rhetorical, Historical and Theological Perspectives." PhD diss., Trinity International University, 2007.

Clines, David J. A., ed. *DCH*. Sheffield, UK: Sheffield Academic, 1993–2011.

Cogan, Mordechai. *First Kings*. AYBC 10. New York: Doubleday, 2001.

Coggins, R. J. *The First and Second Books of the Chronicles*. TCBC 13–14. Cambridge, UK: Cambridge University Press, 1976.

Collins, John J. "Cognitive Dissonance and Eschatological Violence: Fantasized Solutions to a Theological Dilemma in Second Temple Judaism." In *Monotheism in Late Prophetic and Early Apocalyptic Literature*, edited by Nathan MacDonald and Ken Brown, 201–17. Studies of the Sofja Kovalevskaja Research Group on Early Jewish Monotheism 3. Tübingen, Germ.: Mohr Siebeck, 2014.

———. *The Invention of Judaism: Torah and Jewish Identity from Deuteronomy to Paul*. TLJS 7. Oakland, CA: University of California Press, 2017.

Corvin, Jack. "A Stylistic and Functional Study of the Prose Prayers in the Historical Narratives of the Old Testament." PhD diss., Emory University, 1972.

Cowley, A. *Aramaic Papyri of the Fifth Century B.C.* London: Oxford University Press, 1923.

Cross, Frank Moore. "A Reconstruction of the Judean Restoration." *JBL* 94 (1975) 4–18.

Crouch, Carly L. *The Making of Israel*. VTSup 162. Leiden, Neth.: Brill, 2016.

Cudworth, Troy D. "The 'God of the Fathers' in Chronicles." *JBL* 135, no. 3 (2016) 483–91.

———. *War in Chronicles: Temple Faithfulness and Israel's Place in the Land*. LHBOTS 627. New York: T&T Clark, 2016.

Curtis, Edward Lewis, and Albert Alonzo Madsen. *A Critical and Exegetical Commentary on the Books of Chronicles*. Edinburgh: T&T Clark, 1910.

Daffern, I. J. Megan. "The Semantic Field of 'Remembering' in the Psalms." *JSOT* 41, no. 1 (2016) 79–97.

Dahood, Mitchell S. J. *Psalms Two: 51–100*. AYBC 17. New Haven, CT: Yale University Press, 1995.

David, Ohad, and Daniel Bar-Tal. "A Sociopsychological Conception of Collective Identity: The Case of National Identity as Example." *PSPR* 13, no. 4 (2009) 354–79.

Davidson, Robert. *The Validity of Worship: A Commentary on the Book of Psalms*. Grand Rapids: Eerdmans, 1998.

DeClaissé-Walford, Nancy L., et al. *The Book of Psalms*. NICOT. Grand Rapids: Eerdmans, 2014.

Deems, Edward Mark, et al., eds. *First Chronicles*. Vol. 23 of *The Pulpit Commentary*. New ed. New York: Funk & Wagnalls Company, 1950.

Dever, William G. *What Did the Biblical Writers Know and When Did They Know it?: What Archaeology Can Tell Us about the Reality of Ancient Israel*. Grand Rapids: Eerdmans, 2001.

DeVries, Simon J. "Festival Ideology in Chronicles." In *Problems in Biblical Theology: Essays in Honor of Rolf Knierim*, edited by Henry T. C. Sun and Keith L. Eades, 104–24. Grand Rapids: Eerdmans, 1997.
———. *First and Second Chronicles*. Edited by Rolf P. Knierim and Gene M. Tucker. FOTL 11. Grand Rapids: Eerdmans, 1989.
———. "Moses and David as Cult Founder in Chronicles." *JBL* 107 (Dec. 1988) 619–39.
———. "Temporal Terms as Structural Elements in the Holy-War Tradition." *VT* 25, no. 1 (1975) 80–105.
Dillard, Raymond B. "The Chronicler's Jehoshaphat." *TrinJ* 7, no. 1 (1986) 17–22.
———. "The Literary Structure of the Chronicler's Solomon Narrative." *JSOT* 30 (1984) 85–93.
———. "The Reign of Asa (2 Chronicles 14–16): An Example of the Chronicler's Theological Method." *JETS* 23, no. 3 (1980) 207–18.
———. *Second Chronicles*. WBC 15. Waco, TX: Word, 1987.
Dirksen, P. B. *First Chronicles*. HCOT. Dudley, MA: Peeters, 2005.
Doan, William, and Terry Giles. "The Song of Asaph: A Performance-Critical Analysis of 1 Chronicles 16:8–36." *CBQ* 70, no. 1 (2008) 29–43.
Driver, S. R. "The Speeches in Chronicles." *The Expositor I* (1895) 241–56.
———. "The Speeches in Chronicles." *The Expositor II* (1895) 286–308.
Duke, Rodkey K. *The Persuasive Appeal of the Chronicler: A Rhetorical Analysis*. JSOTSup 88. Sheffield, UK: Almond, 1990.
———. "Recent Research in Chronicles." *CR:BS* 8, no. 1 (2009) 10–50.
Dumbrell, William J. *Covenant and Creation: An Old Testament Covenant Theology*. Rev. ed. Milton Keynes, UK: Paternoster, 2013.
———. "The Davidic Covenant." *RTR* 39, no. 2 (1980) 40–47.
———. "The Purpose of the Books of Chronicles." *JETS* 27 (1984) 257–66.
Durant, Alan. *Ezra Pound, Identity in Crisis: A Fundamental Reassessment of the Poet and His Work*. Sussex, UK: Harvester, 1981.
Dyck, Jonathan E. *Ethnicity and the Bible*. Edited by Mark G. Brett. Boston: Brill, 2002.
———. *The Theocratic Ideology of the Chronicler*. BIS 33. Leiden, Neth.: Brill, 1998.
Edelman, Diana V. "Hezekiah's Alleged Cultic Centralization." *JSOT* 32, no. 4 (2008) 395–434.
Edelman, Diana V., et al., eds. *History, Memory, Hebrew Scriptures: A Festschrift for Ehud Ben Zvi*. Winona Lake, IN: Eisenbrauns, 2015.
———. *A Palimpsest: Rhetoric, Ideology, Stylistics, and Language Relating to Persian Israel*. PHSC 5. Piscataway, NJ: Gorgias, 2009.
Eichrodt, Walther. *Theology of the Old Testament*. 2 vols. OTL. Philadelphia: Westminster John Knox, 1967.
Endres, John C., et al., eds. *Chronicles and Its Synoptic Parallels in Samuel, Kings, and Related Biblical Texts*. Collegeville, MN: Liturgical, 1998.
Eskenazi, Tamara C. *In an Age of Prose: A Literary Approach to Ezra-Nehemiah*. SBLMS 36. Atlanta: Scholars, 1988.
———. "Nehemiah 9–10: Structure and Significance." *JHS* 3, no. 8 (2001) §1.1—4.3.
———. "The Structure of Ezra-Nehemiah and the Integrity of the Book." *JBL* 107, no. 4 (1988) 641–56.

Eskenazi, Tamara C., and Kent Harold Richards, eds. *Second Temple Studies 2: Temple and Community in the Persian Period.* JSOTSup 175, 146–52. Sheffield, UK: JSOT, 1994.

Esler, Philip F. "Ezra-Nehemiah as a Narrative of (Re-Invented) Israelite Identity." *BI* 11, no. 3 (2003) 413–26.

Estes, Daniel J. "Metaphorical Sojourning in 1 Chronicles 29:15." *CBQ* 53, no. 1 (1991) 45–49.

Evans, Paul S. "The Function of the Chronicler's Temple Despoliation Notices in Light of Imperial Realities in Yehud." *JBL* 129, no. 1 (2010) 31–47.

Evans, Paul S., and Tyler F. Williams, eds. *Chronicling the Chronicler: The Book of Chronicles and Early Second Temple Historiography.* Winona Lake, IN: Eisenbrauns, 2013.

Finkelstein, Israel. "Archaeology and the List of Returnees in the Books of Ezra and Nehemiah." *PEQ* 140, no. 1 (2008) 7–16.

———. "Persian Period Jerusalem and Yehud: A Rejoinder." *JHS* 9, no. 24 (2009) 2–13.

Fishbane, Michael. *Biblical Interpretation in Ancient Israel.* New York: Oxford University Press, 1985.

FitzGerald, William. *Spiritual Modalities: Prayer as Rhetoric and Performance.* University Park, PA: Pennsylvania State University Press, 2012.

Frankel, David. *The Land of Canaan and the Destiny of Israel: Theologies of Territory in the Hebrew Bible.* Winona Lake, IN: Eisenbrauns, 2011.

Freedman, David Noel. "The Chronicler's Purpose." *CBQ* 23 (1961) 436–42.

French, Blaire A. *Chronicles through the Centuries.* WBBC. Sussex, UK: John Wiley & Sons, 2017.

Fretheim, Terence E. "Psalm 132: A Form-Critical Study." *JBL* 86, no. 3 (1967) 289–300.

Fried, Lisbeth S. *The Priest and the Great King: Temple-Palace Relations in the Persian Empire.* BJSUCSD 10. Winona Lake, IN: Eisenbrauns, 2004.

Gentry, Peter John, and Stephen J. Wellum. *Kingdom through Covenant: A Biblical-Theological Understanding of the Covenants.* Wheaton, IL: Crossway, 2012.

Giffone, Benjamin D. "The Timeless, Unifying Rhetoric of Lamentations." *OTE* 25, no. 3 (2012) 534–58.

Gillmayr-Bucher, Susanne, and Maria Häusl, eds. *Prayers and the Construction of Israelite Identity.* AIL 35. Atlanta: SBL, 2019.

Gilmour, Rachelle. *Representing the Past: A Literary Analysis of Narrative Historiography in the Book of Samuel.* VTSup 143. Leiden, Neth.: Brill, 2011.

Glueck, Nelson. *Hesed in the Bible* [Das Wort Hesed im alttestamentlichen Sprachgebrauche als menschliche und göttliche gemeinschaftsgemässe Verhaltungsweise]. Translated by Alfred Gottschalk. Cincinnati: Hebrew Union College Press, 1967.

Goldingay, John. "The Chronicler as a Theologian." *BTB* 5 (1975) 99–126.

———. *Psalms: 90–150.* BCOT 3. Grand Rapids: Baker Academic, 2008.

Good, Robert M. "The Just War in Ancient Israel." *JBL* 104, no. 3 (1985) 385–400.

Gosse, Bernard. *David and Abraham: Persian Period Traditions.* Edited by J. Elayi and J. Sapin. Transeuphratène Supplement 16. Pendé, Fr.: Gabalda, 2010.

Goswell, Gregory. "The Absence of Davidic Hope in Ezra-Nehemiah." *TrinJ* 33 (2012) 19–31.

Grabbe, Lester L. *Yehud: A History of the Perisan Province of Judah.* Vol. 1 of *A History of the Jews and Judaism in the Second Temple Period.* LSTS 47. London: T&T Clark, 2006.

———. *An Introduction to Second Temple Judaism: History and Religion of the Jews in the Time of Nehemiah, the Maccabees, Hillel, and Jesus*. New York: T&T Clark, 2010.

Graham, M. Patrick, and Steven L. McKenzie, eds. *The Chronicler as Author: Studies in Text and Texture*. JSOTSup 263. Sheffield, UK: Sheffield Academic, 1999.

Graham, M. Patrick, et al., eds. *The Chronicler as Historian*. JSOTSup 238. Sheffield, UK: Sheffield Academic, 1997.

———. *Worship and the Hebrew Bible: Essays in Honour of John T. Willis*. JSOTSup 284. Sheffield, UK: Sheffield Academic, 1999.

Granerød, Gard. *Dimensions of Yahwism in the Persian Period: Studies in the Religion and Society of the Judaean Community at Elephantine*. BZAW 488. Berlin: Walter de Gruyter, 2016.

Greenberg, Moshe. *Biblical Prose Prayer: As a Window to the Popular Religion of Ancient Israel*. Taubman Lectures in Jewish Studies 1. Berkeley, CA: University of California Press, 1983.

Greenspahn, Frederick E., ed. *The Hebrew Bible: New Insights and Scholarship*. Jewish Studies in the Twenty-First Century. New York: New York University Press, 2008.

Gring, Mark A. "Rhetoric and Ideology: An Analysis of Interaction among Epistemology, Praxis and Power." PhD diss., The Ohio University, 1993.

Grisanti, Michael A. "The Davidic Covenant." *MSJ* 10, no. 2 (1999) 233–50.

Grisanti, Michael A., and Joseph Blenkinsopp, eds. *Judah and the Judeans in the Neo-Babylonian Period*. Winona Lake, IN: Eisenbrauns, 2003.

Grisanti, Michael A., and David M. Howard, eds. *Giving the Sense: Understanding and Using Old Testament Historical Texts*. Leicester, UK: Apollos, 2003.

Gunneweg, Antonius H. J., and Otto Kaiser, eds. *Textgemäss: Aufsätze und Beiträge zur Hermeneutik des Alten Testaments; Festschrift Für Ernst Würthwein zum 70. Geburtstag*. Göttingen, Germ: Vandenhoeck & Ruprecht, 1979.

Hafemann, Scott J., and Paul R. House, eds. *Central Themes in Biblical Theology: Mapping Unity in Diversity*. Grand Rapids: Baker Academic, 2007.

Hahn, Scott. *The Kingdom of God as Liturgical Empire: A Theological Commentary on 1–2 Chronicles*. Grand Rapids: Baker Academic, 2012.

Hamilton, Mark W. "Who Was a Jew?: Jewish Ethnicity During the Achaemenid Period." *RQ* 37 (1995) 102–17.

Handy, Lowell K., ed. *The Age of Solomon: Scholarship at the Turn of the Millennium*. Studies in the History and Culture of the Ancient Near East 11. Leiden, Neth.: Brill, 1997.

Harris, R. Laird, et al., eds. *TWOT*. Chicago: Moody, 1999.

Heard, R. Christopher. "Echoes of Genesis in 1 Chronicles 4:9–10: An Intertextual and Contextual Reading of Jabez's Prayer." *JHS* 4, no. 2 (2002) §1.1—5.7.

Heiler, Friedrich. *Prayer: A Study in the History and Psychology of Religion*. Translated by Samuel McComb. London: Oxford University Press, 1938.

Hendel, R. "The Exodus in Biblical Memory." *JBL* 120, no. 4 (2001) 601–21.

Heschel, Abraham Joshua. *The Prophets*. Perennial Classics. New York: Perennial, 2001.

Hess, Richard S. *The Old Testament: A Historical, Theological, and Critical Introduction*. Grand Rapids: Baker Academic, 2016.

Hicks, John Mark. *First and Second Chronicles*. CPNIVC. Joplin, MS: College, 2001.

Hill, Andrew E. *First and Second Chronicles*. NIVAC. Grand Rapids: Zondervan, 2003.

———. "Patchwork Poetry or Reasoned Verse? Connective Structure in 1 Chronicles XVI." *VT* 33, no. 1 (1983) 97–101.

Hirst, William, and Gerald Echterhoff. "Creating Shared Memories in Conversation: Toward a Psychology of Collective Memory." *Soc.Res.* 75, no. 1 (2008) 183–216.

Hoffman, Yair, et al., eds. *Politics and Theopolitics in the Bible and Postbiblical Literature*. JSOTSup 171. Sheffield, UK: Sheffield, 1994.

Hognesius, Kjell. *The Text of 2 Chronicles 1–16: A Critical Edition with Textual Commentary*. CBOT 51. Stockholm [Sweden]: Almqvist & Wiksell International, 2003.

Hooker, Paul K. *First and Second Chronicles*. Westminster Bible Companion. 1st ed. Louisville, KY: Westminster John Knox, 2001.

Horbury, William. *Jewish Messianism and the Cult of Christ*. London: SCM, 1998.

———, ed. *Templum Amicitiae: Essays on the Second Temple Presented to Ernst Bammel*. Sheffield, UK: JSOT, 1990.

Hossfeld, Frank-Lothar, and Erich Zenger. *Psalms Three: A Commentary on Psalms 101–150*. Edited by Klaus Baltzer. Translated by Linda M. Maloney. Herm. Minneapolis: Fortress, 2011.

Hwang, Sunwoo. "Coexistence of Unconditionality and Conditionality of the Davidic Covenant in Chronicles." *HJ* 58, no. 2 (2017) 239–46.

———. *The Hope for the Restoration of the Davidic Kingdom in the Light of the Davidic Covenant in Chronicles*. Lewiston, NY: Edwin Mellen, 2014.

Jamieson, Robert, et al. *Commentary Critical and Explanatory on the Whole Bible*. New York: George H. Doran, 1871.

Janzen, David. *Chronicles and the Politics of Davidic Restoration: A Quiet Revolution*. LHBOTS 655. New York: T&T Clark, 2017.

———. *Witch-Hunts, Purity and Social Boundaries: The Expulsion of the Foreign Women in Ezra 9–10*. JSOTSup 350. New York: Sheffield Academic, 2002.

———. "Yahwistic Appropriation of Achaemenid Ideology and the Function of Nehemiah 9 in Ezra-Nehemiah." *JBL* 136, no. 4 (2017) 839–56.

Japhet, Sara. *First and Second Chronicles: A Commentary*. OTL. Louisville, KY: Westminster John Knox, 1993.

———. *From the Rivers of Babylon to the Highlands of Judah: Collected Studies on the Restoration Period*. Winona Lake, IN: Eisenbrauns, 2006.

———. *The Ideology of the Book of Chronicles and Its Place in Biblical Thought*. Winona Lake, IN: Eisenbrauns, 2009.

———. "Sheshbazzar and Zerubbabel against the Background of the Historical and Religious Tendencies of Ezra-Nehemiah." *ZAW* 94 (1982) 66–98.

Jarick, John. *First Chronicles*. 2nd ed. Readings: A New Biblical Commentary. Sheffield, UK: Phoenix, 2007.

Jenni, Ernst, and Claus Westermann. *TLOT*. Peabody, MA: Hendrickson, 1997.

Johnstone, William. *Chronicles and Exodus: An Analogy and Its Application*. JSOTSup 275. Sheffield, UK: JSOT, 1998.

———. *First and Second Chronicles*. 2 vols. LHBOTS 253–54. Sheffield, UK: Sheffield Academic, 1997.

Jones, Gwilym H. *First and Second Chronicles*. Sheffield, UK: Sheffield Academic, 1993.

Jonker, Louis C. "The Chronicler's Portrayal of Solomon as the King of Peace within the Context of the International Peace Discourses of the Persian Era." *OTE* 21 (2008) 653–69.

———. "Chronicles in an (Un)Changing World: The 'Persian Context' in Biblical Studies." *JSOT* 42, no. 3 (2018) 267–83.

———. *Defining All-Israel in Chronicles: Multi-Levelled Identity Negotiation in Late Persian-Period Yehud*. FAT 106. Tübingen, Germ.: Mohr Siebeck, 2016.

———. *First and Second Chronicles*. UBC. Grand Rapids: Baker Academic, 2013.

———, ed. *Historiography and Identity (Re)Formulation in Second Temple Historiographical Literature*. LHBOTS 534. New York: T&T Clark, 2010.

———. *Reflections of King Josiah in Chronicles: Late Stages of the Josiah Reception in II Chr. 34f*. Gütersloh, Germ.: Gütersloher Verlagshaus, 2003.

———. "Reforming History: The Hermeneutical Significance of the Books of Chronicles." *VT* 57, no. 1 (2007) 21–44.

———. "The Rhetoric of Finding a New Identity in a Multi-Religious and Multi-Ethnic Society: The Case of the Book of Chronicles." *VE* 24 (2003) 396–416.

———. *Texts, Contexts and Readings in Postexilic Literature: Explorations into Historiography and Identity Negotiation in Hebrew Bible and Related Texts*. FAT 2, no. 53. Tübingen, Germ.: Mohr Siebeck, 2011.

———. "Was the Chronicler More Deuteronomic than the Deuteronomist?: Explorations into the Chronicler's Relationship with Deuteronomistic Legal Traditions." *SJOT* 27, no. 2 (2013) 185–97.

———. "Who Constitutes Society?: Yehud's Self-Understanding in the Late Persian Era as Reflected in the Books of Chronicles." *JBL* 127, no. 4 (2008) 703–24.

———. "Within Hearing Distance?: Recent Developments in Pentateuch and Chronicles Research." *OTE* 27, no. 1 (2014) 123–46.

Joo, Samantha. "Past No Longer Present: Revision of David's Legacy in Chronicles." *SJOT* 26, no. 2 (2012) 235–58.

Joüon, Paul. *A Grammar of Biblical Hebrew*. Edited by T. Muraoka. Reprint, Rome: Editrice Pontificio Istituto Biblico, 2005.

Kalimi, Isaac. *The Reshaping of Ancient Israelite History in Chronicles*. Winona Lake, IN: Eisenbrauns, 2005.

———, ed. *New Perspectives on Ezra-Nehemiah: History and Historiography, Text, Literature, and Interpretation*. Winona Lake, IN: Eisenbrauns, 2012.

Kartveit, Magnar. *Motive und Schichten der Landtheologie in I Chronik 1–9*. CBOT 28. Stockholm, Swed.: Almqvist & Wiksell International, 1989.

Kaufmann, Yehezkel. "The Messianic Idea: The Real and the Hidden Son of David." *JBQ* 22, no. 3 (1994) 141–50.

———. *The Religion of Israel: From Its Beginnings to the Babylonian Exile*. Translated by M. Greenberg. Chicago: University of Chicago Press, 1960.

Kellermann, Ulrich. *Messias und Gesetz: Grundlinien einer alttestamentlichen Heiserwarung: Eine traditionsgeschichtliche Einführung*. Biblische Studien 61. Neukirchen-Vluyn, Germ.: Neukirchener, 1971.

Kelly, Brian E. *Retribution and Eschatology in Chronicles*. JSOTSup 211. Sheffield, UK: Sheffield Academic, 1996.

Kennedy, Elisabeth Robertson. *Seeking a Homeland Sojourn and Ethnic Identity in the Ancestral Narratives of Genesis*. BIS 106. Boston: Brill, 2011.

Kennedy, George A. *New Testament Interpretation through Rhetorical Criticism*. Chapel Hill, NC: University of North Carolina Press, 1984.

Kim, Brittany. "'We Do Not Know What We Should Do, but Our Eyes Are on You': The Prayer of King Jehoshaphat in 2 Chronicles 20:6–12." In *Speaking with God: Probing Old Testament Prayers for Contemporary Significance*, edited by Phillip G. Camp and Elaine A. Phillips, 81–98. Eugene, OR: Pickwick, forthcoming.

Kim, Jong-Hoon. "열왕기와 역대기 평행본문의 칠십인경 본문 형태에 관한 연구: 열왕기상 8장 1–53절과 역대하 5장 2절–6장 42절을 중심으로 [Observations on the LXX Parallel Text Forms: A Focus on 1 Kings 8:1–53 and 2 Chronicles 5:2—6:42]." *KJOTS* 22, no. 2 (2016) 10–37.

Kim, Kiyoung. "The Chronicler's View of Forgiveness in 2 Chronicles 6 and 7:14." Unpublished manuscript.

Kim, Yeong Seon. *The Temple Administration and the Levites in Chronicles*. CBQMS 51. Washington, DC: Catholic Biblical Association, 2014.

Kim, Youngjin. "포로기와 포로기 이후의 신학사상 [Theological Paradigms during the Exilic and the Post-Exilic Period]." *KJOTS* 21 (2006) 33–50.

Klein, George L. *Zechariah*. NAC 21B. Nashville: Broadman & Holman, 2008.

Klein, Ralph W. *First Chronicles: A Commentary*. Edited by Thomas Krüger. Herm. Minneapolis: Fortress, 2006.

———. "The Last Words of David." *CurTM* 31, no. 1 (2004) 15–23.

———. *Second Chronicles: A Commentary*. Edited by Paul D. Hanson. Herm. Minneapolis: Fortress, 2012.

Kleinig, John W. *The Lord's Song: The Basis, Function and Significance of Choral Music in Chronicles*. Sheffield, UK: Sheffield Academic, 1993.

Knight, Douglas A. "Wellhausen and the Interpretation of Israel's Literature." *Semeia* 25 (1982) 21–36.

Knoppers, Gary N. "The Construction of Judean Diasporic Identity in Ezra-Nehemiah." *JHS* 15, no. 3 (2015) 1–29.

———. *First Chronicles 1–9*. AYBC, n.s., 12. New York: Doubleday, 2004.

———. *First Chronicles 10–29*. AYBC, n.s., 12A. New Haven, CT: Yale University Press, 2008.

———. "Hierodules, Priests, or Janitors?: The Levites in Chronicles and the History of the Israelite Priesthood," *JBL* 118, no.1 (1999) 49–72.

———. "Images of David in Early Judaism: David as Repentant Sinner in Chronicles." *Bib* 76, no. 4 (1995) 449–70.

———. "Jehoshaphat's Judiciary and 'the Scroll of YHWH's Torah.'" *JBL* 113, no. 1 (1994) 59–80.

———. "Jerusalem at War in Chronicles." In *Zion, City of Our God*, edited by Richard S. Hess and Gordon J. Wenham, 57–76. Grand Rapids: Eerdmans, 1999.

———. *Jews and Samaritans: The Origins and History of Their Early Relations*. Oxford: Oxford University Press, 2013.

———. "Mt. Gerizim and Mt. Zion: A Study in the Early History of the Samaritans and Jews." *SR* 34, no. 3–4 (2005) 309–37.

———. "Nathan's Oracle and the Davidic Monarchy." In *Shai Le-Sarah Japhet: Studies in the Bible, Its Exegesis and Its Languages*, edited by Moshe Bar-Asher et al., 99–123. Jerusalem: Bialik Institute, 2007.

———. "Of Rewritten Bibles, Archaeology, Peace, Kings, and Chronicles." *JHS* 5, no. 20 (2005) 69–94.

———. "Reform and Regression: The Chronicler's Presentation of Jehoshaphat." *Biblica* 72, no. 4 (1991) 500–524.

———. "Yhwh Is Not with Israel: Alliances as a *Topos* in Chronicles." *CBQ* 58, no. 4 (1996) 601–26.

Knoppers, Gary N., and Richard J. Bautch, eds. *Covenant in the Persian Period: From Genesis to Chronicles*. Winona Lake, IN: Eisenbrauns, 2015.

Knoppers, Gary N., and Bernard M. Levinson, eds. *The Pentateuch as Torah: New Models for Understanding Its Promulgation and Acceptance*. Winona Lake, IN: Eisenbrauns, 2007.

Knoppers, Gary N., and J. G. McConville, eds. *Reconsidering Israel and Judah: Recent Studies on the Deuteronomistic History*. Winona Lake, IN: Eisenbrauns, 2000.

Knoppers, Gary N., and Kenneth A. Ristau, eds. *Community Identity in Judean Historiography: Biblical and Comparative Perspectives*. Winona Lake, IN: Eisenbrauns, 2009.

Knoppers, Gary N., et al., eds. *The Chronicler as Theologian: Essays in Honor of Ralph W. Klein*. JSOTSup 371. New York: T&T Clark, 2003.

Knowles, Melody D. *Centrality Practiced: Jerusalem in the Religious Practice of Yehud and the Diaspora during the Persian*. Archaeology and Biblical Studies 16. Atlanta: SBL, 2006.

Köhler, Ludwig, et al. *HALOT*. Leiden, Neth.: Brill, 1994–2000.

Kraus, Hans-Joachim. *Psalms 1–59*. Translated by Hilton C. Oswald. ContC. Minneapolis: Fortress, 1993.

———. *Psalms 60–150*. Translated by Hilton C. Oswald. ContC. Minneapolis: Fortress, 1993.

Krinetzki, Leo. *Israels Gebet im Alten Testament*. Vol. 5 of *Der Christ in der Welt: Das Buch der Bücher*. Aschaffenburg, Germ.: Paul Pattloch, 1965.

Kruse, Heinz. "David's Covenant." *VT* 35, no. 2 (1985) 139–64.

Kugel, James L., ed. *Prayers That Cite Scripture*. Harvard University Center for Jewish Studies. Cambridge, MA: Harvard University Press, 2006.

Kugel, James L., and Rowan A. Greer. *Early Biblical Interpretation*. Philadelphia: Westminster John Knox, 1986.

Laato, Antti. *A Star Is Rising: The Historical Development of the Old Testament Royal Ideology and the Rise of the Jewish Messianic Expectations*. USFISFCJ 5. Atlanta: Scholars, 1997.

Lau, Peter H. W. *Identity and Ethics in the Book of Ruth: A Social Identity Approach*. BZAW 416. Berlin: Walter de Gruyter, 2011.

Leary, Mark R., and June Price Tangney, eds. *Handbook of Self and Identity*. New York: Guilford, 2003.

Lee, Hee-Hak. "Studies on the Meanings of 'the Assembly, Israel and Sojourners' in 2 Chronicles 30:25." *KJOTS* 16, no. 2 (2016) 10–29.

Lee, Kyong-Jin. *The Authority and Authorization of Torah in the Persian Period*. Contributions to Biblical Exegesis & Theology 64. Leuven, Belg.: Peeters, 2011.

Levenson, Jon D. "The Davidic Covenant and its Modern Interpreters." *CBQ* 41, no. 2 (1979) 205–19.

Levin, Yigal. *The Chronicles of the Kings of Judah: Second Chronicles 10–36*. NTC. New York: T&T Clark, 2017.

Lipschits, Oded, et al., eds. *Judah and the Judeans in the Achaemenid Period: Negotiating Identity in an International Context*. Winona Lake, IN: Eisenbrauns, 2011.

———. *Judah and the Judeans in the Fourth Century B.C.E.* Winona Lake, IN: Eisenbrauns, 2007.

———. *Judah and the Judeans in the Persian Period*. Winona Lake, IN: Eisenbrauns, 2006.

Long, Burke O. *First Kings: With an Introduction to Historical Literature*. FOTL 9. Grand Rapids: William B. Eerdmans, 1984.

Long, V. Philips, et al. *A Biblical History of Israel.* Louisville, KY: Westminster John Knox, 2003.

Longman, Tremper, III. *Literary Approaches to Biblical Interpretation.* Grand Rapids: Academie, 1987.

Luttikhuizen, Gerard P., ed. *Eve's Children: The Biblical Stories Retold and Interpreted in Jewish and Christian Traditions.* TBN 5. Leiden, Neth.: Brill, 2003.

Lynch, Matthew. "Mapping Monotheism: Modes of Monotheistic Rhetoric in the Hebrew Bible." *VT* 64 (2014) 47–68.

———. *Monotheism and Institutions in the Book of Chronicles: Temple, Priesthood, and Kingship in Post-Exilic Perspective.* FAT 2, no. 64. Tübingen, Germ.: Mohr Siebeck, 2014.

Mabie, Frederick. *First, Second Chronicles–Job.* EBC 4. Rev. ed. Grand Rapids: Zondervan, 2010.

MacArthur, John. *Elements of True Prayer.* MBS. Chicago: Moody, 1988.

MacDonald, Nathan, ed. *Covenant and Election in Exile and Post-Exilic Judaism.* Studies of the Sofja Kovalevskaja Research Group on Early Jewish Monotheism V. FAT 2, no. 79. Tübingen, Germ.: Mohr Siebeck, 2015.

MacDonald, Nathan, and Ken Brown, eds. *Monotheism in Late Prophetic and Early Apocalyptic Literature.* Studies of the Sofja Kovalevskaja Research Group on Early Jewish Monotheism 3. Tübingen, Germ.: Mohr Siebeck, 2014.

Maier, Christel M., ed. *Congress Volume Munich 2013.* VTSup 163. Leiden, Neth.: Brill, 2014.

Maier, Walter A., III. "The Divine Presence within the Cloud." *CTQ* 79, no. 1 (2015) 79–102.

Mason, Rex. *Preaching the Tradition: Homily and Hermeneutics after the Exile: Based on the "Addresses" in Chronicles, the "Speeches" in the Books of Ezra and Nehemiah, and the Post-Exilic Prophetic Books.* Cambridge, UK: Cambridge University Press, 1990.

Matlock, Michael D. *Discovering the Traditions of Prose Prayers in Early Jewish Literature.* LSTS 81. New York: T&T Clark, 2012.

———. "The Function of Psalmic Prayers in Chronicles: Literary-Rhetorical Method in Conversation with Ritual Theory." *Asbury Journal* 72, no. 2 (2017) 91–106.

———. "Traditions of Prose Prayer in Early Jewish Literature." PhD diss., Hebrew Union College: Jewish Institute of Religion, 2009.

Mays, James Luther. *Psalms Interpretation: A Bible Commentary for Teaching and Preaching.* Louisville, KY: Westminster John Knox, 2011.

McCarthy, Dennis J. "Covenant and Law in Chronicles-Nehemiah." *CBQ* 44, no. 1 (1982) 25–44.

McConville, J. G. "First Chronicles 28:9: Yahweh 'Seeks Out' Solomon." *JTS* 37, no. 1 (1986) 105–8.

McKenzie, Steven L. *The Chronicler's Use of the Deuteronomistic History.* Atlanta: Scholars, 1985.

———. *Covenant.* Understanding Biblical Themes. St. Louis, MO: Chalice, 2000.

———. *First and Second Chronicles.* AOTC. Nashville: Abingdon, 2004.

Mermelstein, Ari. *Creation, Covenant, and the Beginnings of Judaism: Reconceiving Historical Time in the Second Temple Period.* JSJSup 168. Leiden, Neth.: Brill, 2014.

Merrill, Eugene H. "The Chronicler: What Kind of Historian Was He Anyway?" *BibSac* 165 (2008) 397–412.

———. *A Commentary on First and Second Chronicles*. Grand Rapids: Kregel Academic, 2015.

———. *Haggai, Zechariah, Malachi: An Exegetical Commentary*. Dallas: Biblical Studies Press, 2003.

———. *Kingdom of Priests: A History of Old Testament Israel*. 2nd ed. Grand Rapids: Baker Academic, 2008.

———. "Remembering: A Central Theme in Biblical Worship." *JETS* 43, no. 1 (2000) 27–36.

Millar, J. G. *Calling on the Name of the Lord: A Biblical Theology of Prayer*. NSBT 38. Downers Grove, IL: InterVarsity, 2016.

Miller, Cynthia L. *The Representation of Speech in Biblical Hebrew Narrative: A Linguistic Analysis*. HSM 55. Leiden, Neth.: Brill, 1996.

Miller, Patrick D. *They Cried to the Lord: The Form and Theology of Biblical Prayer*. Minneapolis: Fortress, 1994.

Min, Kyung-Jin. *The Levitical Authorship of Ezra-Nehemiah*. LHBOTS 204. Sheffield, UK: Bloomsbury Academy, 2004.

Mirau, Neil A., et al., eds. *Urbanism in Antiquity: From Mesopotamia to Crete*. JSOTSup. Sheffield, UK: Sheffield Academic, 1997.

Mitchell, Christine. "Transformations in Meaning: Solomon's Accession in Chronicles." *JHS* 4, no. 3 (2002) §1.1—4.1.

Moffat, Donald P. *Ezra's Social Drama: Identity Formation, Marriage and Social Conflict in Ezra 9 and 10*. TCLBS 579. New York: T&T Clark, 2013.

Mor, Menachem, and Freidrich V. Reiterer, eds. *Samaritans: Past and Present: Current Studies*. New York: De Gruyer, 2010.

Moriarty, Frederick L. "Chronicler's Account of Hezekiah's Reform." *CBQ* 27, no. 4 (1965) 399–406.

Moshavi, Adina. "Can a Positive Rhetorical Question Have a Positive Answer in the Bible?" *JSS* 56, no. 2 (2011) 253–73.

———. "What Can I Say?: Implications and Communicative Functions of Rhetorical 'WH' Questions in Classical Biblical Hebrew Prose." *VT* 64, no. 1 (2014) 93–108.

Mosis, Rudolf. *Untersuchungen zur Theologie des chronistischen Geschichtswerkes*. FrThst 92. Freiburg, Germ.: Herder, 1973.

Mowinckel, Sigmund. *The Psalms in Israel's Worship*. Grand Rapids: Eerdmans, 2004.

Mtshiselwa, V. Ndikhokele N. "Remembering and Constructing Israelite Identity in Postexilic Yehud: Some Remarks on the Penitential Prayer of Nehemiah 9:6–37." *VE* 37, no. 1 (2016) 1–6.

Murray, Donald F. "Dynasty, People, and the Future: The Message of Chronicles." *JSOT* 58 (1993) 71–92.

———. "Under YHWH's Veto: David as Shedder of Blood in Chronicles." *Biblica* 82, no. 4 (2001) 457–76.

Myers, Jacob M. *First Chronicles*. AYBC 12. Garden City, NY: Doubleday, 1965.

———. *Second Chronicles*. AYBC 13. Garden City, NY: Doubleday, 1965.

Nel, H. W. "The Davidic Covenant in First and Second Chronicles: A New Theme for an Old Song." *In die Skriflig* 28, no. 3 (1994) 429–44.

———. "Theopolitics in the Davidic Monarchal System: A Pilot Study." *In die Skriflig* 31, no. 4 (1997) 421–34.

Newman, Judith H. *Praying by the Book: The Scripturalization of Prayer in Second Temple Judaism*. EJL 14. Atlanta: Scholars, 1999.

Newsome, James D. "Toward a New Understanding of the Chronicler and His Purposes." *JBL* 94 (1975) 201–17.
North, Robert Grady. "Theology of the Chronicler." *JBL* 82 (1963) 369–81.
Noth, Martin. *The History of Israel*. Translated by P. R. Ackroyd. 2nd ed. Edinburgh: A&C Black, 1960.
Nurmela, Risto. *The Levites: Their Emergence as a Second-Class Priesthood*. South Florida Studies in the History of Judaism 193. Atlanta: Scholars, 1998.
O'Kennedy, Daniel F. "Prayer in the Post-Exilic Prophetic Books of Haggai, Zechariah and Malachi." *Scriptura* 113 (2014) 1–13.
———. "Twee Weergawes Van Die Gebed Van Salomo (1 Kon. 8 En 2 Kron. 6): 'N Vergelykende Studie [Two Versions of Solomon's Prayer (1 Kings 8 and 2 Chronicles 6): A Comparative Study]." *AT* 26, no. 2 (2006) 155–77.
Olley, John W. "'The God of Heaven': A Look at Attitudes to Other Religions in the Old Testament." *Colloquium* 24, no. 2 (1995) 76–94.
Olyan, Saul M. "Purity Ideology in Ezra-Nehemiah as a Tool to Reconstitute the Community." *JSJ* 35, no. 1 (2004) 1–16.
Oswalt, John N. *The Book of Isaiah: Chapters 40–66*. NICOT. Grand Rapids: Eerdmans, 1998.
Pagán, Samuel. "Poor and Poverty: Social Distance and Bible Translation." *Semeia* 76 (1996) 69–80.
Pechawer, Larry. *The Lost Prayer of Jabez*. Joplin, MO: Mireh, 2001.
Penner, Jeremy. *Patterns of Daily Prayer in Second Temple Period Judaism*. STDJ 104. Leiden, Neth.: Brill, 2012.
Perdue, Leo G. "'Yahweh is King Over all the Earth': An Exegesis of Psalm 47." *RQ* 17, no. 2 (1974) 85–98.
Peterson, Paul Birch. "The Theology and the Function of the Prayers in the Book of Daniel." PhD diss., Andrews University: Seventh-day Adventist Theological Seminary, 1998.
Plöger, Otto. *Theocracy and Eschatology*. Translated by S. Rudman. Oxford: Blackwell, 1968.
Pratt, Richard L. *First and Second Chronicles: A Mentor Commentary*. Tain, UK: Mentor, 2006.
———. "Royal Prayer and the Chronicler's Program." PhD diss., Harvard University, 1987.
Pury, A. de, et al., eds. *Israël construit son histoire: L'historiographie eutéronomiste à la lumière des recherches récentes*. Le monde de la Bible 34. Geneva: Labor et Fides, 1996.
Raison, Stephen John. "From Theocracy to Kingdom: Royalist Hope in Chronicles." PhD diss., Westminster Theological Seminary, 1992.
Ramírez Kidd, José E. *Alterity and Identity in Israel: The "Ger" in the Old Testament*. BZAW 283. Berlin: Walter de Gruyter, 1999.
Rata, Tiberius. *Ezra and Nehemiah*. Mentor Commentary. Ross-shire, UK: Mentor, 2010.
Redditt, Paul L. "Prophecy and the Monarchy in Haggai and Zechariah." *CBQ* 76, no. 3 (2014) 436–49.
Reif, Stefan C. *Judaism and Hebrew Prayer: New Perspectives on Jewish Liturgical History*. Cambridge, UK: Cambridge University Press, 1993.

Reif, Stefan C., and Renate Egger-Wenzel, eds. *Ancient Jewish Prayers and Emotions: Emotions Associated with Jewish Prayers in and around the Second Temple Period*. Berlin: Walter de Gruyter, 2015.

Rendtorff, R., and K. Koch, eds. *Studien zur Theologie der alttestamentlichen Überlieferungen*. Festschrift Gerhard von Rad. Neukrichen-Vluyn, Germ.: Neukirchener, 1961.

Riley, William. *King and Cultus in Chronicles: Worship and the Reinterpretation of History*. JSOTSup 160. Sheffield, UK: JSOT, 1993.

Rigsby, Richard O. "The Historiography of Speeches and Prayers in the Books of Chronicles." ThD diss., Southern Baptist Theological Seminary, 1973.

Ristau, Kenneth A. "Reading and Rereading Josiah: The Chronicler's Representation of Josiah for the Postexilic Community." In *Community Identity in Judean Historiography: Biblical and Comparative Perspectives*, edited by Gary N. Knoppers and Kenneth A. Ristau, 219–48. Winona Lake, IN: Eisenbrauns, 2009.

Ross, Allen P. *A Commentary on the Psalms: Volume 3 (90–150)*. Kregel Exegetical Library. 3rd ed. Grand Rapids: Kregel, 2011.

———. *Recalling the Hope of Glory: Biblical Worship from the Garden to the New Creation*. Grand Rapids: Kregel, 2006.

Roth, Ronald D. "Characteristics of Joyful Giving: A Stewardship Study of 1 Chronicles 29:1–20." *WLQ* 90, no. 3 (1993) 199–207.

Rudolph, Von W. "Zur Theologie des Chronisten." *TLZ* 79 (1954) 285–86.

Rudolph, Wilhelm. *Chronikbücher*. HAT 21. Tübingen, Germ.: Mohr Siebeck, 1955.

Sailhamer, John H. *First and Second Chronicles*. Chicago: Moody, 1983.

Satterwaite, Philippe E., and Gordon McConville. *Exploring the Old Testament: A Guide to the Historical Books*. Exploring the Bible 2. London: SPCK, 2007.

Schaefer, Glenn E. "The Significance of Seeking God in the Purpose of the Chronicler." ThD diss., Southern Baptist Theological Seminary, 1972.

Schoville, Keith N. *Ezra-Nehemiah*. CPNIVC. Joplin, MO: College, 2001.

Schreinder, David B. "Zerubbabel, Persia, and Inner-Biblical Exegesis." *JESOT* 4, no. 2 (2015) 191–204.

Schweitzer, Steven J. *Reading Utopia in Chronicles*. LHBOTS 442. New York: T&T Clark International, 2007.

Schweitzer, Steven J., and Frauke Uhlenbruch, eds. *Worlds That Could Not Be: Utopia in Chronicles, Ezra, and Nehemiah*. LHBOTS 620. New York: T&T Clark, 2016.

Selman, Martin J. *First Chronicles: An Introduction and Commentary*. TOTC. Downers Grove, IL: InterVarsity, 1994.

———. *Second Chronicles: An Introduction and Commentary*. TOTC. Downers Grove, IL: InterVarsity, 1994.

Seybold, Klaus. *Studien zur Psalmenauslegung*. Stuttgart, Germ.: Kohlhammer, 1998.

Shaver, Judson Rayford. *Torah and the Chronicler's History Work: An Inquiry into the Chronicler's References to Laws, Festivals, and Cultic Institutions in Relationship to Pentateuchal Legislation*. Ann Arbor, MI: University Microfilms International, 1988.

Silverman, Jason M. *Persepolis and Jerusalem Iranian Influence on the Apocalyptic Hermeneutic*. LHBOTS 558. New York: T&T Clark, 2012.

Southwood, Katherine. E. "'And They Could Not Understand Jewish Speech': Language, Ethnicity, and Nehemiah's Intermarriage Crisis." *JTS* 62, no. 1 (2011) 1–19.

Sparks, James T. *The Chronicler's Genealogies: Towards an Understanding of 1 Chronicles 1–9*. SBL Academia Biblica 28. Atlanta: SBL, 2008.

Stafford, John K. "Temple? What Temple?: Eschatology in the Book of Chronicles." *Perichoresis* 4, no. 1 (2006) 31–52.
Staudt, Edwin E. "Prayer and the People in the Deuteronomist." PhD diss., Vandervilt University, 1980.
Steinmann, Andrew E. *Ezra and Nehemiah*. Concordia Commentary. St. Louis, MO: Concordia, 2010.
———. "What Did David Understand about the Promises in the Davidic Covenant?" *BibSac* 171, no. 681 (2014) 19–29.
Stern, Menahem, ed. *Jewish Identities in Antiquity: Studies in Memory of Menahem Stern*. TSAJ 130. Tübingen, Germ.: Mohr Siebeck, 2009.
Sternberg, Meir. *The Poetics of Biblical Narrative: Ideological Literature and the Drama of Reading*. ISBLS. Bloomington, IN: Indiana University Press, 1985.
Stinespring, W. F. "Eschatology in Chronicles." *JBL* 80 (1960) 209–19.
Street, James M. "The Significance of the Ark Narrative of 1 Chronicles to the History of Israel's Religion." PhD diss., Dallas Theological Seminary, 2006.
Stuart, Douglas K. *Exodus*. NAC 2. Nashville: Broadman & Holman, 2006.
Talstra, E. *Solomon's Prayer: Synchrony and Diachrony in the Composition of I Kings 8,14–61*. Translated by Gonni Runia-Deenick. CBET 3. Kampen, Neth.: Kok Pharos, 1993.
Tavani, Jean Louis, et al. "Tell Me What You Remember and I Will Know Who You Are: The Link between Collective Memory and Social Categorization." *Group Processes & Intergroup Relations* 20, no. 1 (2017) 91–108.
Taylor, Jonathan G. "The Application of 2 Chronicles 7:13–15." *BibSac* 168, no. 670 (2011) 146–61.
Thiessen, Matthew. "The Function of a Conjunction: Inclusivist or Exclusivist Strategies in Ezra 6.19–21 and Nehemiah 10.29–30?" *JSOT* 34, no. 1 (2009) 63–79.
Thistlethwaite, Susan Brooks. "'You May Enjoy the Spoil of Your Enemies': Rape as a Biblical Metaphor for War." *Semeia* 61 (1993) 59–75.
Thompson, J. A. *First, Second Chronicles*. NAC 9. Edited by E. Ray Clendenen. Nashville: Broadman & Holman, 1994.
Thompson, Michael E. W. *I Have Heard Your Prayer: The Old Testament and Prayer*. Peterborough, UK: Epworth, 1996.
Throntveit, Mark A. *Ezra-Nehemiah*. Interpretation: A Biblical Commentary for Teaching and Preaching. Louisville, KY: Westminster John Knox, 1992.
———. *The Significance of the Royal Speeches and Prayers for the Structure and Theology of the Chronicler*. Ann Arbor, MI: University Microfilms International, 1987.
———. "Was the Chronicler a Spin Doctor? David in the Books of Chronicles," *Word & World* 23 no.4 (2003) 374–81.
———. *When Kings Speak: Royal Speech and Royal Prayer in Chronicles*. SBLDS 93. Atlanta: Scholars, 1987.
Tiemeyer, Lena-Sofia. *Ezra-Nehemiah: An Introduction and Study Guide: Israel's Quest for Identity*. Edited by Adrian H. Curtis. TCSGOT. New York: T&T Clark, 2017.
Tiňo, Jozef. *King and Temple in Chronicles: A Contextual Approach to Their Relations*. Göttingen, Germ.: Vandenhoeck & Ruprecht, 2010.
Tollefson, Kenneth D., and H. G. M. Williamson. "Nehemiah as Cultural Revitalization: An Anthropological Perspective." *JSOT* 56 (1992) 41–68.
Tournay, Raymond Jacques. *Seeing and Hearing God with the Psalms: The Prophetic Liturgy of the Second Temple in Jerusalem*. Sheffield, UK: JSOT, 1991.

Tozer, A. W. *The Attributes of God: A Journey into the Father's Heart.* Camp Hill, PA: Wing Spread, 1997.
Tucker, W. Dennis. *Constructing and Deconstructing Power in Psalms 107–150.* AIL 19. Atlanta: SBL, 2014.
Tuell, Steven Shawn. *First and Second Chronicles.* Interpretation: A Bible Commentary for Teaching and Preaching. Louisville, KY: Westminster John Knox, 2001.
Ulrich, Dean R. "David in Ezra-Nehemiah." *WTJ* 78 (2016) 49–63.
Van den Brom, Luco Johan. *Divine Presence in the World: A Critical Analysis of the Notion of Divine Omnipresence.* SPT 5. Kampen, Neth.: Kok Pharos, 1993.
Van Keulen, P. S. F. *Manasseh through the Eyes of the Deuteronomists: The Manasseh Account (2 Kings 21:1–18) and the Final Chapters of the Deuteronomistic History.* Leiden, Neth.: Brill, 1996.
Van Pelt Campbell, George. "Structure, Themes, and Theology in Ezra-Nehemiah." *BibSac* 174 (2017) 394–411.
VanGemeren, Willem. *Interpreting the Prophetic Word: An Introduction to the Prophetic Literature of the Old Testament.* Grand Rapids: Zondervan, 1990.
von Rad, Gerhard. *Das Geschichtsbild des chronistischen Werkes.* BWANT 4, no. 3. Stuttgart, Germ.: W. Kohlhammer, 1930.
———. *Old Testament Theology.* Vol. 2. Translated by D. M. G. Stalker. Edinburgh: Oliver & Boyd, 1965.
———. *The Problem of the Hexateuch and Other Essays.* Translated by E. W. Trueman Dicken. Edinburgh: Oliver & Boyd, 1966.
Wagner, Andreas. "Struckturen des Gebets im Alten Testament." In *Orakel und Gebete: Interdisziplinäre Studien zur Sprache der Religion in Ägypten, Vorderasien und Griechenland in hellenistischer Zeit,* edited by Markus Witte and Johannes F. Diehl, FAT 2, no. 38, 197–215. Tübingen, Germ.: Mohr Siebeck, 2009.
Wallenstein, Meir. "Lexical Material in the Judean Scrolls." *VT* 4, no. 2 (1954) 211–14.
Walsh, Jerome T. *Style and Structure in Biblical Hebrew Narrative.* Collegeville, MN: Liturgical, 2001.
Waltke, Bruce K., and M. O'Connor. *An Introduction to Biblical Hebrew Syntax.* Winona Lake, IN: Eisenbrauns, 1989.
Waltner, James H. *Psalms.* BCBC. Scottdale, PA: Herald, 2006.
Washington, Harold C. "Israel's Holy Seed and the Foreign Women of Ezra-Nehemiah: A Kristevan Reading." *BI* 11, nos. 3–4 (2003) 427–37.
Watts, James W. *Persia and Torah: The Theory of Imperial Authorization of the Pentateuch.* SBLSS 17. Atlanta: SBL, 2001.
———. *Psalm and Story: Inset Hymns in Hebrew Narrative.* JSOTSup 139. Sheffield, UK: JSOT, 1992.
———. "Ritual Legitimacy and Scriptural Authority." *JBL* 124, no. 3 (2005) 401–17.
———. "Scripturalization and the Aaronide Dynastism." *JHS* 13, no. 6 (2013) 1–15.
Weinberg, Joel. *Citizen-Temple Community.* JSOTSup 151. Sheffield, UK: JSOT, 1992.
Weinfeld, Moshe. "The Covenant of Grant in the Old Testament and the Ancient Near East." *JAOS* 90, no. 2 (1970) 184–203.
———. *Deuteronomy and the Deuteronomy School.* Winona Lake, IN: Eisenbrauns, 1992.
Welch, A. C. *Post-Exilic Judaism.* London: Blackwood, 1935.
Wellhausen, Julius. *Prolegomena to the History of Israel.* Atlanta: Scholars, 1994.

Wendel, Adolf. *Das freie Laiengebet im vorexilischen Israel.* Leipzig, Germ.: E. Pfeiffer, 1931.

Wenham, Gordon J., and Richard S. Hess, eds. *Zion, City of Our God.* Grand Rapids: Eerdmans, 1999.

Wenham, J. W. "Large Numbers in the Old Testament." *TynBul* 18 (1967) 19–53.

Werline, Rondey A. "Prayer, Politics, and Power in the Hebrew Bible." *Interpretation* 68, no. 1 (2014) 5–16.

Widmer, Michael. *The Message of Psalms: Songs for the People of God.* Downers Grove, IL: InterVarsity, 2001.

———. *Moses, God, and the Dynamics of Intercessory Prayer: A Study of Exodus 32–34 and Numbers 13–14.* FAT 2, no. 8. Tübingen, Germ.: Mohr Siebeck, 2004.

Wilcock, Michael. *The Message of Chronicles: One Church, One Faith, One Lord.* Bible Speaks Today. Downers Grove, IL: InterVarsity, 1987.

Wilkinson, Bruce. *The Prayer of Jabez: Breaking Through to the Blessed Life.* Sisters, OR: Multnomah, 2000.

Willi, Thomas. *Die Chronik als Auslegung: Untersuchungen zur literarischen Gestaltung der historischen Überlieferung Israel.* Göttingen, Germ.: Vandenhoeck & Ruprecht, 1972.

———. *Judah-Jehud-Israel:Studien zum Selbstverständnis des Judentums in persischer Zeit.* FAT 12. Tübingen, Germ.: Mohr Siebeck, 1995.

———. "Zwei Jahrzehnte Forschung an Chronik und Esra-Nehemia." *TR* 67, no. 1 (2002) 61–104.

Williams, Ronald J. *Williams' Hebrew Syntax.* 3rd ed. Toronto: University of Toronto Press, 2007.

Williamson, H. G. M. "Eschatology in Chronicles." *TynBul* 28 (1977) 115–54.

———. *Ezra and Nehemiah.* Sheffield Old Testament Guides. Sheffield, UK: JSOT, 1987.

———. *Ezra, Nehemiah.* WBC 16. Dallas: Word, 1985.

———. *First and Second Chronicles.* New Century Bible Commentary. Reprint, Eugene, OR: Wipf & Stock, 2010.

———. *Israel in the Books of Chronicles.* Cambridge, UK: Cambridge University Press, 1977.

———. "Sources and Redaction in the Chronicler's Genealogy of Judah." *JBL* 98, no. 3 (1979) 351–59.

———. "The Temple in the Books of Chronicles." In *Templum Amicitiae: Essays on the Second Temple Presented to Ernst Bammel,* edited by William Horbury, 15–31. Sheffield, UK: JSOT, 1991.

Wilson, Gerald H. *Psalms, Volume 1.* NIVAC. Grand Rapids: Zondervan, 2002.

Wilson, Robert R. *Genealogy and History in the Biblical World.* New Haven, CT: Yale University Press, 1977.

Wirzba, Norman., and Bruce Ellis Benson, eds. *The Phenomenology of Prayer.* PCP 46. New York: Fordham University Press, 2005.

Wood, C. R. *Sermon Outlines on Great Doctrinal Themes.* Grand Rapids: Kregel, 1994.

Wright, Jacob L. *Rebuilding Identity: The Nehemiah-Memoir and Its Earliest Readers.* BZAW 348. Berlin: Walter de Gruyter, 2004.

Wright, John W. "A Commentary on Commentaries on Chronicles." *JHS* 5, no. 20 (2005) 58–68.

———. "The Founding Father: The Structure of the Chronicler's David Narrative." *JBL* 117, no. 1 (1998) 45–59.
Yamauchi, Edwin M. *Persia and the Bible*. Grand Rapids: Baker Academic, 1990.
Yona, S. E. L. Greenstein, et al., eds. *Marbeh Ḥokmah: Studies in the Bible and the Ancient Near East in Loving Memory of Victor Avigdor Hurowitz*. Winona Lake, IN: Eisenbrauns, 2015.
Zevit, Ziony. "Is There an Archaeological Case for Phantom Settlements in the Persian Period?" *PEQ* 141, no. 2 (2009) 124–37.
Zucker, David J. "Downplaying the Davidic Dynasty." *JBQ* 42, no. 3 (2014) 185–91.

Subject Index

King Abijah, 144n83, 147n97
abnormal situation, praying in, 118
"above all gods," 45–46n59
Abraham
    Chronicler replacing with Israel, 43
    God granted land to the
        descendants of, 101
    God's promise to, 20, 20n20, 100
    Jehoshaphat's reference to, 99–100
Abrahamic covenant, 44, 45n57. *See also*
    covenant
Achaemenid empire, 119, 123–29, 149
Achar, 31n15
activism, 149, 150
King Ahaz, 115n279, 140n68
Ahura Mazda, 130n36, 131
all-Israel
    accountable to worship Yhwh,
        172–73
    as the community identity, 10
    King Hezekiah eager to worship
        with, 117
    including the northern tribes, 144
    offering sacrifices and prayers, 118
    response to Hezekiah's invitation,
        110n268
    temple dedication, gathering for, 87
    theme of, 109n264
    understanding of, 144n84
    as a united group of tribes, 117
    worship by, 39n37, 124, 170
anthropo-metaphorical context, of
    prayer, 17n9
apocryphal literatures, attesting to
    prayer, 159n136

Aram, 140n68
archaeological artifacts or inscriptions,
    120n3
ark
    placed in the temple, 34, 86, 87, 88
    representing the presence of God, 41
King Asa, 89–95, 140n68
Asa's Prayer (Second Chronicles 14:10),
    88–95
Athaliah, 154n118
atonement, 108, 108n258, 112
attitude, transforming through prayer,
    21–22
audience. *See also* post-exilic audience
    of Chronicles, 3–4n8
    confirmations giving hope to, 23
    internalizing roles and
        characteristics, 15
    motivating to become active
        supplicants, 77
    persuading to become supplicants, 89
    responding to the invitation to pray,
        16–17
    of Solomon's worship among all-
        Israel, 110n268
authoritative resources, Chronicles' use
    of, 166n161
authority
    creating discrimination, 142
    of God over the universe, 134
    priests' misuse of, 138n63
Azubah, 31n15

Babylonian exile, 1, 137

Babylonians, wiped out their enemies, 125n21
battle, 94n212, 102, 150
Beersheba to Dan, as the entire territory of Israel, 110n266
benefactor, God as, 70
biblical historiographies, on prayer practices, 159n136
biblical literature, 121, 122, 167
biblical "ring," providing, 166
biblical writers, on the existence of other divine beings, 11n32
biblical writings, on the hope of restoration, 155

characteristics. *See* roles and characteristics
characterization
    by the Chronicler, 24
    of Hezekiah, 109n263, 117
    of Jabez, 30
    of supplicants, 23
characters, evaluating in a prayer, 23
choral music, significance of, 38n33
Chronicler
    actualizing the community through the Levites, 36
    adding God's response to Solomon's prayer, 77n154
    adopting from Psalm 132, 87
    assigning more space to Hezekiah's story, 107n256
    associating petitioners' prayer with either heaven or God, 161
    audience of. *see* post-exilic audience
    characterization of King Hezekiah, 108, 117
    encouraging the community to depend solely upon Yhwh, 135
    esteem of Jabez among his brothers, 28
    on the existence of other divine beings, 11n32
    favoring the name "Israel" over "Jacob," 43n51
    on God as hearing from heaven, 162n145
    on the good nature of God, 114
    on heaven not containing God, 162n145
    historical and rhetorical circumstances of, 113n274
    hope for the Yehud community, 51
    hopeful perspectives through the history of Israel, 3–4
    on Israel as a liturgical community, 11
    on joyful worship, 49n67
    model prayers for post-exilic readers, 19–20
    on the musical duties of the Levites and priests, 39
    not abandoning hope for the future Israel, 173
    not mentioning Egypt or the exodus event, 101n235
    not omitting the exodus event from his *Vorlage*, 57
    on obligation to the law and ordinances, 114
    perspective of differing from its *Vorlage*, 3
    portraying Israel without slavery in Egypt, 133n44
    prayer conveying the ideology of, 16
    providing words for prayer, 50
    psalms teaching the community how to sing (pray), 35n24
    on repentance, 79–80, 164
    replacing Abraham with Israel, 43
    replacing Judah with house of David, 147n97
    report of Asa's reign, 89
    reviewing the history of Israel, 44
    roles or characteristics for community members, 119n1
    on Solomon's blamelessness, 83n176
    on the status and roles of Levites, 124
    on supplicants praying for God's forgiveness, 125
    teaching the effectiveness of prayer, 114
    theological significance of music, 38n33
    on the verbal formulation of prayers, 18

Subject Index

vision for a society unified around the Temple, 82
  on the worship of God by all-Israel, 39n37
  on Yhwh as their God, 43
Chronicles
  bridging the past and the present, 168
  concerns with worshipers or the worshiping community, 139
  as an eschatological text, 148n100
  exemplary kings in, 140n68
  on hope for the revival of the Davidic kingdom, 157
  on Israel's identity through prayers, 125
  prayer in, 14–15, 158n132
  on the proper functioning of the temple, 146
  on the restoration of the Davidic kingdom, 155
cleansing, 108, 108n258
cloud, signifying God's presence, 162
collective identity, 10n29
commercialization, in the Persian Empire, 123n14
communal prayer, power of, 100–101, 170
communication, by a human to God, 13–14
community, 9n28, 49–51, 147, 151
community identity
  Chronicler's desired, 168
  Chronicler's picture of all-Israel, 10, 10n29
  constructed by roles or characteristics, 151
  in the sociohistorical context of Yehud, 12, 171
  as a whole, 169
congregation, witnessing God's presence through music, 38
consecration, 108, 108n258
covenant
  Davidic. *see* Davidic covenant
  as everlasting, 44
  made between God and Israel, 132–33
  mentioning with reference to the patriarchs, 44n56
  renewing bringing hope, 72
covenant curses, Solomon alluding to, 84
covenantal relationship, of God with Israel, 49, 172
creation, recognizing God's sovereignty, 48
creator, God as, 46
crying out, act of, 99
cultic sites, in the days of David and Solomon, 144n86
Cushite army, King Asa'a battle against, 88
Cushites, military strength of, 93–94
Cyrus of Persia, 123, 138, 152

David
  abasing himself before God, 53
  appointing Levites and priests, 38
  appointing Solomon as the temple builder, 67
  demonstrating the attitude of a giver, 73
  desiring to receive God's promise, 55
  establishing and operating Israel's cult, 142
  as an exemplary figure, 66
  on failure of seeking God, 40n43
  as a faithful supplicant, 65–66
  on God's salvific deeds in Israel's history, 55
  on God's sovereignty over the universe, 68–69
  on God's special relationship with his people, 58
  honored and remembered in the community, 156
  implementing and operating Israel's cult, 117
  as a man of war, 88n193
  as a monotheistic believer, 52–58
  praying with faith in God's promise, 160
  as preparer of the temple, 64n110
  on the purpose of worship, 38
  recognizing God's position, 55

David (*cont.*)
    references to in Ezra and Nehemiah, 155n121
    referring to God as Yhwh and God of Israel, 68
    teaching Israel the songs to sing, 35n24
    on transference of the ark to Jerusalem, 86

Davidic citizenship
    actualization of, 171
    in close relation to the status of the temple, 151
    dwelling in the revived Davidic kingdom, 12
    future Israel maintaining, 173
    hope of, 58–65
    motivating, 85, 170–71

Davidic covenant
    conditionality of, 83n176
    continuing fulfillment of, 78n157
    as hope of Davidic citizenship, 58–65
    not playing a significant role in Malachi, 157
    recent research, 52n75
    scholars having different opinions on, 83n176
    unconditional nature of, 83n176

Davidic dynasty, 60n103, 65, 82–88, 153n115

Davidic kingdom
    Chronicler's desire regarding, 128
    citizens of, 11, 115, 147–57
    meaning of the nature of, 60n102
    perpetuity of, 60, 132
    responsible for maintaining the temple, 147n97
    revival of, 58, 107, 129, 147, 168

Davidic kings, 139, 148–49n100

Davidic promise
    as grounding for appeals to God, 160n137
    hope of the actualization of, 85n182
    hoping for the fulfillment of, 88
    in Psalm 132, 87
    Solomon's prayer beginning with, 87n191
    unconditionality of, 154

Davidic promises and kingdom, emphasizing, 127

Davidic royal line, everlasting nature of, 59

Davidic temple citizen, 60–65

David's final prayer (First Chronicles 29:10–19), 67–75
    sections of, 67n121

David's oath, with Yhwh's oath in Psalm 132, 86n188

David's Prayer (First Chronicles 17:16–27), 52–66
    as affirmation of the Davidic dynasty, 170–71
    given in response to Nathan's prophecy, 59n99
    presenting God's dynastic promises to David, 66
    showing David's inner mind, 19n17

deliberative rhetoric, prayer as a genre of, 68n123

demographic composition, 124

deportees, returning to their homeland, 124, 132n44, 139

desired Israel, 7, 10

diachronic tracing, of identity, 174

dialogue, differentiating prayer from, 14

diaspora synagogue, 161n141

disasters and diseases, receiving because of sin, 78–79

discontinuity, between the post-exilic period and the Israelites' past, 2

distinctiveness, of Yhwh, 129

distress, caused by a hostile attack, 102n238

distressing situations, 78, 98

divine assistance, inward attitude possible through, 74

divine beings, other than God as human-made, weak, and vulnerable, 46

divine discipline, people repenting through, 165

divine election and covenant, responsibilities of, 141n70

divine governance, accentuating God's, 70

divine help, Asa'a direct request for, 92

Subject Index

divine judgment, benchmarks for, 105
divine plan, successful completion of, 136n57
divine response, to prayer, 17
divine wisdom, 131
divine-human analogy, 17–18
divinity, community maintaining perception of, 131

effectiveness, of prayer, 22–23, 24, 30n13, 96, 111–14
election, rooted and grounded in love, 100n232
Elephantine, syncretism and, 137n60
Elephantine Judaism, 138n60
priest Eliashib, 143
embedded prayer, emphasizing the contents of, 50–51
end of days, Chronicles not referencing, 148n100
Er, as evil in the eyes of the Lord, 31n15
eschatology, using as a term, 148n100
etiological presentation, effectiveness of prayer and, 30n13
"everlasting covenant," in the Old Testament, 44n55
exegetical/literary indicators, enabling readers to perceive identity, 24
exile, 84–85, 84n181, 153n115
exile returnees. *See* deportees
exodus event, 57, 133n44
external influences, upon members of community, 120
"eyes," referring to the Lord, 162n145
Ezra, 159, 160
Ezra (book of), 1n1, 136n57, 146
Ezra-Nehemiah, 136, 136n57, 145, 155
Ezra's prayer, 2, 160n138

faith, 169
faithfulness, describing Asa's, 94
fasting, 97, 98n227, 101
finiteness, of human beings, 72
foreign nations, 130, 134, 135. *See also* nations
foreigners, 79, 79n163, 80–81, 82
forgiveness
    asking Yhwh for, 170
    receiving, 76, 79n166
    referring to God's restoration, 78n159
    Solomon clearly asking for God, 98
    supplicants asking God's, 77–80
"free-form phenomenon," by supplicants, 166
future Israel, defined by religious practices, 173–74

genealogy, 132–33n44, 147n97
genealogy section (chs. 1–9), in Chronicles, 26
Gibeon, 144n86
glory and strength, recognizing the source of, 46
glory of God, in the temple, 162
God. *See also* Yhwh
    of Abraham, Isaac, and Israel, 110, 110n267, 116n280
    actions of in first person singular verbs, 80n166
    as the agent of remembering, 19n15
    answering Jabez's prayer, 32
    Asa's perception of, 91–95
    chose Solomon as the temple builder, 64
    communicating with Solomon, 77
    David's recognition of his greatness and plan, 53
    defeating Israel's enemy, 101
    direct relationship to his people, Israel, 58n95
    discerning the heart of a giver, 73
    dominion over the world, 162n145
    election of Israel, 56
    establishing David's kingdom, 59
    establishing Solomon's kingdom, 64
    of the fathers, 114–15, 115n279, 118
    forgiving sins wherever people are located, 163
    gave the land of Canaan in perpetuity, 102
    greatness of, 53n81, 67, 69n126
    hands of, 33, 33n20
    as the healer in Solomon's dream, 111
    interacting with what Solomon asks for, 77

God (*cont.*)
  intervening in battle, 92, 104
  intervening in human affairs, 103
  of Israel, 32, 33, 42–44, 57, 68, 74, 101–5
  keeping his promise to David, 87n190
  making David a greater figure, 62n106
  making himself accessible through his name, 40n41
  as a mighty warrior, 91
  not requiring Judah to fight, 149
  possessing everything in the heaven and the earth, 46n61, 69
  praising for his protection of Israel, 20
  praying to during war, 90
  preeminence and uniqueness of, 80–82
  presence of, 139
  promising Israel that he would present himself, 39
  promising Solomon, 63n110, 98
  promising to watch the temple, 163
  psalm recording David's praise to, 37n31
  punishing his people and foreign nations, 130n36
  referring to his name as Yhwh, 55n87
  rejecting David's appeal to construct the temple, 52–53n77
  reliance upon, 93–95
  remembrance of David's deeds, 86
  reminding of his promise to David, 84n177
  requiring Solomon's obedience to the law, 84n177
  responding to a supplicant's prayer, 117–18
  response of, 76, 95, 97, 162n145
  returning the deportees through Cyrus, 134
  as special and unique, 35
  standing on Judah's side, 102
  supremacy of, 35, 68–74, 81, 103
  as the sustainer of memories, 18
  as uncontainable, 162n145
  universe recognizing the sovereignty of, 46n61, 48–49
  work of, 113
  worshipers focusing on, 37
"God created heaven," implying God rules over the universe, 46n61
God's name
  as access to divine power, 39n41
  bestowing the authorization of God, 40n41
  calling upon and glorifying/boasting in, 39
  David calling on during his prayer, 65
  as an expression of divine presence, 162n143
  as good, 114n277
  as the source of power, 40n41
  special attention to, 39n38
  temple bearing, 81, 161
  worshipers relating to, 39n39
God's people
  contemplating their united identity and role, 124
  Israel as, 42–43, 55–56, 57–58, 80
governors, Persian, 123n14, 128, 135

Haggai, 134, 137, 156
healer, image of God as, 111
heart of a giver, 73, 75
heart/attitude, for seeking God's presence, 40–41
hearts, asking that God would touch, 74
heaven, 46n61, 102–3, 163n145
King Hezekiah
  authority of, 110n267, 171
  commanding restoration of the temple, 140n68
  as eager to worship with all-Israel, 117
  as an ideal king, 115, 118
  as a model figure, 108–11, 170
  purifying and restoring Israel's worship, 106–7
  reestablishing Israel's religion, 117n282
  reformation of, 115n279

requesting God's intervention, 108n259
as the second David or Solomon, 116n280
on serving the priests and Levites, 111n269
supervising the Levites, 109
as the supplicant, 111–14
walking the opposite path of Ahaz, 140n68
Hezekiah's Prayer (Second Chronicles 30:18–20), 106–18, 107n257
Hezron, death of, 31n15
"hierocracy," 63n109
high priests, restricting the authority of, 141, 143
historian, Chronicler as, 8n23
historical figures, adopting the prayers of, 169
historical prayer, assimilating, 18
historical process, hand of God behind, 132n44
historical timeline, for Israel, 22
historical value, of biblical literature, 121
historiography, 7–8
history, Chronicler recalling, 9
holy war
    development of the ideology of, 96n218
    motif of, 104, 104n242, 151n107
    theme of in Jehoshaphat's battle, 95–96n218
    worshipping Yhwh as one element of, 150
    "Yhwh war" as more appropriate than, 104n247
hope, 4n9, 19, 72n139
House of David, God's blessing on, 65n116
house of prayer, for all people, 79n162
house of Yhwh, building, 73
human actions, as responses to God's judgment, 80n166
human beings, as agents of remembering, 19n15
human heart, preserved in a right manner, 74
human life, as transitory, 72

human productions, literature and history as, 121n5
human response, in third person plural verbs, 80n166
human-human conversation, differentiating prayer from, 14
humility, 52, 53, 72

I am who I am, 55n87
identity
    concepts concerning, 10
    determining within the text, 7
    as not always revealed explicitly, 22
    of the post-exilic community, 119, 174
    post-exilic community searching for, 168
    in prayer, 23–24
    reconstruction, 3, 20–21
    shaping through prayer, 15–24
    sharing with other community members, 10n29
    Solomon's prayer shaping, 75
identity formation
    discovering, 174
    rhetoric of prayer in relation to, 25, 169
    through biblical texts, 5
    in the Yehud community, 120, 122
ideology, 8n23, 16, 16n6, 123n12
idols, worshiped by other nations, 135
images, concerning God, 103
imperial mechanisms, of the Persian Empire, 123–24
imperial policies, responses to, 120
inheritance, Israel's right of, 101–2
institutions, 82n171, 137. *See also* religious institutions
intercession, basic principles of, 78n157
internal voices, biblical texts exhibiting, 127
invaders, reversing Yahweh's divine plan, 105
inward attitude of worshipers, seeking Yhwh, 40
Isaac, not making a covenant with God, 45n57
Isaiah, 100

Israel
  as active supplicants, 76–80
  better future linked to the identity of, 4
  centralization of the cult of, 144n86
  consisting of the twelve tribes, 43n52
  denoting as God's people, 55–56
  dependent on God, 72n139
  desired, 7, 10
  God making the covenant with, 115
  as God's elected people, 44, 56, 57–58
  God's special relation with, 100, 102
  having ability, 71–72
  history of, 71, 152
  identity of, 96, 119–67
  as the kingdom of Yhwh, 63n109
  as monotheistic believers, 41–49
  as a nation created by God, 56
  no ability without God, 72
  referring to the people of Israel, 1n1
  relationship with God, 35, 42–44, 49, 68
  settlement in, 57n93
  as substitution for "Abraham," 43n51
  ultimate prayer and final acclaim, 50–51
  witnessing God's supremacy, 5n12
  as Yhwh's chosen people, 170
Israelites
  choosing to worship either Yhwh or idols, 136
  as God's special and chosen group, 49
  roles or characteristics of, 9
  second chance for errant, 155n118
  shaping as active supplicants, 28–33
Israel's Jubilant Overture (First Chronicles 16:8–36), 34–51

Jabez
  as a model figure, 28, 28n4, 34
  name of, 30n11
  overcame his sinister omen, 29
  praying like, 31–33
Jabez's Prayer (First Chronicles 4:9–10), 26–34
Jacob, not making a covenant with God, 45n57
King Jehoshaphat
  account of compared to 1 Kings, 95n217
  achieving victory through God's intervention, 98
  on the act of prayer, 21
  adopting David's prayer as a model, 70
  alluding to Solomon's prayer and the prophecy of Isaiah, 167
  bringing God's promise with Abraham into his war context, 100
  calling for a fast throughout all Judah, 97
  dependence upon God, 96
  engaging God in Judah's warfare, 105
  expecting God to be just, 106
  identifying Israel as God's people, 21
  as a model supplicant, 97–101, 106
  modification of Solomon's prayer, 99
  as not the only one praying, 101
  praying with all the people of Judah, 106
  reliance on Ahab, king of Israel, 96
  reporting the victory of, 103
  responding to Jahaziel's prophecy, 150n104
  royal hope of, 155
  transforming past prayer into his own, 96
Jehoshaphat's Prayer (Second Chronicles 20:5–13), 95–106
  as active supplicant and monotheistic believer, 106
  communicating with the post-exilic audience, 167
  constructing a new theological system, 100
  conveying being a witness, 149
  expecting God to be just, 18, 104
  God responding to, 97
  indicating those who pray to God, 99
  as a model prayer, 20, 165
  motivating his audience to be active supplicants, 97
  on the name of God being in the temple, 162n143
  scene of, 21n22

Jerusalem, 126, 127n24, 138n60
Jerusalem temple, 144n86, 145, 172
Jesus, as the Temple, 163n146
Jewish syncretism, 137n60
King Joash, 140n68, 154n118
John the Baptist, 157
Josiah, 140n68, 144n83
joy, as a core element of worship, 48n67
Judah
    God defeating the enemies of, 102
    invaded by enemies as unjust, 105
    responding to the king's summons to join in the prayer, 97
    standing on Yhwh's side, 90
    weak status against the Cushites, 91
justice, 103, 104, 104n248

kingdom, security of, 60, 64
kingdoms of the earth, God granting, 103
kings, 140n68, 152n112
Kugel, James L., 21n21

lacuna, concept of, 154
lament, answering, 102n238
land, as God's permanent bestowal, 105n253
law
    as central for worship, 146
    codification of in the Persian Empire, 123n14
    God as the one giving, 115
    God requiring Solomon's obedience to, 84n177
    people's obligation to, 114
leadership (priests), solidifying their authority, 149
Levites
    consecrating unpurified people, 108n259
    encouraging to be consecrated, 109
    on praising Yhwh along with their names, 150n104
    responsibilities of, 142
    roles as musicians, 38, 38n33
    roles of, 96n218, 110–11, 124, 126, 141, 173
Levites and the priest, unique position in the worshiping community, 11

Levitical groups, experiencing continual changes, 141
Levitical music, 38n33, 104, 150. *See also* music
life
    God having the ability to restore, 103
    of Jabez as prosperous, 30
life stories, 30
life-threatening moment, overcoming, 99
literary analysis, of the Solomon narrative, 64n112
literary and rhetorical analysis, of recorded prayers, 12
literary evidence, on issues in the lives of the people, 121
literary historical situation, analyzing, 23–24
literary rhetorical analysis, of recorded prayers, 26–118
literary structure, 54n81, 69, 92n203, 110n268
literature
    role of, 121n5
    on social and historical realities, 121
liturgical community, 10, 11, 168, 173
Lynch, Matthew, 11

maintenance of the temple, 152n112
Malachi, 146, 157
master/servant relationship, clarifying, 55
memories, 18–19, 18n15
message, of a particular prayer, 22
migration and grouping, in the Persian Empire, 123n14
militarization, in the Persian Empire, 123n14
military personnel, referenced by Asa, 93–94
military strength, 88, 104
miserable circumstances, of Jabez, 33
model figure(s)
    Hezekiah as, 113, 117n282
    King Asa as, 93
    motivating the community to follow, 153
model prayers
    applying to contemporary context, 96
    Chronicler providing, 50
    past prayers as, 19–21, 98–100

monotheism, 11, 52n76
monotheistic belief
  of Asa, 89, 90, 92, 95
  characteristics of, 171
  embodying prayer and worship, 172
  expressing, 73
  principles of, 49–50
monotheistic believer(s)
  aspect of in relation to the nature of the temple, 81
  belief that Yhwh still remembers his people, 170
  characteristic of, 11
  David as, 52–58, 65
  expecting God to be just, 104–5
  Hezekiah as, 114
  Israel as, 41–49
  motivating the audience to become, 75
  outward and inward expressions of, 70–74
  prayer motivating to become active, 68
  shaping, 170, 172
  Solomon as, 75
monotheistic believing community, 129–35
Mosaic covenant, 160n137
Moses, 30n13, 55n87, 139, 142n78, 145–46
mother of Jabez, 32
Mt. Gerizim, 145n87
music, 37, 38–39, 51. *See also* Levitical music

name, of Jabez, 28, 29n6
name etiology, 29n8
Nathan, 62n108, 65–66
Nathan's oracle, 52, 59, 60, 61–64, 151
national crises, 89, 96, 152
nations, 47n64, 104, 124–25. *See also* foreign nations
nationwide response, to Hezekiah's invitation, 110n268
Nehemiah, 134, 136n57, 143, 159–60
Nehemiah 9, expressing eschatological hope, 2n5
Nehemiah's prayer, 127, 159n136

non-Israelites, Solomon praying for, 79
northern people, 109, 110, 143–44, 144n83

object of prayer, 32n17, 114, 115
object of worship or sacrifice, God as, 115
offering, as an outward expression of believers, 71–73
omnipotence, of God, 91n199, 93n209
omnipresence, of God, 162n145
other gods, as inferior to God, 162n145
"our Father," added to the title "the God of Israel," 68n124
outward and inward expressions, of David, 70–74
ownership, depicting God's, 69

pain, of Jabez, 27, 29, 29n7
participating process, in prayer, 17, 18
passages, rules of diagramming, 31n16
Passover, 107, 109, 109n265, 110
past history, remembering of, 8–9
past prayer(s). *See also* prayer(s)
  community employing, 173
  contextualization of, 100, 165
  cultivating in light of their own circumstances, 106
  on the king's interpretation and application of, 96
  as a model, 19–21, 98–100
  retrieving core doctrines of, 100
  transformation of, 167, 171
past records, allowing vision of future possibilities, 168
past Scripture, citing of, 21n21
patriarchal origins, of the covenant, 44
penitential prayer
  accompanied by proper behavior, 165
  development of, 163–64
  features of, 164n148
  looking forward to covenant renewal, 2
  scholarly research or debate on, 163n148
perception, of roles or characteristics of prayer, 15

Persian colony, Yehud community as a, 126
Persian empire, 123, 123n14, 124, 126
Persian period, 6, 122
Persian world, post-exilic community relating to, 120
Persians
    affinities between the Judaeans and, 130n35
    habitation of the Palestine area, 130n34
    harsh against rebellions, 128
    on history having its particular purpose, 130n36
    increasing authority of priests, 138n63
    sought to stabilize the Mediterranean coast, 126
    spoke the phrase "God of heaven," 134n50
personification, of the heaven and the earth, 48
"philosophy," of history in Chronicles, 8n23
political identity, 127
political leaders of Yehud, priests and, 143
population, of Achaemenid Jerusalem, 94n215
portal, by "which prayer finds its way to God," 161n140
possession (*merism*), emphasizing the totality of God's, 70
post-exilic audience, 15, 16–17, 75, 81–82, 94, 97, 131, 167, 168
post-exilic biblical literature, testimony of, 120–22
post-exilic community
    as active supplicants, 90
    adopting and transforming past prayers, 98, 99
    awaiting God's intervention, 150n103
    becoming monotheistic believers, 80, 95
    becoming worshipers, 51
    behavioral changes required by, 164
    as citizens of the Davidic kingdom, 52
    communicating with neighboring religious-cultural influences, 131
    constructing their own prayer, 100
    David as a model figure for, 65
    dependent on perceiving God's promise, 154
    depicting an overall picture of, 121n7
    encouraging to be Davidic citizens, 82
    encouraging to become worshipers, 35
    expecting that God listens to their prayers, 97–98
    expressing hope to God, 19
    God's promise as still in effect, 83n176
    hoping for a Davidic king and his kingdom, 115
    hoping for God's intervention, 85
    identifying as a liturgical community, 172
    inner voice of, 120
    interpreting Nathan's oracle, 151
    interpreting the message of the Chronicler, 24
    inviting to temple reconstruction, 161n140
    Jabez's prayer and, 33
    joining in the prayers of David, 59–60
    motivating to become active supplicants, 89
    not engaged in fierce, nationwide battle, 17
    not in a different context from David, 66
    offering of sacrifices, 111
    participation in temple worship, 172–73
    perceiving their deity, 129, 133
    praying actively, 160
    praying for the revival of the Davidic kingdom, 65
    praying like historic supplicants, 167
    praying toward/at/in the temple, 167
    reassuring of what they learned from Scripture, 102n238

post-exilic community (cont.)
  reconstructing identity, 1
  remembering the covenant, 44
  retrieving the past, 2
  reviewing their history, 132n43
  shaping into actively praying people, 34
  as a small province under the Persian Empire, 129
  standing in line with pre-exilic Israel, 132n44
  surrounded by foreign powers, 105
  understanding of their own identity, 11
  various prayer practices in, 159
  witnessing David and Solomon affirming God's supremacy, 81
  witnessing Levites and priests leading the worship, 36
post-exilic high priests, Chronicler warned against, 141, 143
post-exilic Judah, expanding the territories of, 33n21
post-exilic people, 56, 165n157
post-exilic Yehud community, surrounded by great powers, 51
power, of communal prayer, 100–101
praising, God, 70
prayer(s). *See also* past prayer(s); recorded prayers
  accentuating a message, 22n25
  analysis of eight in Chronicles, 26
  from the books of Chronicles, 15
  changing the destiny of one's life, 30
  as the Chronicler's strategic literary artifacts, 8
  classification and enumeration in Chronicles, 158n132
  combining different, 20
  contributing to ideology and theology, 8
  definition and identification of, 13–15, 13–14n1
  echoing contemporary issues, 158–59
  effectiveness of, 22–23, 111–14
  identity identification in, 23–24
  importance of in Chronicles, 6–7
  literary structure of, 92n203
  as the major topic of Solomon's prayer, 76
  as memory and hope, 18–19
  not portraying roles or characteristics, 169
  persuading the post-exilic community, 168
  practice of, 158, 159n136
  principles of, 31
  reflecting the inner status or attitude, 173
  regarding worshipers, 139
  rhetoric of, 16–24
  of the Second Temple period, 166n160
  shaping identity through, 15–24
  textual suggestions indicating, 15n4
  transformation of attitude through, 21–22
  as a unique element in Jabez's life, 31
  unique rhetorical effect in Chronicles, 169
The Prayer of Jabez: Breaking Through to the Blessed Life (Wilkinson), 26, 27n1
prayer participants, 16–19, 24
prayer scene, differentiating from prayer, 14–15
prayer text, telling about an author and his ideas, 16n6
praying, like Jabez, 31–33
praying community, 12, 29, 158–67, 171
presence of God, worship manifesting, 150n106
priestly and Levitical groups, return of, 124
priests
  hiding behind God and Moses, 142n78
  increased power of, 142, 143
  misused their authority, 138
  roles of in the temple service, 141n71
promises, 63, 154, 154n118
prophetic warnings, prompting repentance, 165
prophets, as mirrors of the *status quo*, 138n63

Psalm 132, 85, 85n183, 85n184, 86n185, 86n186
psalmist, on the Patriarch narrative, 44n57
psalms, 2, 19n15, 35n23, 159n136
public prayer, 96, 100–101, 106, 160n138
public worship, in Hezekiah's prayer, 109
purification, 112, 130–31
purity status, priests determining, 142

readers, receiving prayers as a part of their lives, 20
rebellions, Persians quelling, 128, 149
recorded prayers, 26–118. *See also* prayer(s)
  assisting to reflect on past experience, 168
  as the Chronicler's literary artifact, 18
  literary and rhetorical analysis of, 169
  reflecting the supplicant's view toward God, 17
  revealing the unique rhetorical effect of, 174
  shaping the identity of readers/ participants, 12
  value of, 2
reformation
  of King Asa, 88
  of Hezekiah, 108–9, 111–12, 112n271
  of Jehoshaphat, 98n227
religion, unifying community members, 129
religious identity, revival of, 125n21
religious institutions, 125, 154, 171. *See also* institutions
religious practice, prayer as a central feature of, 158
religious revitalization, 137
religious-cultic identity, 151n108
religious-juridical hierarchy system, priests establishing, 143
repentance
  bringing hope, 72
  describing again and again, 79n164
  encouragement of, 167
  Malachi calling for, 146

referring to the rejection of sins, 78n159
related to God's disciplinary intention, 164–65
Solomon's prayer highlighting, 79
of supplicants, 170
research, need for future, 174–75
resources
  from God's hands, 72
  transferred from other nations, 134
restoration, Solomon on forgiveness as, 78n159
retribution theology, 89, 113, 113n273
rhetoric of prayer, 16–24, 25
rhetorical features, of prayers, 16, 174
rhetorical force (*anaphora*), creating, 69
rhetorical question
  of David about identity, 71
  definition and types of, 53n78
rhetorical strategies, 16n6, 68n123
righteous king, suffering of, 94n213
rituals, in the Persian Empire, 123n14
roles and characteristics
  as ongoing subjects regarding restoration, 171
  overview of the understanding of, 11
  prayers presenting, 15
  in recorded prayers, 119, 169
  throughout Chronicles, 26
royal prayers, 23, 161n140
ruler of the kingdom of nations, God as, 115

sacrifice-related terms or expressions, in Hezekiah's prayer, 108
sacrifices
  of both meat and grain, 47
  involving the act of prayer, 161n141
  offering proper, 111
  properly keeping, 146
  at the temple of Solomon, 144n86
sacrificial ritual, 11, 109, 145
Samarians, offered their own sacrifices, 144–45
Sanballat, interfering with rebuilding the wall, 160
savior, trust in Yhwh as, 90–95

scholars
- on affirmation of the Davidic covenant, 153n115
- on the Davidic kingdom or covenant, 147–48n98
- on the definition of prayer, 13–14n1
- distinguishing between speeches and prayers, 7
- on the dynastic promise, 148n98
- on the lives of Yehud community members, 121
- on the Persian period, 122
- on the ultimate founder of Israel's cult, 142n76
- on utopia, 4n9

scripturalization, 165, 166
scripture, reuse of, 166
second David, Hezekiah being seen as, 116n280
Second Temple period, act of prayer during, 160
seeking Yhwh, 40, 40n44
Segub and his son Jair, lost their town, 31n15
self-abasement
- of David, 53, 71
- before God, 97

self-governing system, definition of, 128n28
sermon/prayer, common form of, 93n210
servant, David as, 54, 55
service, theological principle on proper, 112
Sheshan, having no sons, 31n15
sins
- forgiving, 78
- repenting of, 171

social and economic diversity, 142n79
social factors, under the Persian Empire, 5
sociohistorical context, Israelite identity in, 24, 129–67
sociohistorical portrait, reconstruction of, 122
sociohistorical reality, literature revealing, 121
sociohistorical situation, roles and characteristics, 119
sociological landscape, 174
sociological methodologies, emergence of, 4–5
sociology, definition of, 4–5n10
socioscientific models, 5–6
sojourners and strangers, having no, 72n139
Solomon
- appealing to God to keep his covenant, 84n177
- building the temple, 64
- connection between Hezekiah and, 116n280
- depending upon David's deeds, 87
- hoping for fulfillment of the Davidic promise, 75
- hoping that God will answer prayer, 77
- as a man of peace/rest, 87, 88n193
- as a model supplicant, 88
- passion for successful worship, 117
- as the petitioner, 76
- praying for God's deliverance of his people, 85
- praying with faith in God's promise, 160
- proclaiming God's supremacy, 81
- requesting security of the Davidic dynasty, 83
- scenario regarding Israel's destiny, 166n160
- specifying God's expected act of response, 76
- as a temple builder, 64n110, 73, 117
- transference of the ark into its final place, 87

Solomon's prayer (Second Chronicles 6:14–42), 75–88
- assuming distressing situations, 98
- on the certainty of God's response, 163
- describing the king as an active supplicant, 76
- on the everlasting Davidic kingdom, 171
- God answering, 23

Subject Index

hoping for the fulfillment of the
  Davidic dynasty, 82
Jehoshaphat bringing up, 21
as Jehoshaphat's and the people's
  own prayer, 99
Jehoshaphat's democratization of,
  99n230
not applicable to Jehoshaphat's
  present circumstances, 98
on repentance, 164
requesting God's forgiveness, 77–78
sections of, 78
still in effect for Jehoshaphat, 97
on the temple as central to lives,
  161n140
temple portrayed as the locus of
  prayer, 160–61
Sondergut, 3n7, 67
sovereign deity, Yhwh as, 170
sovereignty. *See also* supremacy of God
of God over the universe, 134n50
"spaceless being," God as, 162n145
supplicant(s)
  articulating prayer as unique, 173
  asking God's forgiveness, 77–80
  behaving as one who prays to God,
    21n23
  changing for the better through
    prayer, 21
  characterization of, 23
  Chronicler idealizing as model,
    166–67
  David as a faithful, 65–66
  expecting God to respond, 19
  Hezekiah as, 111–14
  instrumentalized as exemplary
    models, 169
  Israel as active, 76–80, 88
  Jehoshaphat's prayer exhibiting
    aspects of, 98
  King Asa as, 89
  perceiving God as divinity, 125
  persuading the audience of
    Chronicles to become, 89
  praying together during a national
    calamity, 100–101
  recognizing the importance of
    maintaining faith, 160
  repenting of sins in order to receive
    forgiveness, 88
  seeking God, 112, 159
  shaping Israelites as active, 28–33
  as those who repent of their sins, 75
  transforming readers into, 18
  unique aspects of Jehoshaphat's
    prayer, 96
supremacy of God, 81
  over other gods, 45
  over the universe, 170, 172
  over the world, 45–49, 68, 80
supreme divine being, God's character
  as, 45
supreme qualities, God's possession
  of, 70
synagogue, as a locus for religious
  practice, 161n141
synchronic approach, to the process of
  identity formation, 174
syncretism, 137, 137n60, 146n95

taxation, temple as an important source
  of, 138
temple
  associating with God's presence, 161
  built for God's name's sake, 102
  as the center of cultic activity, 160
  central significance in Chronicles,
    64n112
  community's participation in service
    and duties, 172
  completed as fulfillment of the
    covenant, 61n103
  completion of related to the security
    of the throne, 64
  dedication of, 75, 87
  as the fulfillment of God's promise
    of restoration, 138
  God not always dwelling in, 162
  maintenance of as critical, 152
  nature and function of, 81–82, 170
  one room diverted for Tobiah's use,
    138
  particularity in relation to God,
    82n172
  as the place for sacrifice, 139,
    161n141

temple (*cont.*)
  as the place of divine oversight, 163
  as the place of sacrificial ritual, 143
  as the point of contact between pre- and post-exilic eras, 132n44
  portraying the nature of, 126
  praying toward/at/in, 160–61n140, 163, 172, 173
  receiving God's special attention, 171
  referring to as a medium, 161n140
  reflecting God's preeminence and uniqueness, 81, 82
  reformation of, 140n68
  role in community identity formation, 172
  sacred courts of, 47n64
  service personnel, 139, 141
  as a symbol of the presence of God, 163n146
  testifying to God's presence, 163
  worship involving an inner heart and sacrificial performance, 173
temple construction
  completion of, 66, 152
  David preparing for, 59n100, 67
  relationship to the Davidic dynasty, 171
  support for in the Persian Empire, 123n14
temples, permitted as symbols by Persian authorities, 129
territory, Jabez's requests for, 33
texts
  as a chance for readers to be attentive to prayers, 18
  as literary theological or ideological documents, 7
  as a medium for identity formation, 8–9
  perceiving identity from, 2
  socio relationships of its origins, 121n5
textual construction, role in identity formation, 9n27
textual markers, 80
thematic unity, of a prayer, 24
themes, in Ezra-Nehemiah, 136–37
theocracy, in Chronicles, 63n109

theological doctrine, modifying past prayers with, 100
theological history, Chronicler writing, 8
theological principles, 18, 24
theology, conveying through prayers, 16
throne at the center of heaven, God sitting on, 103
"to give thanks," appearing throughout Chronicles, 39n37
"to sing," appearing in Chronicles, 39n37
Tobiah and Ammonite, interfering with rebuilding the wall, 160
transformative ability, God providing, 19
transience, of Israel, 71
tribute, bringing to Yhwh, 47
true heart, as believers' inward expression, 73–74
trust, in Yhwh as savior, 90–95
truth claims, about participants' life setting, 17

uncleanness, Hezekiah interceding with God regarding, 108
unconditionality, of the Davidic promise, 154
uniqueness
  of God, 55, 69, 82
  of Israel, 57n93
  temple's sharing in, 82n172
  of Yhwh to Israel, 170, 172
united kingdom, hope of, 115–17
united worship, theme of, 110n268
universal ruling authority, perceiving Yhwh's, 134
universe
  authority of God over, 134
  David on God's sovereignty over, 68–69
  God ruling over, 46n61
  sovereignty of God over, 48–49, 134n50, 135
  supremacy of God over, 68–74, 170, 172
utopia, scholarly discussions regarding, 4n9

vertical relationship, defining the supplicant's identity, 23
victory, illustrating the effectiveness of prayer, 96
vision, of a desired community, 4
visualization, of Solomon spreading out his hands toward heaven, 76
Vorlage (Samuel-Kings), 3, 3n7, 9, 57
vulnerable status, dealing with, 94

warfare, 94, 101–5, 149, 150, 150n103
warrior, performance inviting, 150
wholeheartedness, God granting to Solomon, 74
wisdom, originated from Yhwh, 131
world, God's supremacy over, 45–49, 103
worship
    characterized by the reading of the law, 146
    core of, 173
    Hezekiah as a model figure for, 107, 108–11
    involving the outward expression of worshipers, 37
    involving the worshiper's joyful response, 48n67
    inward attitude of, 40
    manifesting the presence of God, 150n106
    musical nature of, 38
    people of Yehud restoring practices of, 171
    performance of as Judah's own warfare, 150
    principles of, 49–50
    proper practice of, 35, 37–41, 107, 138
    as the proper response to divine provision, 136
    restoration of proper, 146
    scene of, 23
worshipers
    community's role as, 11, 151
    invitation to Israel to be, 36–41
    making God's deeds known, 37
    making offerings to God, 46, 47n62
    manifesting appropriate attitudes, 170
    members of the community as, 150
    outward expression of, 40
    proper practice of worship, 37
    seeking God's presence, 41
    singing music and calling on God's name, 51
worshiping community, 11, 135–46, 170
worshiping Yhwh, 136, 150

Yahweh. *See* Yhwh
Yahwism, dimensions of, 131n41
Yahwistic worshipers, conflict with, 146n95
Yehud, province of, 1n1, 130n34, 145–46
Yehud community
    autonomy of, 128n27
    characteristics of religion in the Persian era, 125n21
    continually influenced by Persian ideology, 130
    identifying as a worshiping community, 135–46
    local governors involved in, 128
    lost the Davidic kingdom, 132
    members of exhibiting particular characteristics, 10
    not reflecting the ideal worship practice, 139
    opportunity to revive religious roles, 125
    under the Persian Empire's influence and control, 171
    Persian Empires' interest in, 126n23
    practiced public or communal prayer, 160
    sociohistorical reality of, 119, 120n3
    suffered economically under oppressive foreign governors, 135
    transformed through internal social formation, 127
    uniqueness of, 5n12
Yhwh. *See also* God
    act of seeking, 97
    alone as Israel's hope, 72
    Asa crying out to, 89–90
    calling upon, 80
    as categorically different, 11
    as the chief god of Judaeans, 131n41

Yhwh (*cont.*)
   as creator, 45
   as a divinity incomparable to other gods, 136
   as the God of gods, 45–46
   as incomparable, 55n86, 90–91, 134
   as Israel's God, 80, 132n43
   Israel's relationship with, 107
   Jehoshaphat praying to, 95
   as the object of prayer, 34n22, 169
   power and might of, 68n122
   promise to Israel's ancestors, 115n279
   receiving what he deserves, 46–47
   relying upon, 91–92
   renewing his relationship with Israel, 157
   struck the Cushites, 90, 91
   supremacy over Israel's enemies, 102, 106
   as supreme, 11, 41, 133–34, 136
   as their special God, 51
   as their unique God, 135
   as the unique and supreme deity, 131
   used the nations as his instruments, 133
   as who is good, 114
   worshiping by following Hezekiah's path, 109–11
"Yhwh has judged," as the meaning of Jehoshaphat's name, 104n248
"Yhwh war," as more appropriate than "holy war," 104n247

Zechariah, 137, 157
Zerah, 88–89, 93n211
Zerubbabel, 156, 156n124, 156n125, 156n127
Zoroastrianism, 130

Ancient Document Index

OLD TESTAMENT

Genesis

3:16	29n6
6:5	74, 74n146
8:21	74n146
9:16	44n55
15:18	45n57
17:3	44n55
17:7, 13, 19	45n57
17:7, 19	44n55
17:13	45n57
17:19	44n55, 45n57
21:32–34	30n10
24:3, 7	134n50
24:7	134n50
26:3	44n57
26:20–22	30n10
27:20–22	30n10
31:50–53	30n10

Exodus

3:6	115
3:11	53
3:13–15	55n87
4:22–23	55n85
5:2	53
12:43–51	107
14	102n238
14:13	102n238
15:17	62n105
15:22–25	30n13
15:26	165n153
16:7, 8	53
16:8	53
20:24	39
23:13	55n86
31:16	44n55
34:14	55n86
40	162n144

Leviticus

1:4	108n258
1–6	145n87
2	47
4:20	108n258
4:26	108n258, 110
4:31	108n258
4:35	108n258
5:6	108n258
5:10	108n258
5:13	108n258
5:16	108n258
5:26	108n258
6:11, 20	108n258
6:23	108n258
7:7	108n258
8:10	108n258
8:11	108n258
8:12	108n258
8:15	108n258, 111
8:15, 34	108n258
8:30	108n258
16:9, 30	108n258
16:19	108n258

Leviticus (cont.)

16:30	108n258
24:8	44n55
25:23	72n139
25:23–24	102
26:14–15	84

Numbers

3:6	141n71
8:6	108n258
8:7	108n258
8:15	108n258
8:21	108n258
8:26	141n71
18:2	141n71
19:12, 19	108n258
31:23, 24	108n258

Deuteronomy

	115n279
1:31	115
2:1–22	101
2:2–22	105
3:24	81
4:29	40n44
4:35, 39	55n86
4:39	55n86, 81
6:4, 14	55n86
7:4	55n86
7:8	56
7:9, 12	80n167
8:5	115
9:26	56
11:8–12	102
11:23–24	62n105
13:2	55n86
13:6 [Eng. v. 5]	56
14:1–2	115
15:15	56
16:19	105n249
17:3	55n86
20:1–20	104
21:8	56
24:18	56
26:15	162n145
28:13	56
28:14	55n86
28:15–60	84
28:20–36	78
28:21	78n160
28:22	78n160
29:22	165n153
31:18, 20	55n86
32:3	47n62
32:6	115
32:39	55n86

Joshua

6:4–20	104
8:2	104
8:7	104
8:12	104
8:14	104
8:19	104
8:21	104
8:24	104
11:4	104

Judges

7:18–20	104
9:28	53
15:19b	30n10
20:26–27	97n224

1 Samuel

3:20	110n266
7:13–14	30n10
17:26	53
18:6	39n37

2 Samuel

3:10	110n266
5:21	30n10
6	86
6:8b	30n10
7:6	57n91
7:14	83n176
7:16	64n110
7:18–29	166n160
7:23	56, 57
7:23 MT	56
7:24	56

Ancient Document Index 217

7:26	58
7:29	65, 65n115
8:2, 6	47n64
17:11	110n266
19:36	39n37
22:50	39n37
23:5	44n55
24:2, 15	110n266

1 Kings

5:5 [Eng. 4:25]	110n266
5:12	39n37
8	8, 79n166
8:23–53	166n160
8:27	81
8:33, 35	39n37
8:40	166n160
8:50–53	85
8:62—9:9	77n154
9:5	147n97
9:13b	30n10
10:1	37
10:12	39n37
15:9–24	89
15:23	140n68
21:3	102
22:1–55 [Eng. vv. 1–50]	95n217

2 Kings

8:13	53
8:19	147n97
17:3–4	47n64
17:24–41	146n95
19:15–19	166n160
22:3—23:27	145
22:32	99n229

1 Chronicles

1–9	4, 26, 27n2
1:19	29n9
2:3	31n15
2:3, 7	28, 30n14
2:7	28, 30n14, 31n15
2:18–19	28, 30n14
2:19	31n15
2:21–23	28, 30n14
2:22–23	31n15
2:24	28, 30n14, 31n15
2:34	28, 30n14, 31n15
2:35	28, 30n14
3:17–19	156
3:17–24	147n97
4:9	27n2, 167
4:9–10	15, 26–34, 30n14, 107n257, 111, 125n22, 131, 169
4:9a–b	28
4:9b	28
4:10	32, 33, 34n21
4:10b	28, 29, 32, 33
5:20	32n17
5:25	115
6:16–17 [Eng. vv. 31–32]	144n86
6:17 [Eng. v. 32]	139, 144n86
6:49	108n258
7:23	29n9
9:6	116n280
10–12	27n2
11:1–3	117
11:3	62n107
12:3	94n212
12:17–18	115
12:29 [Eng. v. 38]	116n280
13	86
13:11b	30n10
13–16	117
14	116n280
14:11 [Eng. v. 10]	170
15	86
15:14	108n258
15:25–28	172
16	20, 21, 97n222, 99, 150n106
16:1–15	52
16:2	144n86
16:4	38, 38n36
16:4, 12, 15	19n15
16:4, 37	144n86
16:4–5	34n22, 142
16:4–6	11, 34n22, 139
16:4–11	139
16:5	38n35, 38n36
16:5–6	38
16:6	38n35

1 Chronicles (*cont.*)

16:6–36	170
16:7	34n22
16:7–11	139
16:8	37, 39n39
16:8–10a	35
16:8–11	35, 37
16:8–13	36
16:8–36	15, 20, 26, 34–51, 34n22, 125n22, 126, 131, 167, 169, 170
16:10b–11	35
16:12	19n15
16:12–14	35
16:12–22	35
16:12–33	35
16:13	20
16:15	19n15, 100
16:15–16	172
16:15–17	132
16:15–22	35
16:16	44n57, 99
16:16–18	20, 132
16:16–23	20
16:21	103, 103n240, 150n106
16:23	20, 37, 39n37
16:23, 34	39n37
16:23–24	36
16:23–26	35
16:23–33	35, 45, 134
16:25	37
16:27	37
16:27–30	36
16:29	37
16:30–33	35, 37
16:33	38
16:34	39n37, 114
16:34–35	36
16:34–36	35, 36
16:35	135
16:35–36	36
16:36	36, 172
16:36b	36n27
16:37	38n36, 144n86
16:37–43	23, 36, 144n86
16:40	144n86
16:41–42	36
16:42	38n36
17	15n4, 64, 66, 81, 147n97, 151, 152n114
17:1–27	127
17:3–15	170
17:4	151n111
17:4–14, 23–24	83
17:5	57n91
17:9	62, 62n105
17:9–14	61
17:10	60
17:10–13	53
17:10a	62
17:10b	62, 63
17:10b–14	59, 59n99
17:11	64
17:11b	62, 63n108
17:11b–12	83n176
17:12	60, 63, 63n108, 63n110
17:12–14	62n108, 64
17:13	63n108, 83n176
17:14	63, 63n108, 63n110
17:16–22	52n76
17:16–27	15, 26, 52–66, 57n91, 125n22, 126, 131, 160, 167, 169, 170
17:16b–19	53
17:17	60
17:19	53n81, 60, 69n127
17:20	81
17:20–22	55
17:21	56, 135
17:22	56, 172
17:23–24	83
17:23–27	60
17:25	65n117, 66
17:27	65, 65n115, 65n116
18—2 Chr 7	64n110
19:10–19	125n22
19:13	114, 114n276
21	164, 165

21:1–30	155n118	28–29	67
21:2	110n266	29	147n97
21:8	15n4, 164	29:1	67
21:8, 17	164	29:2–5	67
21:17	15n4, 164	29:6–9	67
21:26	46n61	29:9	73
22, 28, 29	147n97	29:10	68, 71
22:5	129	29:10, 20	110n268
22:7	161, 162n143	29:10–12	70
22:8	161	29:10–19	15, 26, 67–75,
22:9	88n193		125n22, 131, 167,
22:9–10	83n176		169, 170
22:9–12	83	29:11	69, 103n240
22:9b	30n10	29:11–12	133n47, 134, 135
22:10	59n100, 151n111,	29:11a	69, 69n127
	161	29:11b	69, 70, 103
22:13	116n280	29:12	70
22:19	40, 161	29:12, 16	134
22:24–32	142	29:13	71
23:1—27:24	139	29:13, 16	68
23:3	110n268	29:13–17	71
23:13	108n258	29:13–19	70
23–27	10, 11, 117, 141,	29:14	133n47
	170	29:14–16	71, 71n133
23:28	141n71	29:15	71, 72, 72n139
24:1–19	139	29:16	33, 68, 134, 161
25	141	29:17	68, 73
25:1, 6	139	29:18	68, 71, 74, 110,
25:6	139		110n267, 115,
26:22	116n280		116n280
28	147n97	29:18–19	172
28:1—29:9	139	29:19	73, 83n176,
28:2–8	67		111n269
28:3	161	29:20	115
28:4	151n111	29:22	117
28:4, 7	151n111		
28:4–5	117	**2 Chronicles**	
28:5–10	83n176	1:3	144n86
28:6–10	83	1–7	117
28:7	151n111	1:7–17	131
28:7–8	111n269	1–9	75
28:8	67, 102	1:18	161–62
28:8–9	83n176, 172	1:18—2:17 [Eng. 2:1–16]	73n144
28:9	40, 67, 73, 73n143,	2:3	162
	74	2:4–5 [Eng. vv. 5–6]	81
28:11–21	67	2:5	81, 162n145
28:12	116n280	2:5 [Eng. v. 6]	162n145
28:20	110n268		

2 Chronicles (*cont.*)

2–7	139
2:11–12	131
5	86
5:1–10	87
5:2–10	85n184
5:6	116n280
5–7	75
5:11–14	87
5:12–13	38
5:13	114, 116n280
5:13, 14	162
6	8, 21, 80n166, 81, 84n179, 86, 116n280
6:2	161
6:3	87
6:4, 15	33n20
6–7	164
6:9b	63n108
6:10	83n174
6:10, 15	83
6:11, 14	172
6:12–38	20, 26, 169, 170
6:12–42	82, 102, 160, 161n141, 167
6:13	76
6:14	55, 81, 134, 172
6:14–15, 20	32n17
6:14–16	87n191
6:14–17	160
6:14–42	15, 23, 75–88, 125n22, 126, 127, 131, 170, 171
6:15	33n20, 83
6:16	83, 84
6:17	84
6:18	81, 162n145
6:20	21n22, 32n17, 39n39
6:20, 33, 38	162
6:20–39	145n89
6:21	162, 165
6:22–39	84
6:23	162
6:24–25	116n280
6:25	78n159, 162, 165
6:26	164
6:26, 27	46n61
6:27	46n61, 78n159, 165
6:28	20, 98
6:28–30	97
6:29	99
6:29–30	98n228
6:30	98, 165
6:30, 33, 39	162
6:31	78n159
6:32	33
6:32–33	82, 116n280
6:33	81, 162
6:34	145n89
6:34–35	90
6:36–39	84
6:37	164, 165
6:38	162
6:39	162
6:40	77, 163
6:40–42	85
6:41	41, 86, 87
6:42	87n190
7:1	23
7:1, 4–5	116n280
7:1, 14	46n61
7:1–10	87, 161n141, 167
7:1–11	77n154
7:1–22	77n154
7:3	110n268, 114, 162
7:4–5	116n280
7:5	87n192
7:5–6	38n35
7:6, 10	116n280
7:8	110n268
7:10	116n280
7:11–16	23
7:12	139, 145, 161n141
7:12b–15	116n280
7:13	46n61
7:13–15	77
7:13–16	20, 77, 77n154, 97, 98, 139
7:13b–14	80n166
7:14	32n17, 46n61, 78n159, 79n166, 98n228, 103, 111, 164, 165, 165n153

7:14–16	80n166	15:12	115
7:15	77n155, 163	15:12–15	94
7:16	39, 39n39	15:15	37
7:17–18	83n176	16	152n114
7:18	147n97	16:2	140n68
7:19–22	83n176	16:7	92
8:14–15	139, 141, 143	16:7, 8	91
9	27n2	16:7–10	140n68, 165
9:8	56	16:8	91
10–36	151n108	16:8–9, 12	92
11:6–7	172	16:8–36	22
11:16	115	16:9	133, 162n145
12:1, 5	165	16:12	92, 140n68, 165n153
12:1–12	152		
12:5	165	16:18	100
12:5–12	155n118	17:5	33n20
12:6–7, 12	164	17:10	104
12:12	164	18:1–34	96
13:3–21	104n242	18:12–27	165
13:5	147n97	18:18	46n61, 103
13:8	39n37	18:31	99, 99n229
13:10–12	144n83	19	98n227, 104n248
13:11–12	104, 115	19:1–11	155n118
13:13	104	19:1—20:3	95n217
13:14	89	19:2	96
13:18	91, 92, 115	19:3	165
13:18–21	92	19:4	98n227, 115
14:2–7	94	19:7	105
14:7 [Eng. v. 8]	93	20	20, 95n218, 98n227, 102n238
14:7–13 [Eng. vv. 8–14]	104n242		
14:8 [Eng. v. 9]	93	20:1	70, 98n227
14:8–14 [Eng. vv. 9–15]	89	20:1–30	96
14:9–15	152	20:1–34	94n213, 152
14:10	167	20:2	97
14:10 [Eng. v. 11]	15, 26, 32n17, 88–95, 125n22, 131, 135, 169, 170	20:3	97, 101
		20:3, 4, 20	149
		20:4	97, 149
14:10–11	39	20:5	97n223, 145n89
14:10–14 [Eng. vv. 11–15]	92	20:5–12	20, 23, 26, 169, 170
14:11	23		
14:11–14 [Eng. vv. 12–15]	135	20:5–13	15, 21n22, 95–106, 125n22, 131, 167
14:12	111		
14:12–15	23		
15:1–7	140n68	20:6	33, 46n61, 70, 103, 115, 133
15:2, 12–15	94		
15:8–9, 15	37	20:6–12	70, 89
15:9–15	172	20:6–13	100n233
15:11–15	140n68		

2 Chronicles (*cont.*)

20:7	20, 21, 100n232, 132
20:7, 11	100
20:7–12	20
20:8	81, 162, 162n143
20:8–9	20
20:9	21n22, 98n228, 99, 161
20:11	100, 105
20:12	21n22, 104, 105
20:12–13	21
20:13	21n22, 160n138
20:13–17	96
20:13–30	170
20:14–15	135
20:14–17	97, 100n233
20:15	105n252
20:15, 17	149
20:17	102n238, 149
20:18	150n104
20:19	150n104
20:19, 21	104
20:20	100n233, 149, 150
20:20–30	97, 103
20:21	104, 150n104
20:22	150n104
20:22–23	104, 111, 135
20:22–23, 27–29	98
20:22–30	23
20:24	104
20:26b	30n10
20:27–29	98
20:28–29	37
20:33	115
21:7	59n100, 147n97, 151n111
21:10	115
21:11	145n86
21:18	165n153
22:6	165n153
22:9	96
22:19	87
22:23	164
24:4	140n68
24:5–10	140n68
24:12–13	140n68
24:18, 24	115
24:18–20	162
24:19–20	165
24:23	140n68
24:24	115
25:5–13	104n242, 155n118
28:6, 9	115n279
28:6, 9, 25	115
28:8–15	144
28:9	115, 115n279, 144n83
28:11–19	87
28:19	164
28:22	140n68
28:23	140n68
28:24	140n68
28:25	115, 140n68, 145n86
29:1–19	106n255
29:1—30:27	139
29:2	116n280
29:5	115
29:6	108
29:11–19	164
29:12	33n20, 72n138
29:12–19	110
29:15	139
29:15, 16, 18	108n258
29:16	39n39, 108n258
29:18	108n258, 109
29:19	109
29:20	109n263
29:25	33n20
29:25–28	139
29:25–30	38n35
29–30	140, 143, 144
29–30, 35	136
29–31	106, 108, 110, 111, 112
29–32	106
30:1	117n283
30:1, 5	109n263
30:1–4	164
30:1–12	43n52, 140n68
30:1–27	106n255, 124
30:2, 4, 23	110n268
30:3	108n259, 140n68
30:4	110n268

30:5	109n263, 140n68	32:1–21	152
30:5–9	117	32:1–23	94n213, 116n280
30:5–12	110	32:7	116n280
30:6	116n280, 140n68	32:20, 24	161
30:6, 9	80n166	32:20–23	89
30:6, 11	153	32:21, 24	162n145
30:6–9	116n280	32:23	47
30:7	115	32:24	15n3, 111, 161, 162n145
30:8–19	126		
30:9	80n166	33:8	111n269
30:10	110n266, 116n281	33:10	164
30:11	153, 164	33:10–13	3, 15n3
30:12	33n20, 116n280	33:10–17	155n118
30:13	107, 110n268	33:11–12	165
30:15–16, 22, 24	116n280	33:12	115
30:15–16, 24	111	33:12, 13, 18	161
30:16	139	33:12, 19, 23	164
30:17–19	108	33:12–13	161n140, 167
30:18	107, 108, 111, 114, 116	33:13	111, 114, 161, 162n145
30:18–19	109, 116n280, 117, 125n22, 126, 131	33:15	164
		33:18	161, 165
		33:19	145n86, 164
30:18–20	15, 26, 106, 167, 169, 170, 171	34:1—35:19	144n83
		34:3, 5, 8	108n258
30:19	112, 114, 140n68	34:5	108n258
30:19, 22	115	34:8	108n258
30:20	111, 165, 165n153	34:8–13	140n68
30:21–22	38n35	34:9, 21, 33	153
30:21–23, 26	116n280	34:12	142
30:22	109, 116n280, 139	34:15	140n68
30:22–24	110	34:21	153
30:23	110n268	34:22–28	165
30:23–25	110n268	34:27	140n68
30:24	111, 116n280	34:27–28	164
30:25	111, 144n84	34:28	140n68
30:26	116n280	34:29	140n68
30:27	46n61, 103, 161, 162	34:29–33	140n68
		34:29—35:6	172
31:1, 6	117	34:30	140n68
31:1–21	106n255	34:32–33	115
31:2	38n35	34:33	153
31:4	111n269, 139	35	136
31:6	117	35:1	110
31:11–14	116n280	35:1–19	139, 140, 145
31:20	112	35:2, 4, 10	141
31:21	112, 114	35:4	139, 141
31:25	153	35:6	139

2 Chronicles (*cont.*)

35:10	141
35:18	140n68, 153
36	27n2
36:12	164
36:13	80n166
36:15	115
36:16	165n153
36:17	152
36:17–21	152
36:21–24	3
36:22	152
36:23	46n61, 103, 134n50, 152, 152n114

Ezra

1:1	155
1:1–4	134, 136n57
1:2	131, 133, 134n50
1–2	139
1:5–8, 11	132
1:5–11	124
1:5—Neh 7:72	136n57
1–6	136n57
1:11	132
2:1–2	124
2:1–70	132n44
2:2	1n1
2:41	141
2:59	1n1
2:70	1n1
3:1	1n1
3:1–3	146
3:2	125
3:4	137
3:4–6	146
3–6	125
3:10	155, 155n120
3:11	114
4:1–3	146, 146n95
4:3	131
4:4, 6	1n1
5:11	131
5:13–17	128
5:14, 16	128
5:14–16	124
5:16	128
6:7	128
6:13–22	136, 136n57
6:17	124
6:18	145
6:19	137
6:19–22	132, 146
6:21	1n1, 131, 164
7:1—8:36	124
7:6	159
7:6, 21, 23	134
7:7	1n1
7–8	139
7–10	136n57
7:10	146
7:17	134n50
7:21	134
7:23	134
7:27	131
8:1–20	132n44
8–13	136n57
8:20	155, 155n120
8:21–23	137
8:22	159
8:25, 35	1n1
8:28	146
8:35	1n1, 124
9	3n6, 164n149, 165, 167
9:1	1n1
9:1–15	137, 160
9:2	146
9:6–15	2, 159n136
9–10	124, 144n84
9:10–12	131
9:12	165
10:1	160, 160n138
10:2	72
10:2, 11	164
10:2–3	72
10:3	160
10:6	1n1
10:11	164
10:23–24	141
12:27–43	136n57

Nehemiah

1	164n149, 165, 167
1:1—2:10	136n57
1:4	137
1:4, 5	134n50
1:4–11	159n136
1:5	134n50
1:5–11	160
1:6	1n1, 159n136
1–7	136n57
1:8	160n137
1:9	164
2:1–8	128
2:1–10	136n57
2:4, 20	134n50
2:4–8	126
2:5	134
2:8, 18	134
2:10	1n1
2:18	134
2:20	134n50
3–4	125
3:5	124
3:15–16	155n120
4:8 [Eng. v. 14]	131
5:14–17	128
5:15	135
5:17	124
6:16	131
6:17	1n1
7:5–72	124
7:7	1n1
7:43–45	141
7:72	1n1, 136n57
8	125
8:1–6	160
8:1–11	137
8:6	145
8:7–8, 10–11	146
8:9–12, 14–18	164
8:10	49n67
8:10–11	146
8–13	136n57
8:13–18	139
8:14	145
8:14, 17	1n1
8:14–18	164
8:17	1n1
9	2n5, 134n49, 164n149, 165, 167
9:1	1n1
9:1–38	137
9:2	1n1
9:4–37	3n6
9:5–37	159n136
9:6	134
9:7–8	131, 132
9:17	165
9:26	164
9:28	165
9:31–33	165
9:32	131
9:32–38	2
9:35	164
9:37–38	127
10:28	141
10:40	1n1
11:1, 18	146
11:1–3, 25–36	139
11:4, 25	1n1
11:15–19	141
11:17, 22	141
11:18	146
11:22	141
11:25	1n1
11:25–36	139
12:1–26	137
12:24, 45	155
12:24–40	155n120
12:26	128
12:27–43	137
12:43	49n67
12:45	155
12:47	1n1
13	144n84
13:1–3	131
13:2	1n1
13:4–5	138
13:4–9	143
13:8–9	138
13:16	1n1, 127n24
13:17	1n1
13:22	146
13:26	124

Job

7:11	37n31
7:13	37n31
8:9	72
14:1–2	72
22:27–28	21n23

Psalms

2:7	115
5:3	159n136
5:3 [Eng. v. 2]	19n16
5:4 [Eng. v. 3]	19n16
6:7	159n136
16:7	159n136
17:15	159n136
18:6	55n86
18:22	55n86
24:1–2	133n47
27:8	159n136
29	47n62, 47n64
29:1, 2	47n62
30:6	159n136
34:8	114
35:10	55n86
38:21	55n86
41:14	68n124
42:8	159n136
47:2	133n47
47:8–9	133
50:21	55n86
52:11	114n277
54:8	114n277
55:3, 18	37n31
57:9	159n136
59:15	159n136
63:7	159n136
64:2	37n31
72:19	68n124
74	2
77	19n17
77:4	37n31
77:7	159n136
77:7 [Eng. v. 6]	37n31
77:13	37n31
78:61	41n45
79	2
79:10	130
80:9	62n105
81:9	33n19
83:18	55n86
86:8	55
86:10	55n86
87:9	45n59
88:14	159n136
89	133n45
89:53	68n124
90:14	159n136
92:3	159n136
95:3	45n59
96	20, 34, 47n62, 47n64
96:4	45n59
96:7, 8	47n62
97:2, 7	47n64
99:1, 5	47n64
100:5	114
102:1	37n31
102:12 [Eng. v. 11]	72
105	20, 34, 44n57, 45n57
105:6	20
105:8	42n49
105:9–11	132
105:10	44n55
105–6	133n45, 134
106	20, 34, 164n149, 165
106:1	114
106:45	132
106:46	56, 135
106:48b	36n27
107:1	114
115:2	130
118:1	114
118:29	114
119:12	68n124
119:23, 27	37n31
119:48	37n31
119:62, 148	159n136
119:78	37n31
119:147	159n136
119:148	37n31, 159n136
126	138
130:6	159n136

132	19n15, 85, 85n182, 85n183, 85n184, 86, 86n185, 87, 87n190	2:8, 20	46n60
		2:11, 17, 20	156n126
		2:17	156n126
		2:20	46n60, 156n126
		3:7, 18	156n126
132:1–10	86, 87n191	7:17	133
132:2–5, 14	87	10:5–6	133
132:7	87	10:20–23	92
132:7–8	47n64	24:5	44n55
132:8	87	26:13	55n86
132:8–10	85, 87	31:7	46n60
132:13–14	145n86	37:16	55n86
132:14	87	40:12	81
135:3	114	40:18	46n60
135:4	133	41:8	100, 100n232
135:5–9, 25	135	41:10	102n238
135:12	132	42:6	56
135:15–18	135	43:11	55n86
135:17–20, 23–24	135	44:6	55n86
135:23–24	135	45:5	55, 55n86
135:25	135	45:6	55n86
135–36	134	45:21	55n86
136	49n70	49:6, 8	56
136:1	114	55:3	44n55
136:21	132	56:7	79n162
137	2, 137	61:8	44n55
139:7–10	162n145	63:15	162n145
139:19	33n19		
143:5	37n31	**Jeremiah**	
143:8	159n136	1:18	56
144:4	72	10:6	55
145:4	37n31	10:6, 7	55n86
145:5	37n31	10:7	55n86, 133, 133n47
145:6	37n31	11:20	73
145:18	17n10	14:8	72
		15:20	56
Proverbs		17:10	73
3:5	91	17:13	72
		17:17	72
Ecclesiastes		20:4	56
6:12	72	20:12	73
7:20	84	23:5–6	155
		23:24	162n145
Isaiah		25:11–12	138
1:2	115	29:1	19n18
2:4	133n47	29:10	138

Jeremiah (cont.)

29:13	14n2
31:33	18n15
32:40	44n55
33:2, 6–11	19n19
33:3	14n2, 19n19
33:6	165n153
33:6–11	19n19
33:11	114
33:15–16	155
41:4–6	137
43	19n18
44	19n18
46–51	130n36
50:5	44n55
51:12	104
51:59–62	19n18
52:28–30	137

Ezekiel

11:15	124
16:60	44n55
33:30–32	137
37:26	44n55
40:1—43:12	138

Daniel

2:18, 19	134n50
2:19	134n50
2:37	133
3	137
3:25–45 LXX	159n136
4:17	133
4:27	164
9	165
9:3–19	159n136
9:5–6	164
9:10–11	164
9:13	164
9:24	164

Hosea

2:18, 21	156n126
2:21	156n126
11:1	115
11:1–2	55n85
13:4	55n86

Joel

2:11	81

Amos

8:3, 9	156n126
8:9	156n126

Jonah

1:9	134n50
2:2–11 [Eng. vv. 1–10]	166n160
4:2–3	166n160

Micah

7:18	55n86

Nahum

1:1—3:19	133

Habakkuk

1:2–11	133

Zephaniah

2:4–15	133

Haggai

1:1	156
1:1, 14	128
1:2, 9	137
1:9	137
1:14	128
2:2, 21	128
2:6–7	134
2:6–9	137
2:21	128
2:22–23	156
2:23	156

Zechariah

1:9	133
2:11	157

3–4	157
4:6–10	156n124
4:10	162n145
6:9–15	156n124
7:2	159n136
7–8	137
7:13	159n136
8:8	157
8:20–23	157, 159n136
8:21, 22	159n136
9:7, 10	157
9:9–10	157
9:9–11	157n128
9:10	157
9–14	156n124
10:1	159n136
10:1, 6	159n136
10:2	157n128
10:6	159n136
12:10	159n136
12:10–12	157
13:7	157n128
13:9	157, 159n136
14:1–19	157n128
14:9	133n47, 157
14:10	159n136
14:16–17	159n136
14:16–21	157

Malachi

1:5, 11	134
1:6—2:9	146
1:7	134
1:8	134
1:9	159n136
1:14	157
2:8	157
2:10	157
2:14	157
2:17—3:6	157
3:1	157
3:1–6	146
3:2	81
3:22 [Eng. 4:4]	124

DEUTEROCANONICAL BOOKS

2 Maccabees

1:21–30	161n141
2:2–20	166n160
3:15	161n141

3 Maccabees

2	165

Judith

4:9–15	161n141
8:2–14	166n160
9	165

DEAD SEA SCROLLS

1QHa

	159n136

1QM

13:1—14:15	159n136

1QS

1:16—2:26	159n136

1QSb

	159n136

4Q

372 1	159n136
380–381	159n136
502	159n136
502–9, 512	159n136
503	159n136
504–6	159n136
507–9	159n136
512	159n136

4QHa, b   159n136

4QTLevia   159n136

11QBer   159n136

11QPsa, b, f   159n136

11QPsaZion   159n136

RABBINIC WORKS

Mishnah Tamid
5.1   159n136

NEW TESTAMENT

Matthew
1:12   156
11:10   157

Mark
1:2   157

Luke
1:10   161n141
2:37   161n141
18:10   161n141

John
15:14–15   100n232

James
2:23   100n232

www.ingramcontent.com/pod-product-compliance
Lightning Source LLC
Chambersburg PA
CBHW051636230426
43669CB00013B/2321